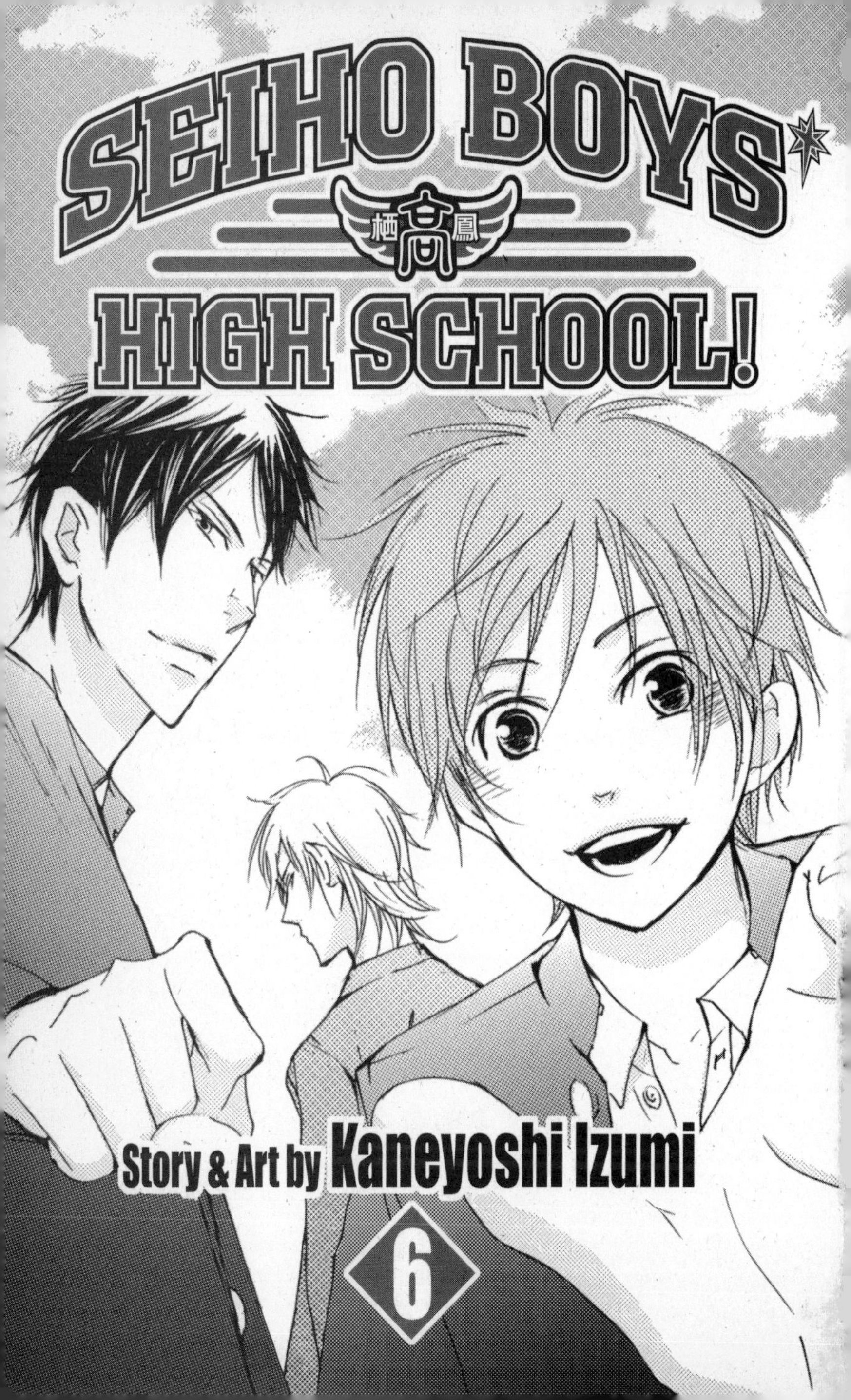
SEIHO BOYS HIGH SCHOOL!
Story & Art by Kaneyoshi Izumi
6

SEIHO BOYS' HIGH SCHOOL!

6

CONTENTS

♠ ♠ ♠ STORY SO FAR ♠ ♠ ♠

Nestled in the distant countryside you'll find Seiho High, a private boys' school surrounded by the mountains and sea. For its students, overflowing with youthful energy and desires, the daily grind of being unable to meet any girls makes their isolated school feel like Alcatraz!

Despite his questionable ideas about courtship, Nogami manages to sweep Miss Fukuhara off her feet. However, the ten-year gap between them inevitably makes things awkward from time to time. As for Maki, he and his new girlfriend, Erika, have finally reached first base. Where will things go from there?

♠ CHARACTERS ♠

■**Maki**■ Adored by men and women of of all ages, Maki is a cute guy and a peacemaker, but he has an unexpected violent streak.

■**Hanai**■ A girl trapped in a boy's body, to put it bluntly. He loves cute accessories and had a girlfriend back in junior high.

■**Kamiki**■ The hottest boy at school. He's got everything it takes to make girls fall for him, but he's surprisingly tactless.

■**Nogami**■ Sees himself as far superior to the other students. He likes the school nurse, Miss Fukuhara.

About This Photo

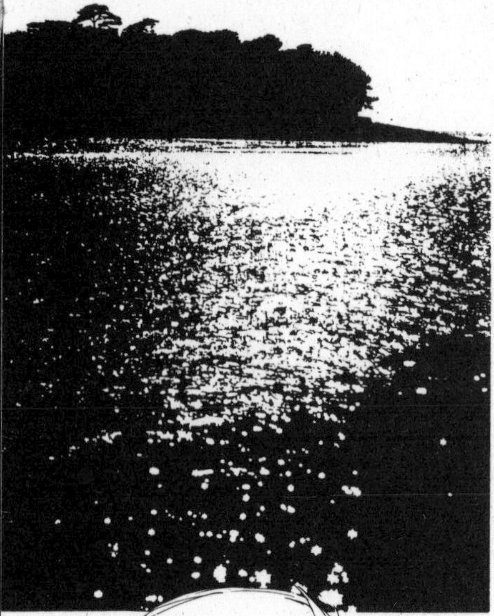

This is a reference photo of a particular place I used as the inspiration for *Seiho Boys' High School*'s setting. I took this picture on a cloudy day, so I had to be super-careful about catching the occasional moment when the sun broke through. And then I fell into the ocean...

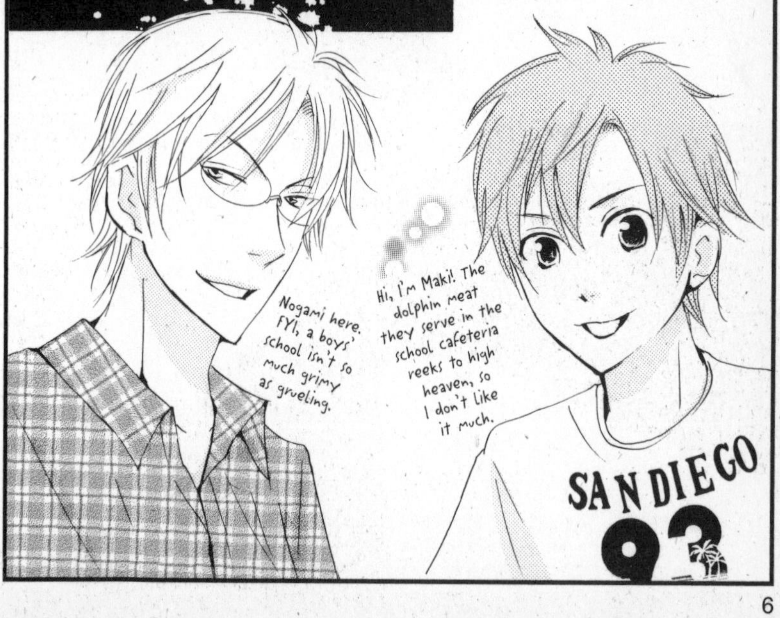
Hi, I'm Maki! The dolphin meat they serve in the school cafeteria reeks to high heaven, so I don't like it much.
Nogami here. FYI, a boys' school isn't so much grimy as grueling.
SAN DIEGO
93

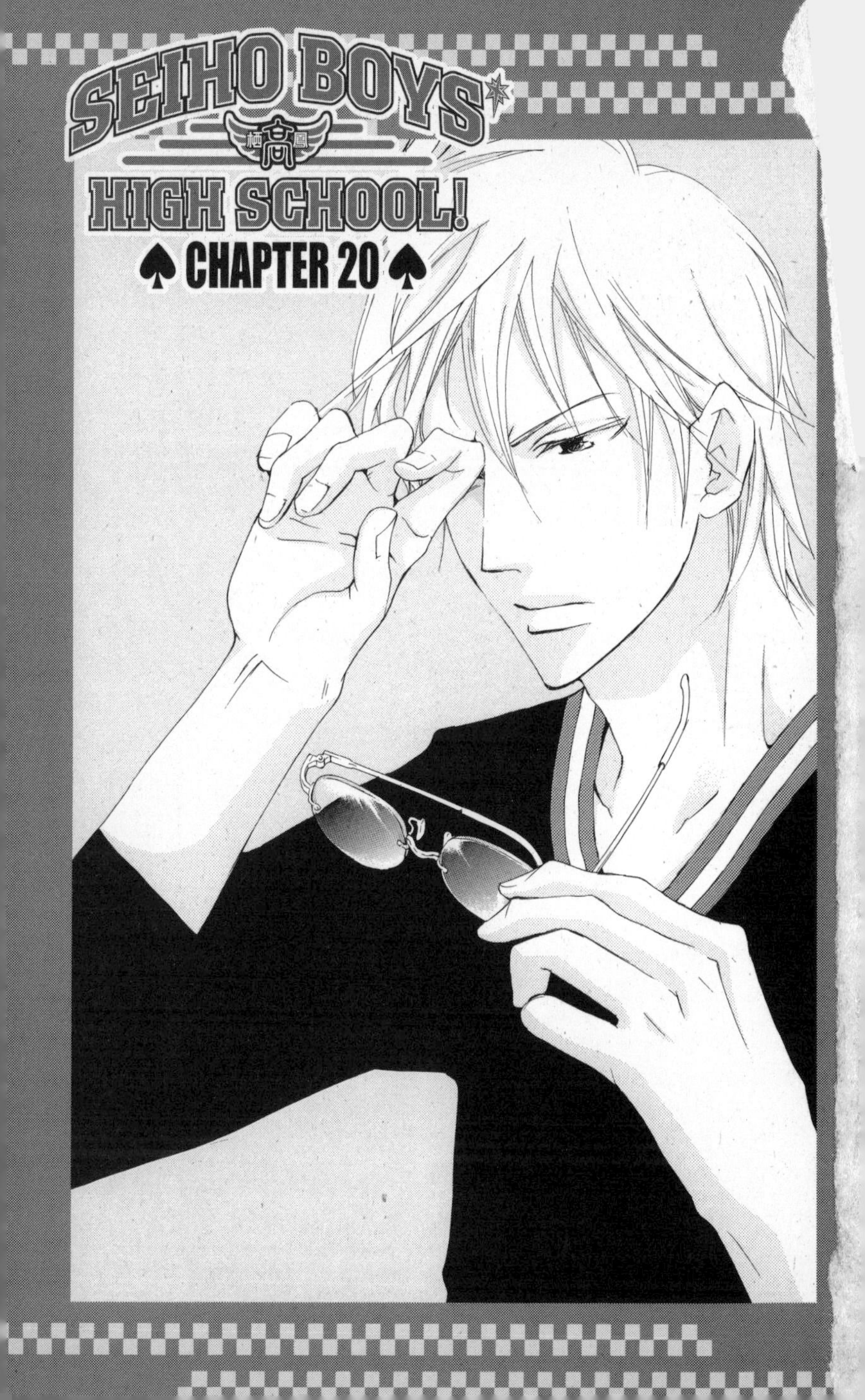
SEIHO BOYS' HIGH SCHOOL!
♠CHAPTER 20♠

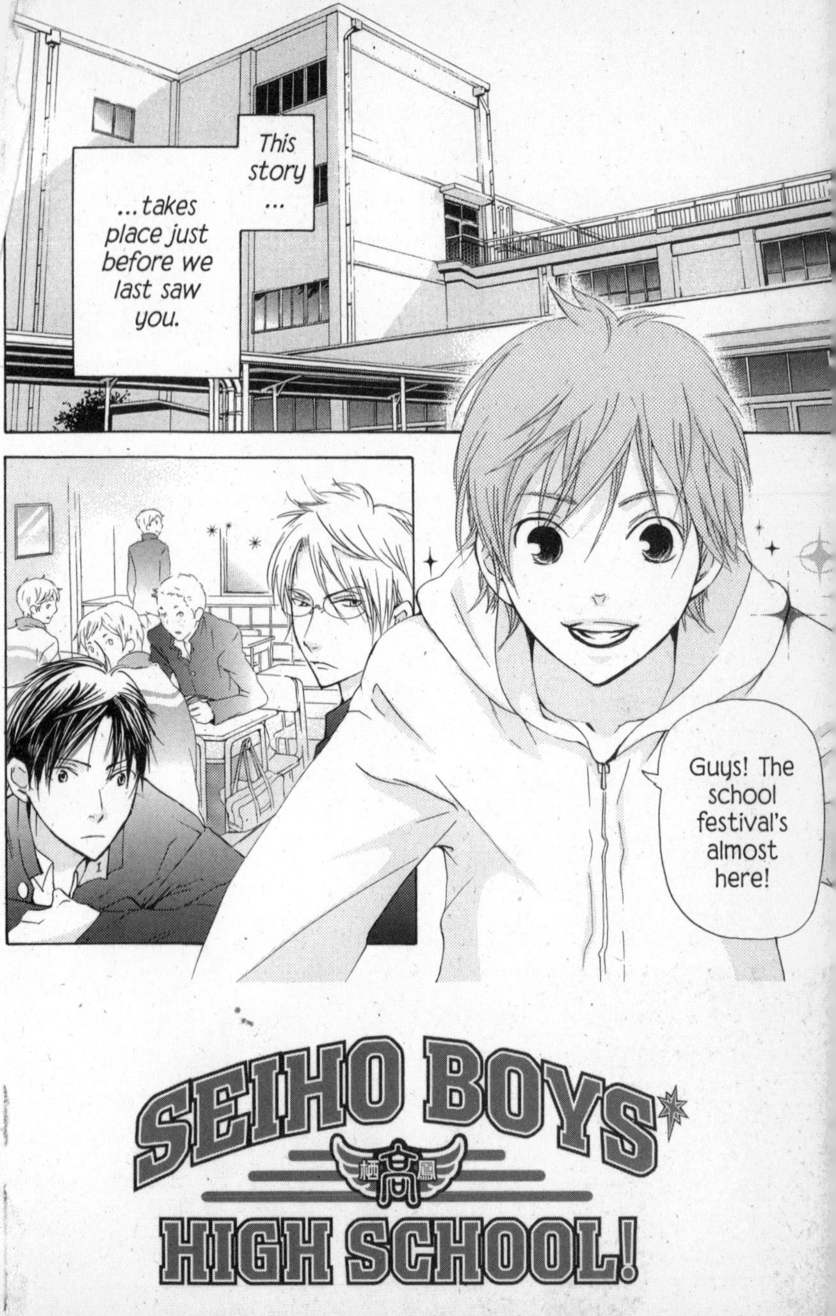
This story ...
...takes place just before we last saw you.
Guys! The school festival's almost here!

SEIHO BOYS HIGH SCHOOL!

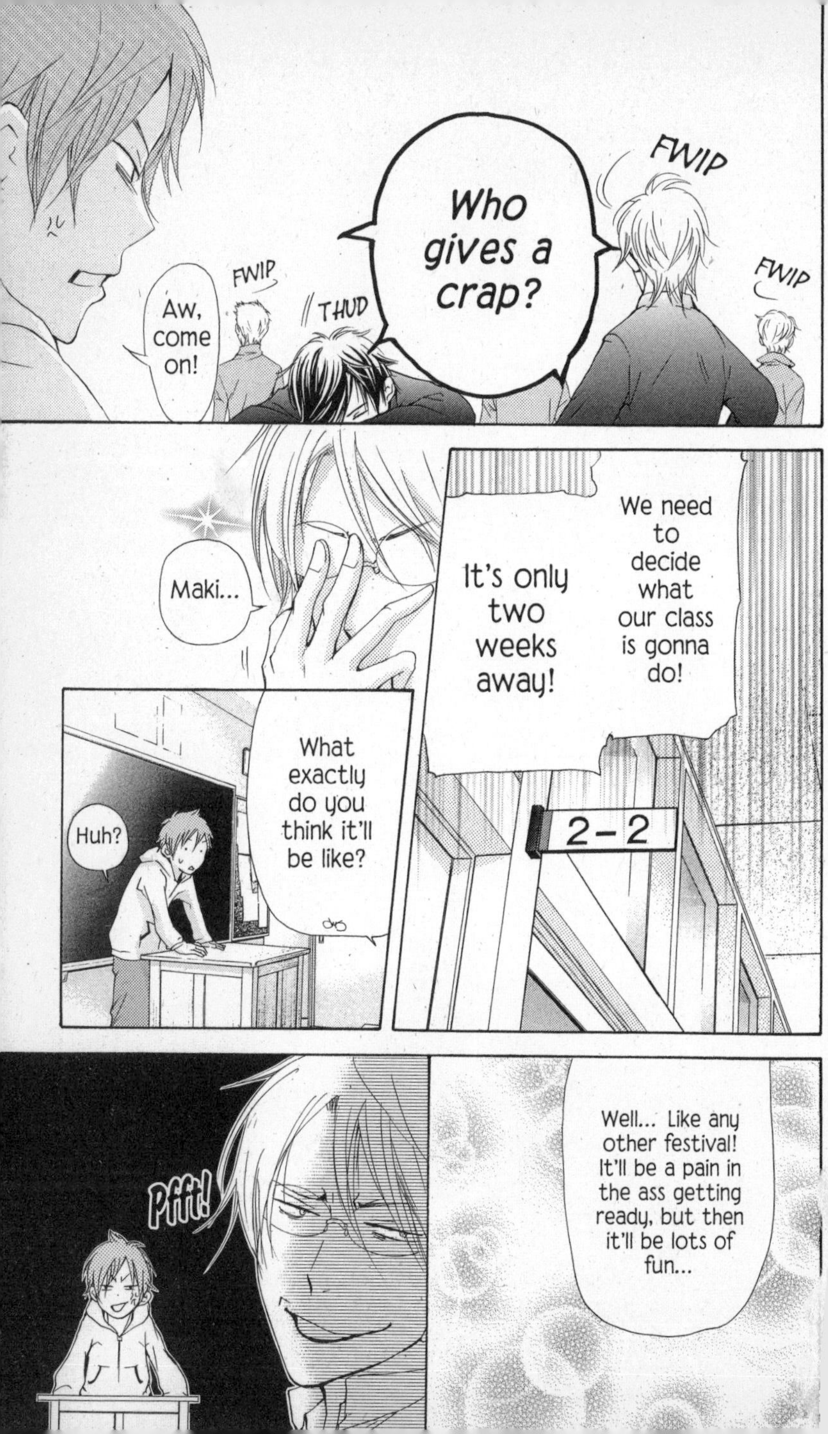
FWIP
FWIP
Who gives a crap?
THUD
FWIP
Aw, come on!
We need to decide what our class is gonna do!
It's only two weeks away!
Maki...
What exactly do you think it'll be like?
Huh?
2-2
Well... Like any other festival! It'll be a pain in the ass getting ready, but then it'll be lots of fun...
Pfft!

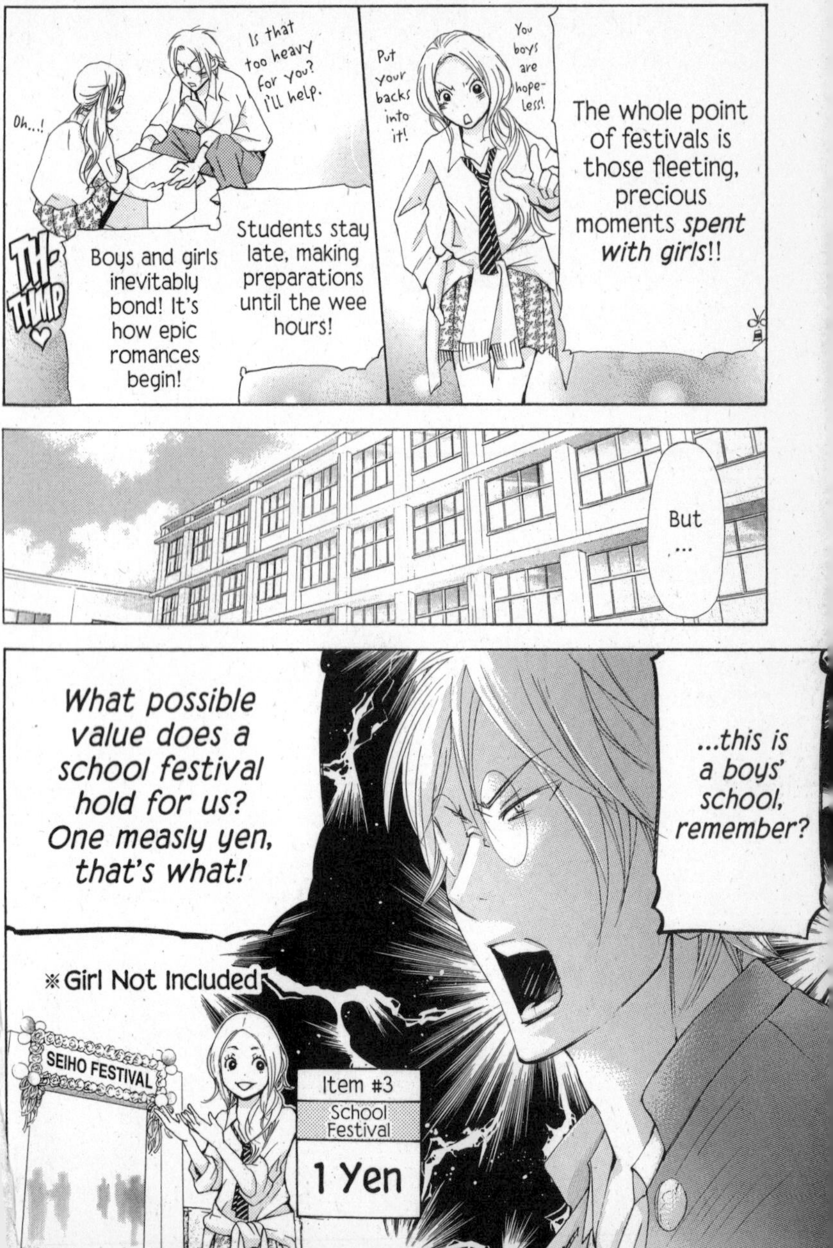
You boys are hope-less!
Put your backs into it!
The whole point of festivals is those fleeting, precious moments *spent with girls*!!
Is that too heavy for you? I'll help.
Oh...!
Students stay late, making preparations until the wee hours!
Boys and girls inevitably bond! It's how epic romances begin!
TH-THMP ♥
But ...
...this is a boys' school, remember?
What possible value does a school festival hold for us? One measly yen, that's what!
※Girl Not Included
SEIHO FESTIVAL
Item #3
School Festival
1 Yen

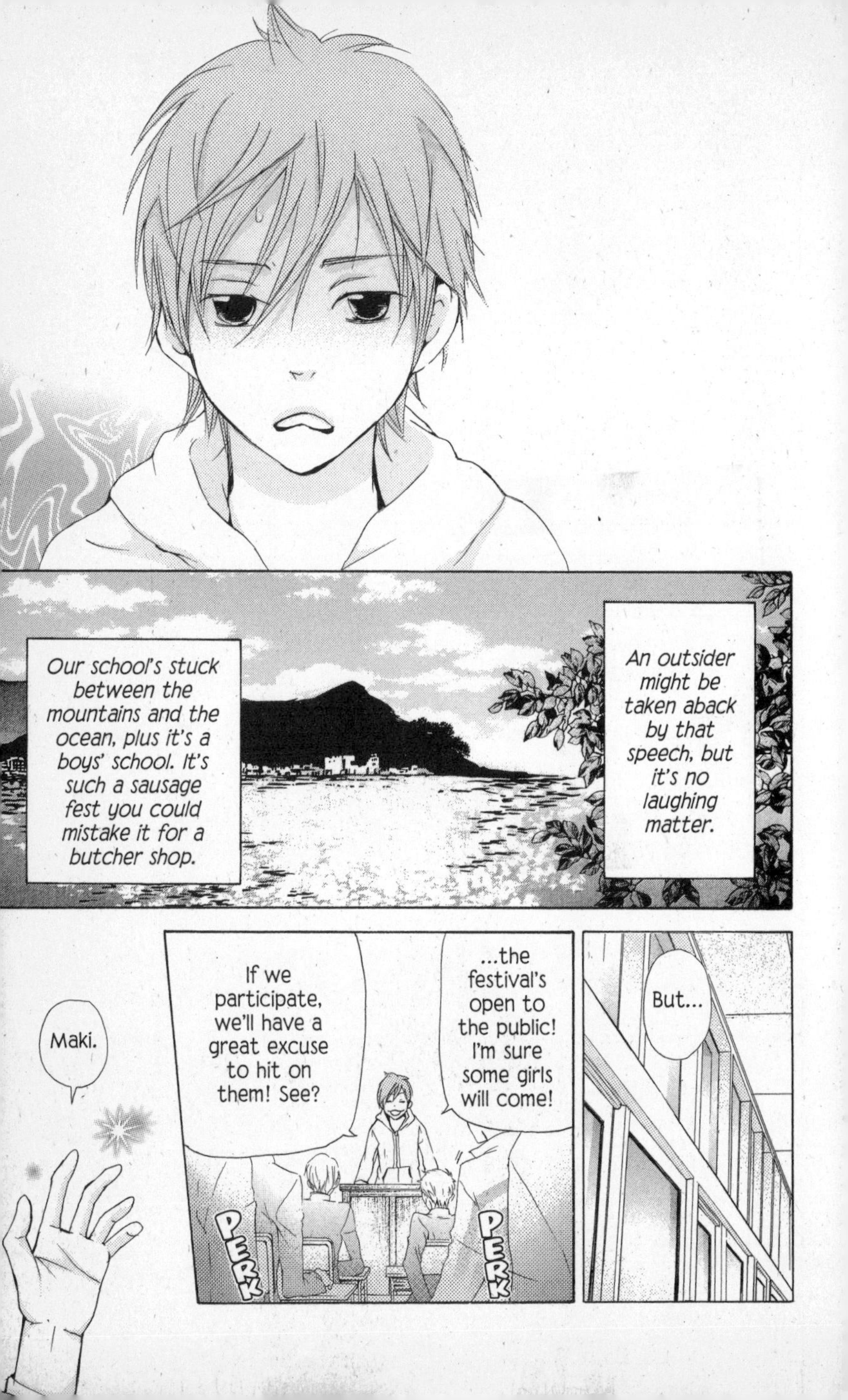
An outsider might be taken aback by that speech, but it's no laughing matter.
Our school's stuck between the mountains and the ocean, plus it's a boys' school. It's such a sausage fest you could mistake it for a butcher shop.
But...
...the festival's open to the public! I'm sure some girls will come!
If we participate, we'll have a great excuse to hit on them! See?
PERK
PERK
Maki.

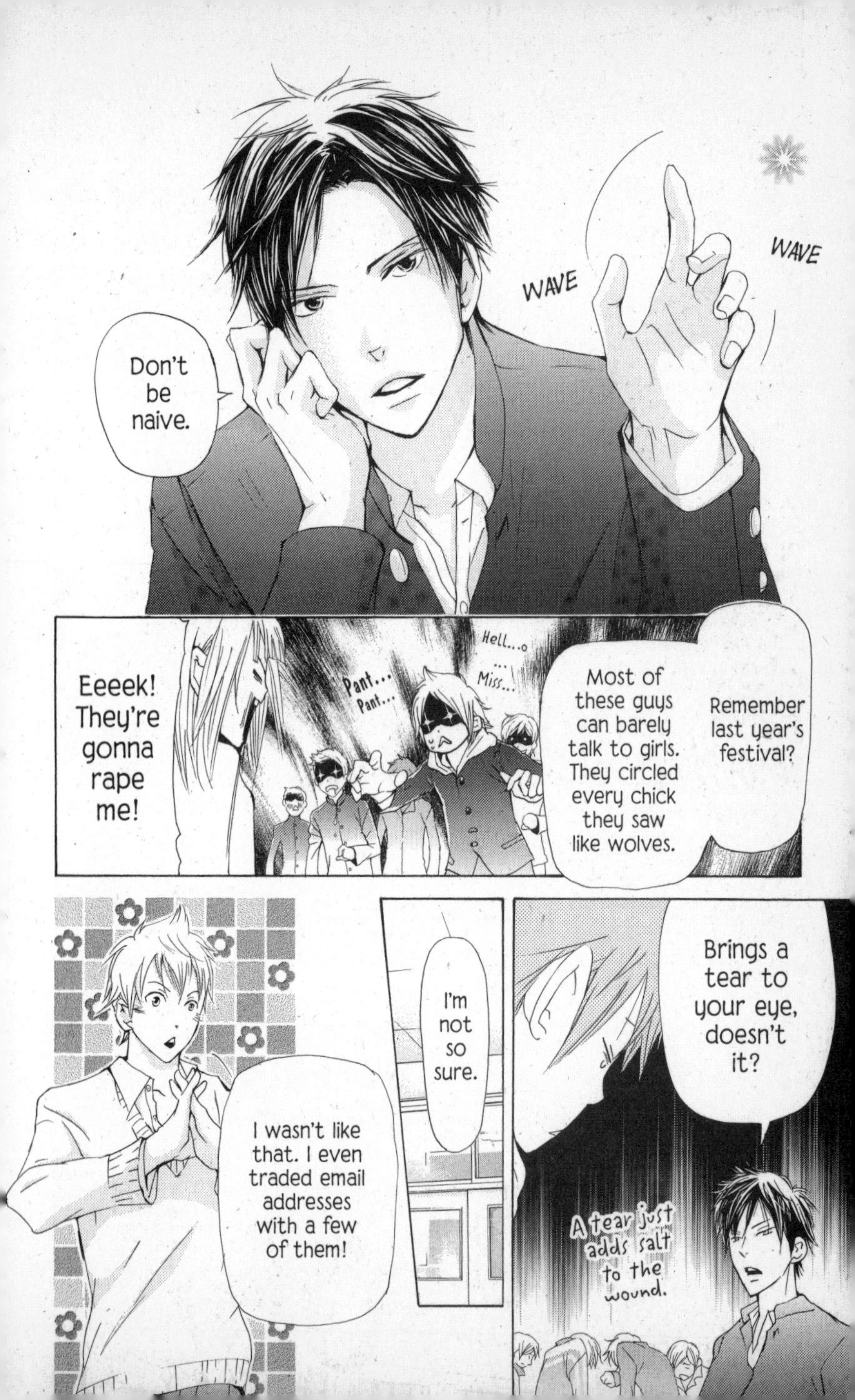
WAVE
WAVE
Don't be naive.
Remember last year's festival?
Most of these guys can barely talk to girls. They circled every chick they saw like wolves.
Hell...o ... Miss...
Pant... Pant...
Eeeek! They're gonna rape me!
Brings a tear to your eye, doesn't it?
A tear just adds salt to the wound.
I'm not so sure.
I wasn't like that. I even traded email addresses with a few of them!

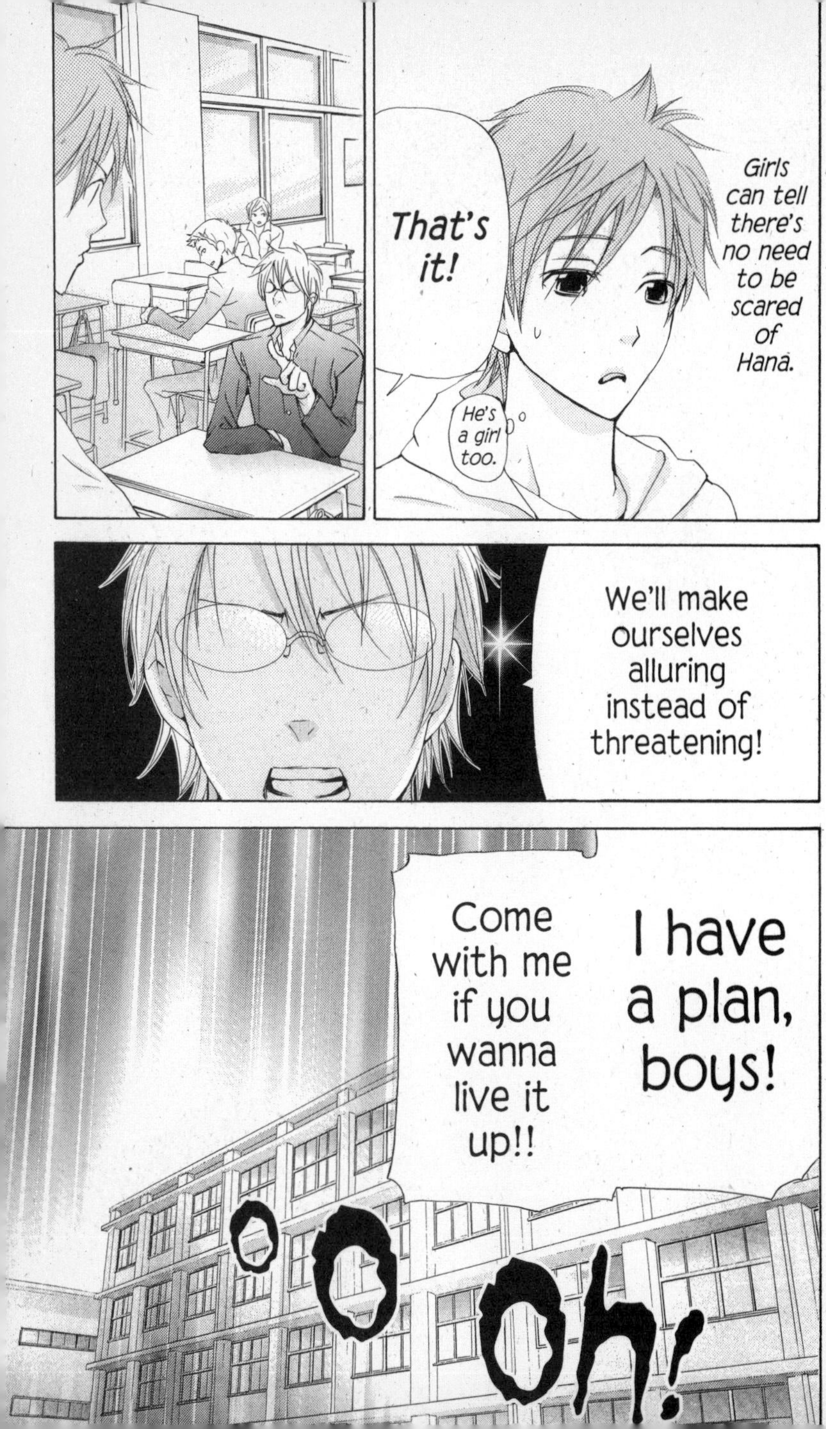
Girls can tell there's no need to be scared of Hana.
That's it!
He's a girl too.
We'll make ourselves alluring instead of threatening!
I have a plan, boys!
Come with me if you wanna live it up!!
Oooh!

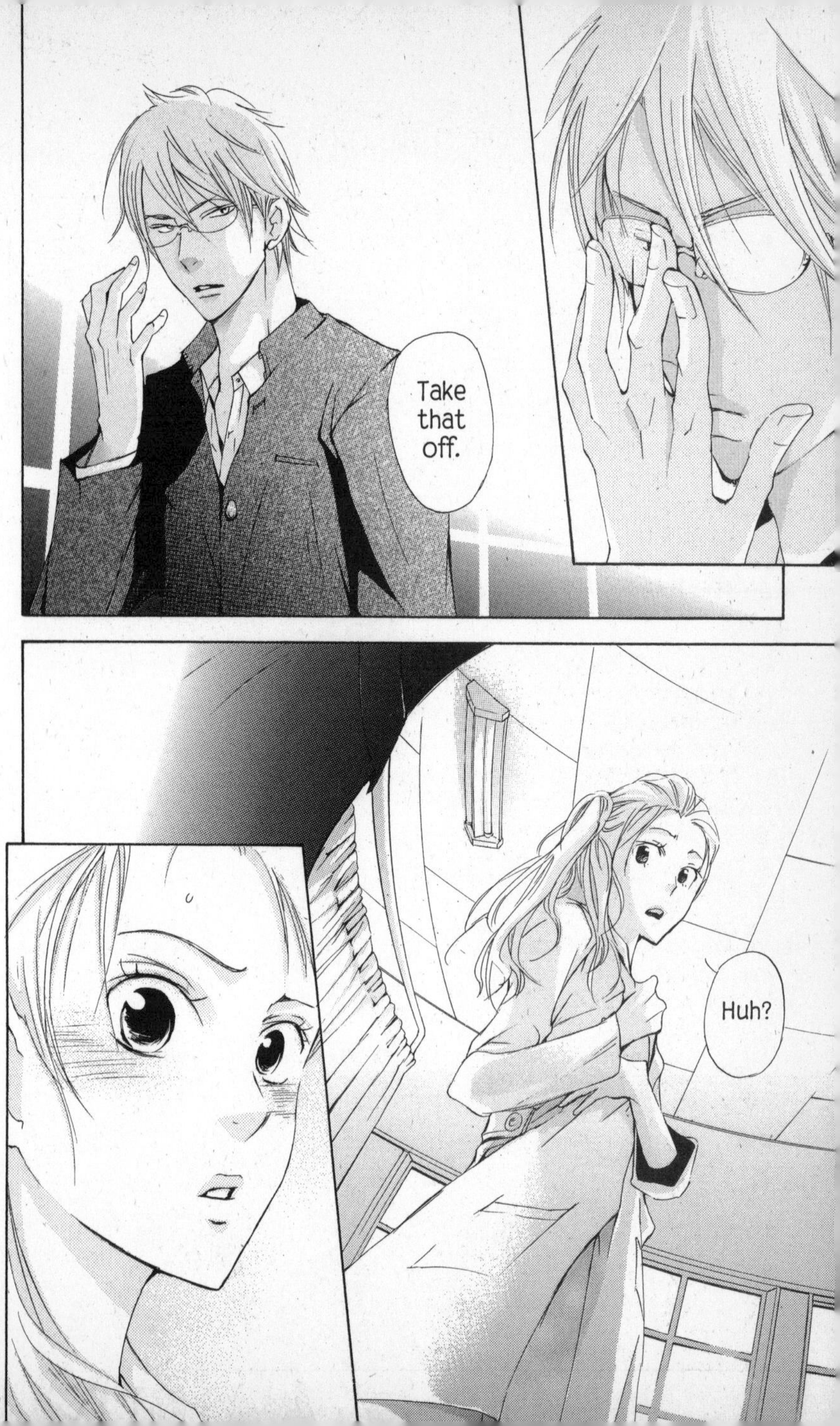
Take that off.
Huh?

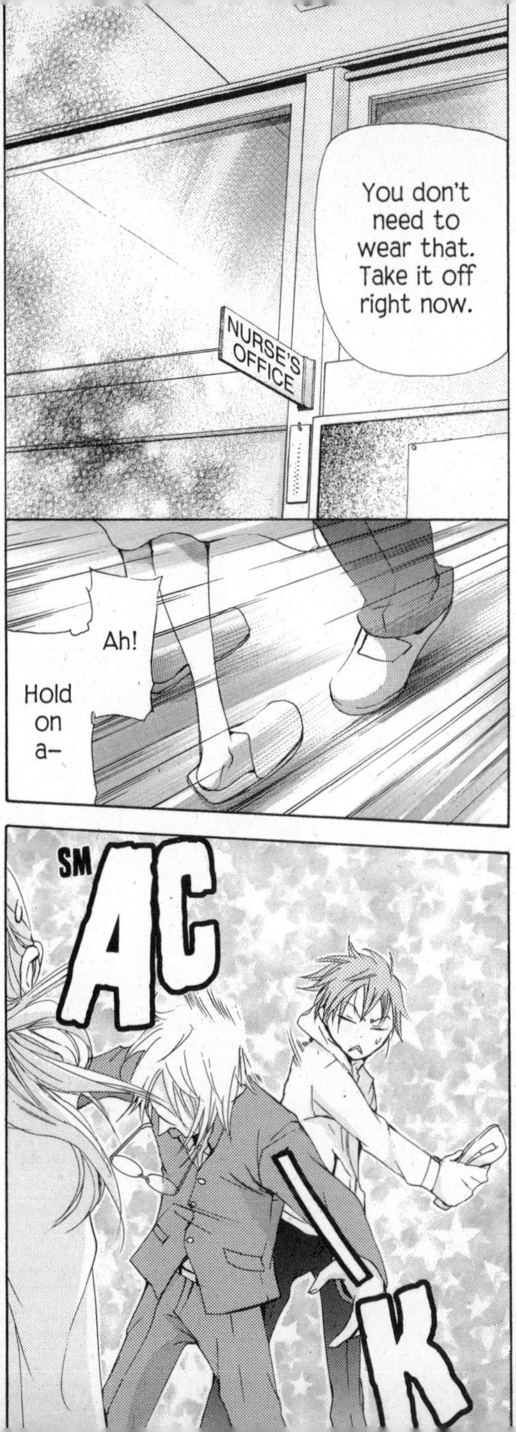
NURSE'S OFFICE
You don't need to wear that. Take it off right now.
Ah!
Hold on a–
SMACK

1/3 Filler Corner

AIRLINE FOOD The Opposite of a Gourmet Journey

When I think travel, I think gourmet! But the truth of the matter is I have lousy taste in food... Just about everything tastes reasonably good to me, so I'm not very picky when it comes to my food...

Heh

But there's food that makes even me turn up my nose, and that's **airline food** served on airplanes!

Case 1

Air C

(China Domestic Flight)

The "snack" they served came in what looked like a lunch box:

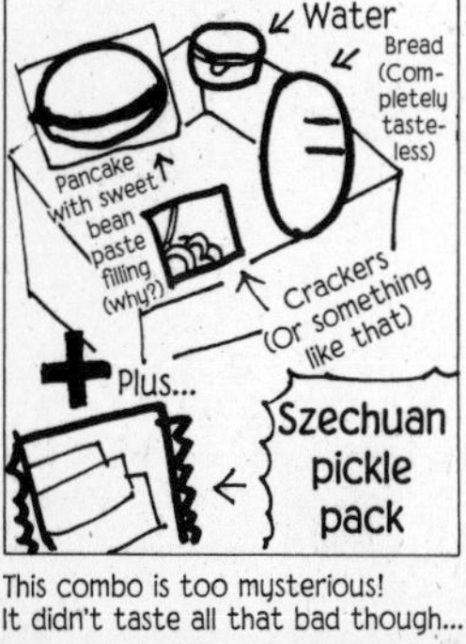
Water
Bread (Completely tasteless)
Pancake with sweet bean paste filling (why?)
Crackers (Or something like that)
Plus...
Szechuan pickle pack

This combo is too mysterious! It didn't taste all that bad though...

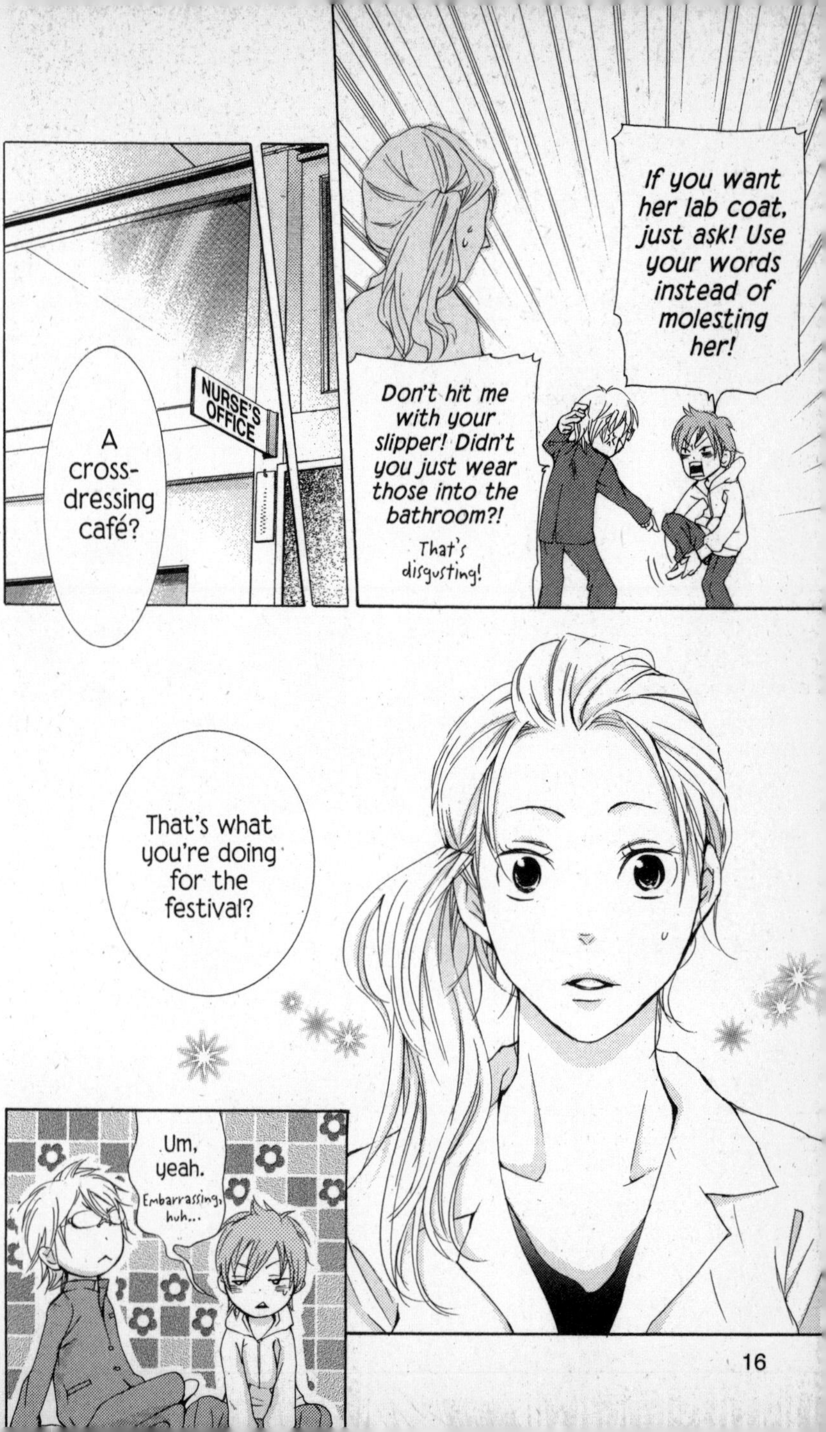

If you want her lab coat, just ask! Use your words instead of molesting her!
Don't hit me with your slipper! Didn't you just wear those into the bathroom?!
That's disgusting!
NURSE'S OFFICE
A cross-dressing café?
That's what you're doing for the festival?
Um, yeah.
Embarrassing, huh...

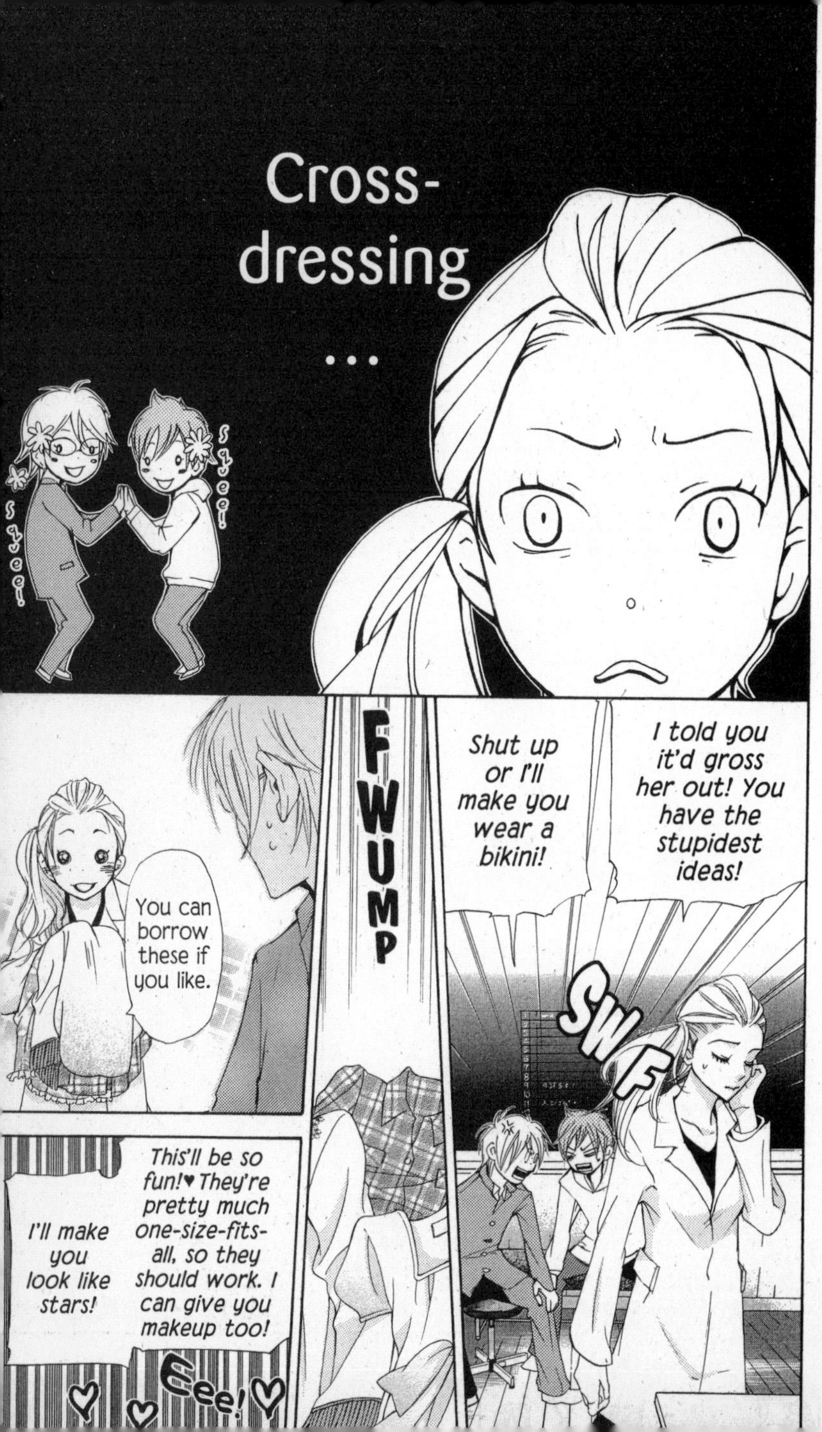
Cross-dressing
...
squee!
squee!
I told you it'd gross her out! You have the stupidest ideas!
Shut up or I'll make you wear a bikini!
SWF
FWUMP
You can borrow these if you like.
This'll be so fun!♥ They're pretty much one-size-fits-all, so they should work. I can give you makeup too!
I'll make you look like stars!
Eee!

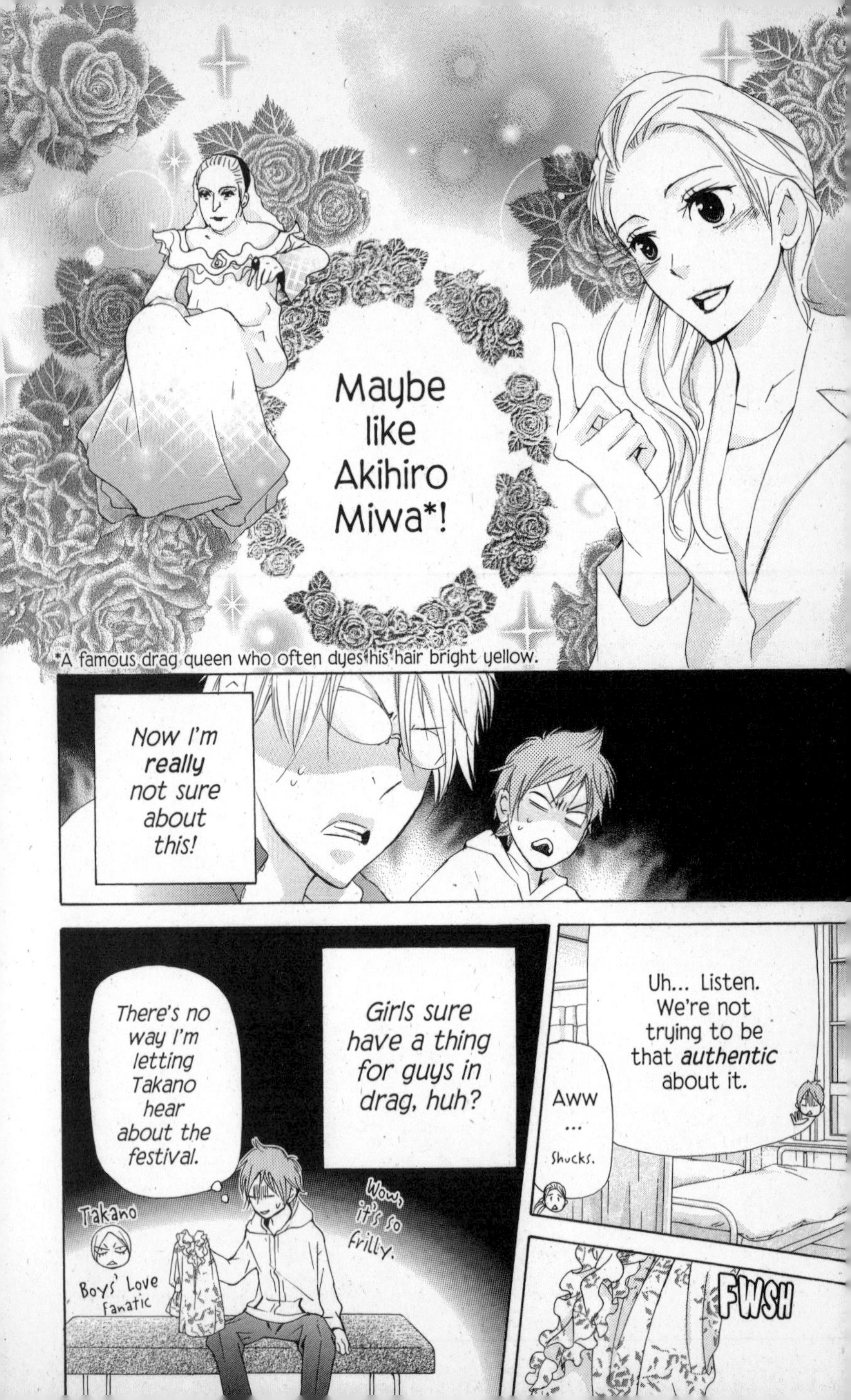
Maybe like Akihiro Miwa*!
*A famous drag queen who often dyes his hair bright yellow.
Now I'm really not sure about this!
Uh... Listen. We're not trying to be that authentic about it.
Aww ...
Shucks.
FWSH
Girls sure have a thing for guys in drag, huh?
Wow it's so frilly.
There's no way I'm letting Takano hear about the festival.
Takano
Boys' Love Fanatic

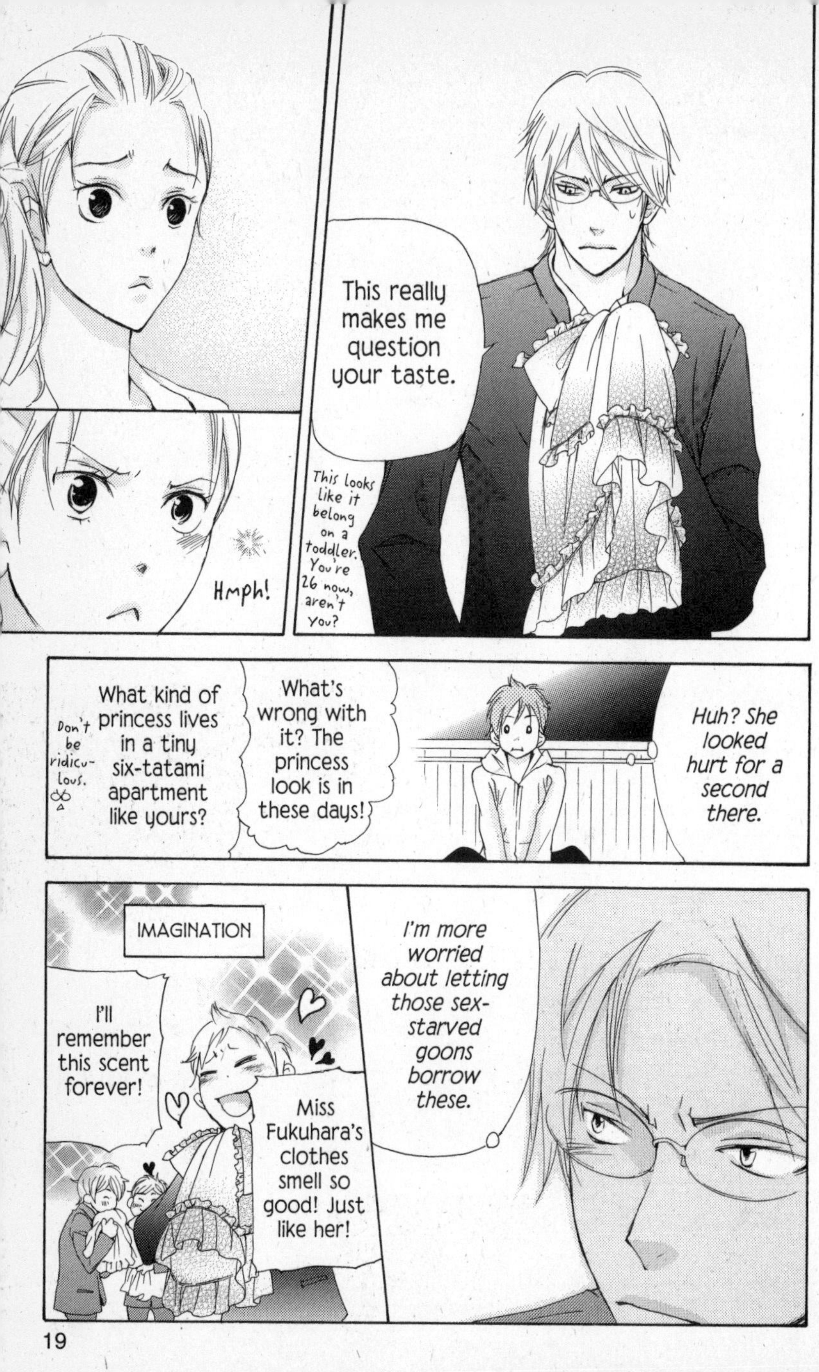
This really makes me question your taste.
This looks like it belong on a toddler. You're 26 now, aren't you?
Hmph!
Huh? She looked hurt for a second there.
What's wrong with it? The princess look is in these days!
What kind of princess lives in a tiny six-tatami apartment like yours?
Don't be ridicu-lous.
I'm more worried about letting those sex-starved goons borrow these.
IMAGINATION
Miss Fukuhara's clothes smell so good! Just like her!
I'll remember this scent forever!

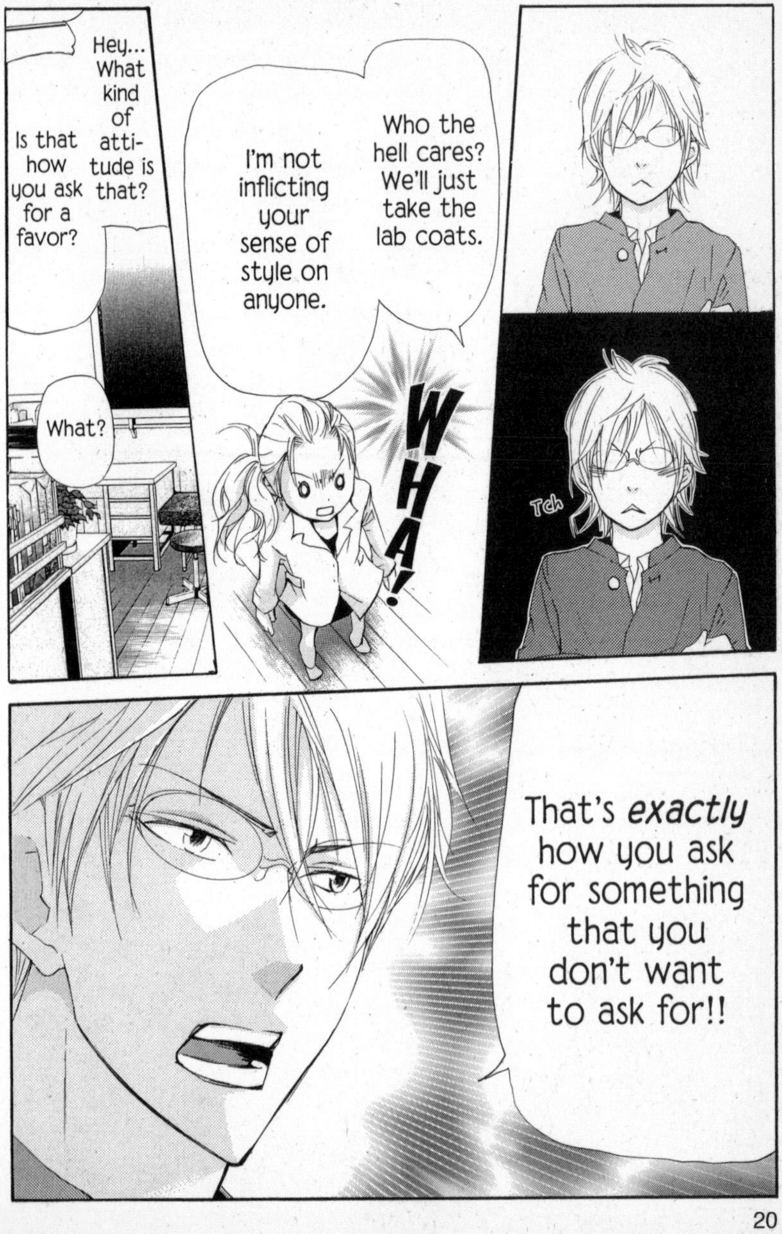
Tch
Who the hell cares? We'll just take the lab coats. I'm not inflicting your sense of style on anyone.
WHA!
Hey... What kind of attitude is that?
Is that how you ask for a favor?
What?
That's *exactly* how you ask for something that you don't want to ask for!!

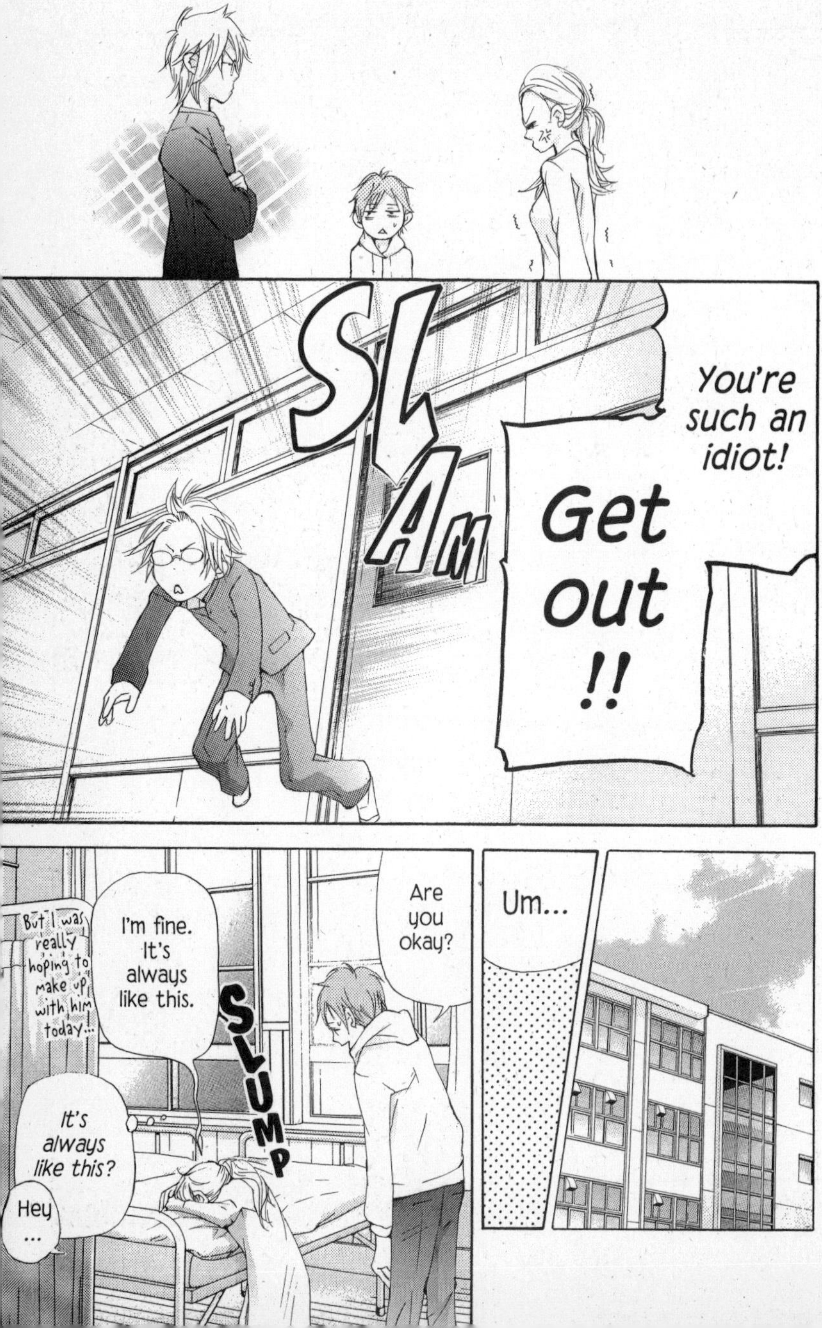
You're such an idiot!
Get out !!
SLAM
Um...
Are you okay?
I'm fine. It's always like this.
But I was really hoping to make up with him today...
SLUMP
It's always like this?
Hey ...

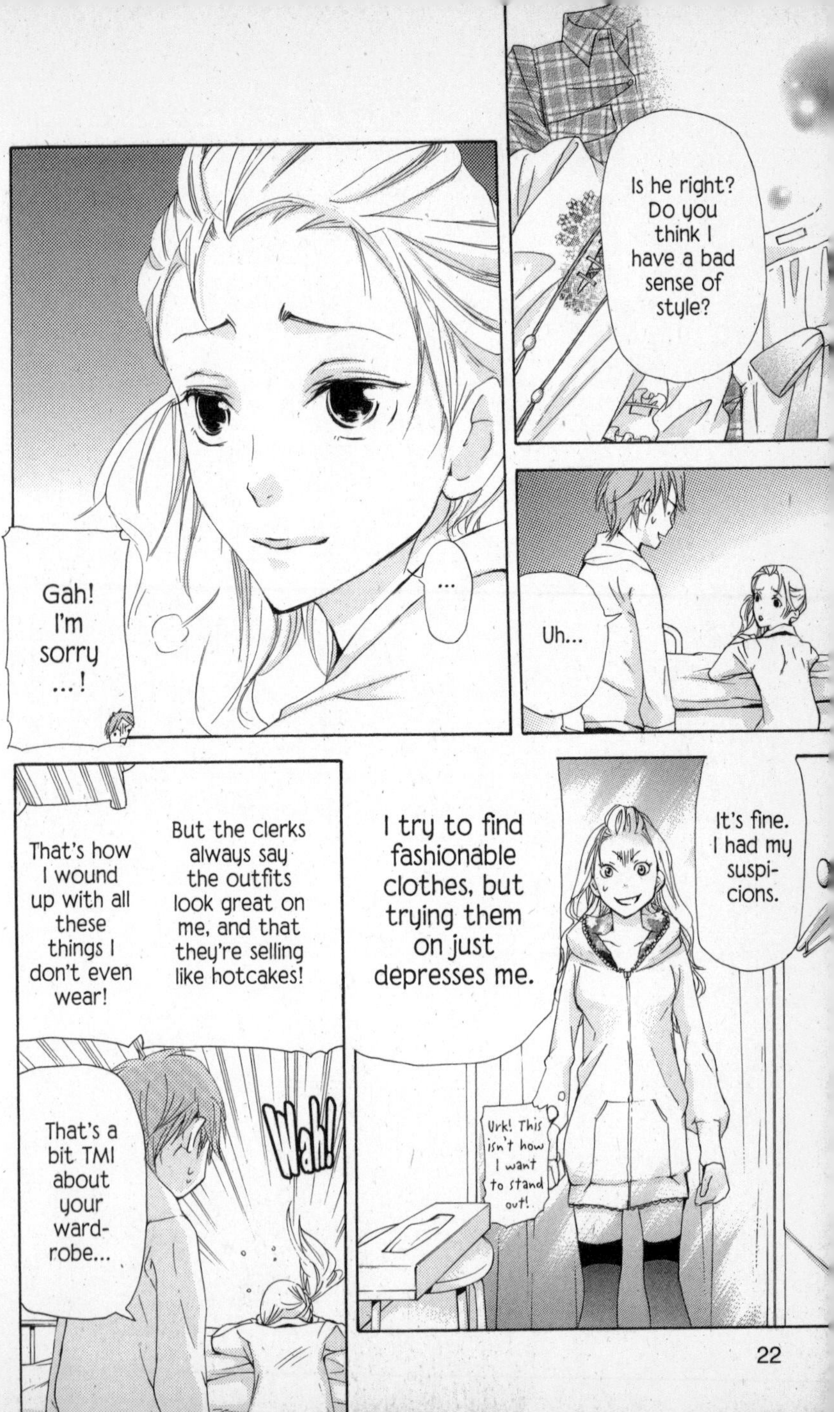
Is he right? Do you think I have a bad sense of style?
Uh...
...
Gah! I'm sorry ...!
It's fine. I had my suspi-cions.
I try to find fashionable clothes, but trying them on just depresses me.
Urk! This isn't how I want to stand out!
But the clerks always say the outfits look great on me, and that they're selling like hotcakes!
That's how I wound up with all these things I don't even wear!
Wah!
That's a bit TMI about your ward-robe...

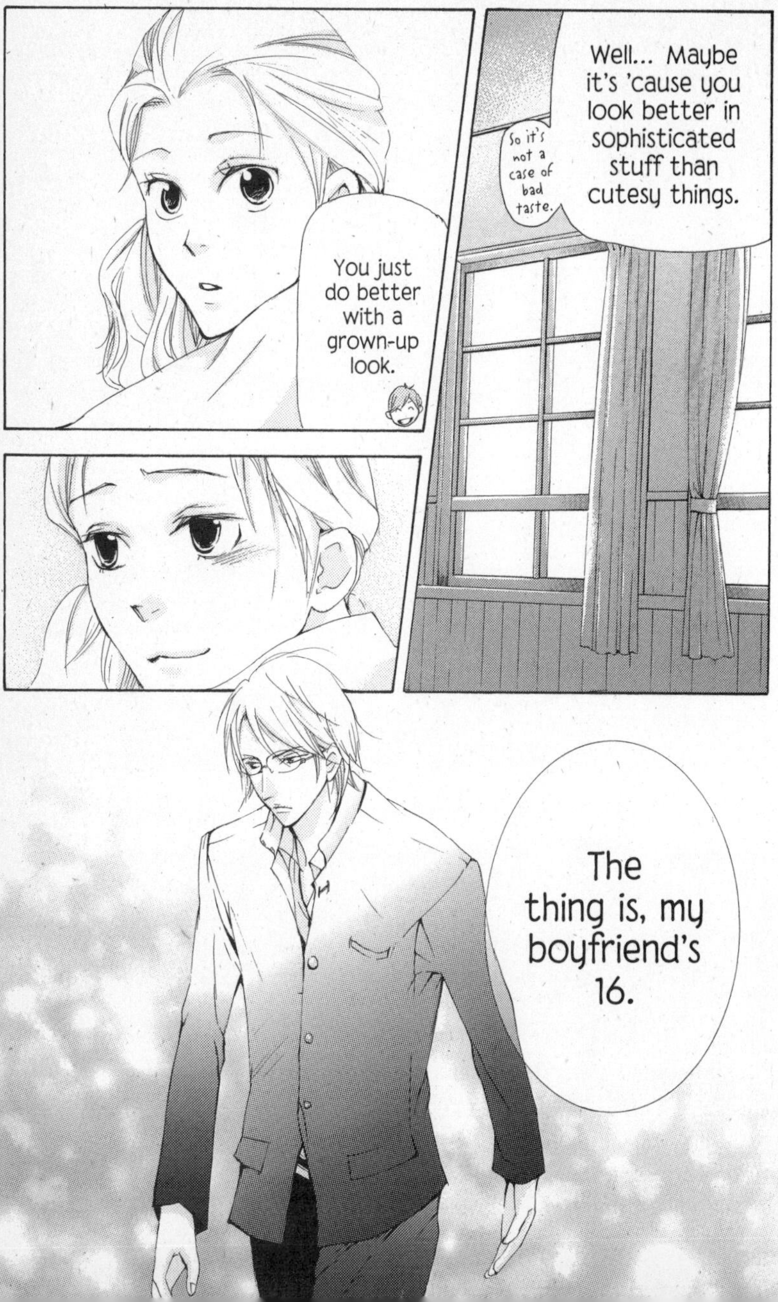
Well... Maybe it's 'cause you look better in sophisticated stuff than cutesy things.
So it's not a case of bad taste.
You just do better with a grown-up look.
The thing is, my boyfriend's 16.

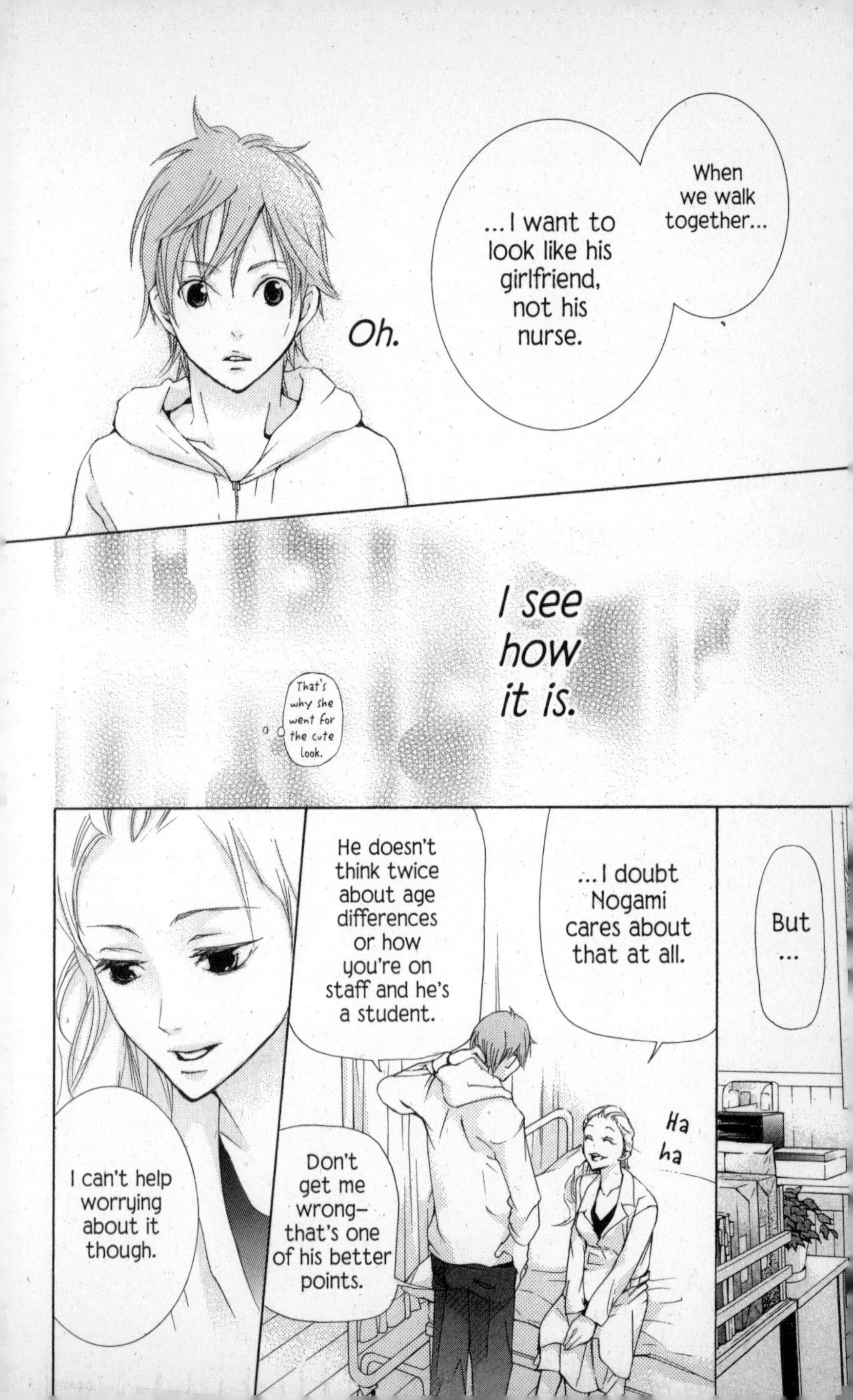
When we walk together...
...I want to look like his girlfriend, not his nurse.
Oh.
I see how it is.
That's why she went for the cute look.
But ...
...I doubt Nogami cares about that at all.
Ha ha
He doesn't think twice about age differences or how you're on staff and he's a student.
Don't get me wrong—that's one of his better points.
I can't help worrying about it though.

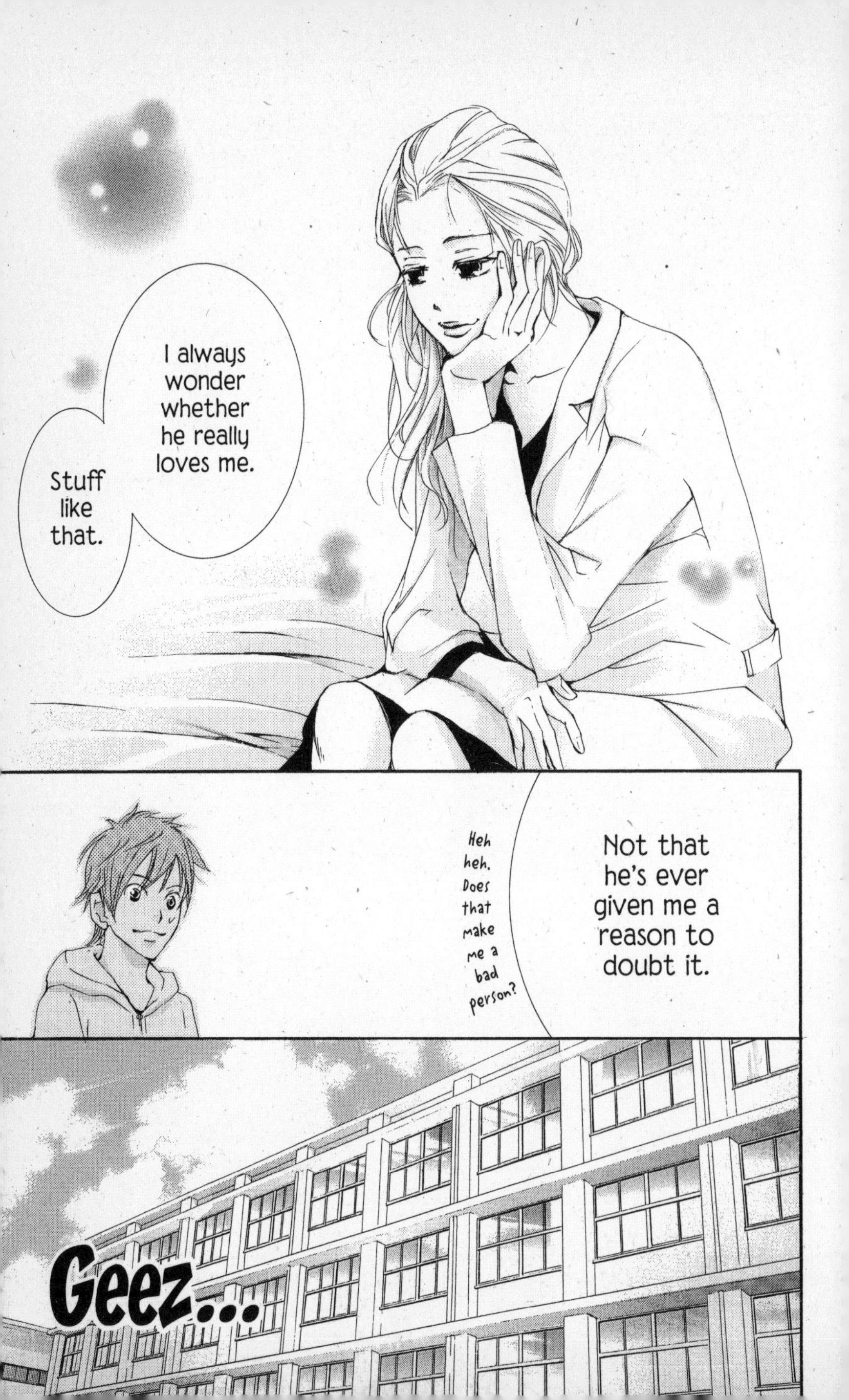
I always wonder whether he really loves me.
Stuff like that.
Not that he's ever given me a reason to doubt it.
Heh heh. Does that make me a bad person?
Geez...

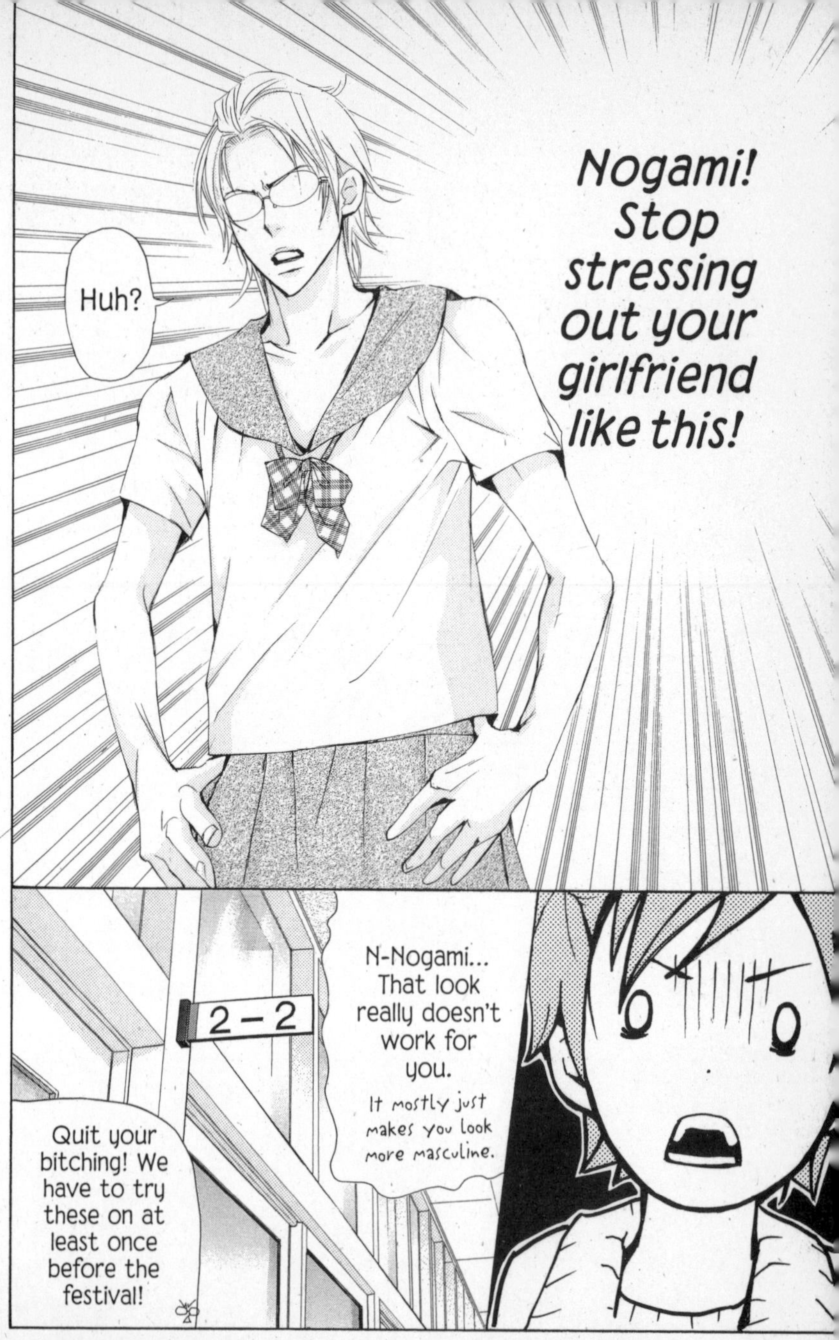
Nogami! Stop stressing out your girlfriend like this!
Huh?
N-Nogami... That look really doesn't work for you.
It mostly just makes you look more masculine.
2 – 2
Quit your bitching! We have to try these on at least once before the festival!

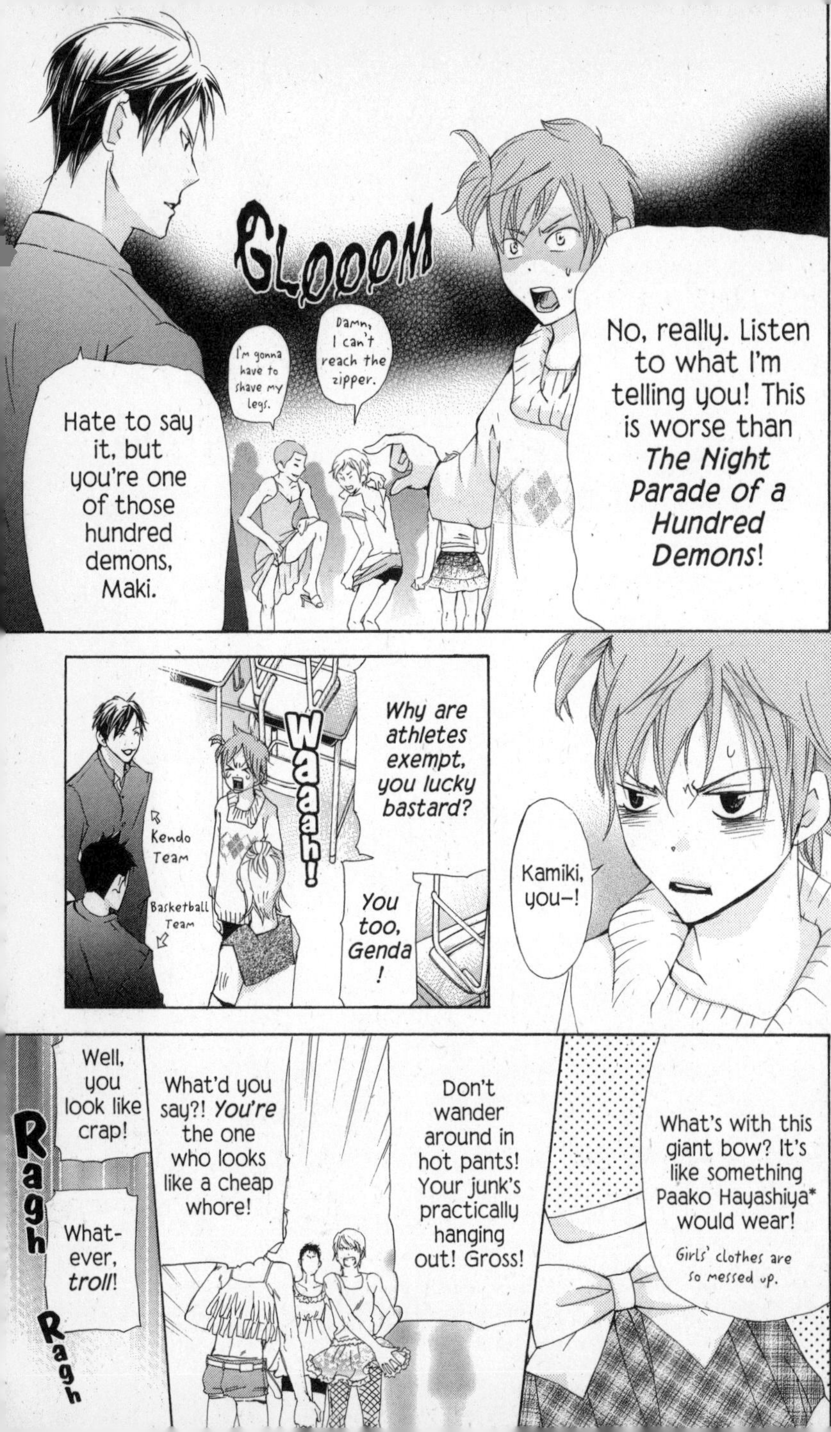
No, really. Listen to what I'm telling you! This is worse than *The Night Parade of a Hundred Demons*!
GLOOOM
Damn, I can't reach the zipper.
I'm gonna have to shave my legs.
Hate to say it, but you're one of those hundred demons, Maki.
Kamiki, you—!
Why are athletes exempt, you lucky bastard?
Waaaah!
You too, Genda!
Kendo Team
Basketball Team
What's with this giant bow? It's like something Paako Hayashiya* would wear!
Girls' clothes are so messed up.
Don't wander around in hot pants! Your junk's practically hanging out! Gross!
What'd you say?! *You're* the one who looks like a cheap whore!
Well, you look like crap!
Whatever, *troll*!
Ragh Ragh

*A comedian who often wears pink frills.

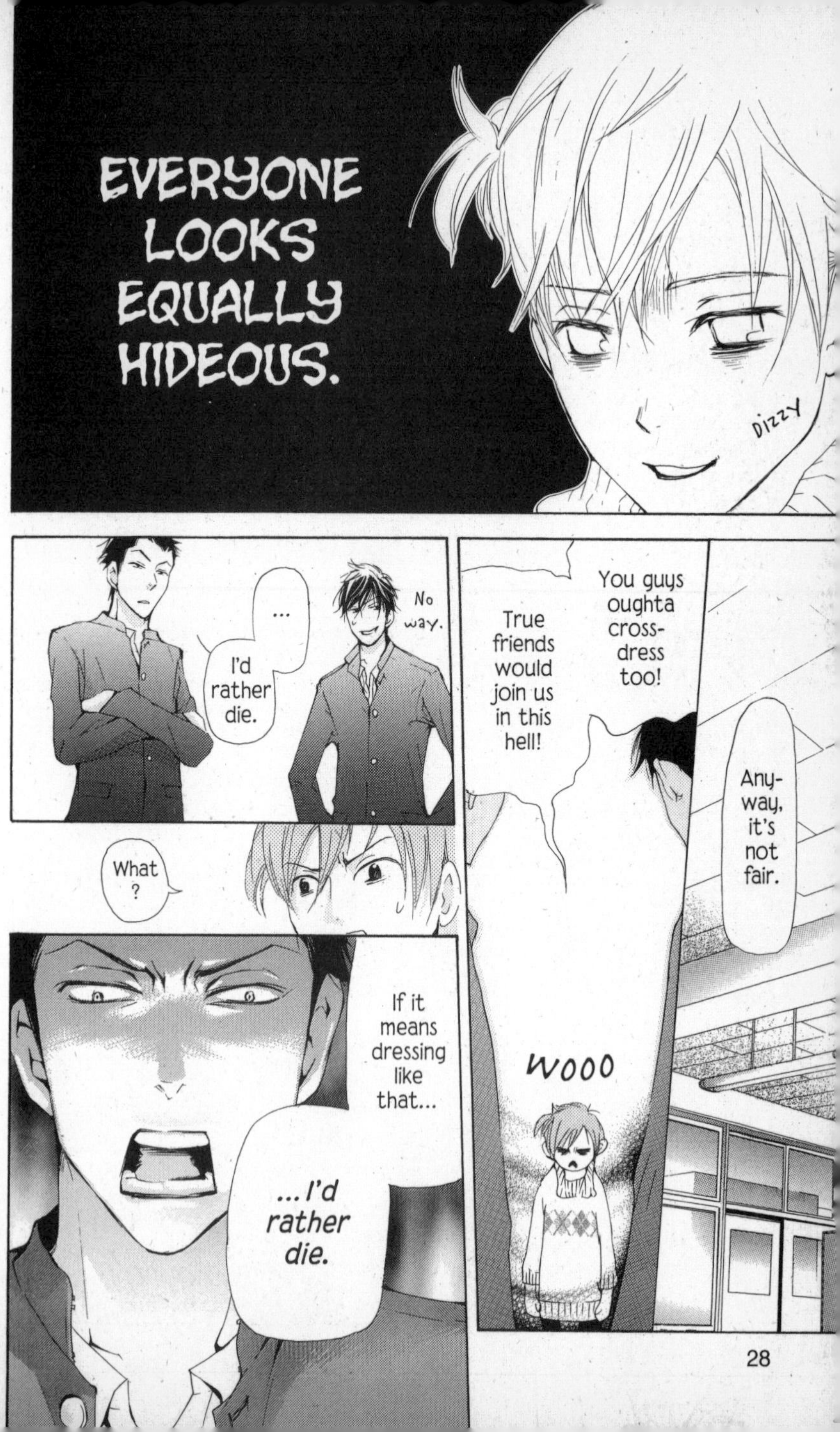
EVERYONE LOOKS EQUALLY HIDEOUS.
Dizzy
Any-way, it's not fair.
You guys oughta cross-dress too!
True friends would join us in this hell!
WOOO
No way.
...
I'd rather die.
What?
If it means dressing like that...
...I'd rather die.

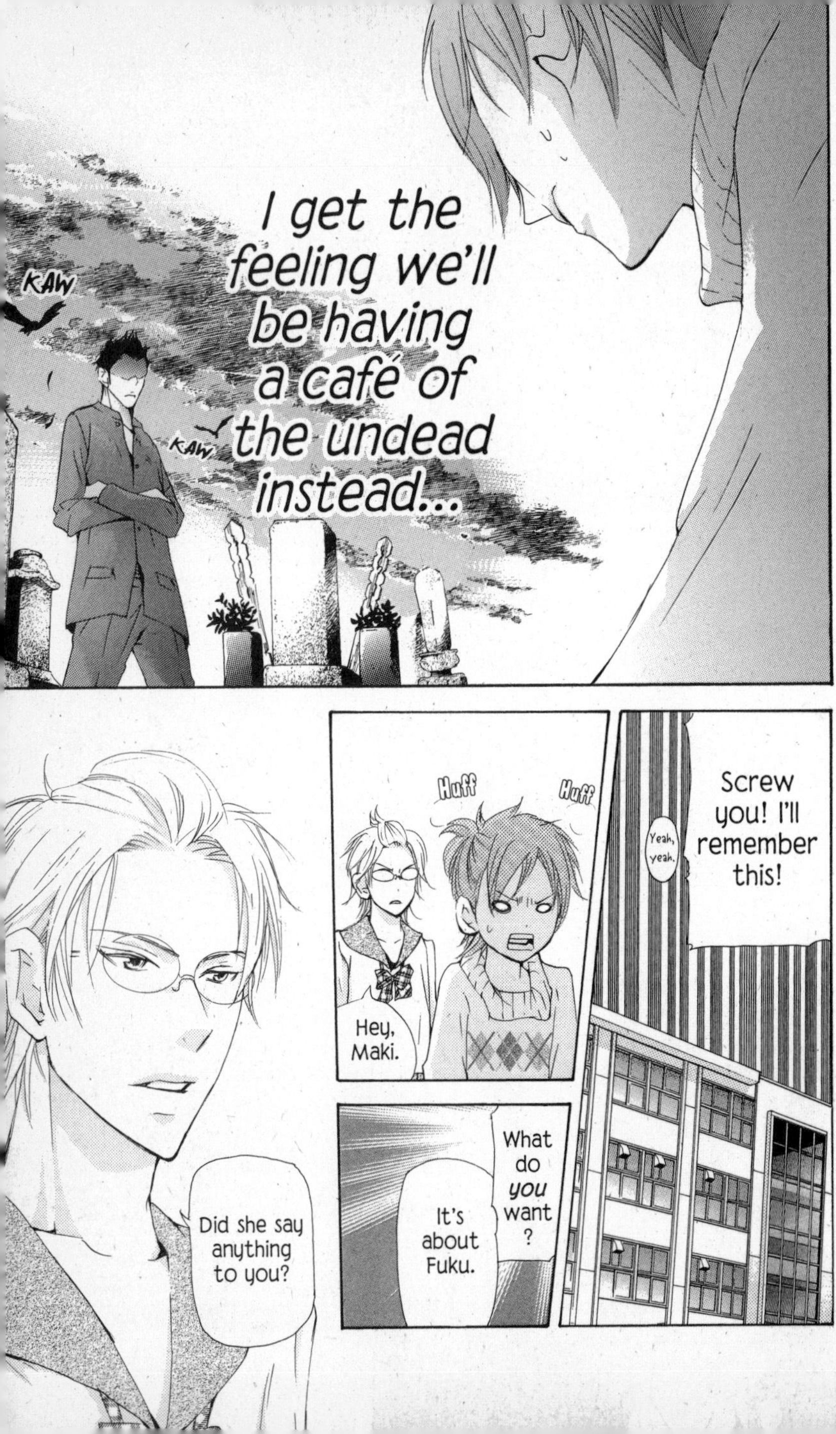
I get the feeling we'll be having a café of the undead instead...
KAW
KAW
Screw you! I'll remember this!
Yeah, yeah.
Huff
Huff
Hey, Maki.
What do *you* want?
It's about Fuku.
Did she say anything to you?

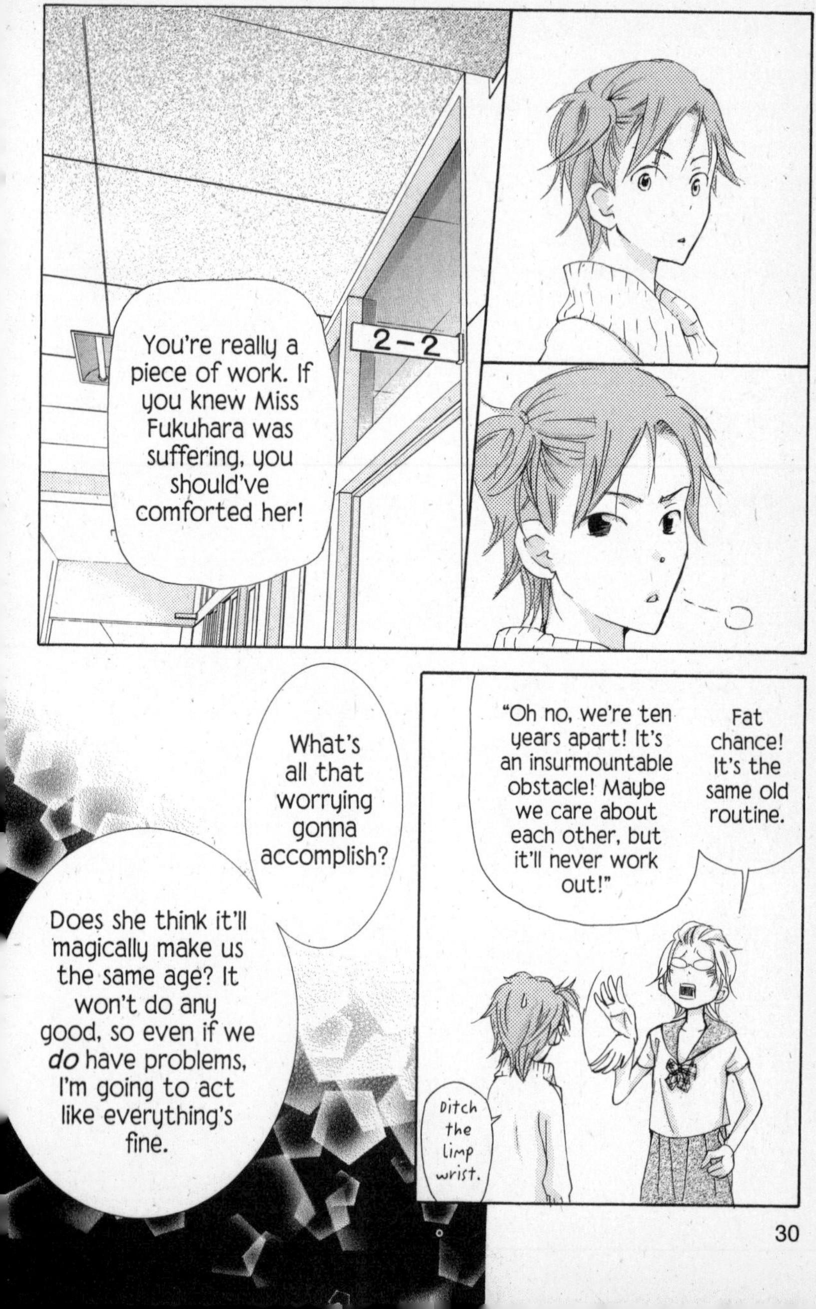
2-2
You're really a piece of work. If you knew Miss Fukuhara was suffering, you should've comforted her!
Fat chance! It's the same old routine.
"Oh no, we're ten years apart! It's an insurmountable obstacle! Maybe we care about each other, but it'll never work out!"
Ditch the limp wrist.
What's all that worrying gonna accomplish?
Does she think it'll magically make us the same age? It won't do any good, so even if we *do* have problems, I'm going to act like everything's fine.

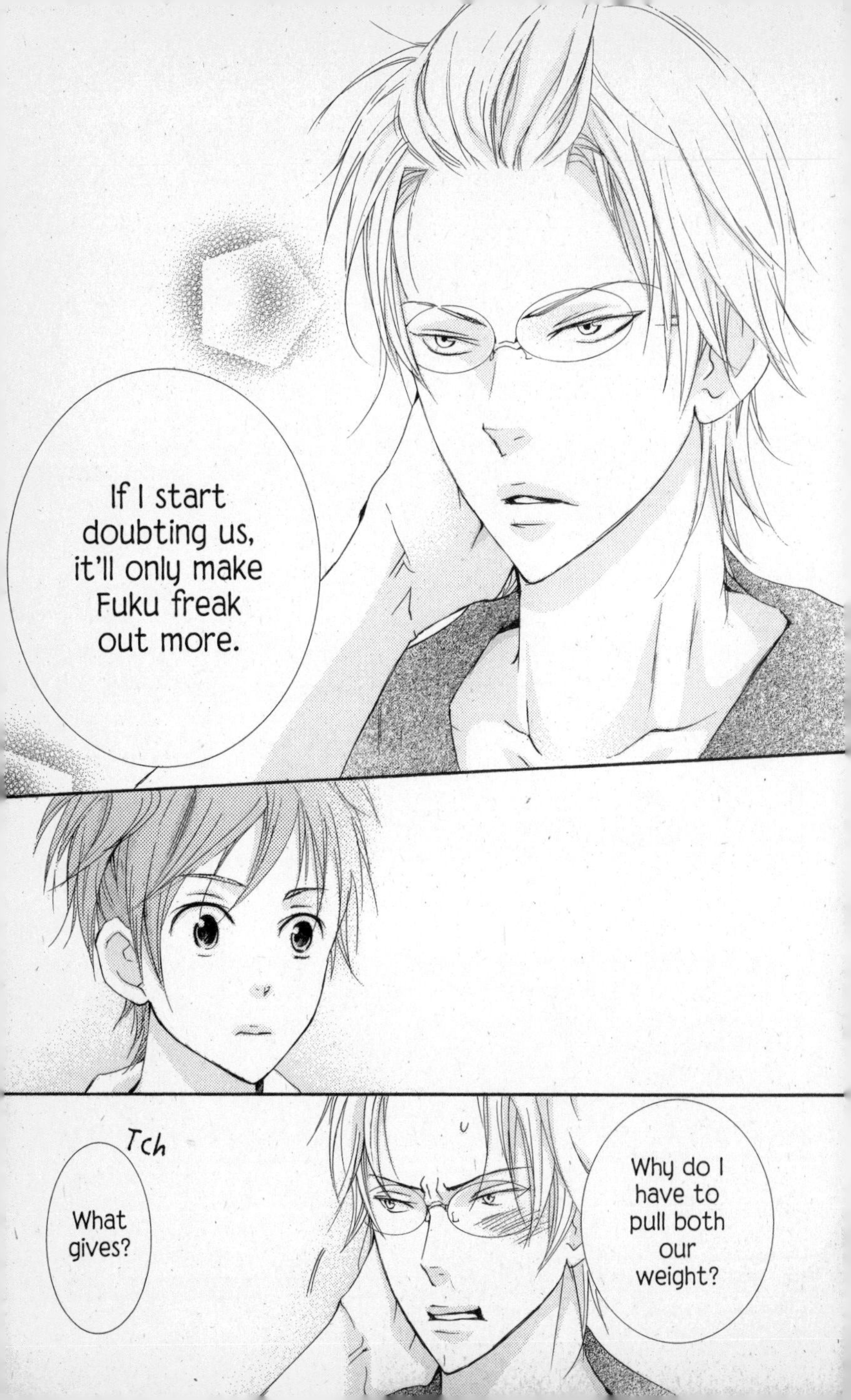
If I start doubting us, it'll only make Fuku freak out more.
Why do I have to pull both our weight?
Tch
What gives?

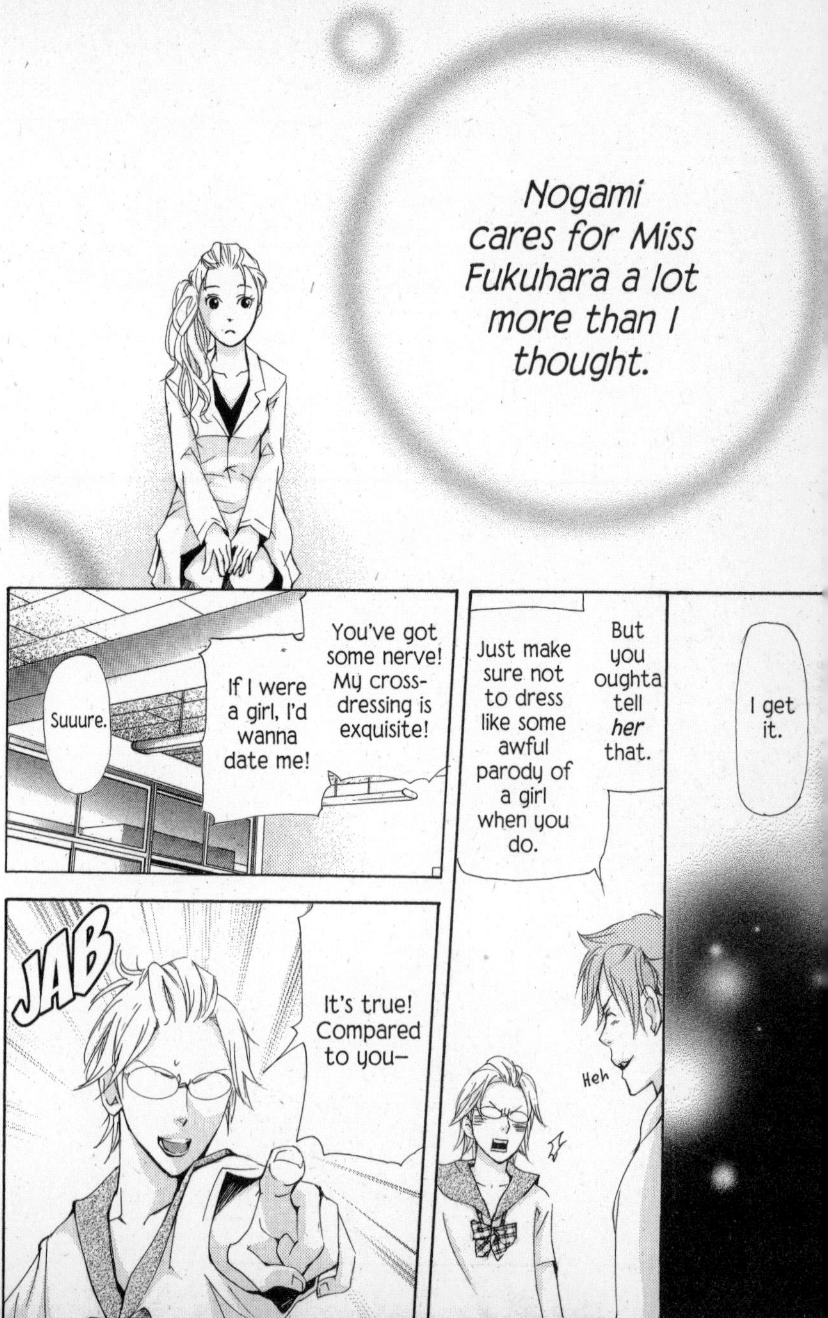
Nogami cares for Miss Fukuhara a lot more than I thought.
I get it.
But you oughta tell *her* that.
Just make sure not to dress like some awful parody of a girl when you do.
Heh
You've got some nerve! My cross-dressing is exquisite!
If I were a girl, I'd wanna date me!
Suuure.
It's true! Compared to you–
JAB

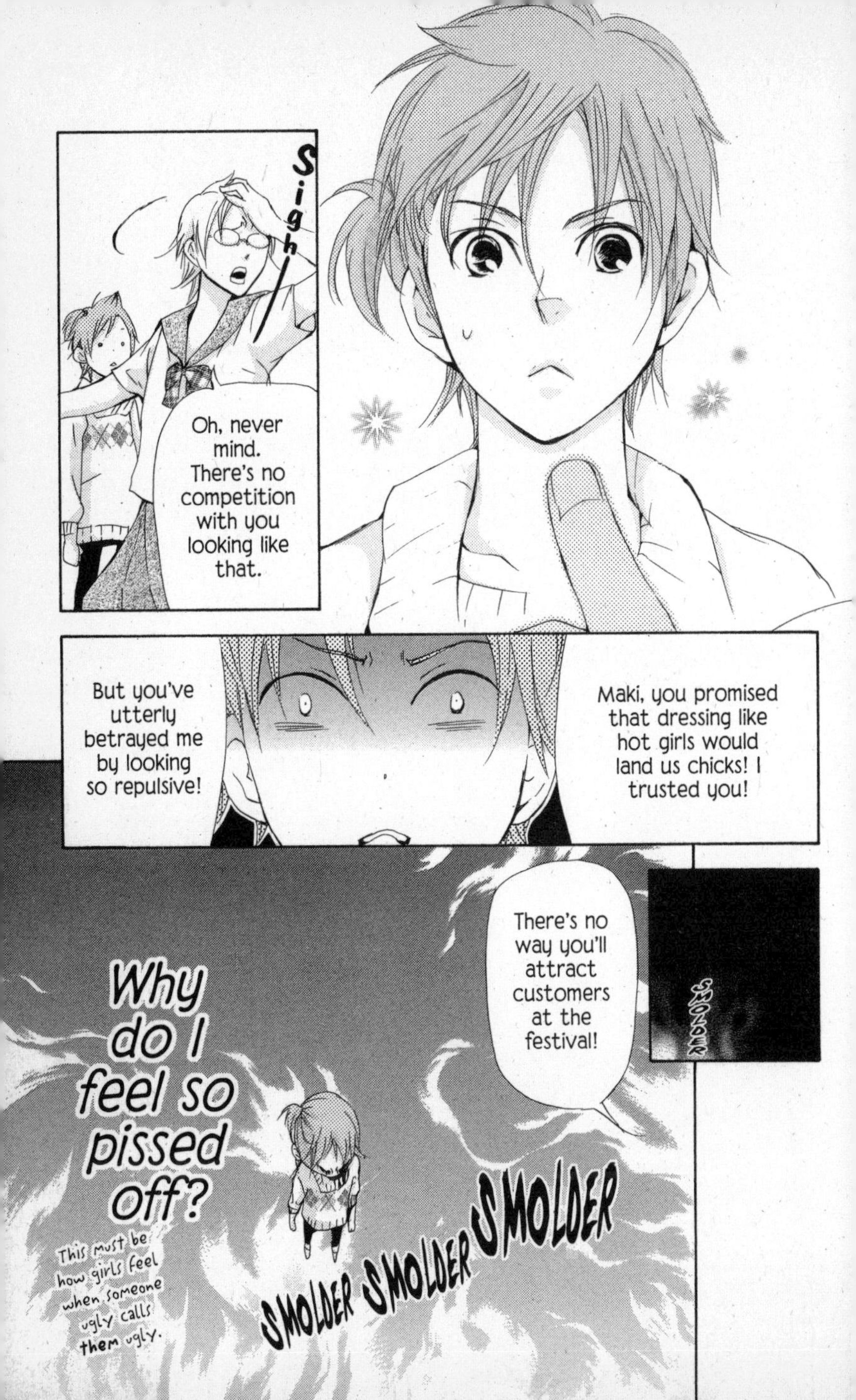
Sigh
Oh, never mind. There's no competition with you looking like that.
Maki, you promised that dressing like hot girls would land us chicks! I trusted you!
But you've utterly betrayed me by looking so repulsive!
SMOLDER
There's no way you'll attract customers at the festival!
Why do I feel so pissed off?
This must be how girls feel when someone ugly calls them ugly.
SMOLDER SMOLDER SMOLDER

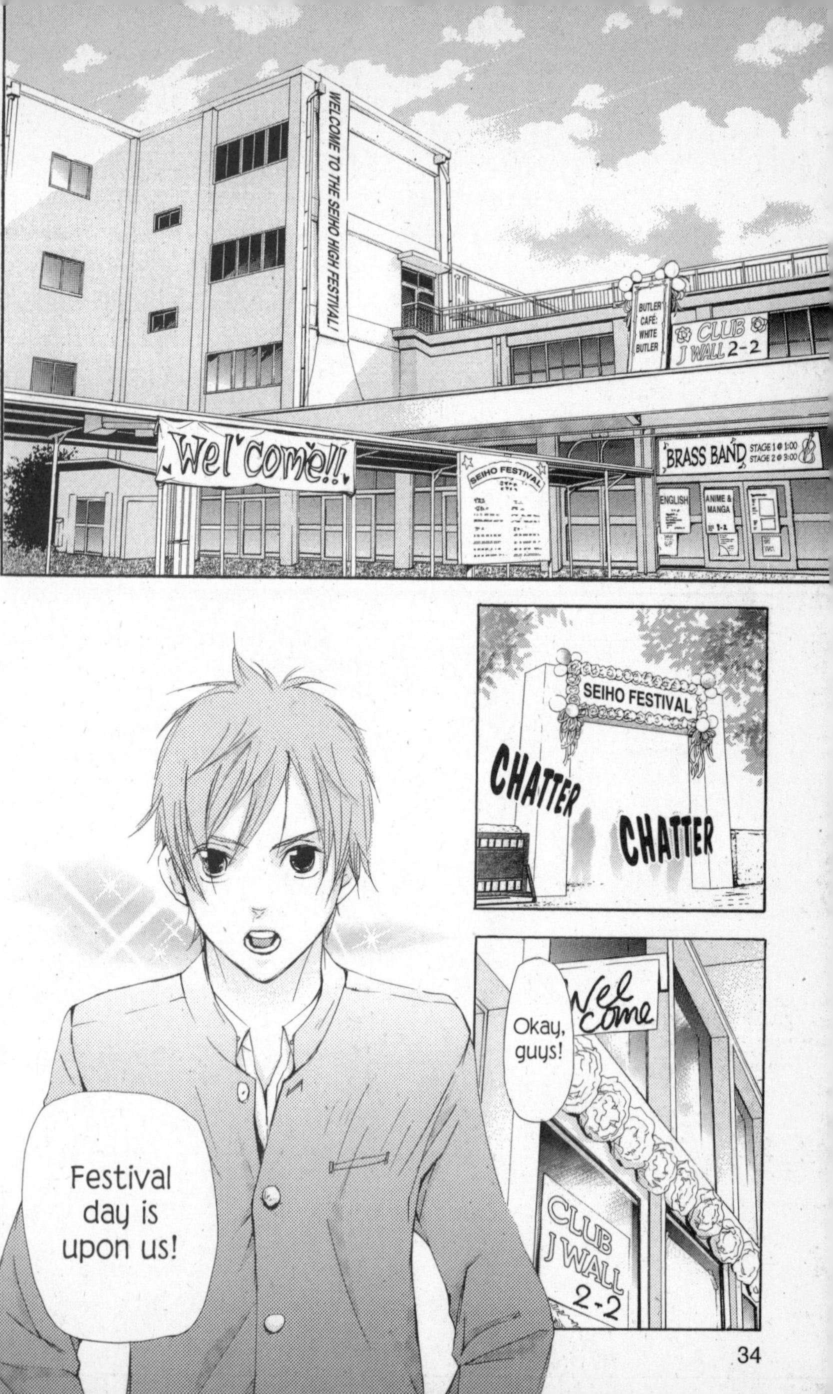

BUTLER CAFÉ: WHITE BUTLER
CLUB J WALL 2-2
WELCOME TO THE SEIHO HIGH FESTIVAL!
BRASS BAND STAGE 1 @ 1:00 STAGE 2 @ 3:00
SEIHO FESTIVAL
Wel come!!
ENGLISH
ANIME & MANGA
SEIHO FESTIVAL
CHATTER
CHATTER
Wel come
Okay, guys!
CLUB J WALL 2-2
Festival day is upon us!

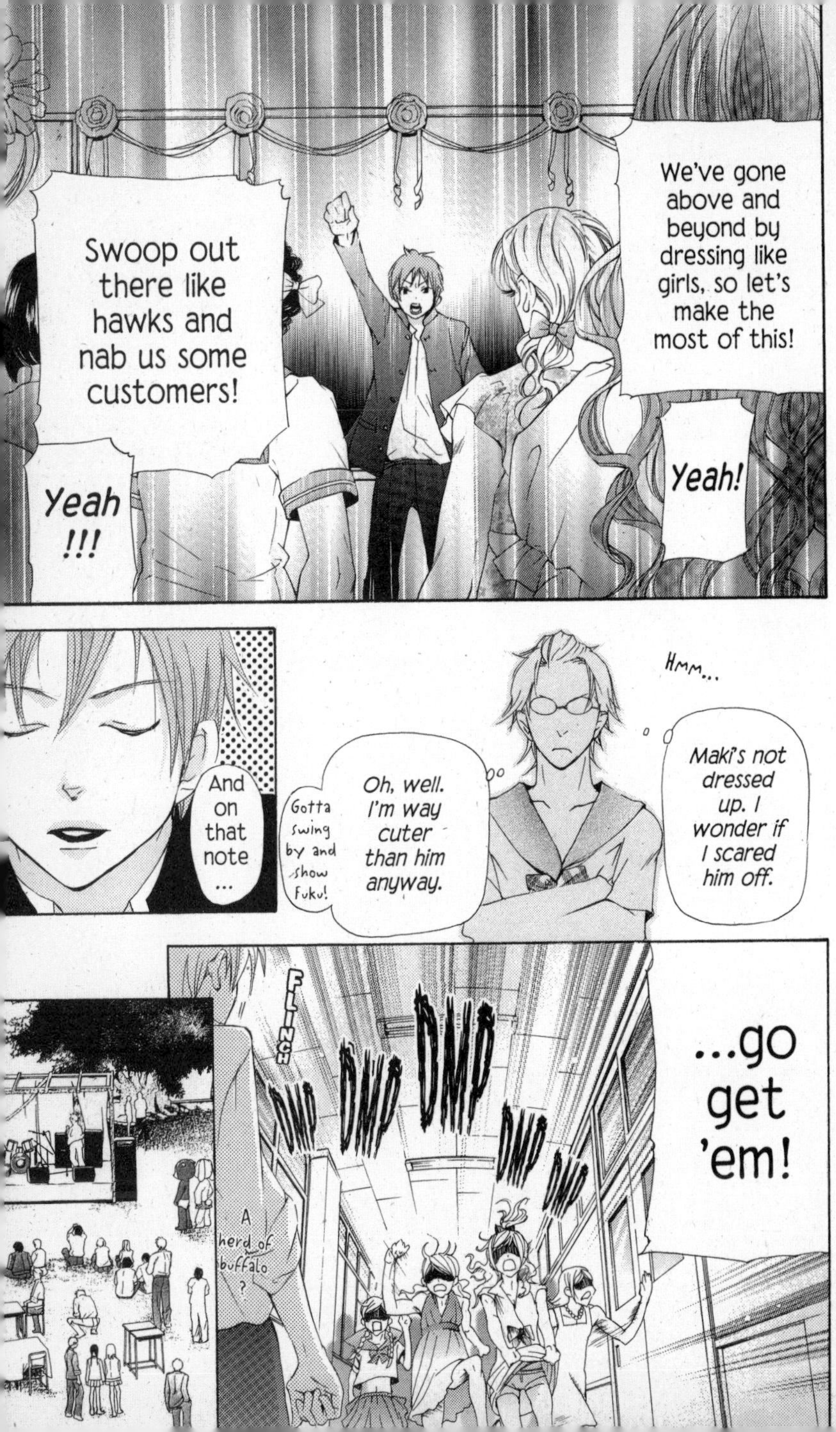

We've gone above and beyond by dressing like girls, so let's make the most of this!
Yeah!
Swoop out there like hawks and nab us some customers!
Yeah!!!
Hmm...
Maki's not dressed up. I wonder if I scared him off.
Oh, well. I'm way cuter than him anyway.
Gotta swing by and show Fuku!
And on that note...
...go get 'em!
DMP DMP DMP DMP DMP DMP
FLINCH
A herd of buffalo?

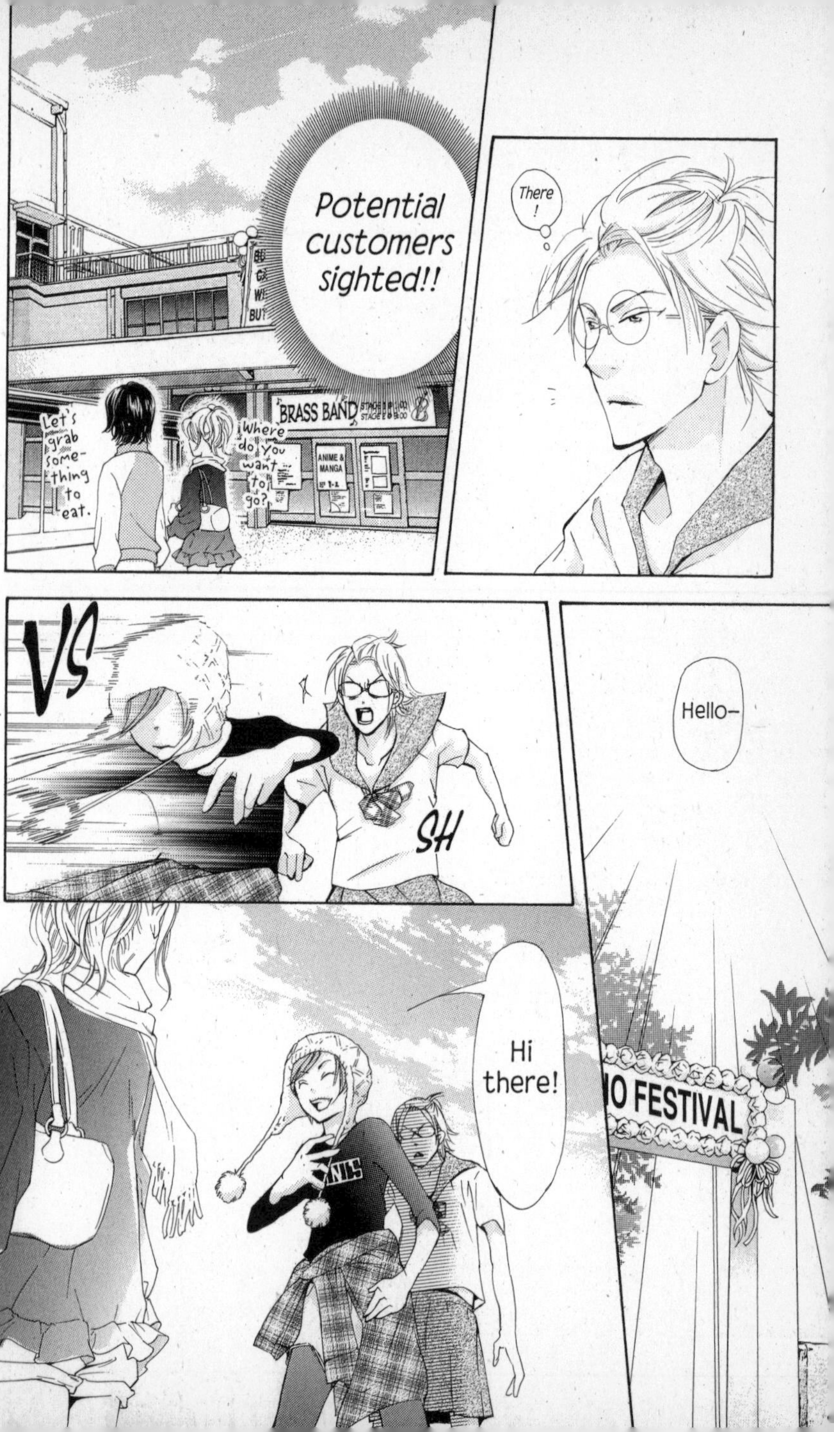
There!
Potential customers sighted!!
BRASS BAND
ANIME & MANGA
Where do you want to go?
Let's grab some-thing to eat.
Hello–
VS
SH
Hi there!
NO FESTIVAL

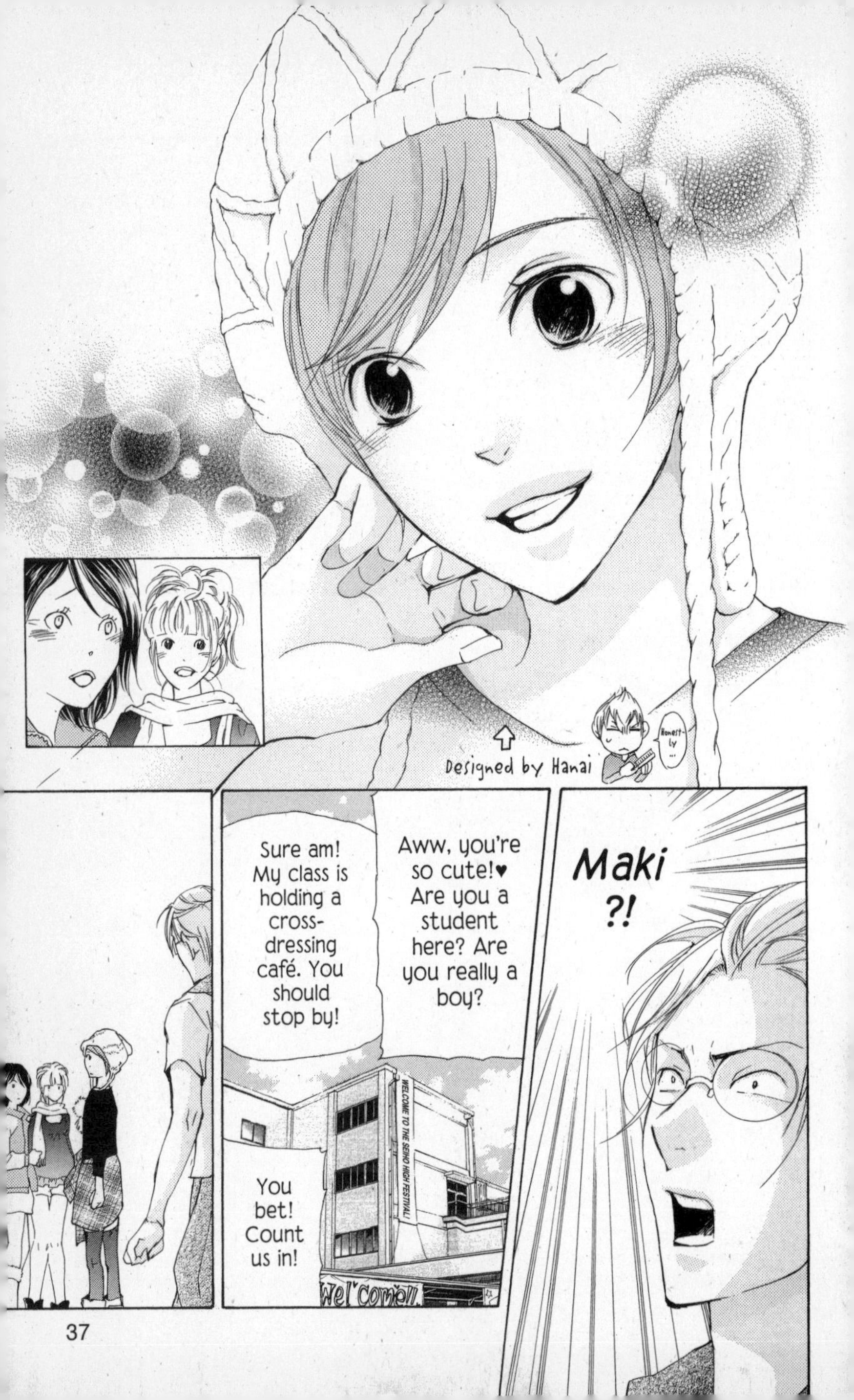
Designed by Hanai
Honestly...
Maki ?!
Aww, you're so cute!♥ Are you a student here? Are you really a boy?
Sure am! My class is holding a cross-dressing café. You should stop by!
WELCOME TO THE SEIHO HIGH FESTIVAL!
Wel'come!!
You bet! Count us in!

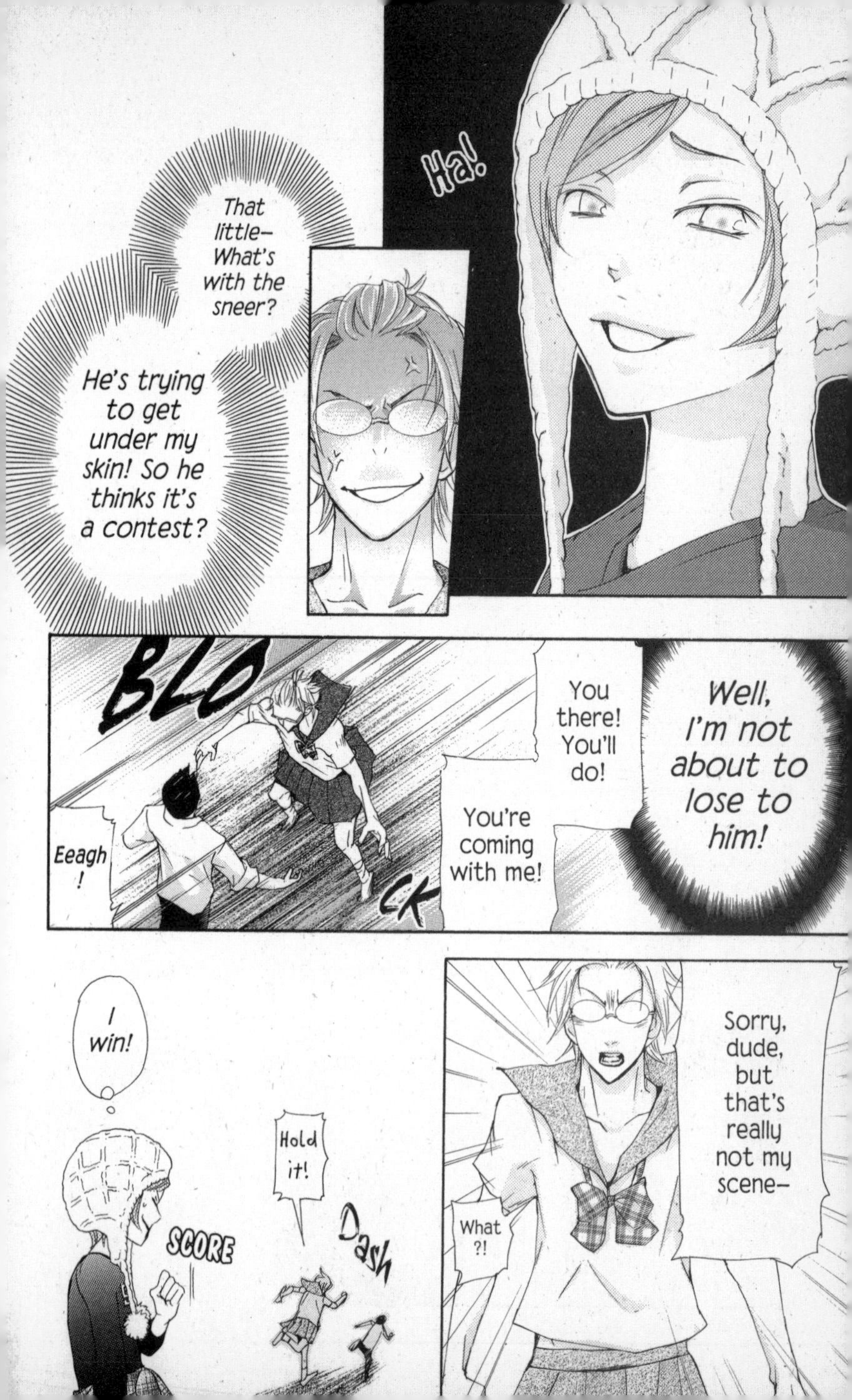
Ha!
That little— What's with the sneer?
He's trying to get under my skin! So he thinks it's a contest?
Well, I'm not about to lose to him!
You there! You'll do!
You're coming with me!
BLO
CK
Eeagh!
Sorry, dude, but that's really not my scene—
What?!
I win!
Hold it!
Dash
SCORE

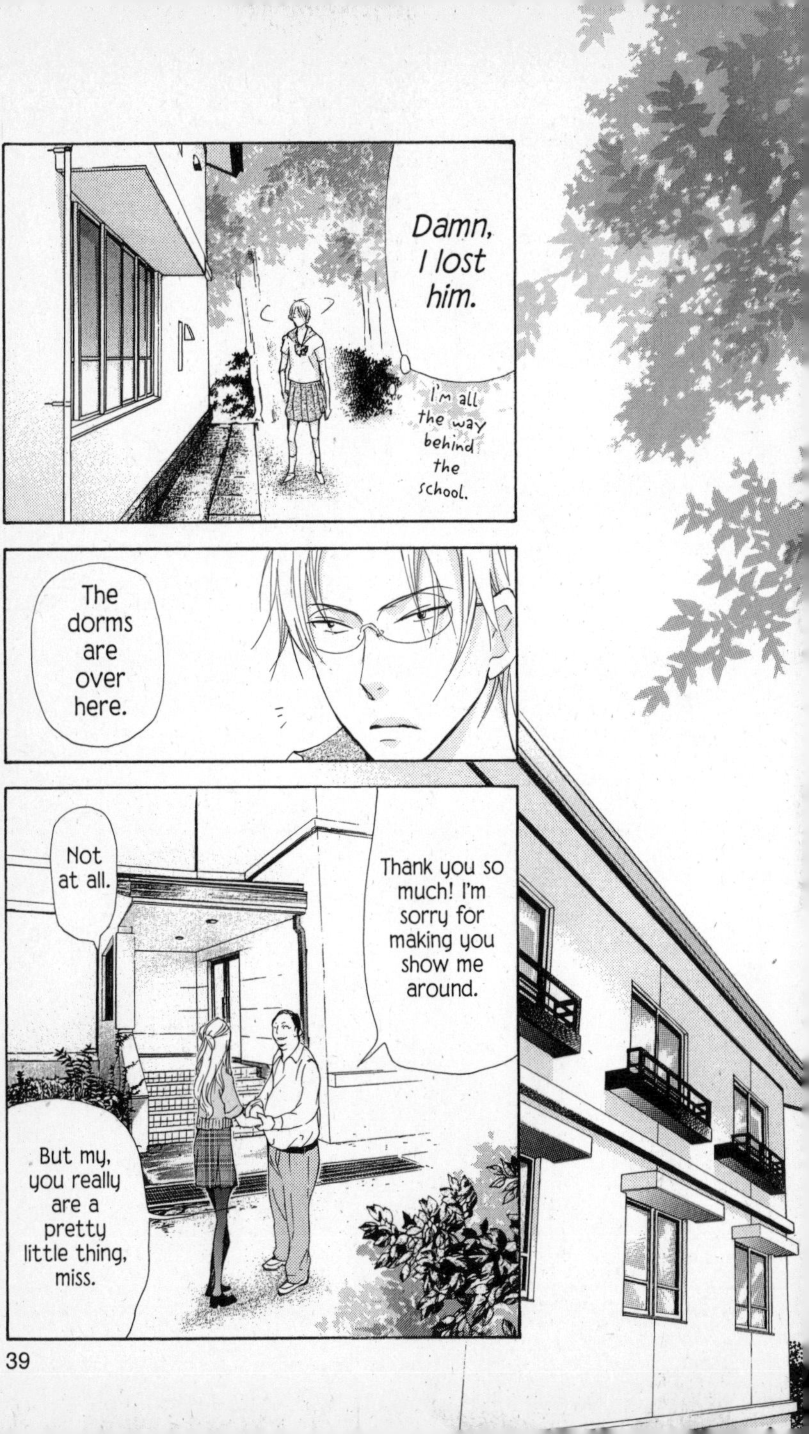
Damn, I lost him.
I'm all the way behind the school.
The dorms are over here.
Thank you so much! I'm sorry for making you show me around.
Not at all.
But my, you really are a pretty little thing, miss.

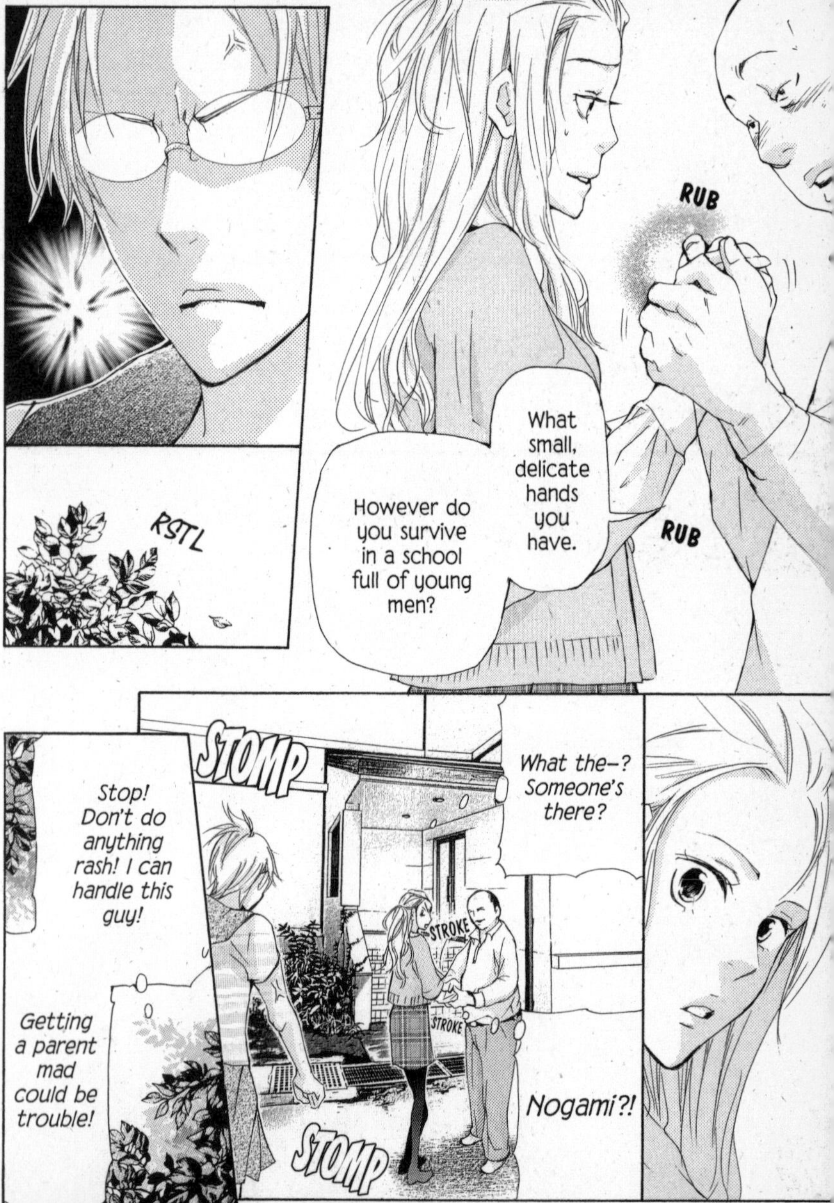
RUB
What small, delicate hands you have.
RUB
However do you survive in a school full of young men?
RSTL
What the–? Someone's there?
STOMP
STROKE
STROKE
Nogami?!
STOMP
Stop! Don't do anything rash! I can handle this guy!
Getting a parent mad could be trouble!

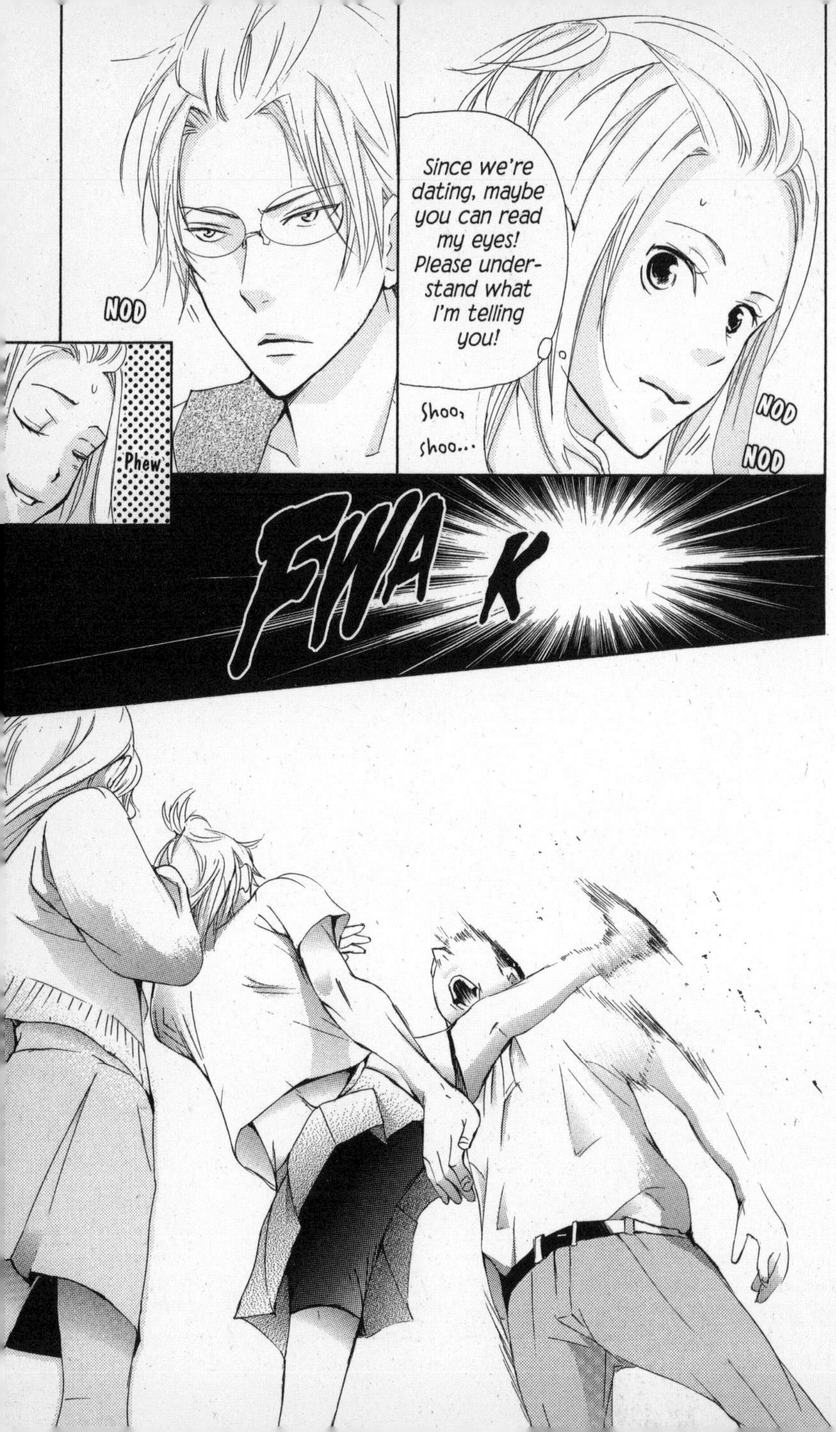
Since we're dating, maybe you can read my eyes! Please under-stand what I'm telling you!
NOD
NOD
Shoo, shoo...
NOD
Phew.
FWAK

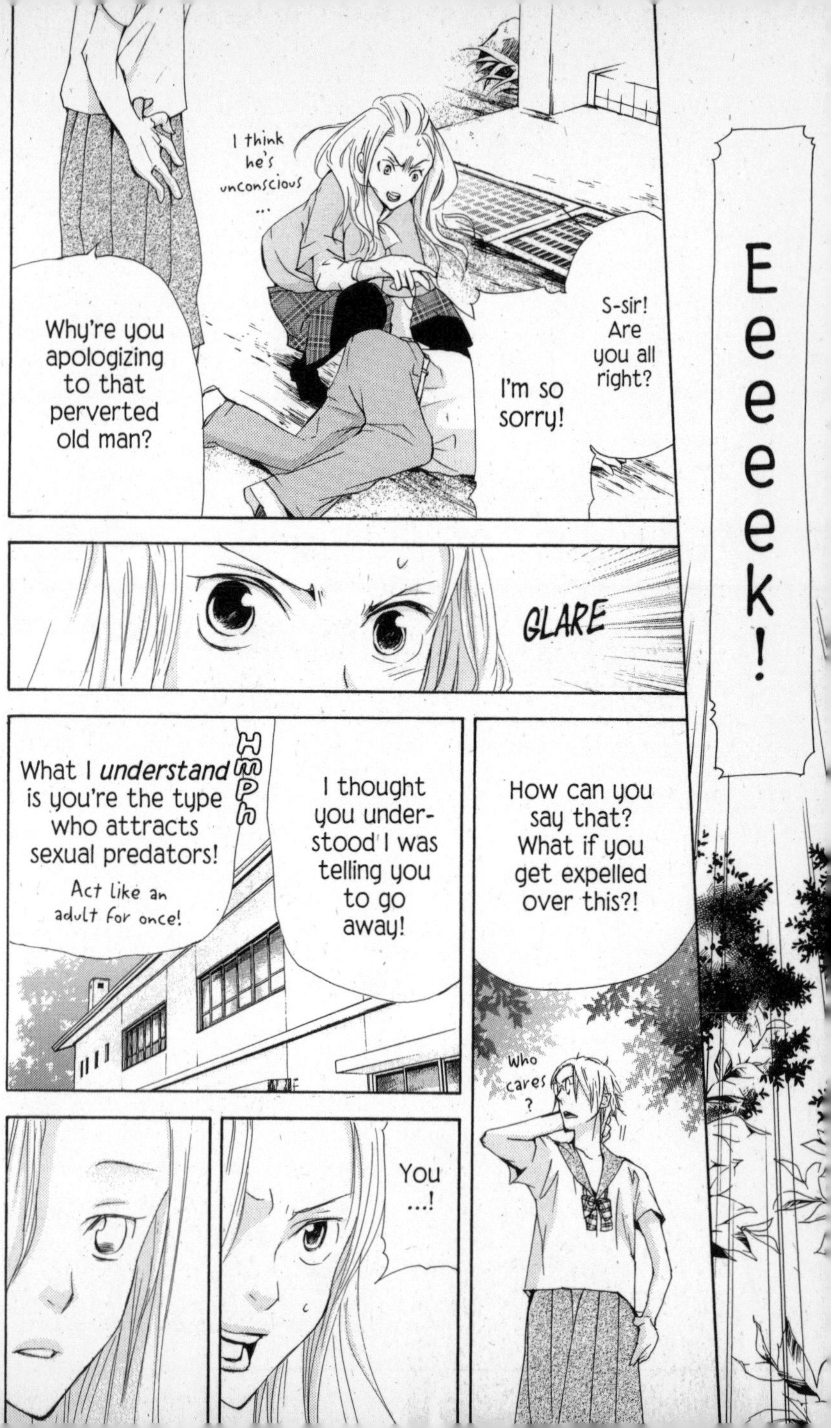
Eeeek!
S-sir! Are you all right?
I'm so sorry!
I think he's unconscious ...
Why're you apologizing to that perverted old man?
GLARE
How can you say that? What if you get expelled over this?!
Who cares?
I thought you understood I was telling you to go away!
Hmph
What I *understand* is you're the type who attracts sexual predators!
Act like an adult for once!
You ...!

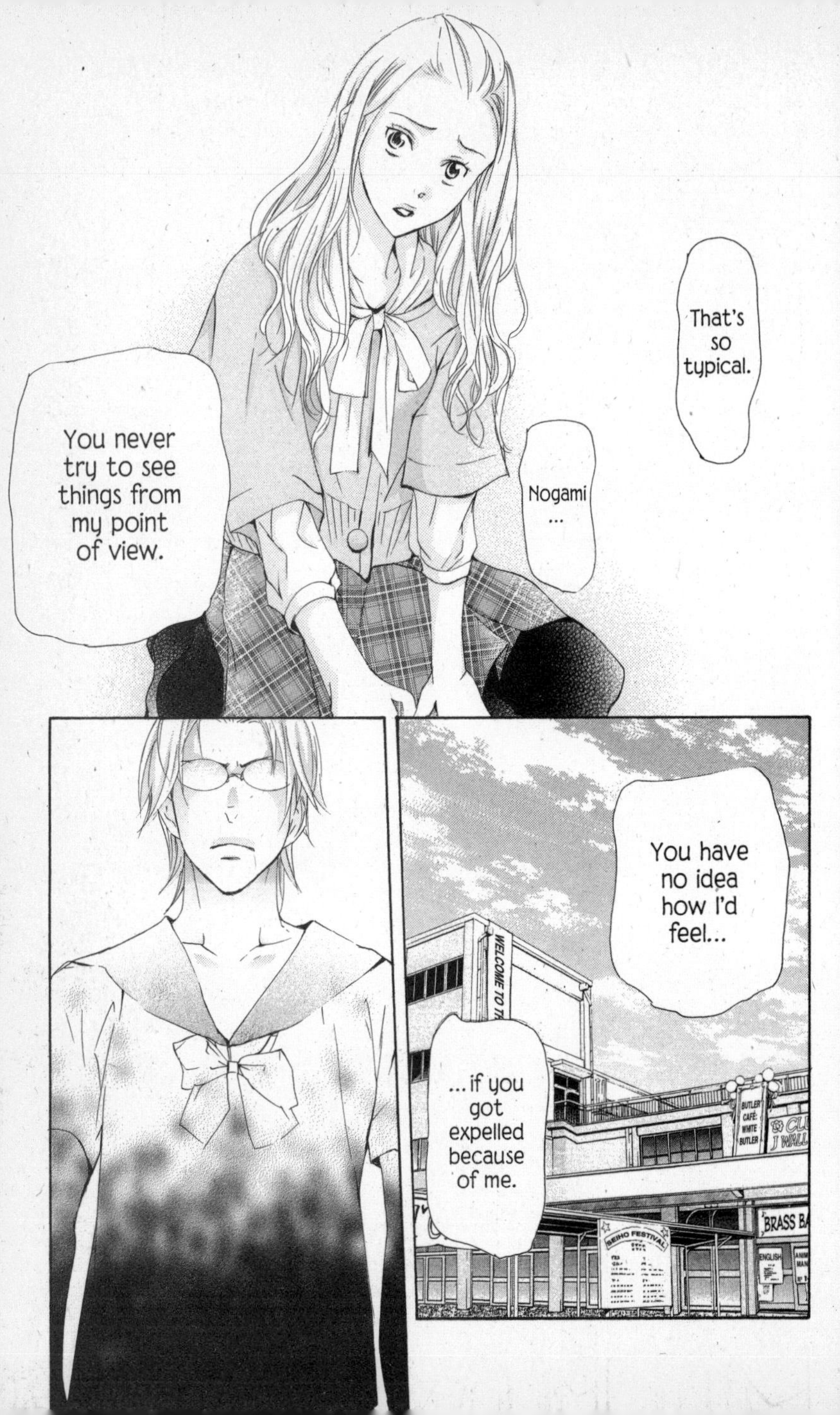
That's so typical.
Nogami...
You never try to see things from my point of view.
You have no idea how I'd feel...
...if you got expelled because of me.
BUTLER CAFÉ: WHITE BUTLER
SEIHO FESTIVAL

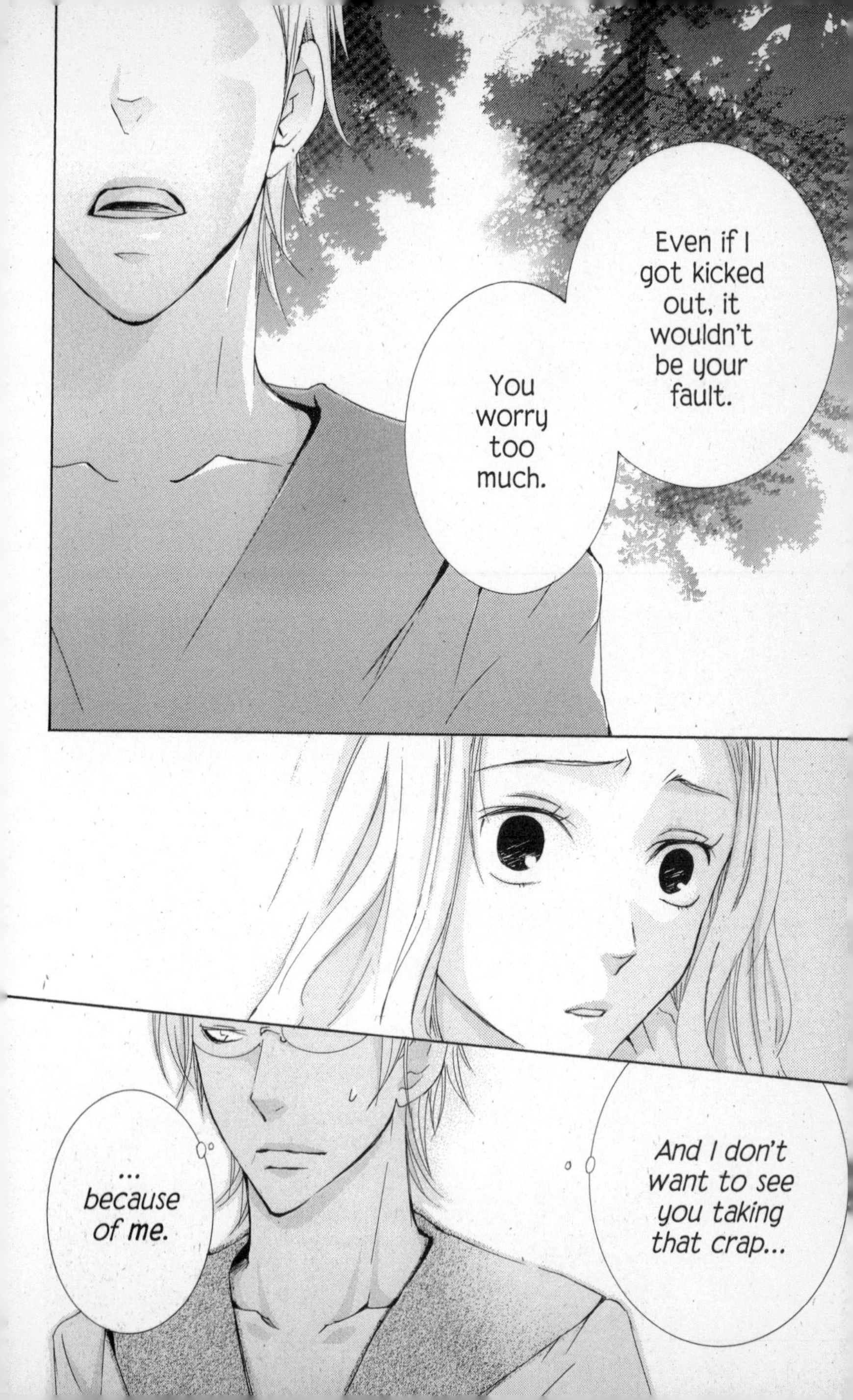
Even if I got kicked out, it wouldn't be your fault.
You worry too much.
And I don't want to see you taking that crap...
... because of me.

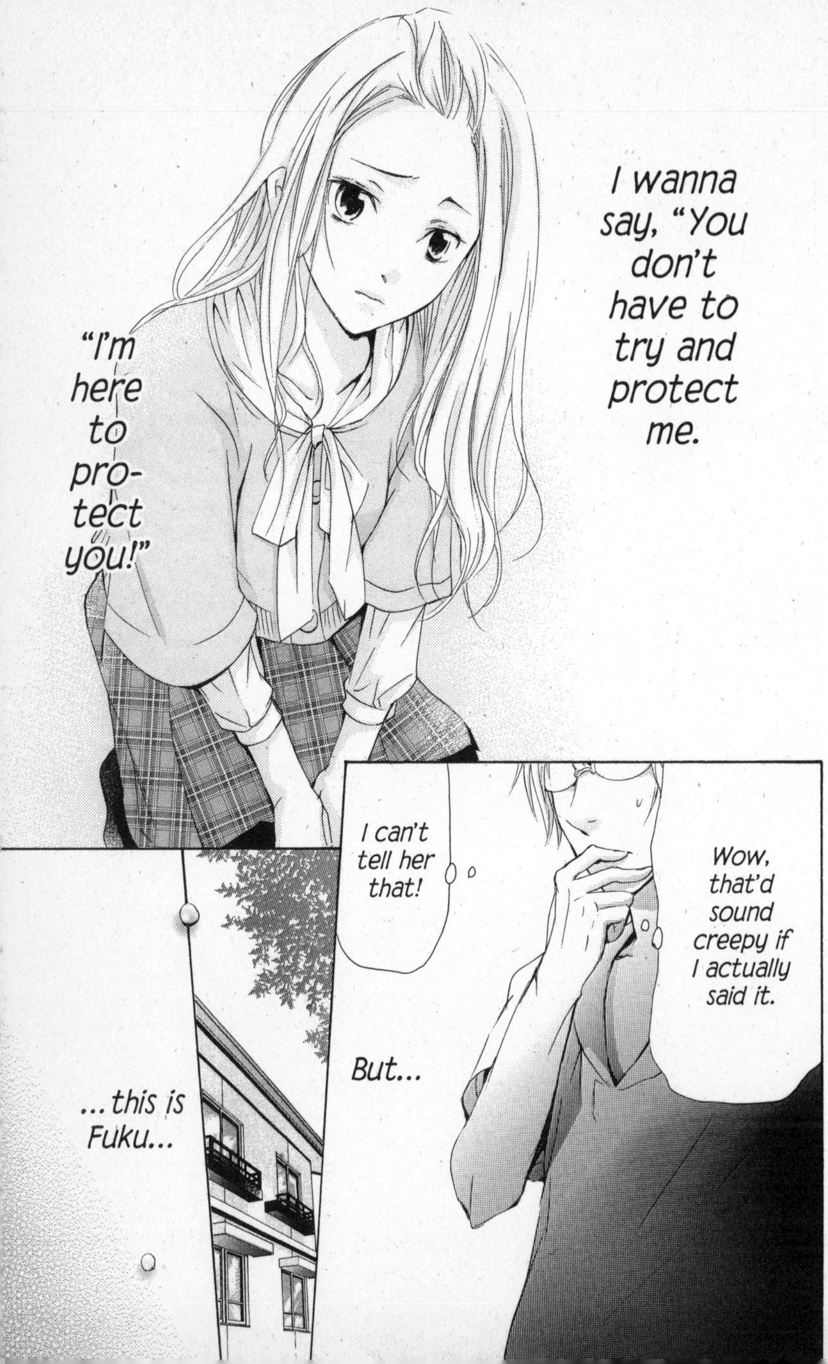
I wanna say, "You don't have to try and protect me.
"I'm here to protect you!"
Wow, that'd sound creepy if I actually said it.
I can't tell her that!
But...
...this is Fuku...

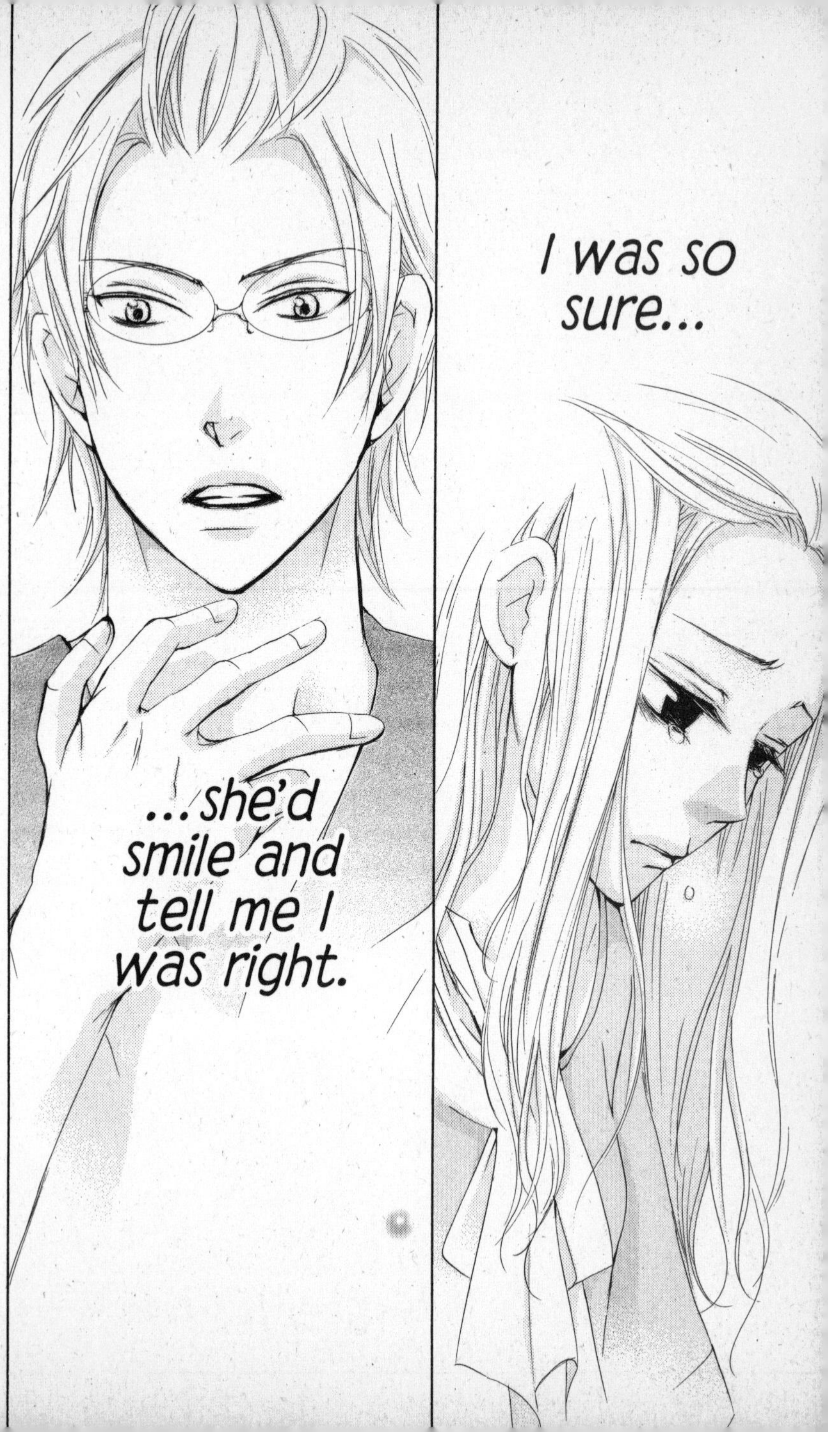
I was so sure...
...she'd smile and tell me I was right.

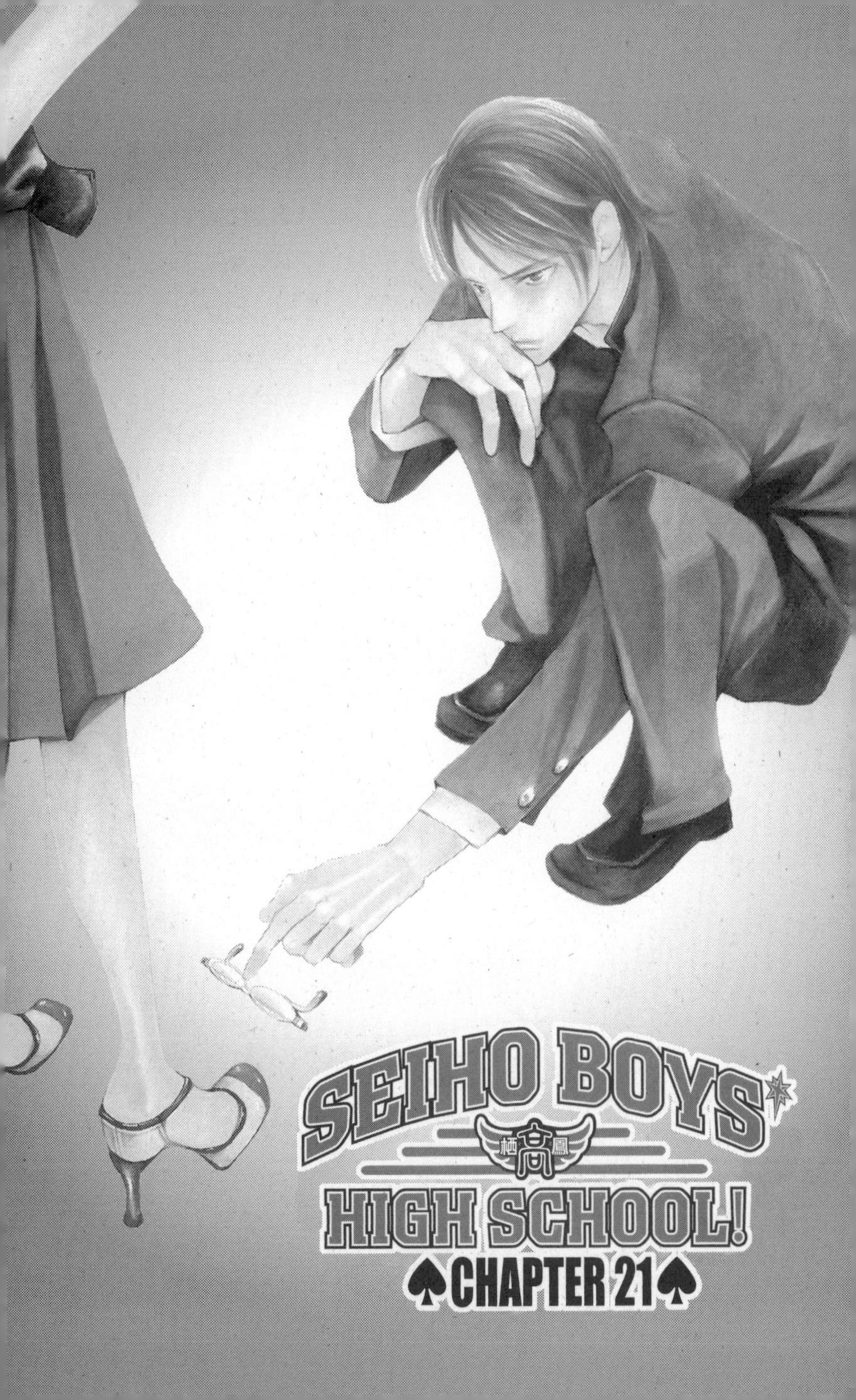
SEIHO BOYS' HIGH SCHOOL!
♠CHAPTER 21♠

When I was a kid, the most important thing was that I was useful to the people around me.

Hidetoshi, you got the highest mark on another test!

That's wonderful! Now your grandpa and grandma won't get snarky with me.

Hidetoshi.

SEIHO BOYS HIGH SCHOOL!

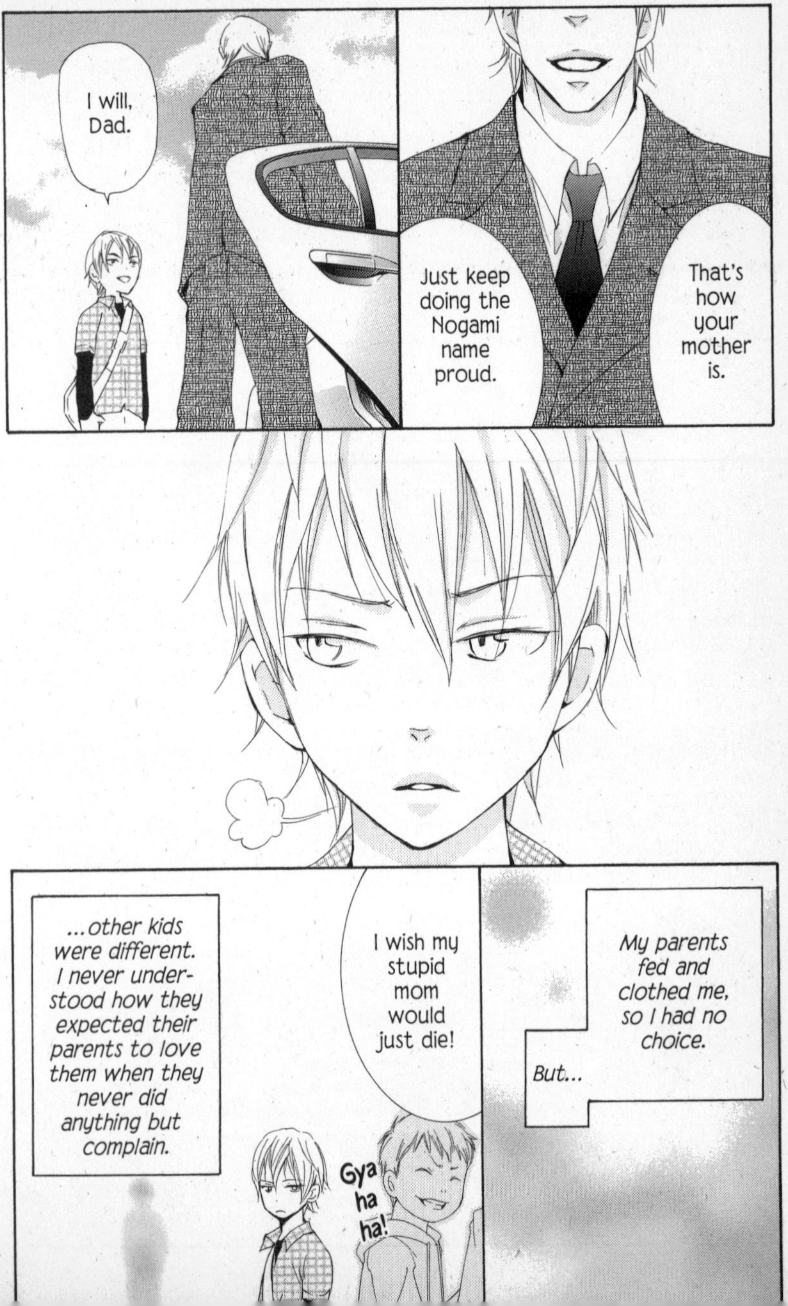
That's how your mother is.
Just keep doing the Nogami name proud.
I will, Dad.
My parents fed and clothed me, so I had no choice.
But...
I wish my stupid mom would just die!
...other kids were different. I never under-stood how they expected their parents to love them when they never did anything but complain.
Gya ha ha!

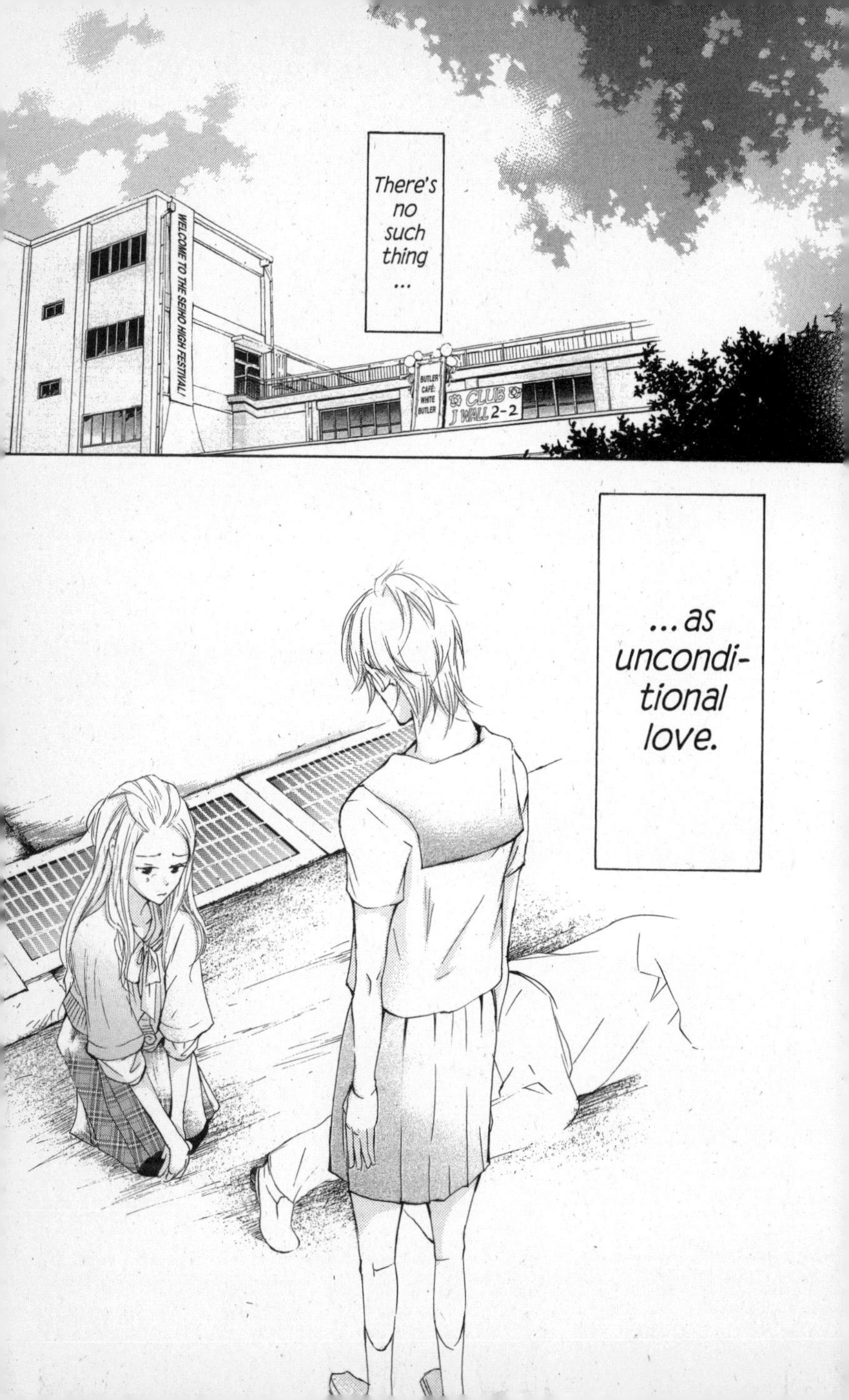
There's no such thing ...
CLUB J WALL 2-2
BUTLER CAFÉ: WHITE BUTLER
WELCOME TO THE SEIHO HIGH FESTIVAL!
...as uncondi-tional love.

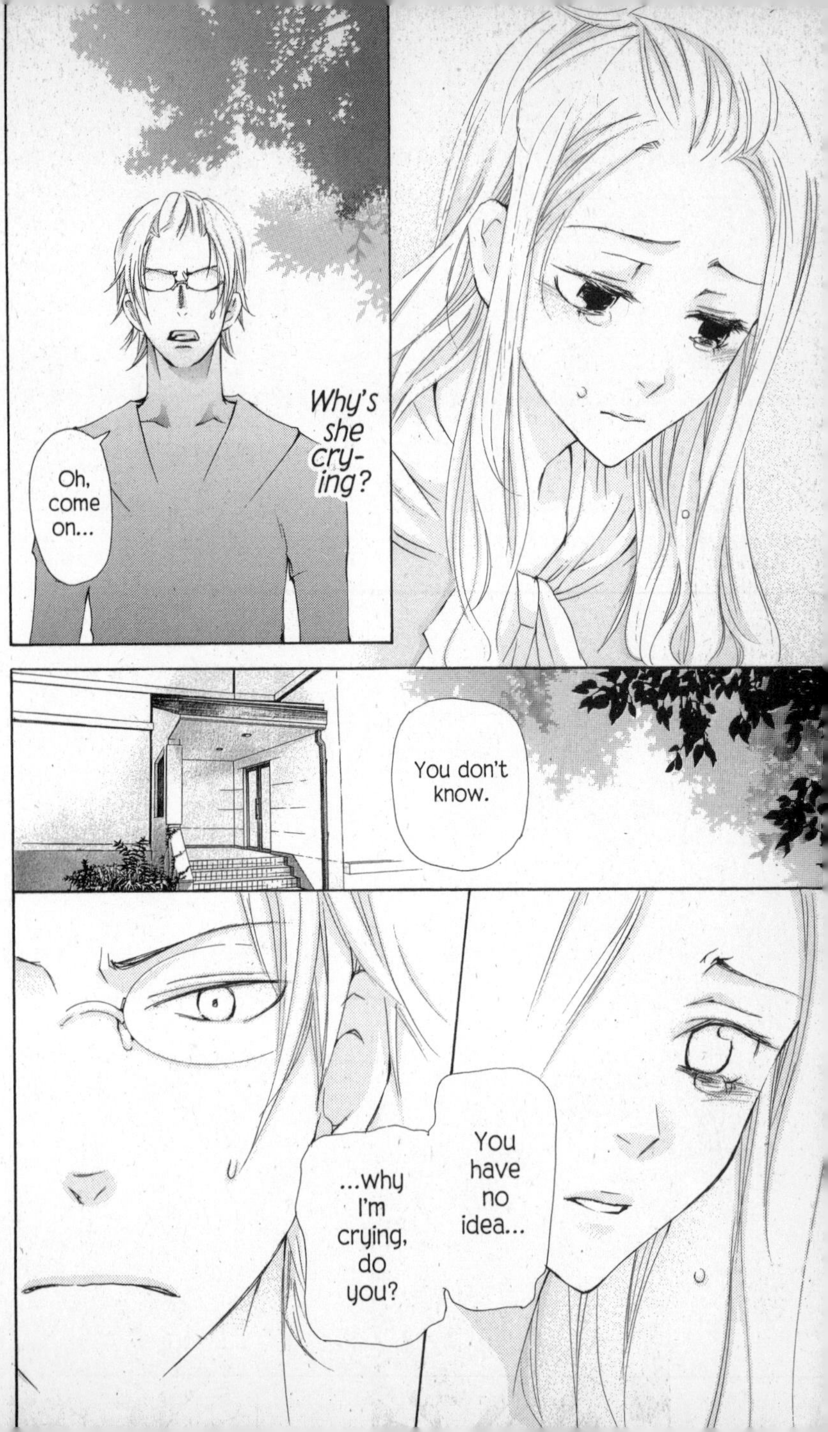
Why's she cry-ing?
Oh, come on...
You don't know.
You have no idea...
...why I'm crying, do you?

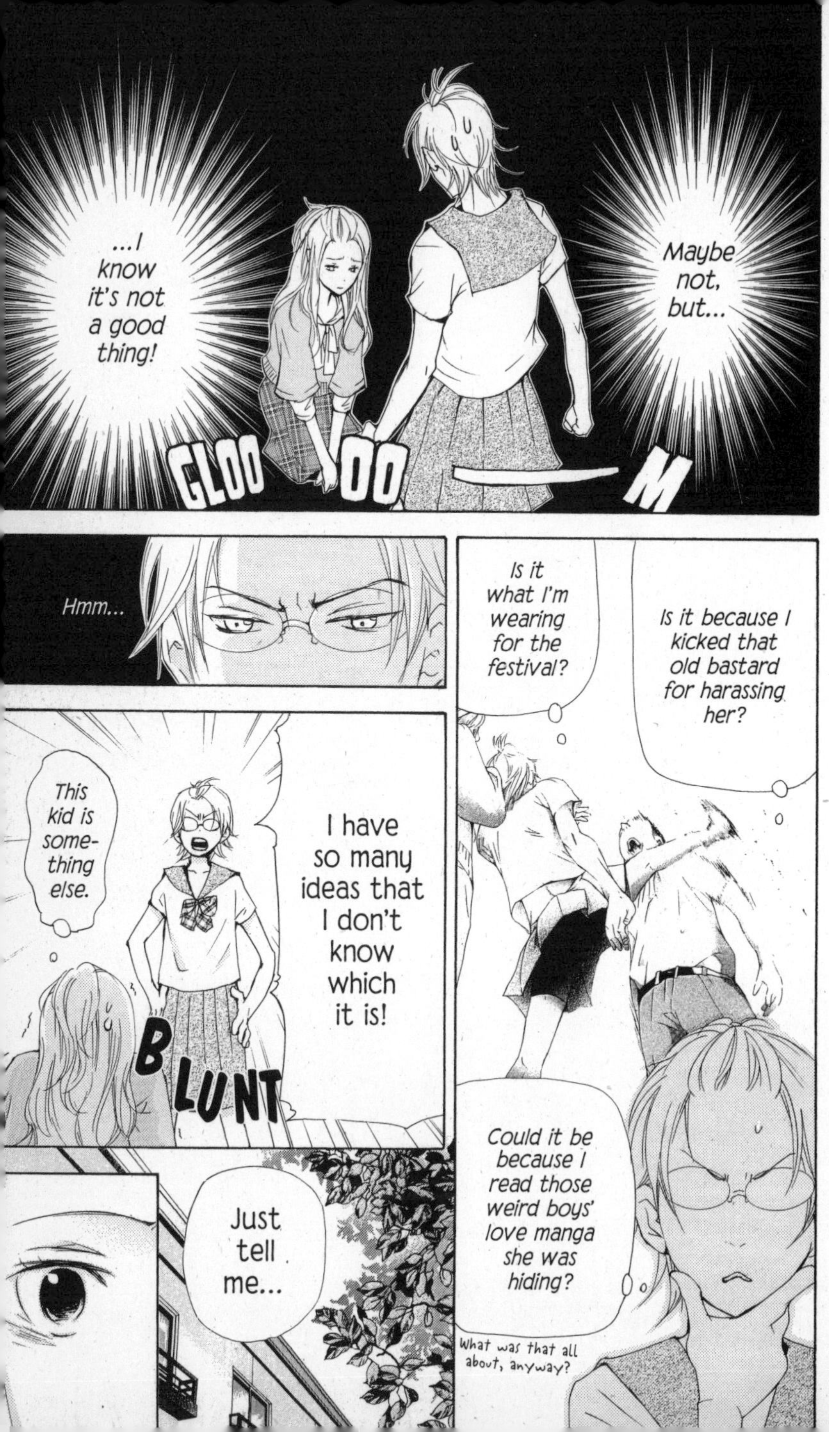
Maybe not, but...
...I know it's not a good thing!
GLOOOOM
Is it because I kicked that old bastard for harassing her?
Is it what I'm wearing for the festival?
Could it be because I read those weird boys' love manga she was hiding?
What was that all about, anyway?
Hmm...
I have so many ideas that I don't know which it is!
This kid is something else.
BLUNT
Just tell me...

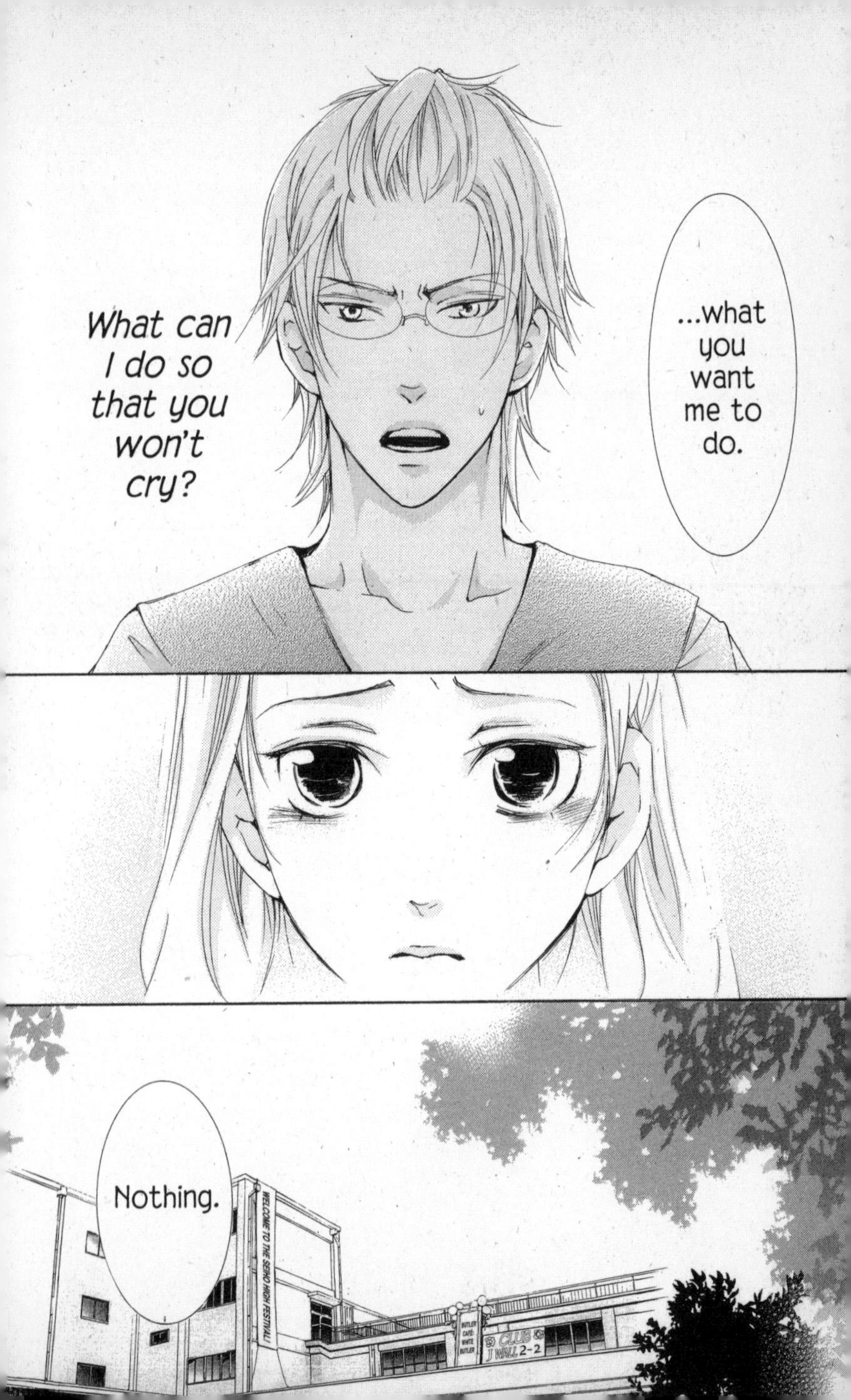
...what you want me to do.
What can I do so that you won't cry?
Nothing.
WELCOME TO THE SEIHO HIGH FESTIVAL!
BUTLER CAFÉ: WHITE BUTLER
CLUB J WALL 2-2

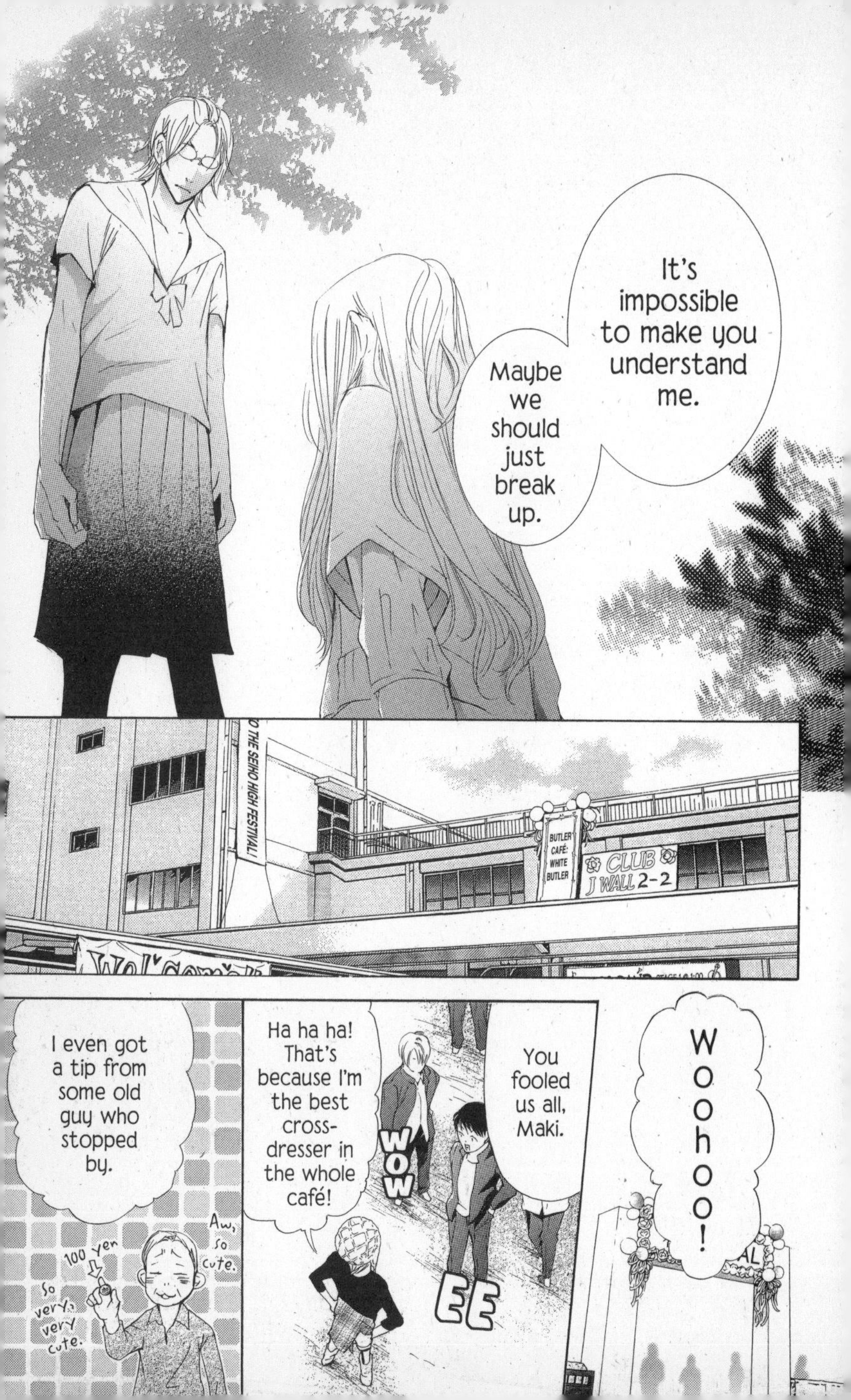
It's impossible to make you understand me.
Maybe we should just break up.
O THE SEIHO HIGH FESTIVAL!
BUTLER CAFÉ: WHITE BUTLER
CLUB J WALL 2-2
Woohoo!
You fooled us all, Maki.
WOW
EE
Ha ha ha! That's because I'm the best cross-dresser in the whole café!
I even got a tip from some old guy who stopped by.
100 yen
Aw, so cute.
So very, very cute.

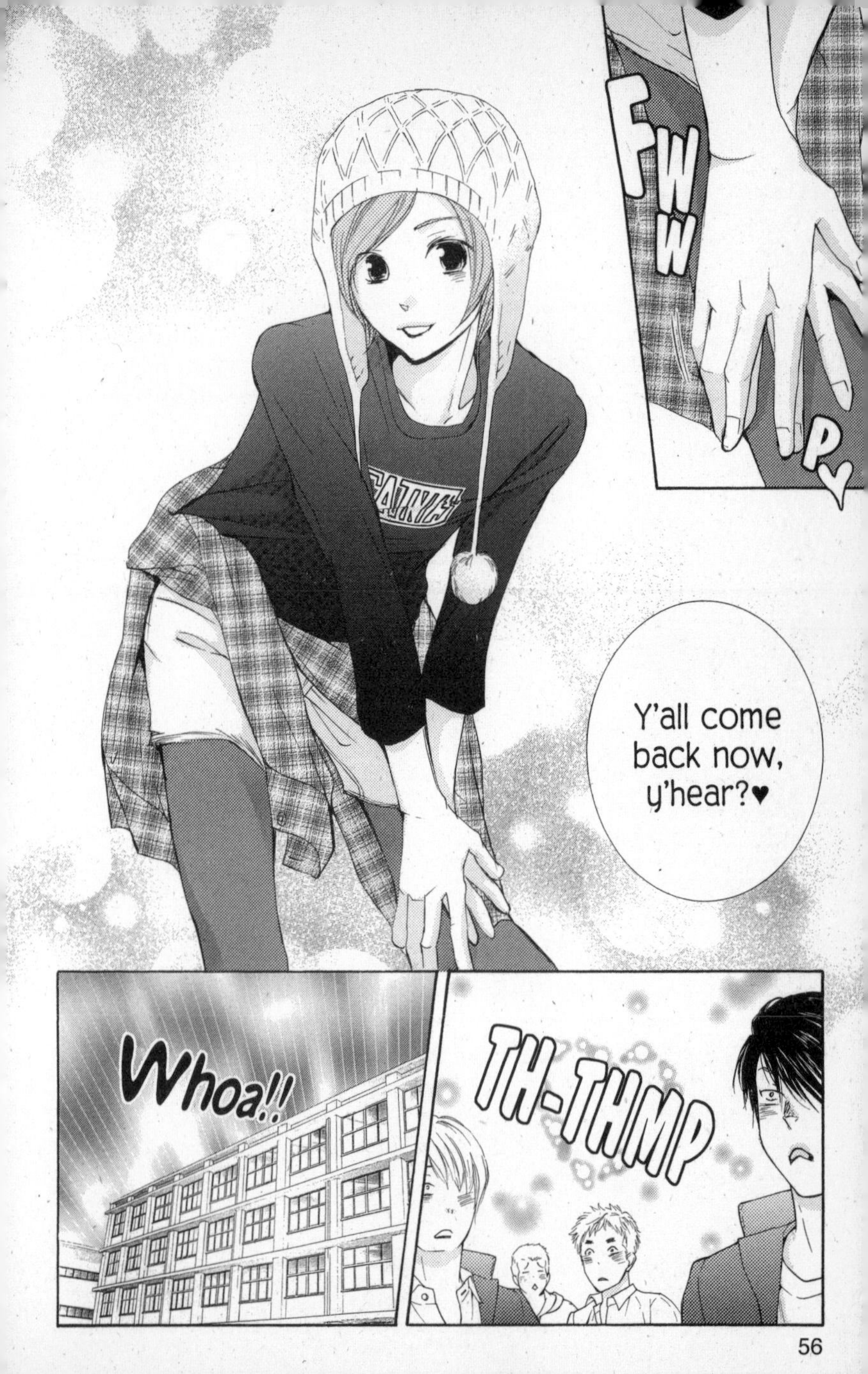
FWW
P♥
Y'all come back now, y'hear?♥
TH-THMP
Whoa!!

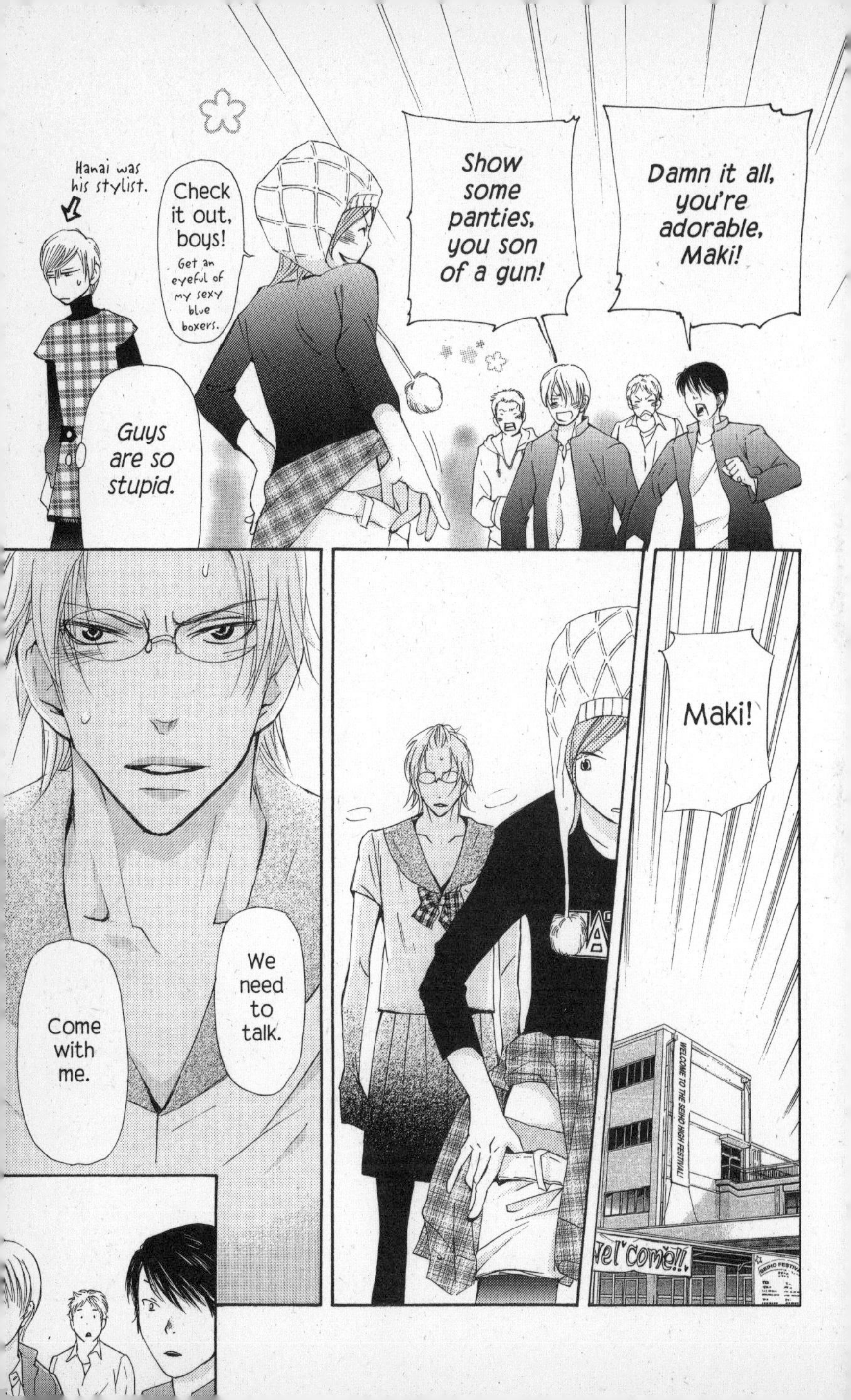
Damn it all, you're adorable, Maki!
Show some panties, you son of a gun!
Check it out, boys!
Get an eyeful of my sexy blue boxers.
Hanai was his stylist.
Guys are so stupid.
Maki!
WELCOME TO THE SEIHO HIGH FESTIVAL!
Wel'come!!
We need to talk.
Come with me.

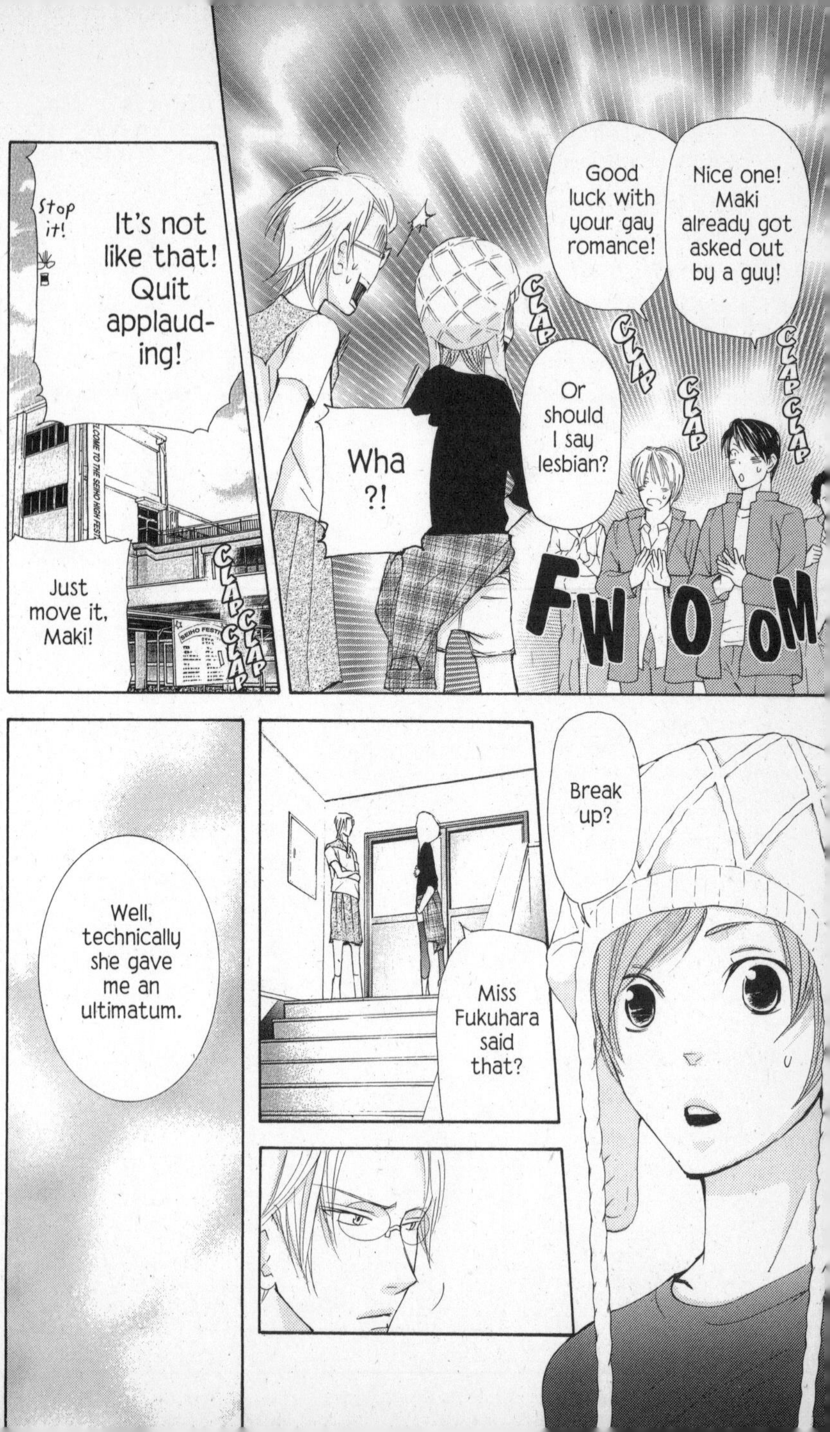
Nice one! Maki already got asked out by a guy!
Good luck with your gay romance!
CLAP CLAP CLAP CLAP CLAP CLAP
Or should I say lesbian?
FWOOM
Wha ?!
It's not like that! Quit applaud-ing!
Stop it!
Just move it, Maki!
CLAP CLAP CLAP
Break up?
Miss Fukuhara said that?
Well, technically she gave me an ultimatum.

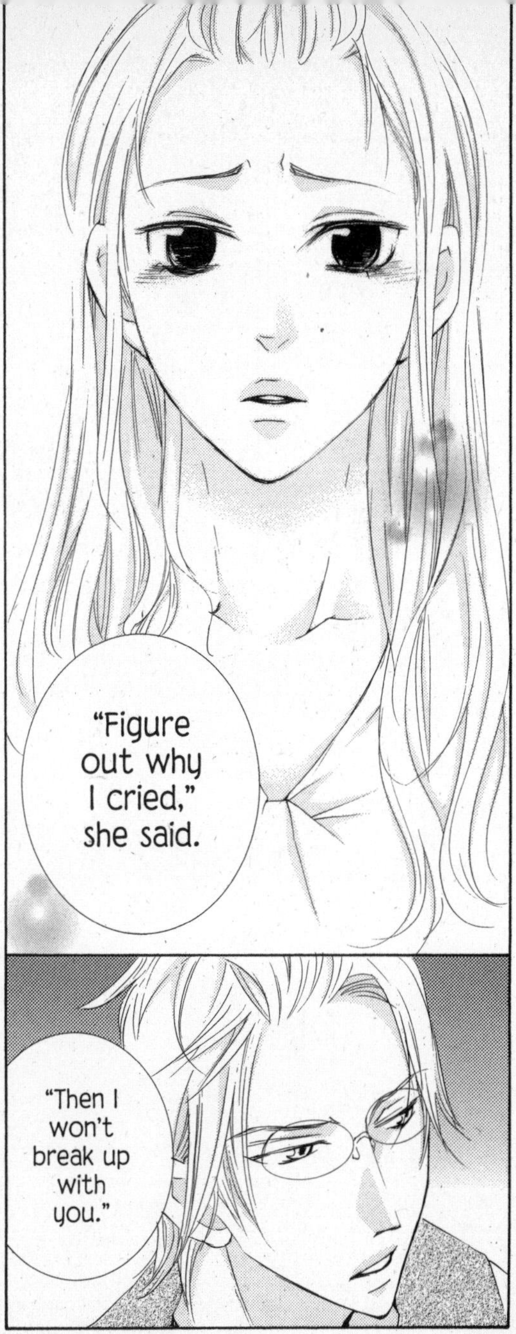
"Figure out why I cried," she said.
"Then I won't break up with you."

1/3 Filler Corner

AIRLINE FOOD The Opposite of a Gourmet Journey

Case 2

Air N

(International FLight)

Staple Menu

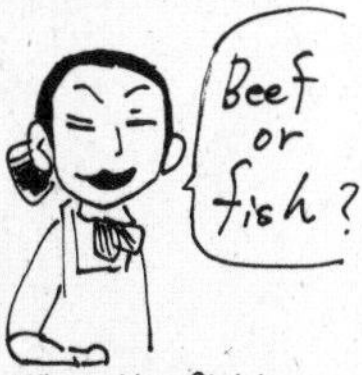
Beef or fish?

When the flight attendant asked what I wanted, I turned to my friend...

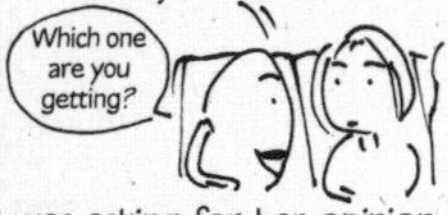
Which one are you getting?

I was asking for her opinion, but then...

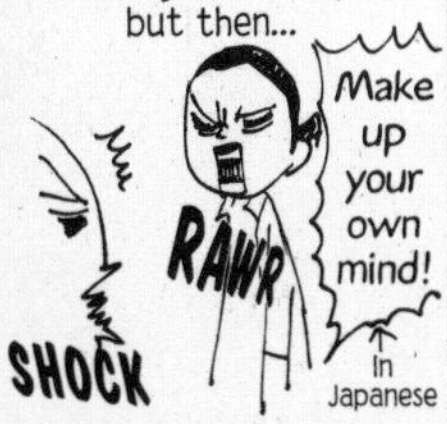
Make up your own mind!
RAWR
SHOCK
In Japanese

I got scorched by the attendant. I was pretty surprised.

But during the rest of the flight, she helped me with my English pronunciation, so she was pretty nice overall. And this happened so long ago that she probably just saw me as a little kid.

Asians often look younger than we actually are...

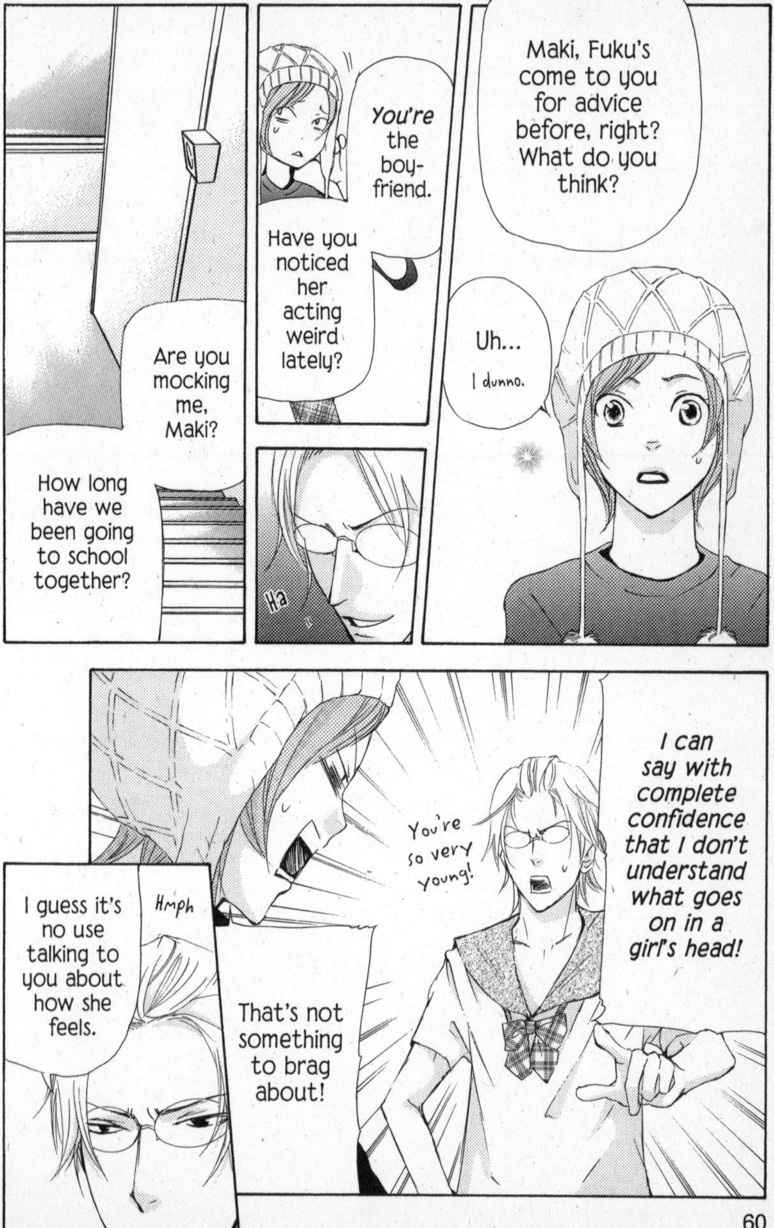

Maki, Fuku's come to you for advice before, right? What do you think?
Uh...
I dunno.
You're the boy-friend.
Have you noticed her acting weird lately?
Ha
Are you mocking me, Maki?
How long have we been going to school together?
I can say with complete confidence that I don't understand what goes on in a girl's head!
You're so very young!
That's not something to brag about!
Hmph
I guess it's no use talking to you about how she feels.

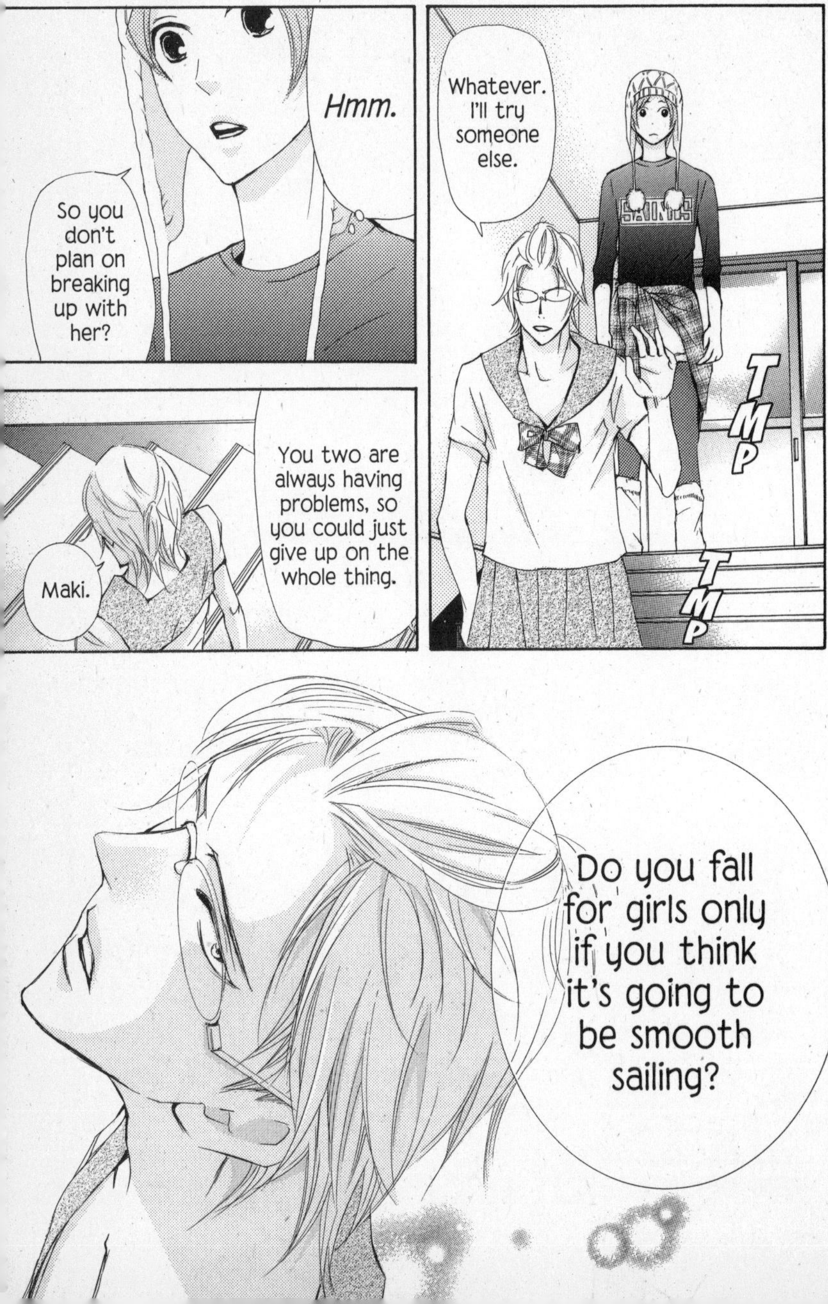
Whatever. I'll try someone else.
TMP
TMP
Hmm.
So you don't plan on breaking up with her?
You two are always having problems, so you could just give up on the whole thing.
Maki.
Do you fall for girls only if you think it's going to be smooth sailing?

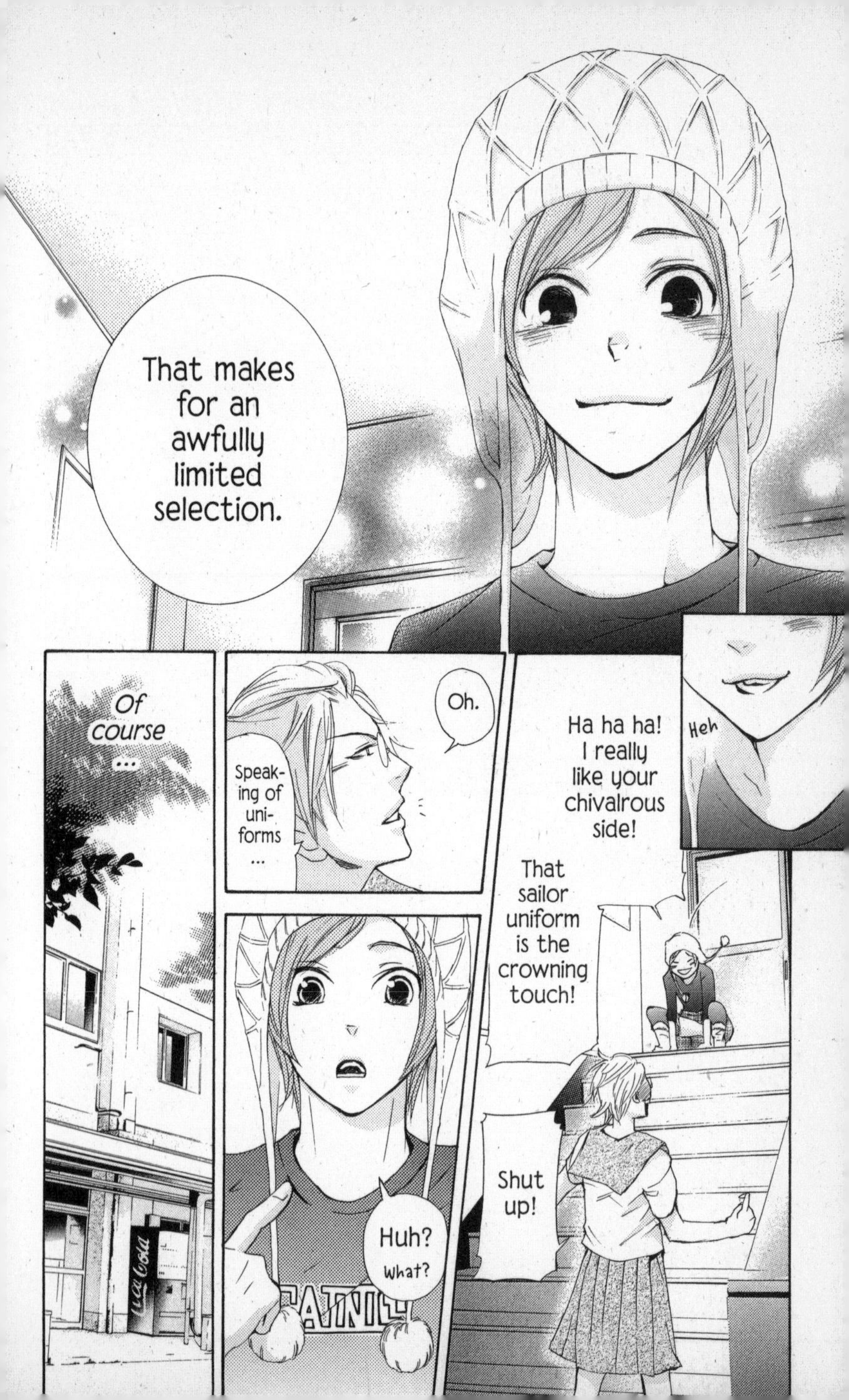
That makes for an awfully limited selection.
Heh
Ha ha ha! I really like your chivalrous side!
That sailor uniform is the crowning touch!
Shut up!
Oh.
Speak-ing of uni-forms ...
Huh? What?
Of course ...

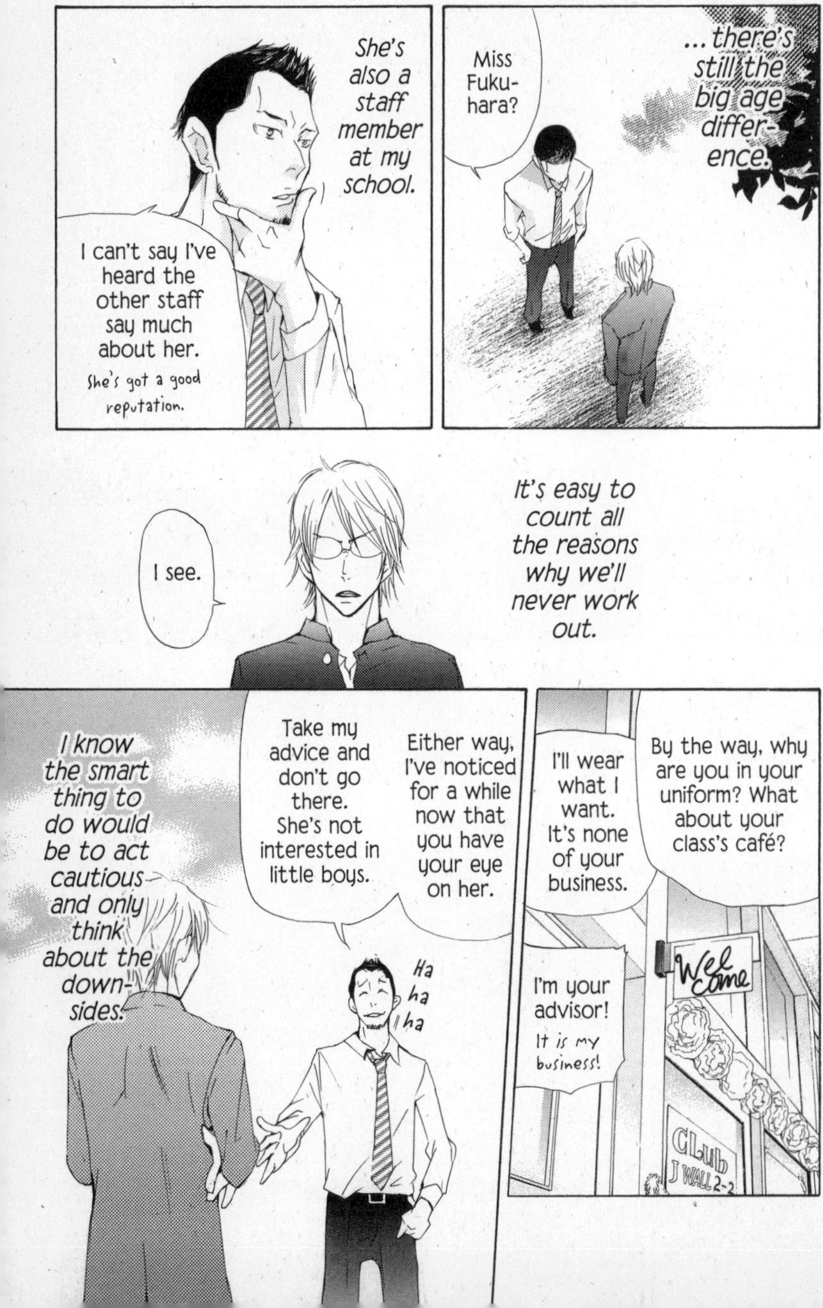
...there's still the big age difference.
Miss Fukuhara?
She's also a staff member at my school.
I can't say I've heard the other staff say much about her.
She's got a good reputation.
It's easy to count all the reasons why we'll never work out.
I see.
By the way, why are you in your uniform? What about your class's café?
I'll wear what I want. It's none of your business.
Welcome
I'm your advisor!
It is my business!
CLub
J WALL 2-2
Either way, I've noticed for a while now that you have your eye on her.
Take my advice and don't go there. She's not interested in little boys.
I know the smart thing to do would be to act cautious and only think about the downsides.
Ha ha ha

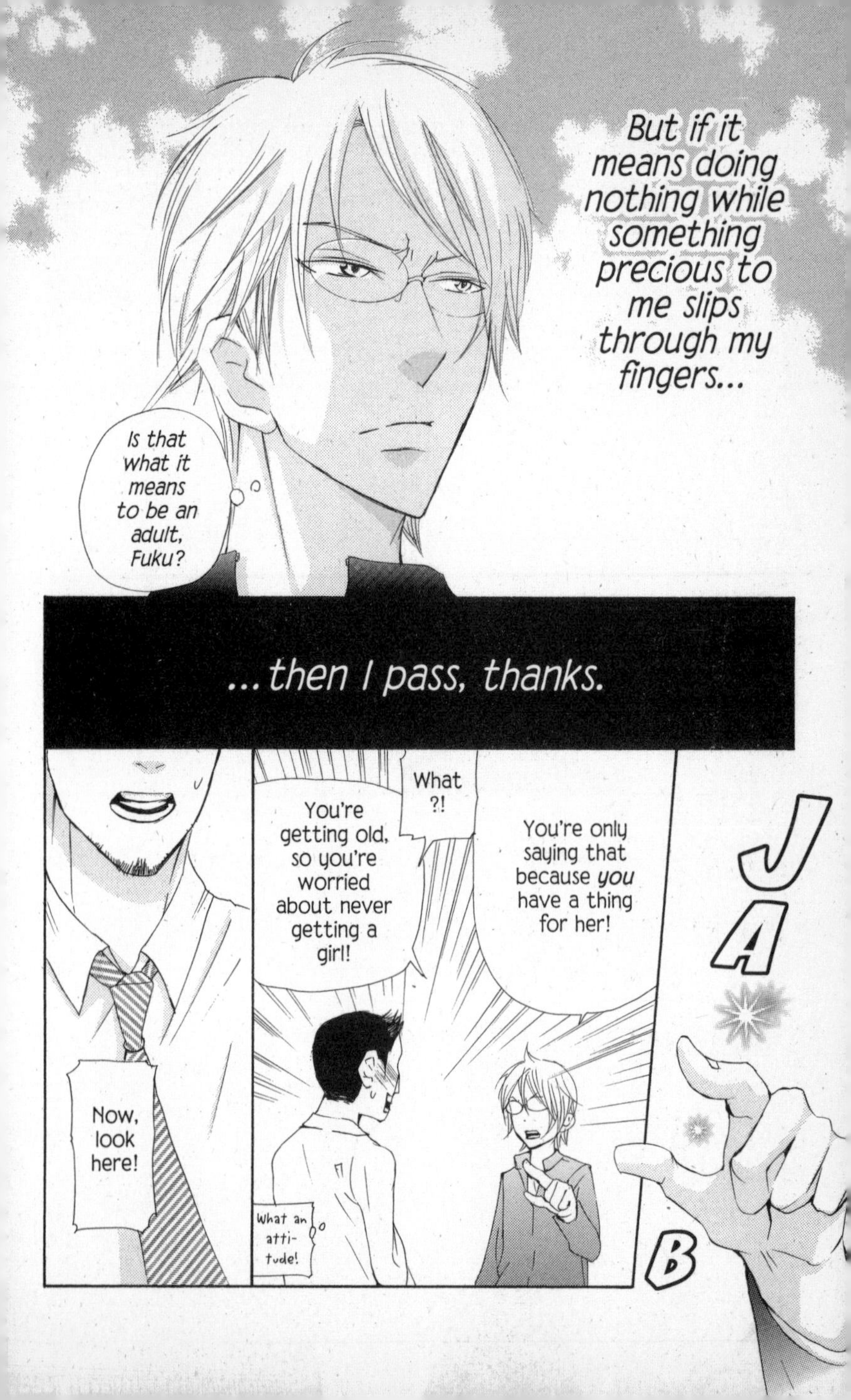
But if it means doing nothing while something precious to me slips through my fingers...
Is that what it means to be an adult, Fuku?
...then I pass, thanks.
JAB
You're only saying that because *you* have a thing for her!
What?!
You're getting old, so you're worried about never getting a girl!
What an atti- tude!
Now, look here!

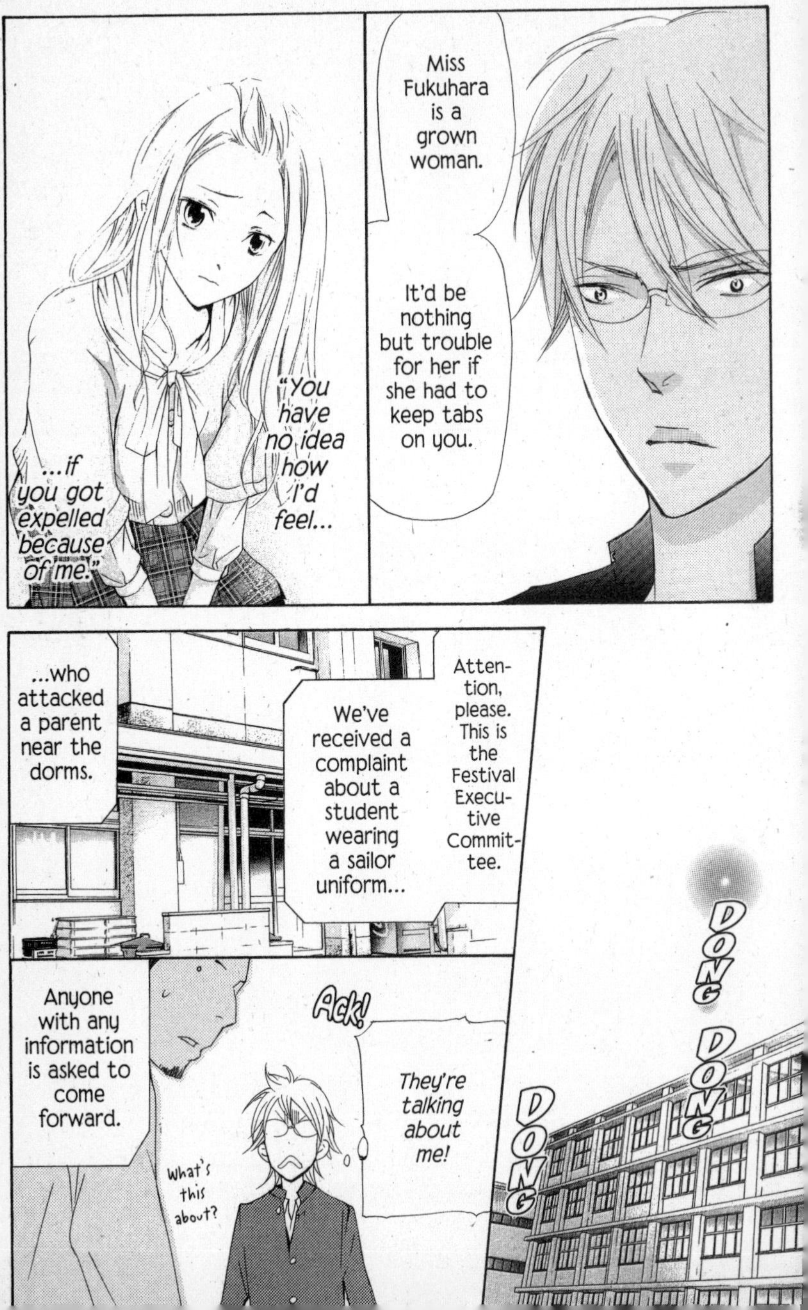

Miss Fukuhara is a grown woman.
It'd be nothing but trouble for her if she had to keep tabs on you.
"You have no idea how I'd feel...
...if you got expelled because of me."
DONG DONG DONG
Atten-tion, please. This is the Festival Execu-tive Commit-tee.
We've received a complaint about a student wearing a sailor uniform...
...who attacked a parent near the dorms.
Ack!
They're talking about me!
Anyone with any information is asked to come forward.
What's this about?

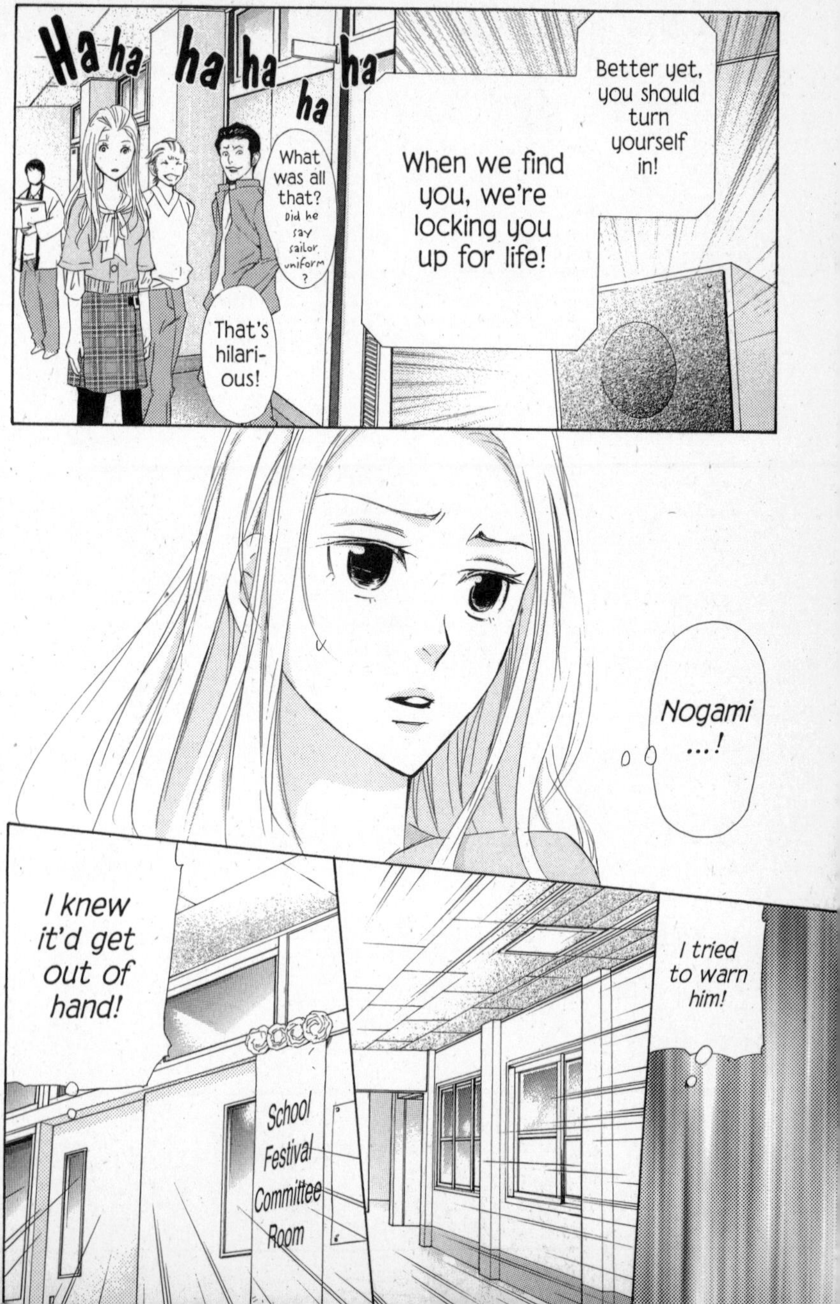
Better yet, you should turn yourself in!
When we find you, we're locking you up for life!
Ha ha ha ha ha ha
What was all that? Did he say sailor uniform?
That's hilarious!
Nogami...!
I tried to warn him!
I knew it'd get out of hand!
School Festival Committee Room

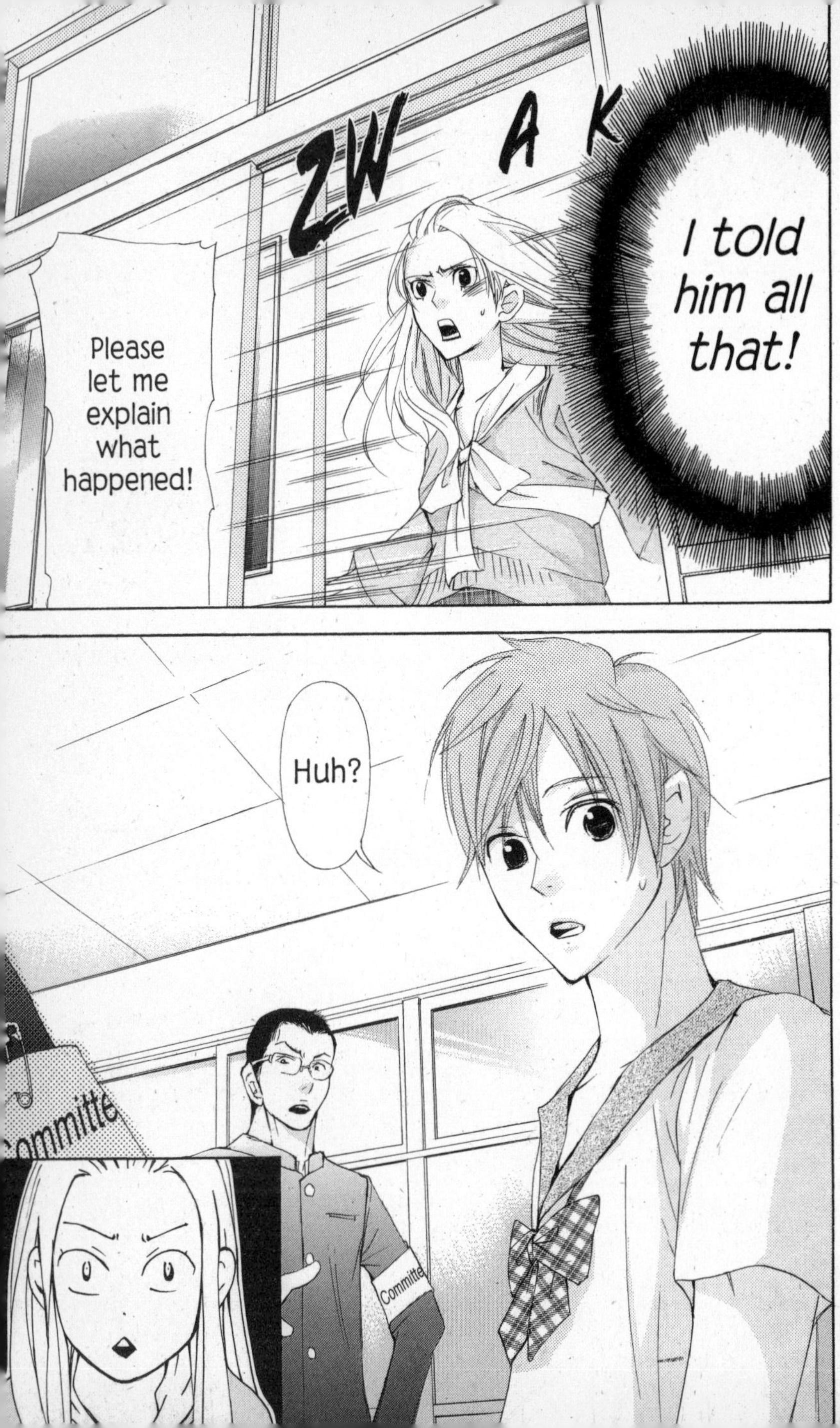
I told him all that!
ZWAK
Please let me explain what happened!
Huh?
Committe
Committe

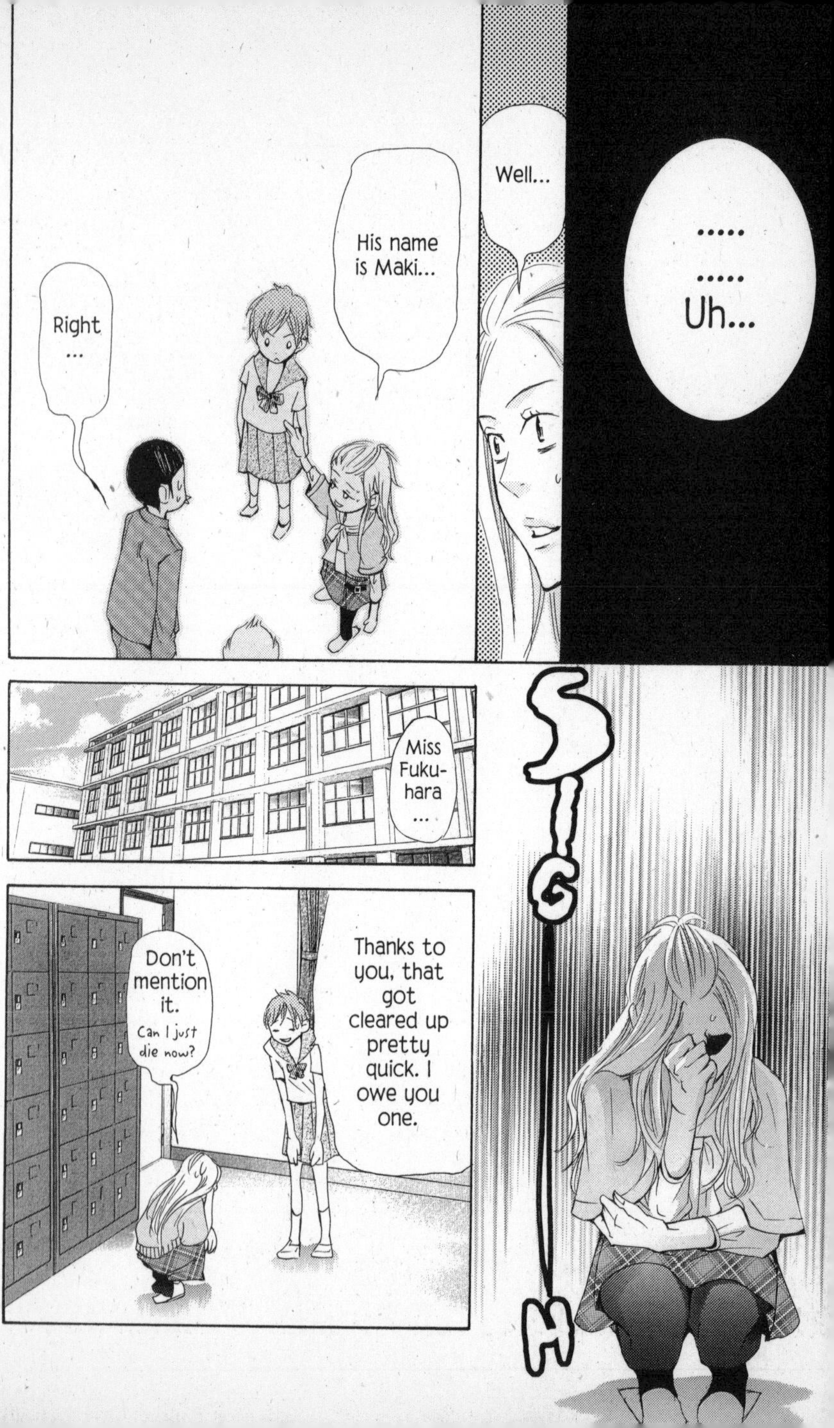
.....
.....
Uh...
Well...
His name is Maki...
Right ...
SIGH
Miss Fuku-hara ...
Thanks to you, that got cleared up pretty quick. I owe you one.
Don't mention it.
Can I just die now?

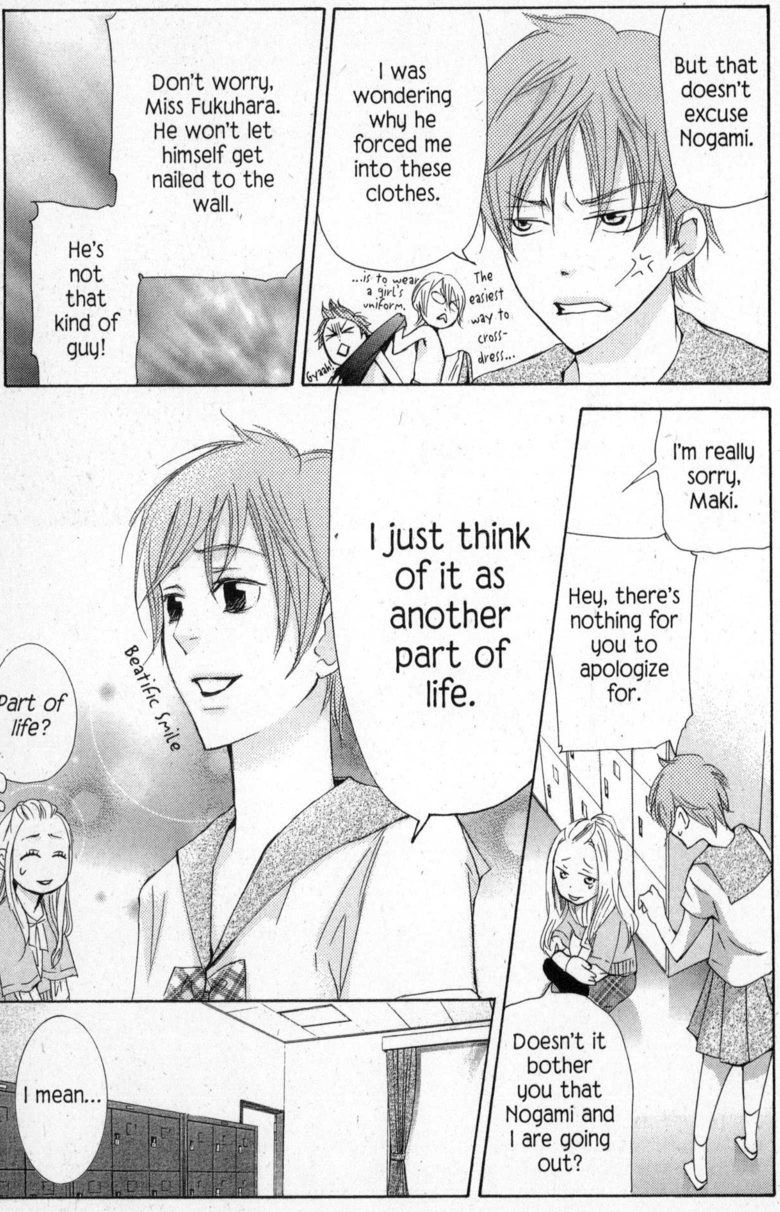
But that doesn't excuse Nogami.
I was wondering why he forced me into these clothes.
The easiest way to cross-dress...
...is to wear a girl's uniform.
Gyaah!
Don't worry, Miss Fukuhara. He won't let himself get nailed to the wall.
He's not that kind of guy!
I'm really sorry, Maki.
Hey, there's nothing for you to apologize for.
Doesn't it bother you that Nogami and I are going out?
I just think of it as another part of life.
Beatific Smile
Part of life?
I mean...

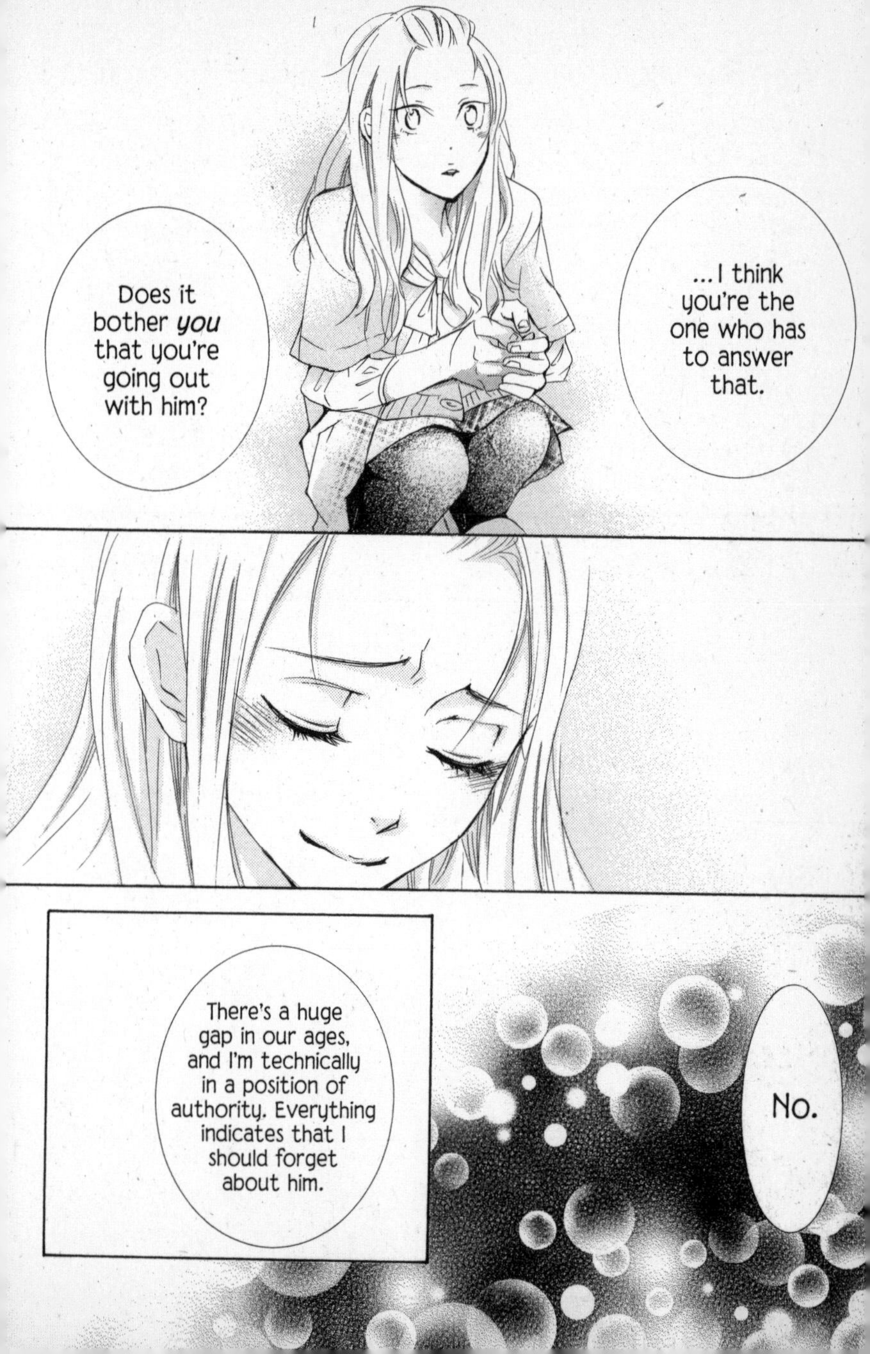
...I think you're the one who has to answer that.
Does it bother *you* that you're going out with him?
No.
There's a huge gap in our ages, and I'm technically in a position of authority. Everything indicates that I should forget about him.

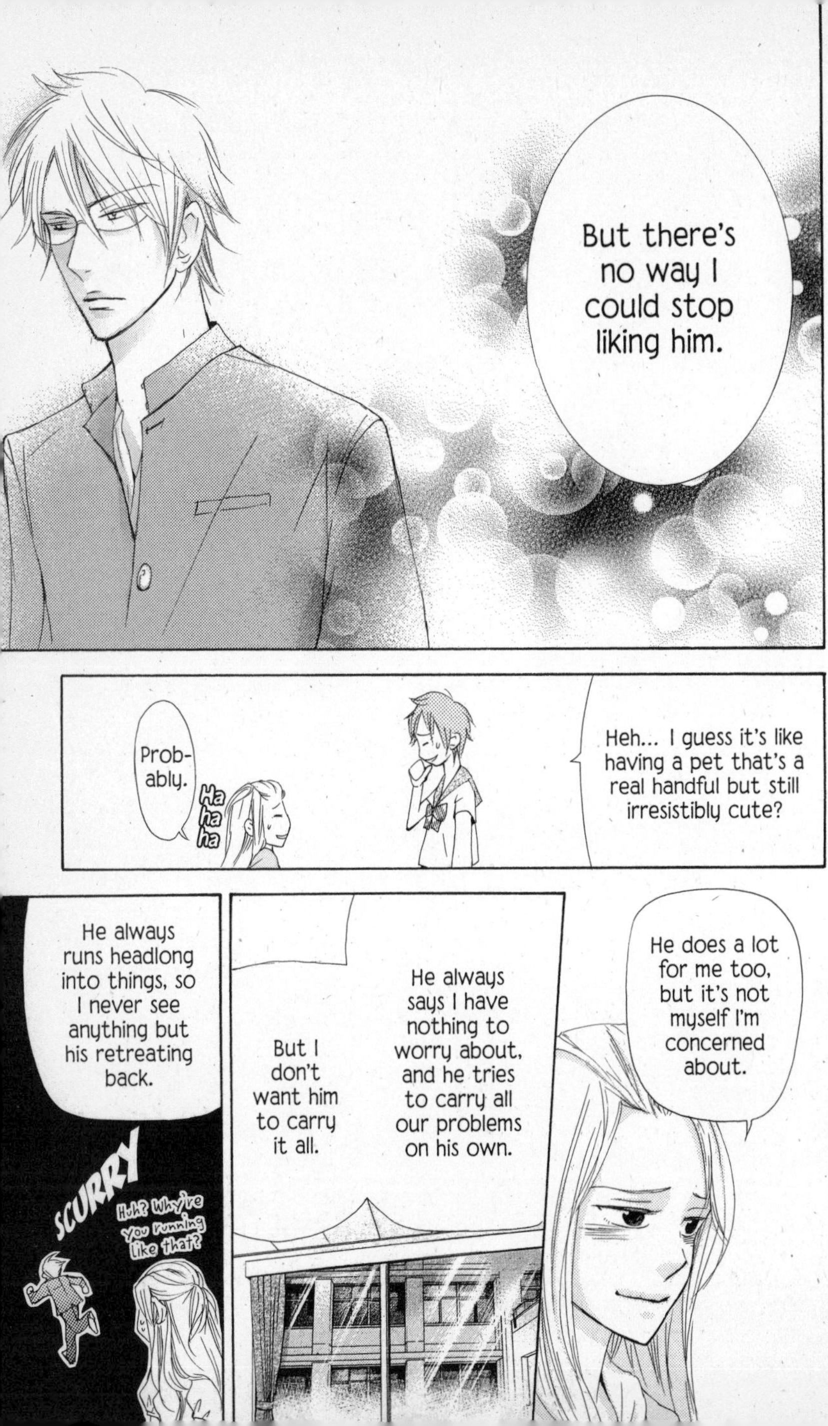
But there's no way I could stop liking him.
Heh... I guess it's like having a pet that's a real handful but still irresistibly cute?
Prob-ably.
Ha ha ha
He does a lot for me too, but it's not myself I'm concerned about.
He always says I have nothing to worry about, and he tries to carry all our problems on his own.
But I don't want him to carry it all.
He always runs headlong into things, so I never see anything but his retreating back.
SCURRY
Huh? Why're you running like that?

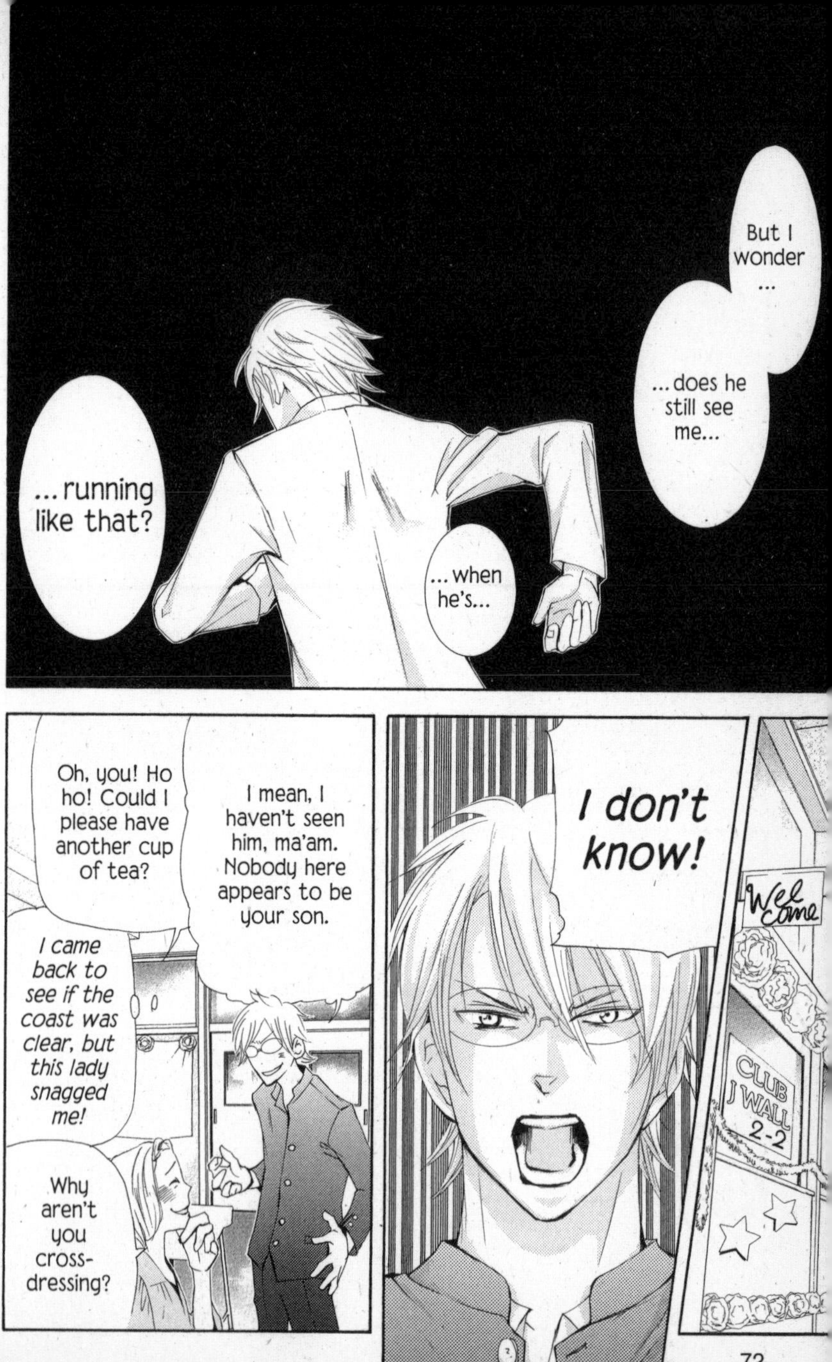
But I wonder ...
...does he still see me...
...when he's...
...running like that?
Welcome
CLUB J WALL 2-2
I don't know!
I mean, I haven't seen him, ma'am. Nobody here appears to be your son.
Oh, you! Ho ho! Could I please have another cup of tea?
I came back to see if the coast was clear, but this lady snagged me!
Why aren't you cross-dressing?

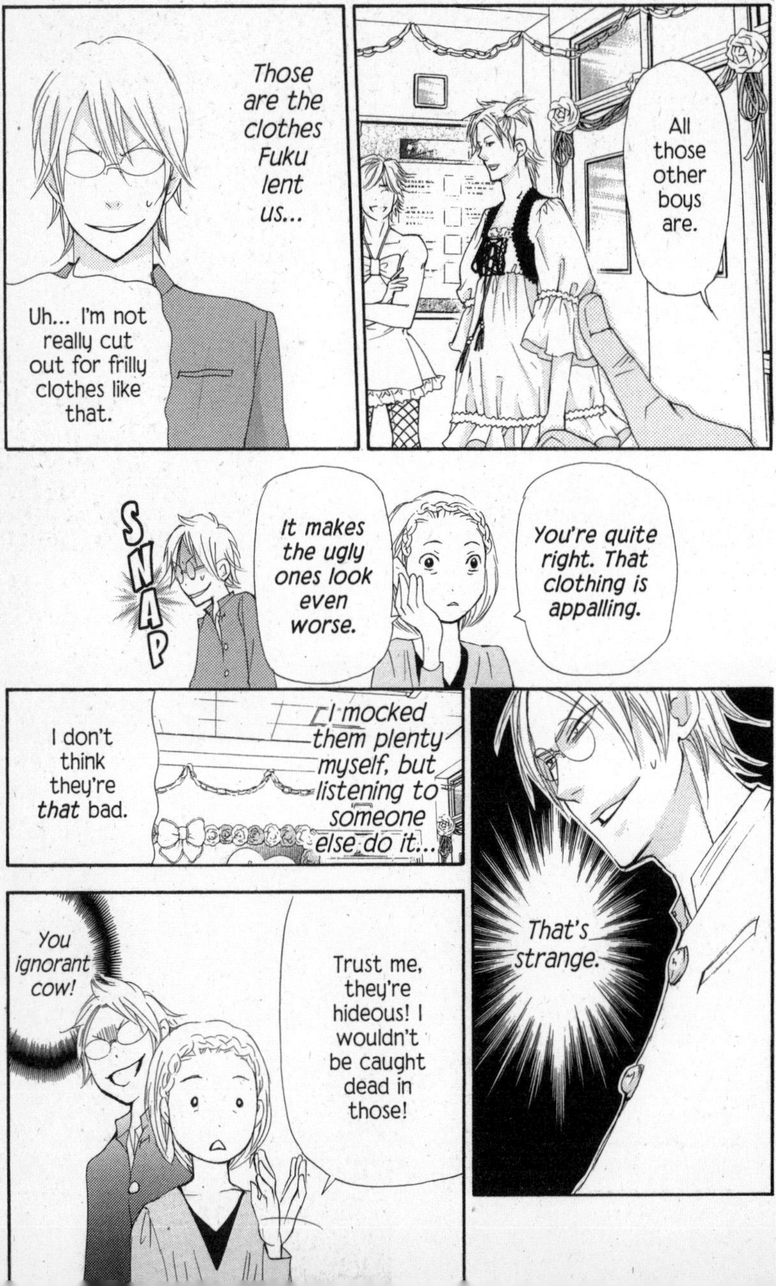
All those other boys are.
Those are the clothes Fuku lent us...
Uh... I'm not really cut out for frilly clothes like that.
You're quite right. That clothing is appalling.
It makes the ugly ones look even worse.
SNAP
That's strange.
I mocked them plenty myself, but listening to someone else do it...
I don't think they're *that* bad.
Trust me, they're hideous! I wouldn't be caught dead in those!
You ignorant cow!

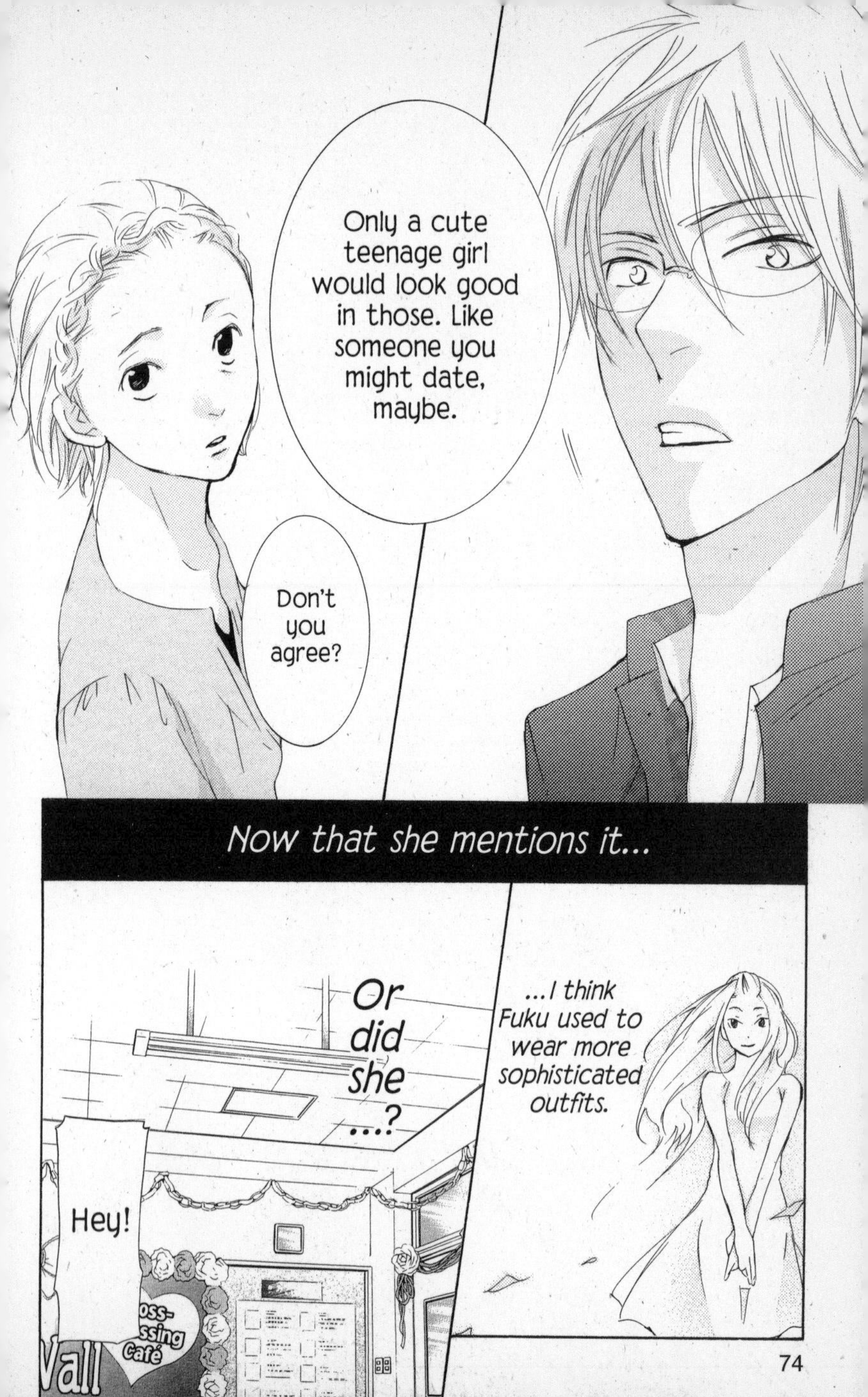
Only a cute teenage girl would look good in those. Like someone you might date, maybe.
Don't you agree?
Now that she mentions it...
...I think Fuku used to wear more sophisticated outfits.
Or did she ...?
Hey!

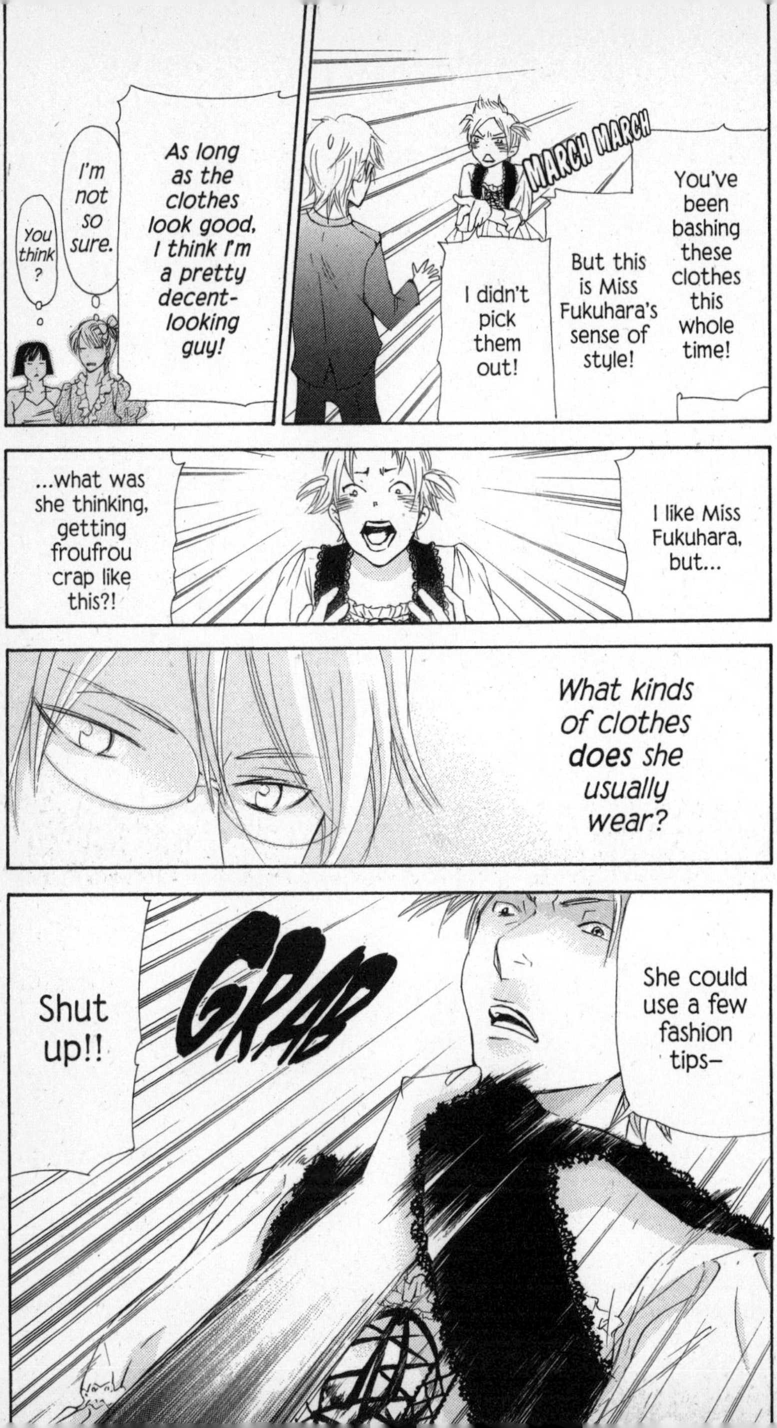
MARCH MARCH
You've been bashing these clothes this whole time!
But this is Miss Fukuhara's sense of style!
I didn't pick them out!
As long as the clothes look good, I think I'm a pretty decent-looking guy!
I'm not so sure.
You think?
I like Miss Fukuhara, but...
...what was she thinking, getting froufrou crap like this?!
What kinds of clothes **does** she usually wear?
She could use a few fashion tips–
GRAB
Shut up!!

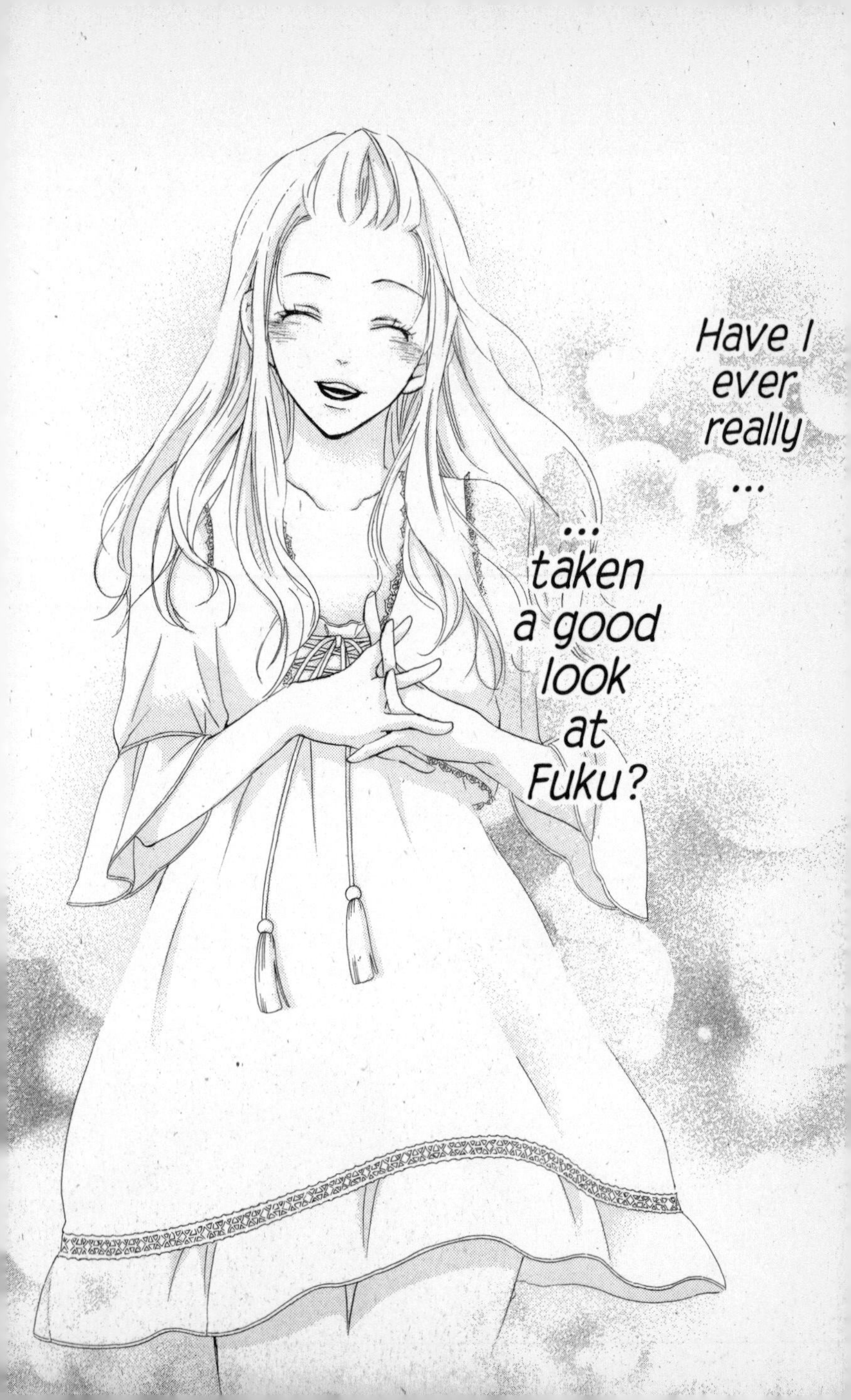
Have I ever really ...
... taken a good look at Fuku?

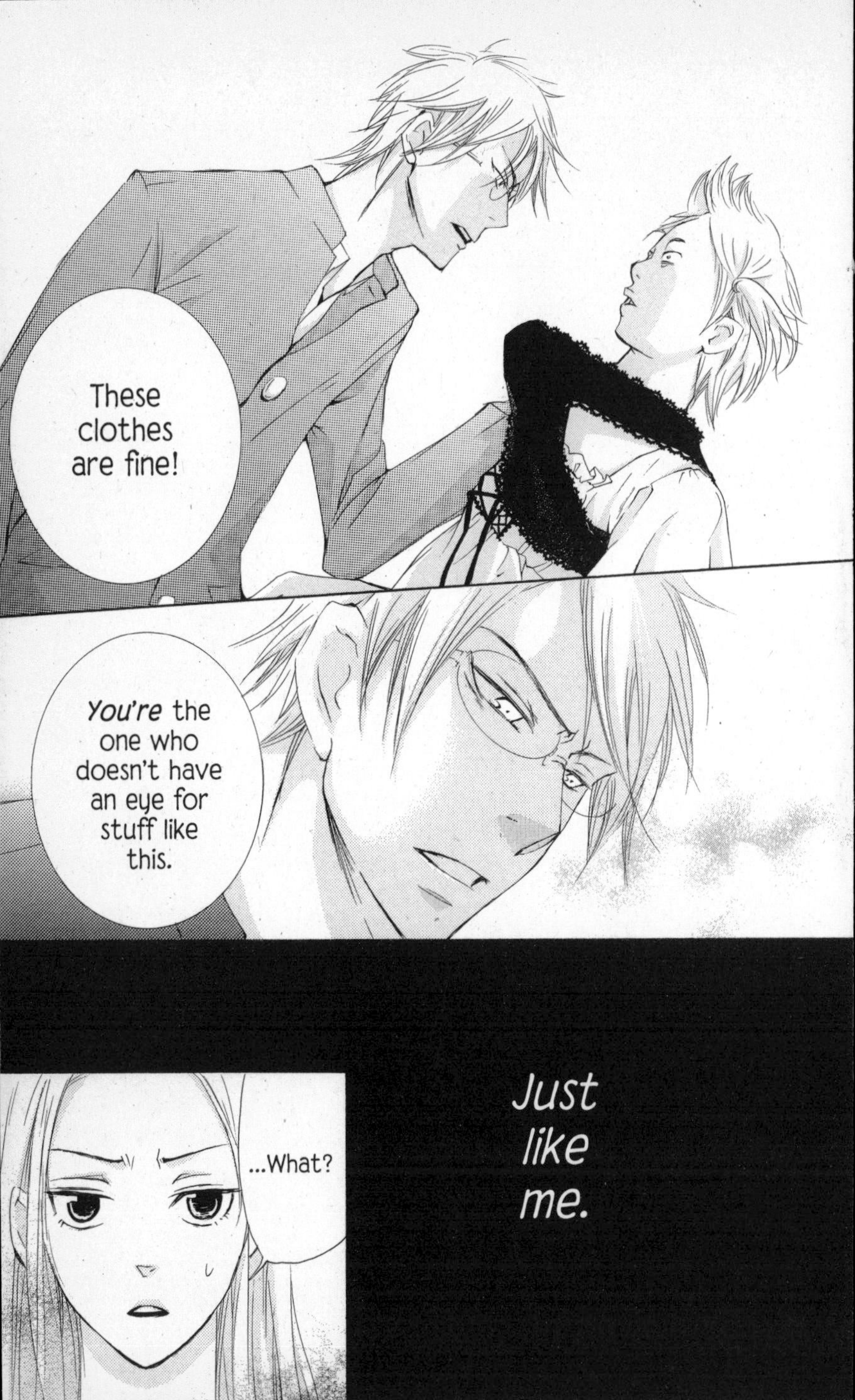
These clothes are fine!
You're the one who doesn't have an eye for stuff like this.
Just like me.
...What?

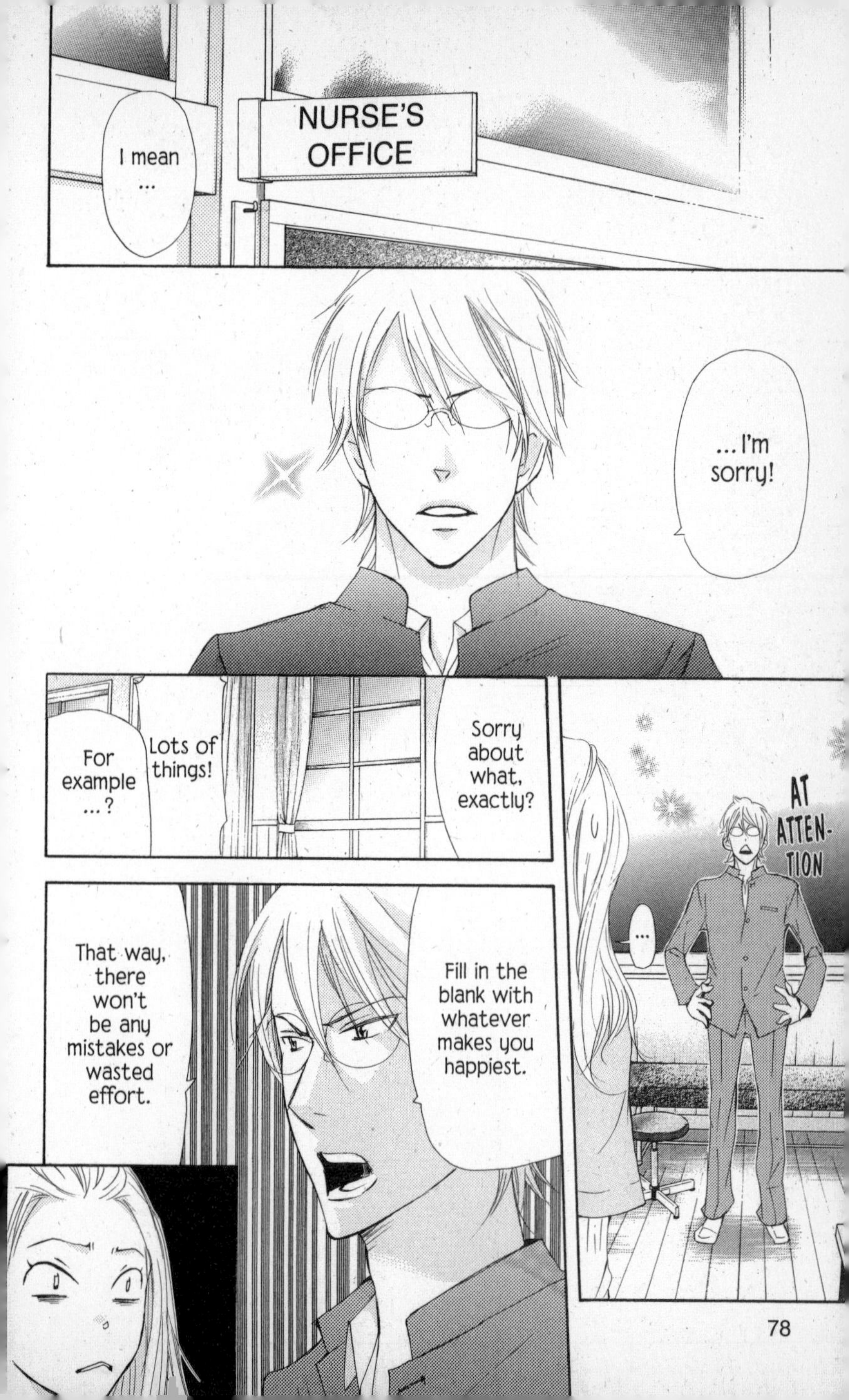
NURSE'S OFFICE
I mean ...
... I'm sorry!
AT ATTEN- TION
...
Sorry about what, exactly?
Lots of things!
For example ...?
Fill in the blank with whatever makes you happiest.
That way, there won't be any mistakes or wasted effort.

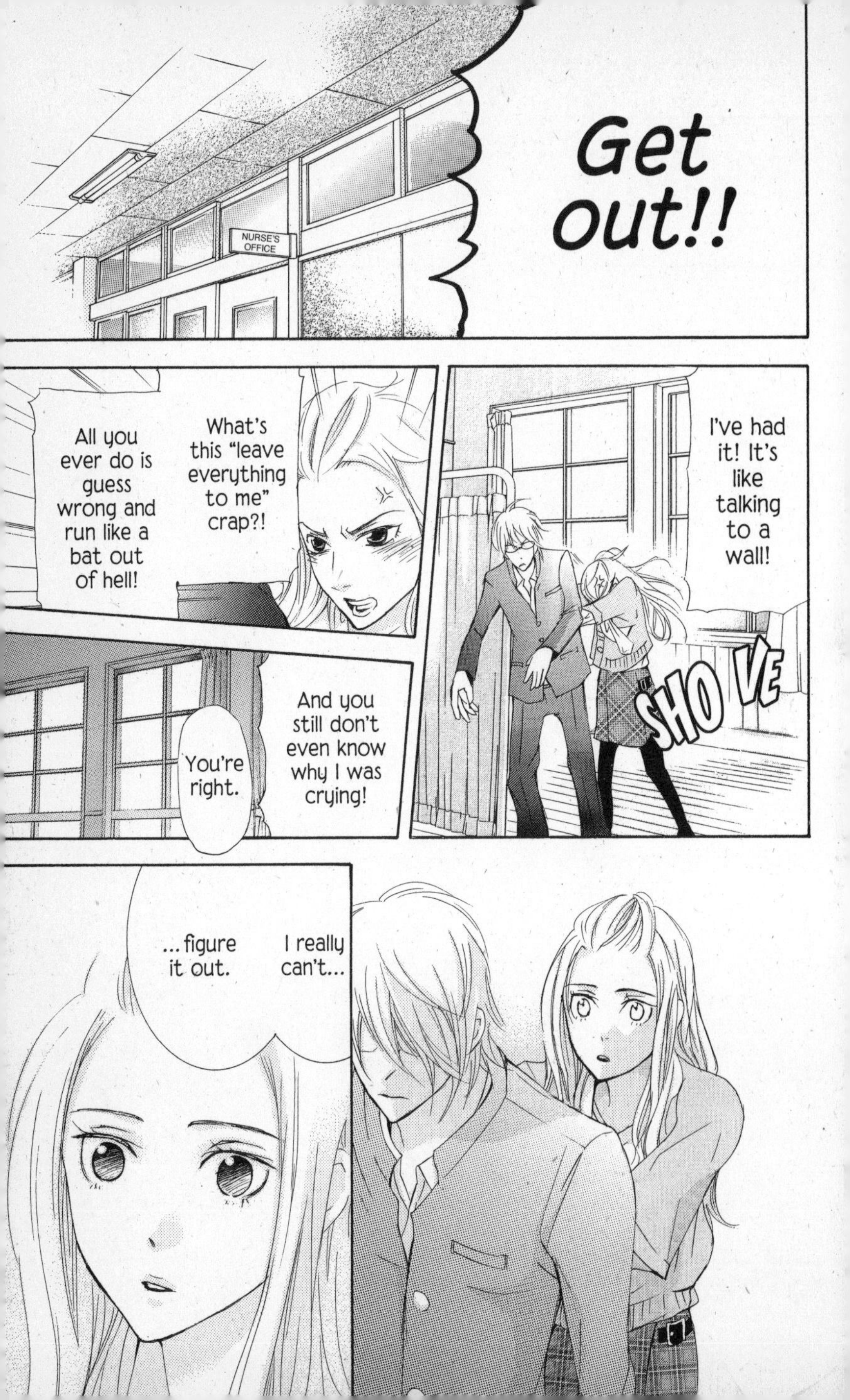
Get out!!
NURSE'S OFFICE
I've had it! It's like talking to a wall!
SHOVE
What's this "leave everything to me" crap?!
All you ever do is guess wrong and run like a bat out of hell!
And you still don't even know why I was crying!
You're right.
I really can't...
...figure it out.

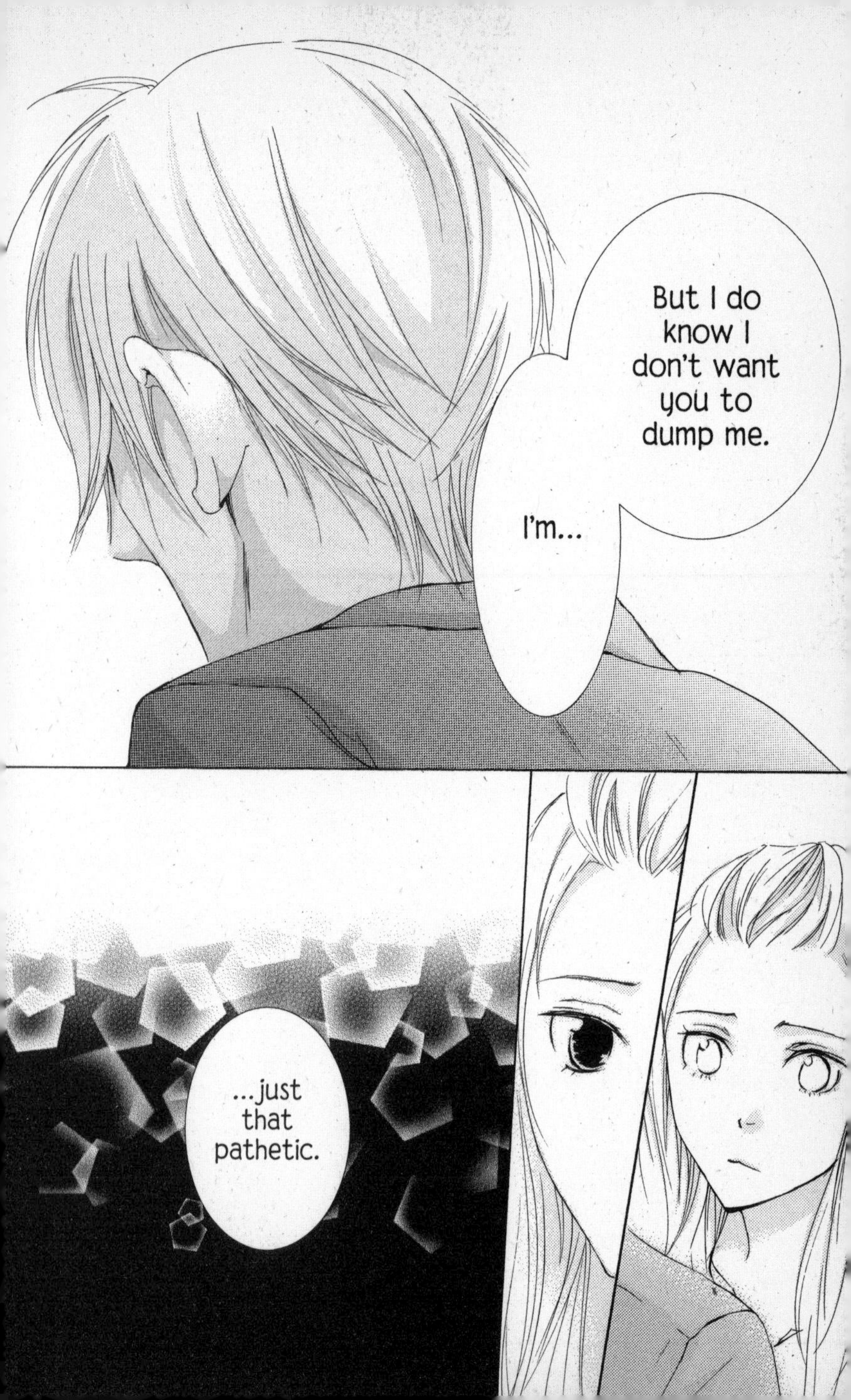
But I do know I don't want you to dump me.
I'm...
...just that pathetic.

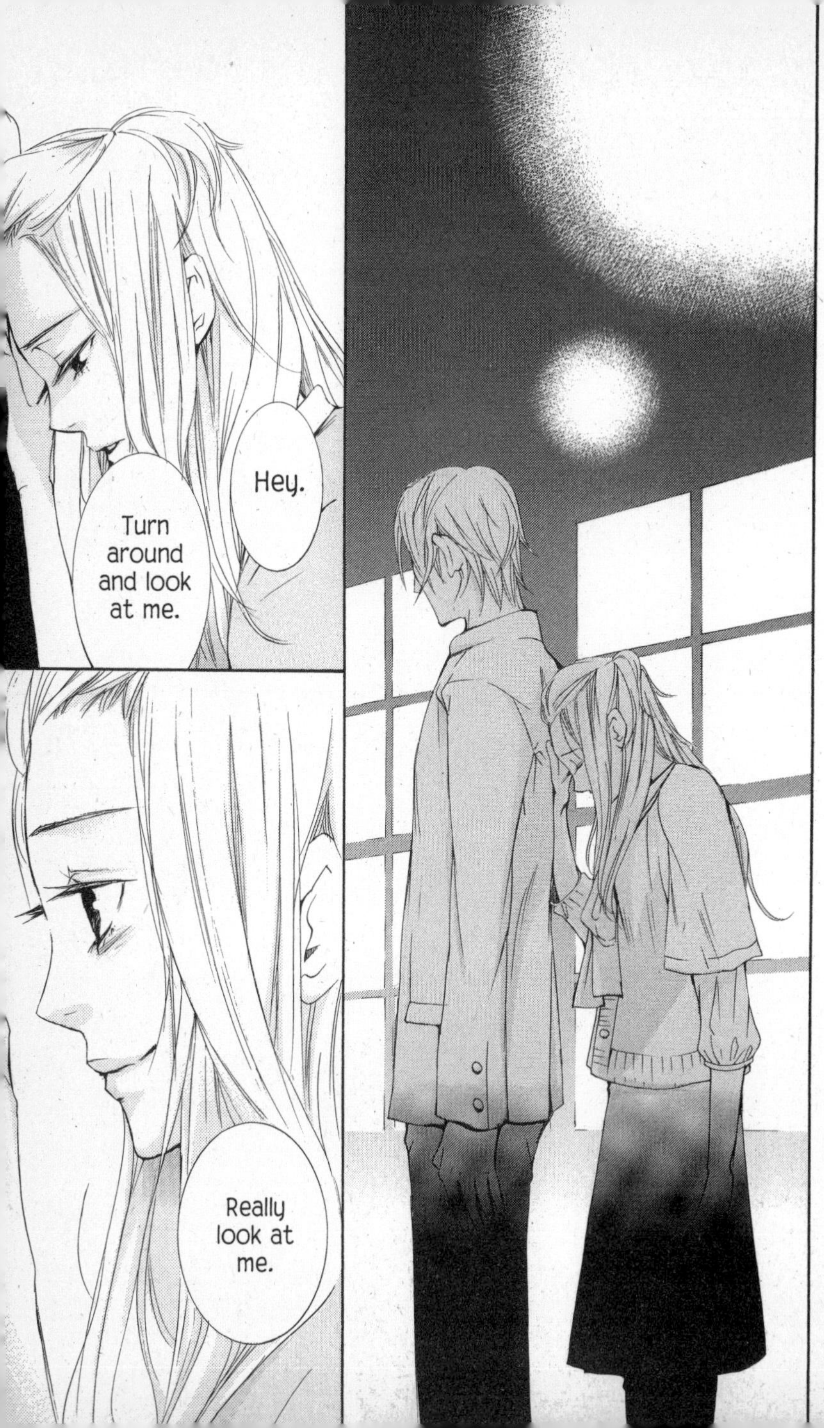
Hey.
Turn around and look at me.
Really look at me.

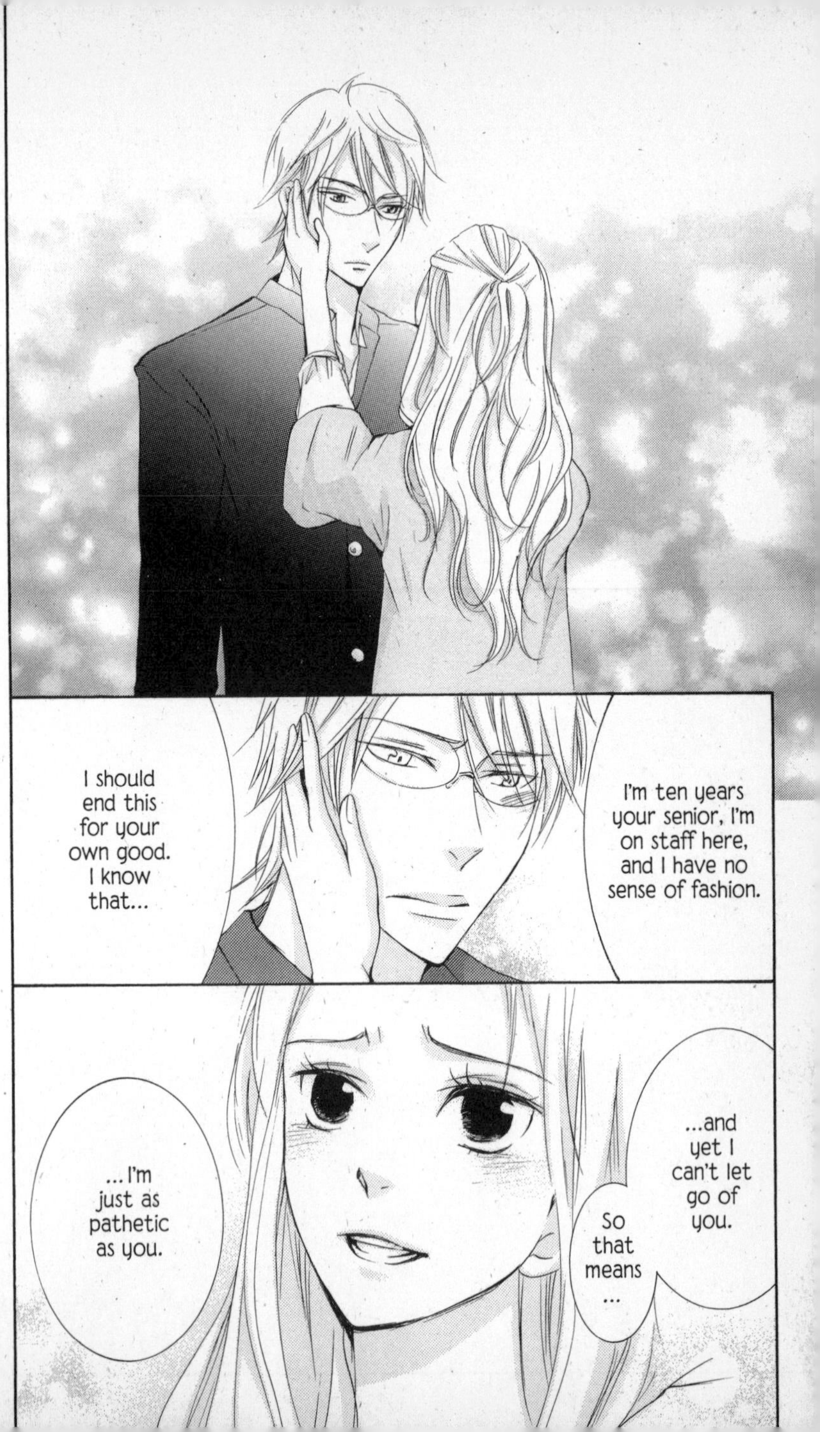
I'm ten years your senior, I'm on staff here, and I have no sense of fashion.
I should end this for your own good. I know that...
...and yet I can't let go of you.
So that means ...
...I'm just as pathetic as you.

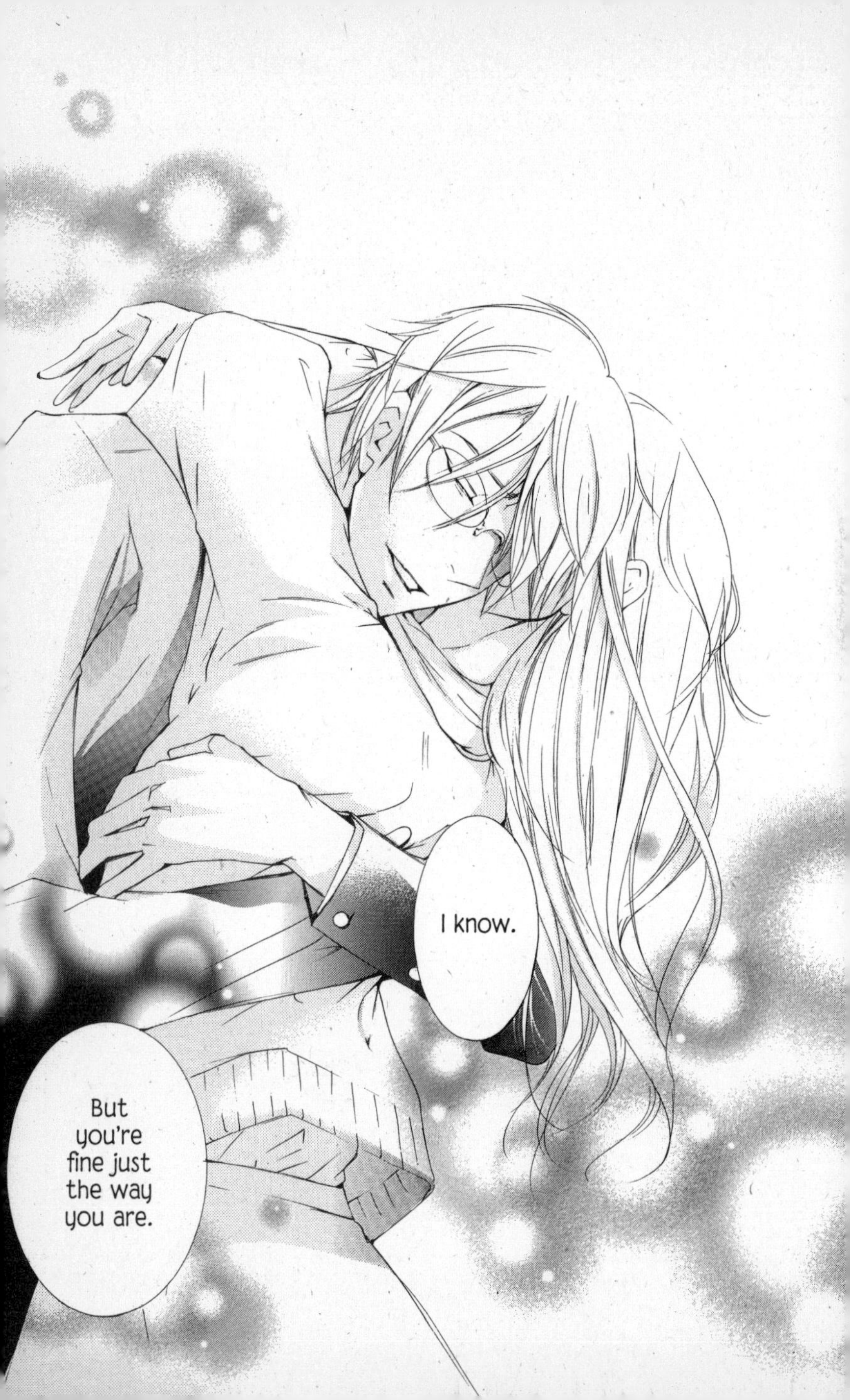
I know.
But you're fine just the way you are.

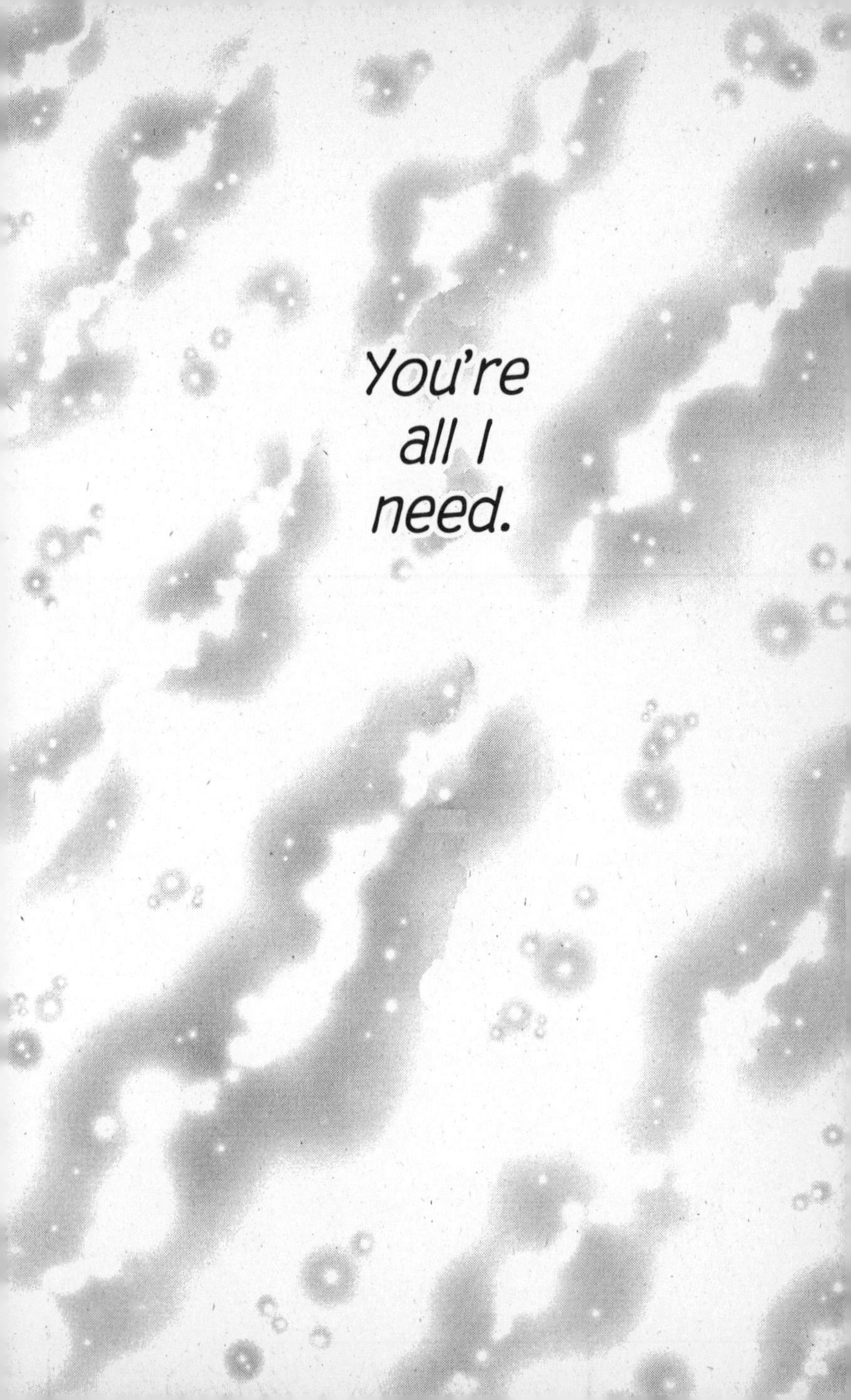
You're all I need.

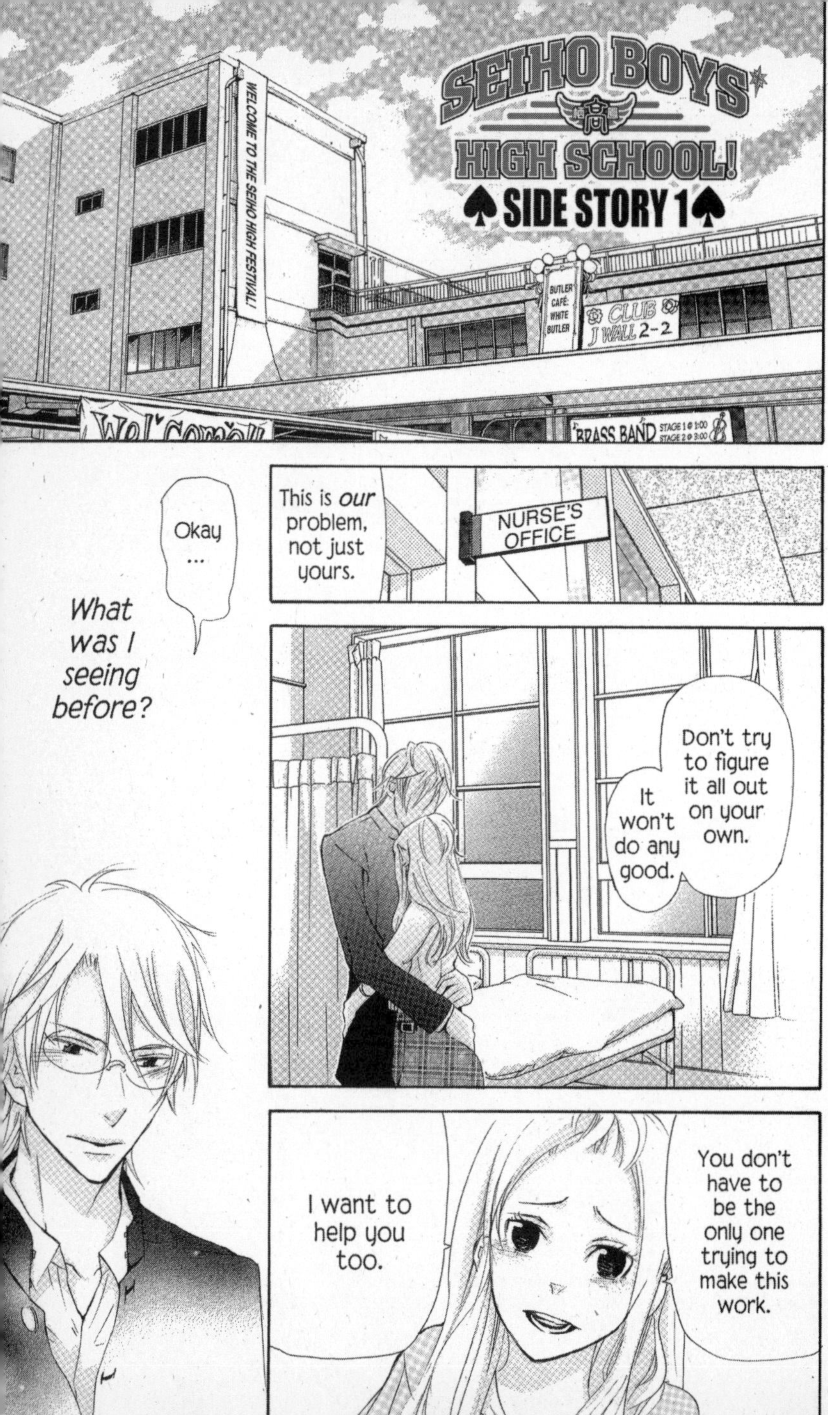
SEIHO BOYS' HIGH SCHOOL!
SIDE STORY 1
WELCOME TO THE SEIHO HIGH FESTIVAL!
BUTLER CAFÉ: WHITE BUTLER
CLUB J WALL 2-2
BRASS BAND STAGE 1 @ 1:00 STAGE 2 @ 3:00
NURSE'S OFFICE
This is *our* problem, not just yours.
Okay ...
What was I seeing before?
Don't try to figure it all out on your own.
It won't do any good.
You don't have to be the only one trying to make this work.
I want to help you too.

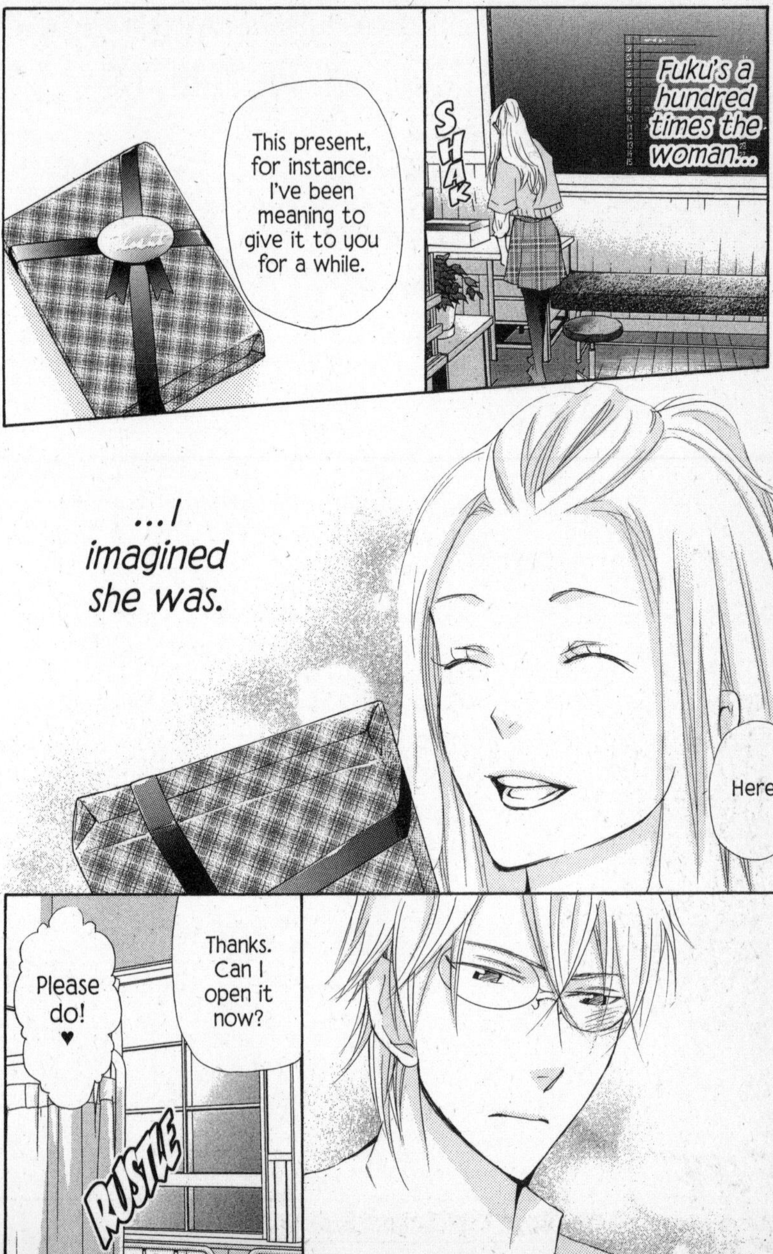
SHAK
Fuku's a hundred times the woman...
This present, for instance. I've been meaning to give it to you for a while.
...I imagined she was.
Here.
Thanks. Can I open it now?
Please do! ♥
RUSTLE

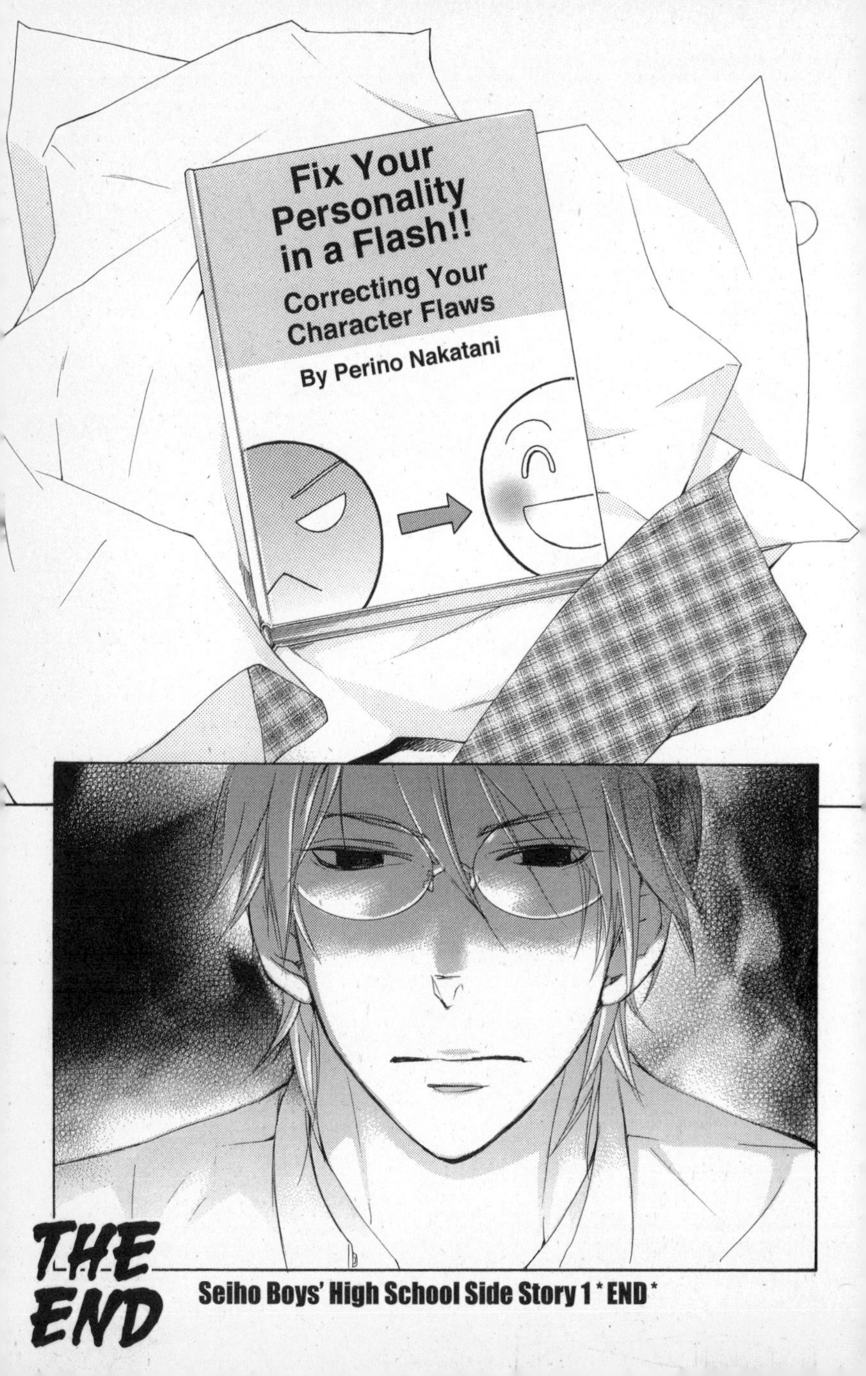
Fix Your Personality in a Flash!!
Correcting Your Character Flaws
By Perino Nakatani
THE END
Seiho Boys' High School Side Story 1 * END *

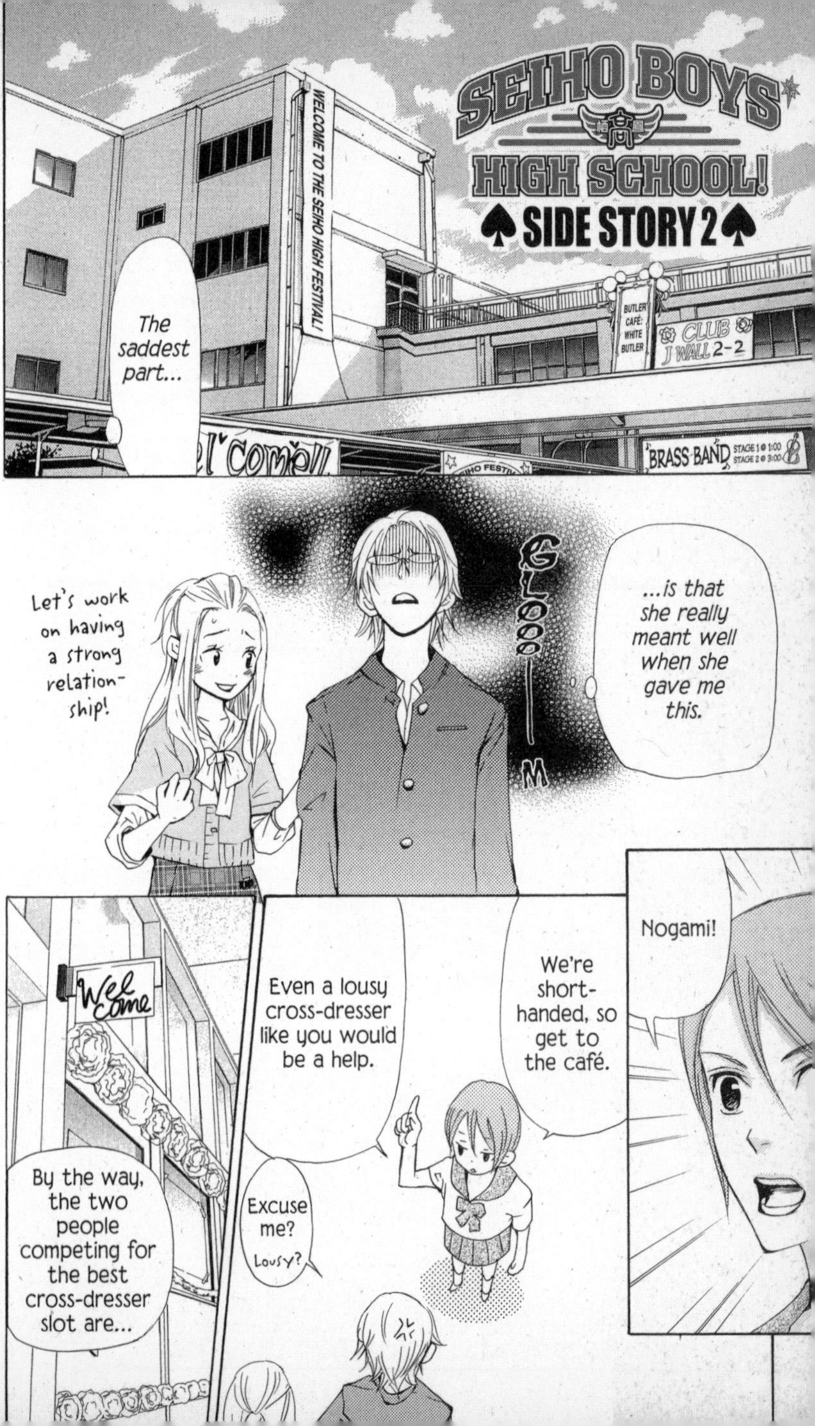
SEIHO BOYS' HIGH SCHOOL!
♠SIDE STORY 2♠
WELCOME TO THE SEIHO HIGH FESTIVAL!
BUTLER CAFÉ: WHITE BUTLER
CLUB J WALL 2-2
The saddest part...
BRASS BAND STAGE 1 @ 1:00 STAGE 2 @ 3:00
...is that she really meant well when she gave me this.
GLOOOO—M
Let's work on having a strong relationship!
Nogami!
We're short-handed, so get to the café.
Even a lousy cross-dresser like you would be a help.
Excuse me?
Lousy?
By the way, the two people competing for the best cross-dresser slot are...

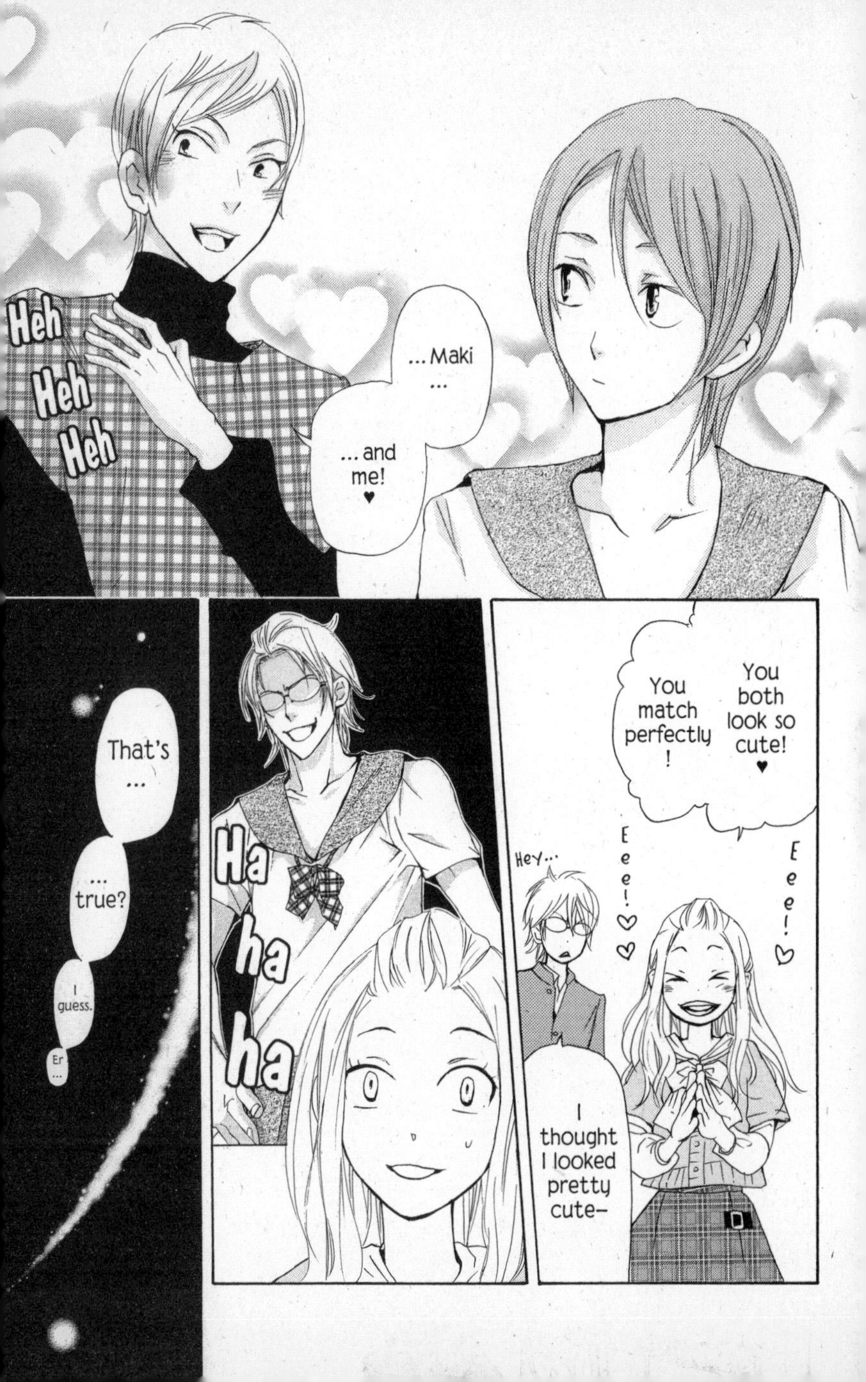
...Maki ... ...and me! ♥
Heh Heh Heh
You both look so cute! ♥
You match perfectly!
Eee! ♡
Eee! ♡
Hey...
I thought I looked pretty cute–
Ha ha ha
That's ...
... true?
I guess.
Er ...

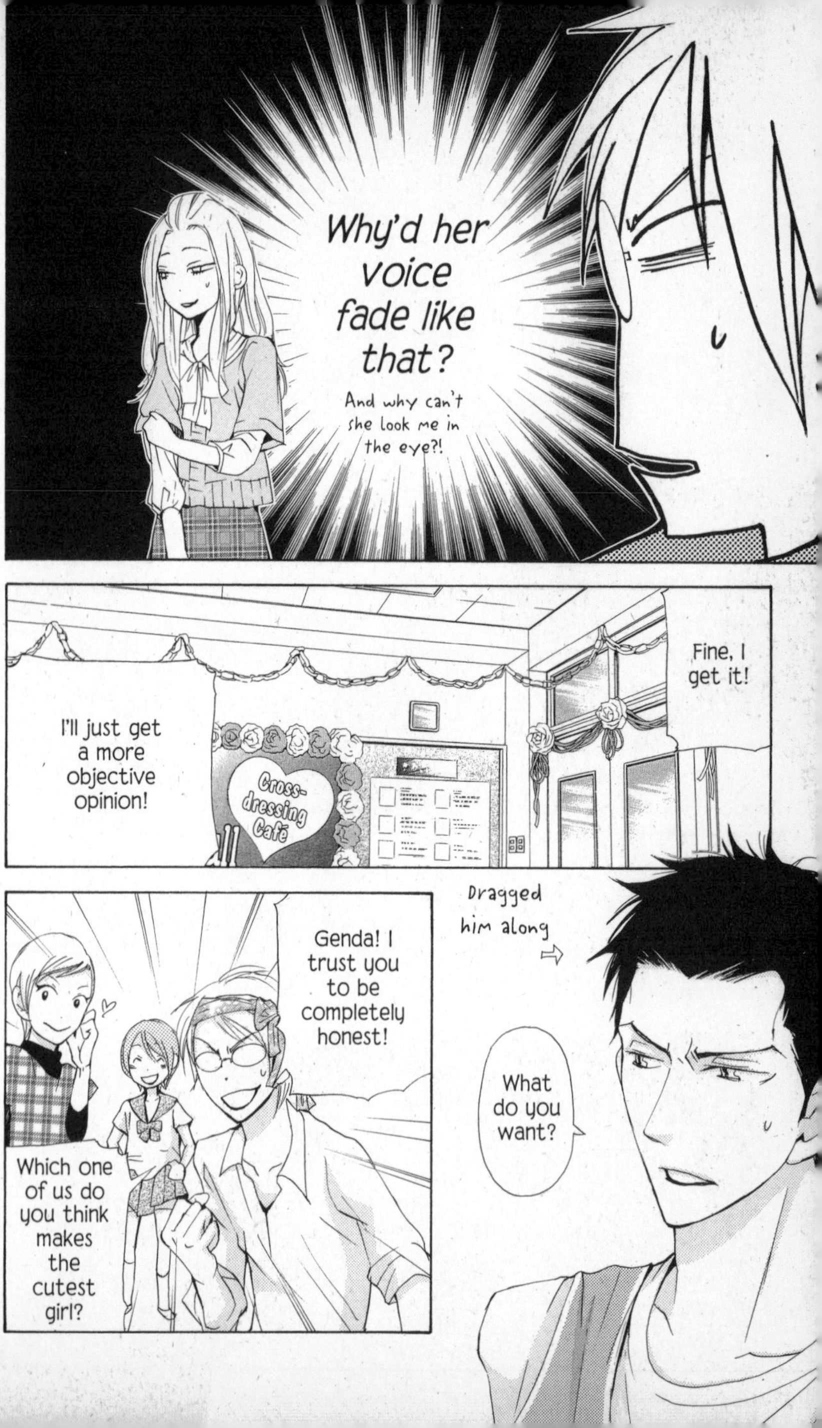
Why'd her voice fade like that?
And why can't she look me in the eye?!
Fine, I get it!
I'll just get a more objective opinion!
Cross-dressing Café
Dragged him along ⇨
What do you want?
Genda! I trust you to be completely honest!
Which one of us do you think makes the cutest girl?

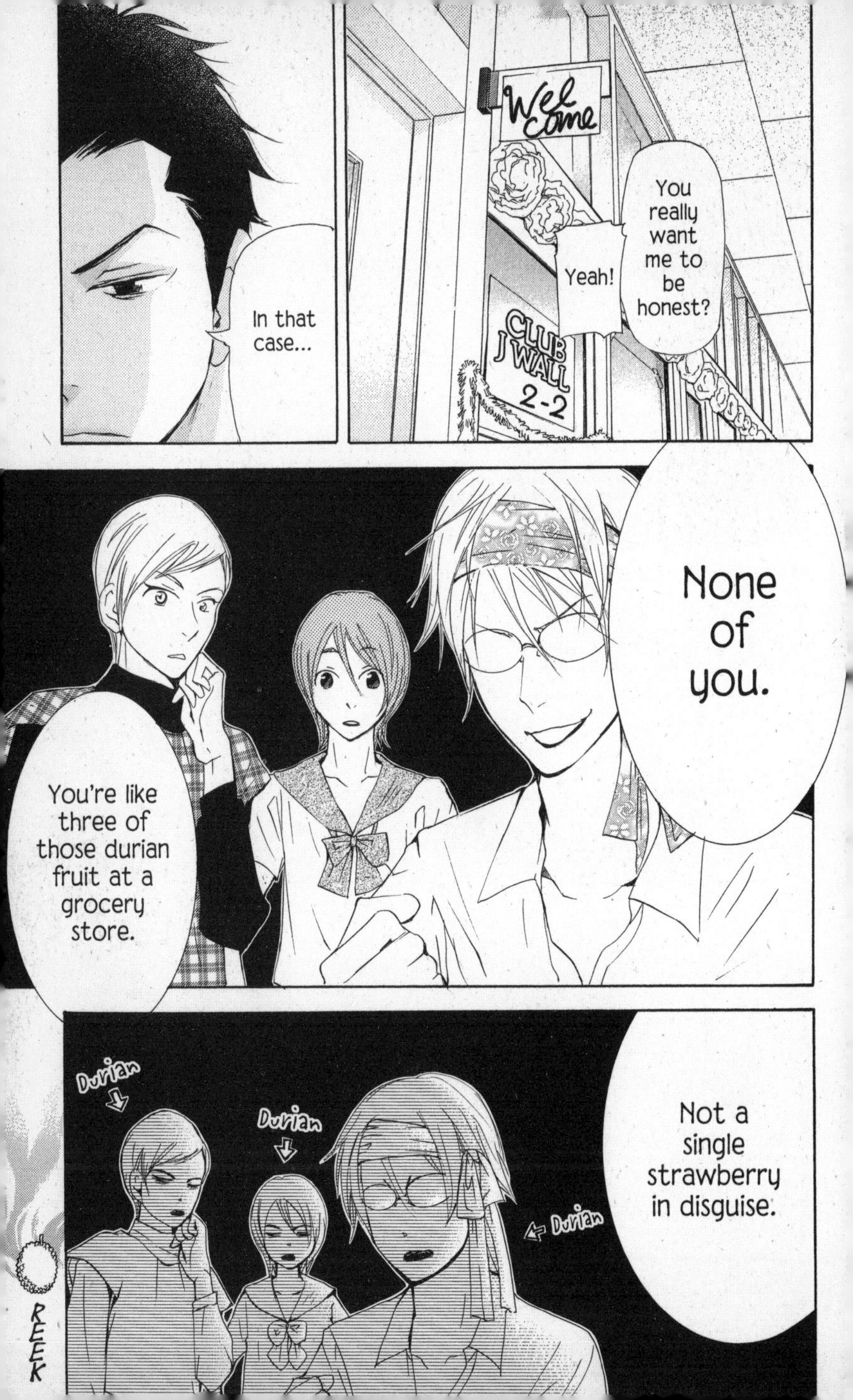
Welcome
CLUB J WALL 2-2
You really want me to be honest?
Yeah!
In that case...
None of you.
You're like three of those durian fruit at a grocery store.
Not a single strawberry in disguise.
Durian
Durian
Durian
REEK

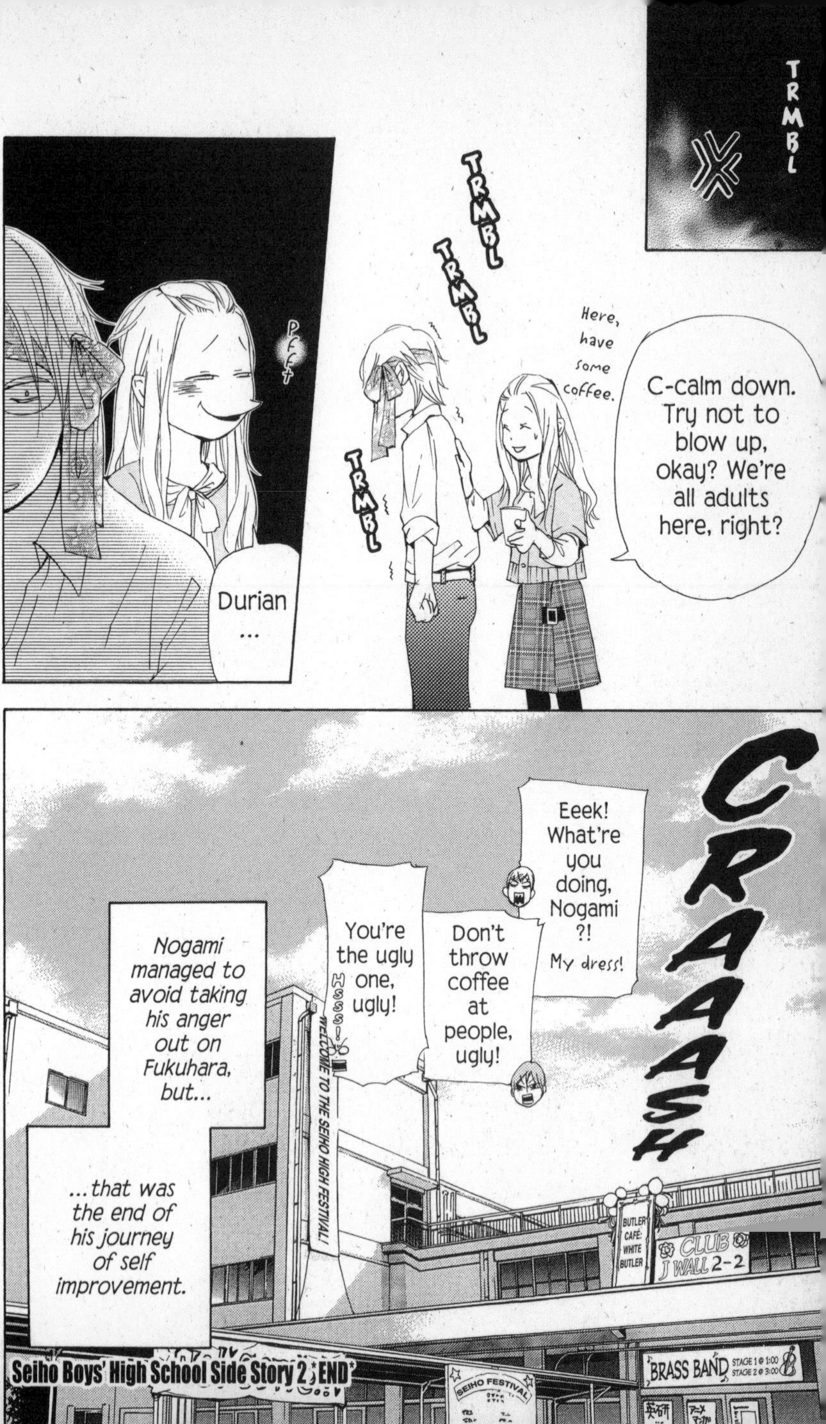
TRMBL
TRMBL
TRMBL
TRMBL
Here, have some coffee.
C-calm down. Try not to blow up, okay? We're all adults here, right?
Pfft
Durian...
CRAAASH
Eeek! What're you doing, Nogami?!
My dress!
Don't throw coffee at people, ugly!
You're the ugly one, ugly!
HSSS!
WELCOME TO THE SEIHO HIGH FESTIVAL!
BUTLER CAFÉ: WHITE BUTLER
CLUB J WALL 2-2
Nogami managed to avoid taking his anger out on Fukuhara, but...
...that was the end of his journey of self improvement.
BRASS BAND STAGE 1 @ 1:00 STAGE 2 @ 3:00
SEIHO FESTIVAL
Seiho Boys' High School Side Story 2 *END*

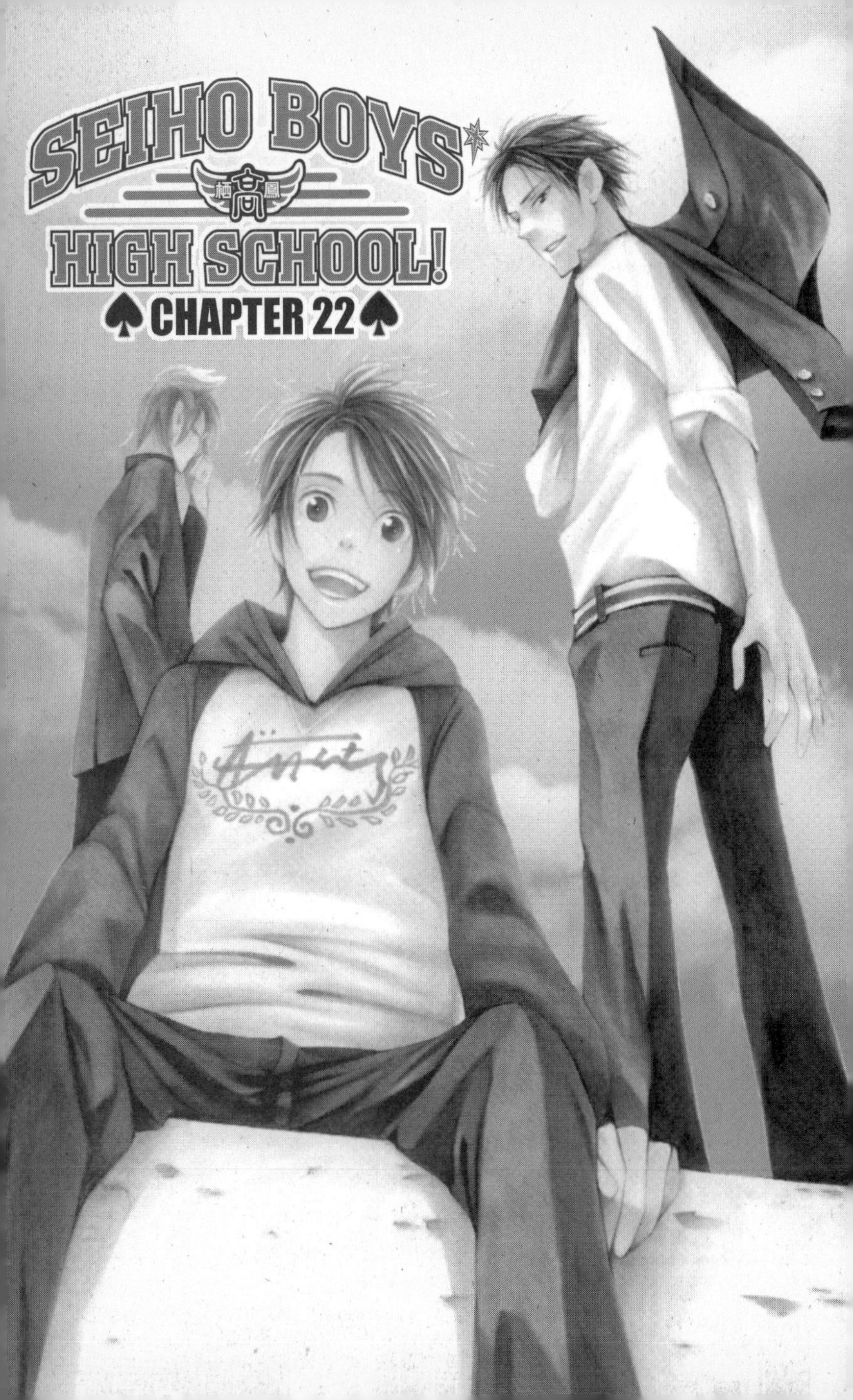
SEIHO BOYS' HIGH SCHOOL!
CHAPTER 22

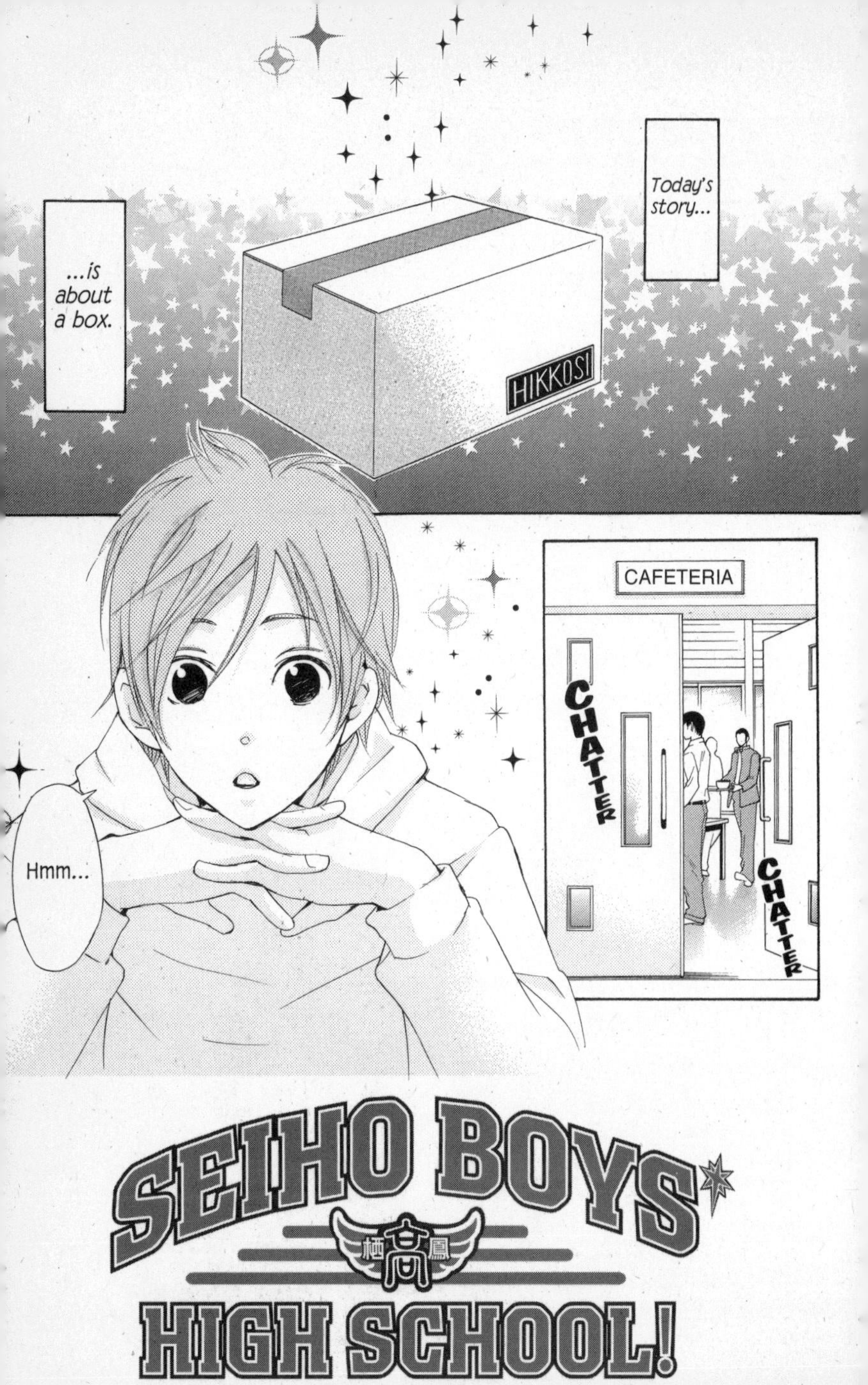
Today's story...
...is about a box.
HIKKOSI
CAFETERIA
CHATTER
CHATTER
Hmm...

SEIHO BOYS HIGH SCHOOL!

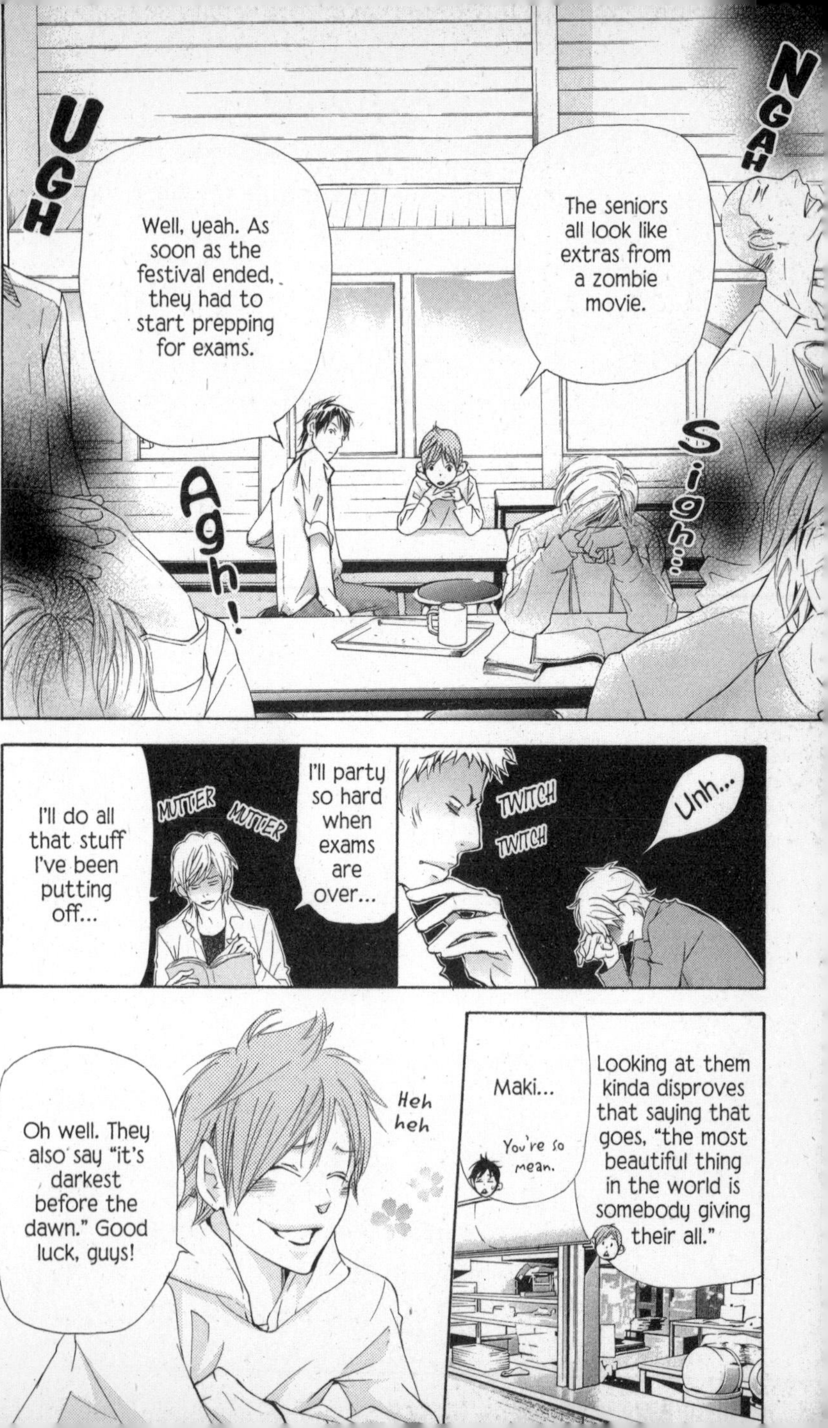
NGAH
The seniors all look like extras from a zombie movie.
Sigh...
UGH
Well, yeah. As soon as the festival ended, they had to start prepping for exams.
Agh!
Unh...
TWITCH
TWITCH
I'll party so hard when exams are over...
MUTTER
MUTTER
I'll do all that stuff I've been putting off...
Looking at them kinda disproves that saying that goes, "the most beautiful thing in the world is somebody giving their all."
Maki...
You're so mean.
Heh heh
Oh well. They also say "it's darkest before the dawn." Good luck, guys!

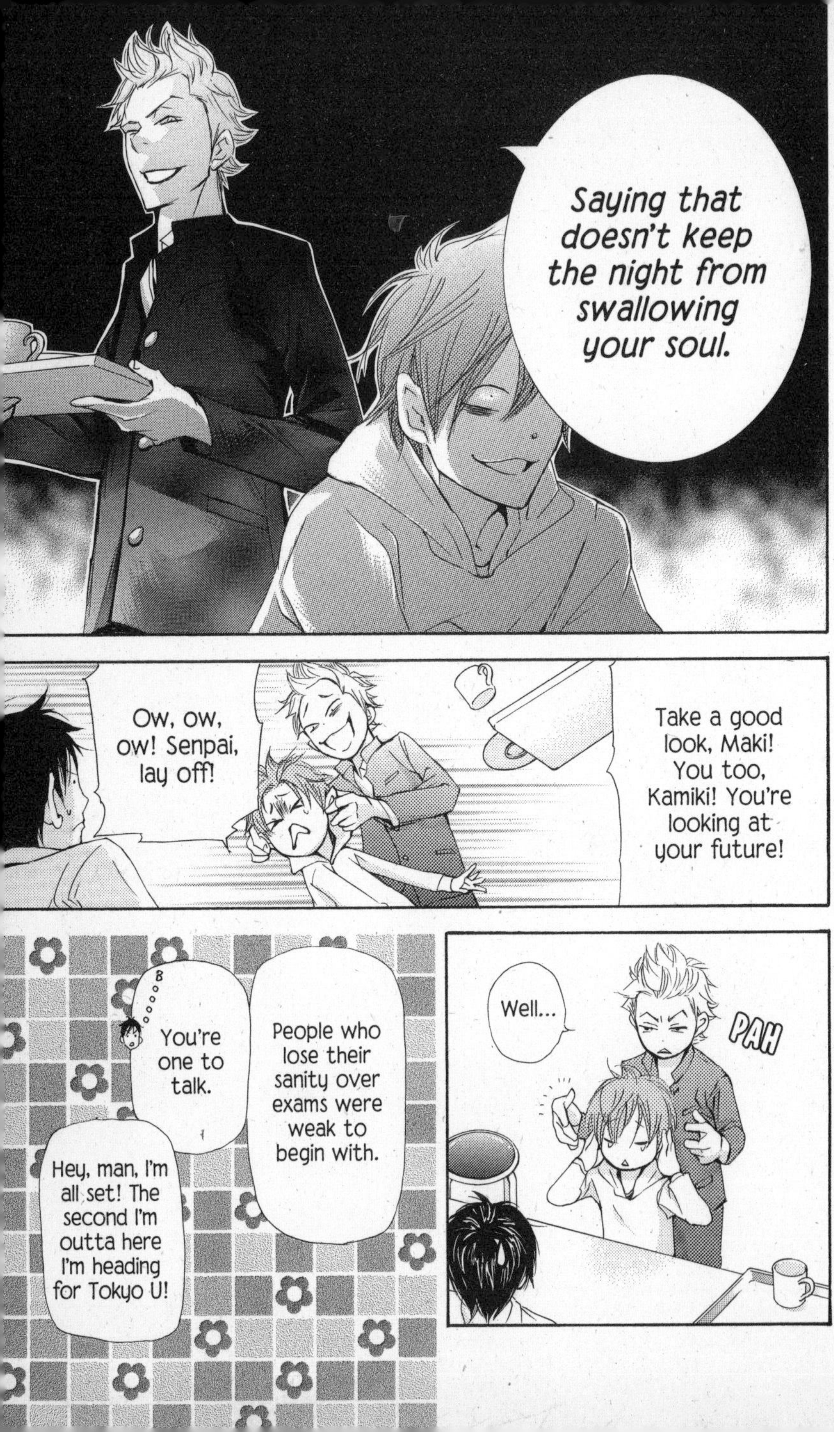
Saying that doesn't keep the night from swallowing your soul.
Take a good look, Maki! You too, Kamiki! You're looking at your future!
Ow, ow, ow! Senpai, lay off!
Well...
PAH
People who lose their sanity over exams were weak to begin with.
You're one to talk.
Hey, man, I'm all set! The second I'm outta here I'm heading for Tokyo U!

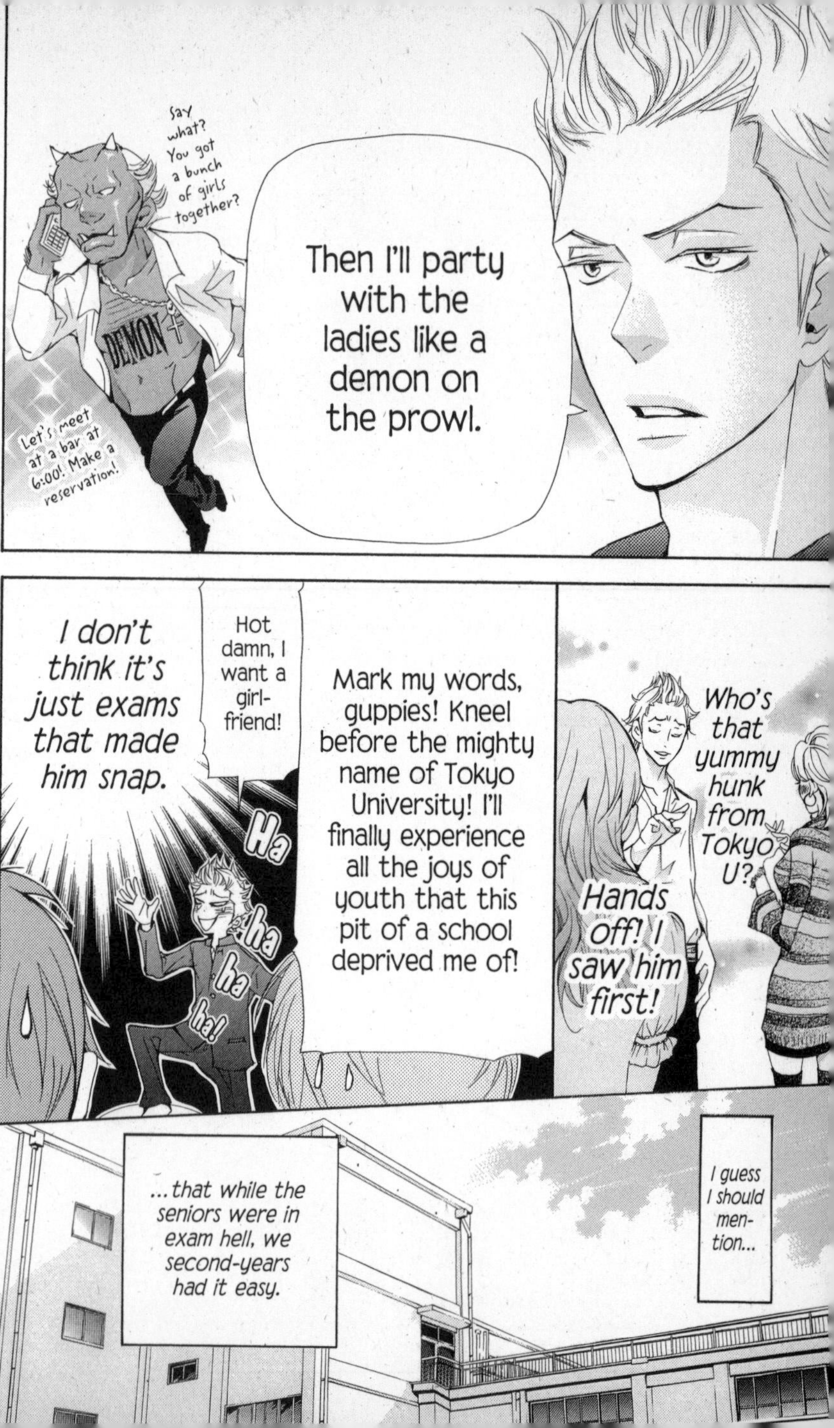
Then I'll party with the ladies like a demon on the prowl.
Say what? You got a bunch of girls together?
DEMON
Let's meet at a bar at 6:00! Make a reservation!
Who's that yummy hunk from Tokyo U?
Hands off! I saw him first!
Mark my words, guppies! Kneel before the mighty name of Tokyo University! I'll finally experience all the joys of youth that this pit of a school deprived me of!
Hot damn, I want a girlfriend!
Ha ha ha ha!
I don't think it's just exams that made him snap.
I guess I should mention...
...that while the seniors were in exam hell, we second-years had it easy.

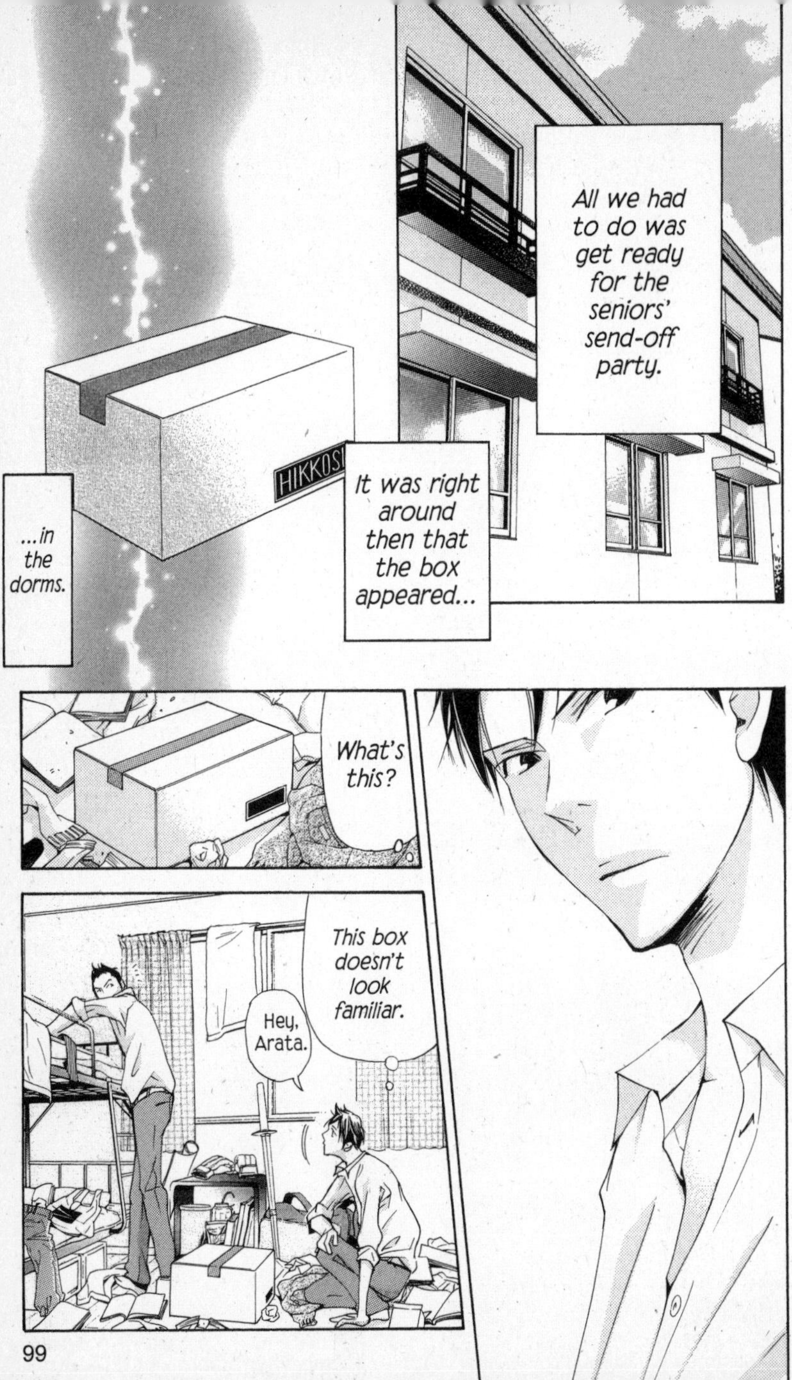
All we had to do was get ready for the seniors' send-off party.
It was right around then that the box appeared...
...in the dorms.
What's this?
This box doesn't look familiar.
Hey, Arata.

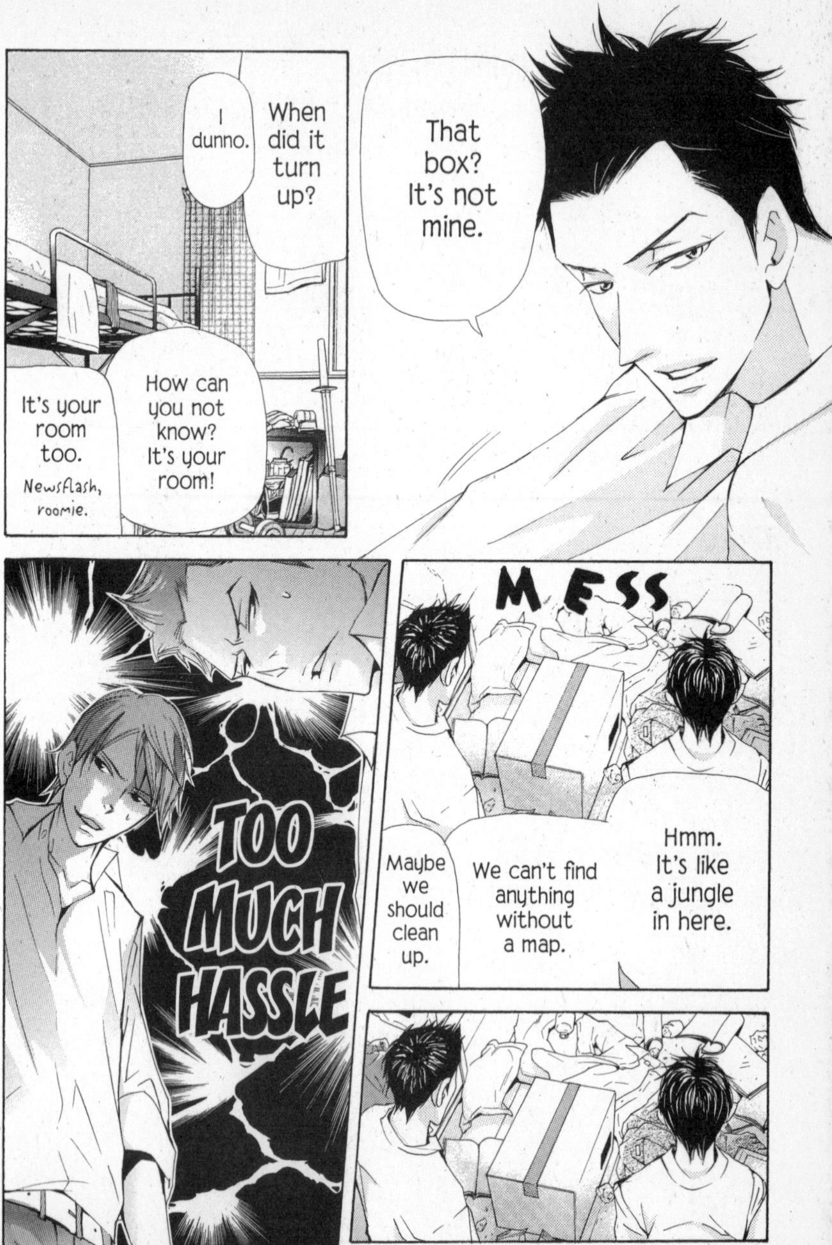
That box? It's not mine.
When did it turn up?
I dunno.
How can you not know? It's your room!
It's your room too.
Newsflash, roomie.
MESS
Hmm. It's like a jungle in here.
We can't find anything without a map.
Maybe we should clean up.
TOO MUCH HASSLE

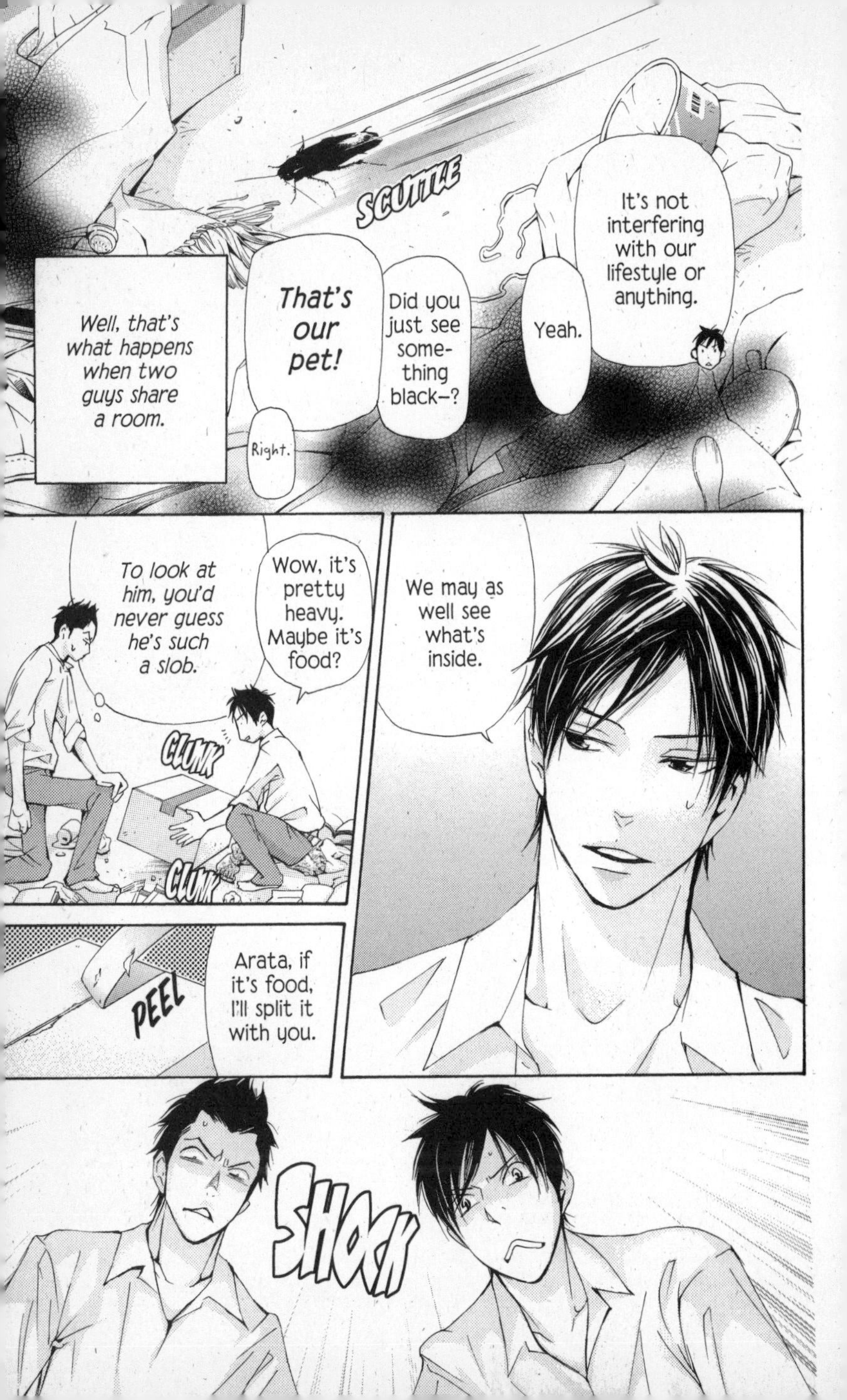
SCUTTLE
It's not interfering with our lifestyle or anything.
Yeah.
Did you just see some-thing black—?
That's our pet!
Right.
Well, that's what happens when two guys share a room.
We may as well see what's inside.
Wow, it's pretty heavy. Maybe it's food?
To look at him, you'd never guess he's such a slob.
CLUNK
CLUNK
Arata, if it's food, I'll split it with you.
PEEL
SHOCK

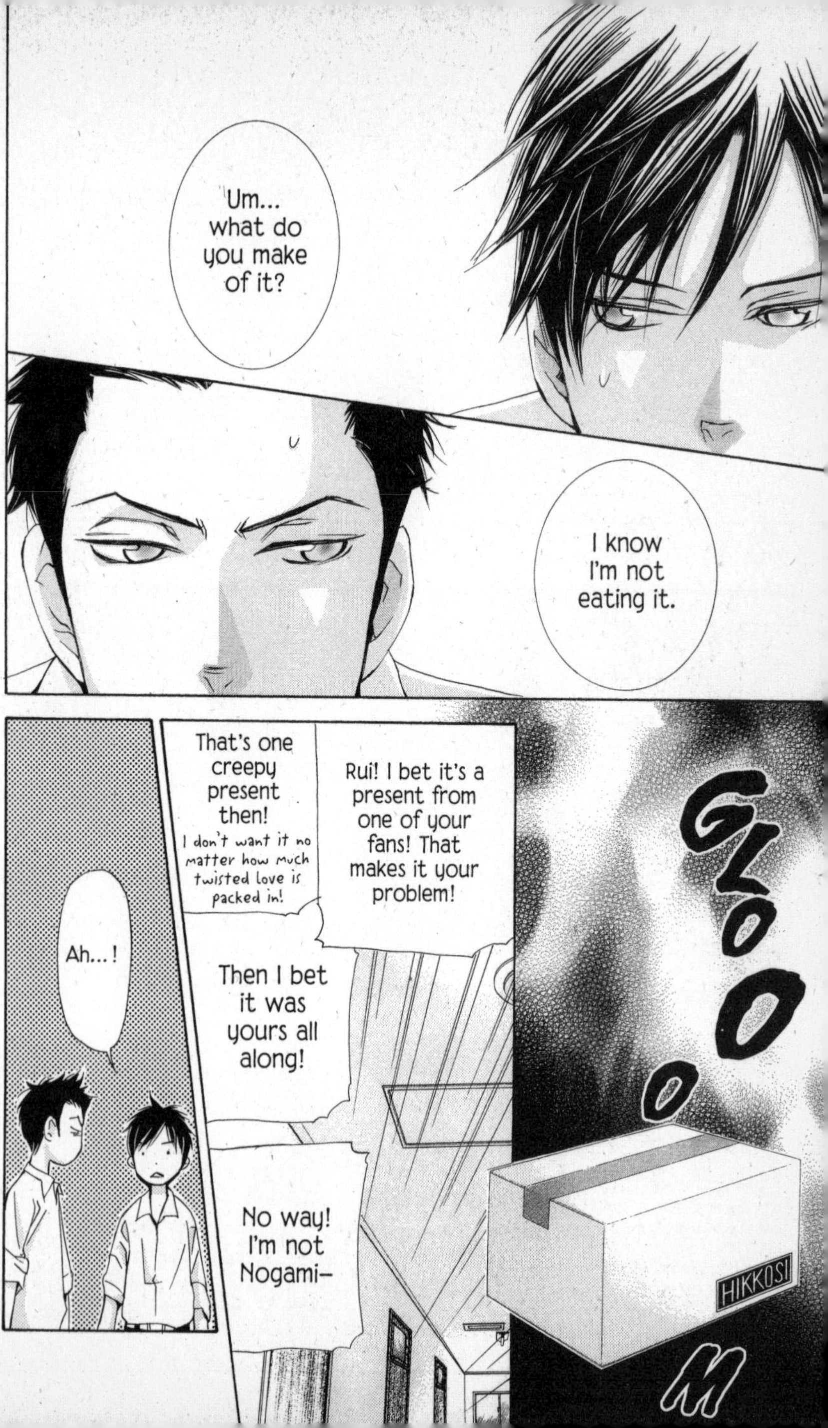

Um... what do you make of it?
I know I'm not eating it.
GLOOOOM
HIKKOSI
Rui! I bet it's a present from one of your fans! That makes it your problem!
That's one creepy present then!
I don't want it no matter how much twisted love is packed in!
Then I bet it was yours all along!
No way! I'm not Nogami-
Ah...!

1/3 Filler Corner

AIRLINE FOOD
The Opposite of a Gourmet Journey

Case 3
Air D
(U.S. Domestic Flight)

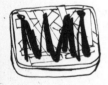

Boiled macaroni (soggy) topped with cheese (flavorless) and ketchup (tasted artificial).
And **that's it.**

I was ravenous, but after just one bite...

CONCEDES DEFEAT

...

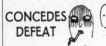

After that, the flight attendant kept saying, "Eat!" to me several times, but I pretended to be asleep instead. Or let's be blunt— **I played dead** and made it through...

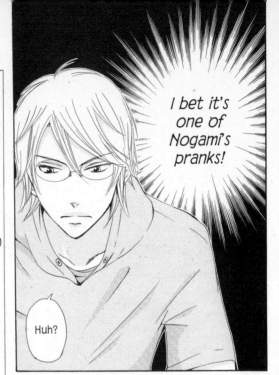

I bet it's one of Nogami's pranks!
Huh?
HIKKOSI
And so the box made its way from Kamiki to Nogami.
What's this? A special delivery?
There's no return address ...

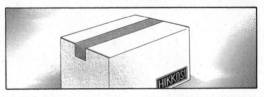

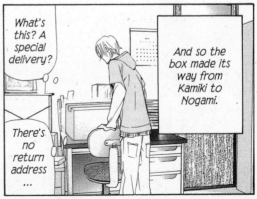

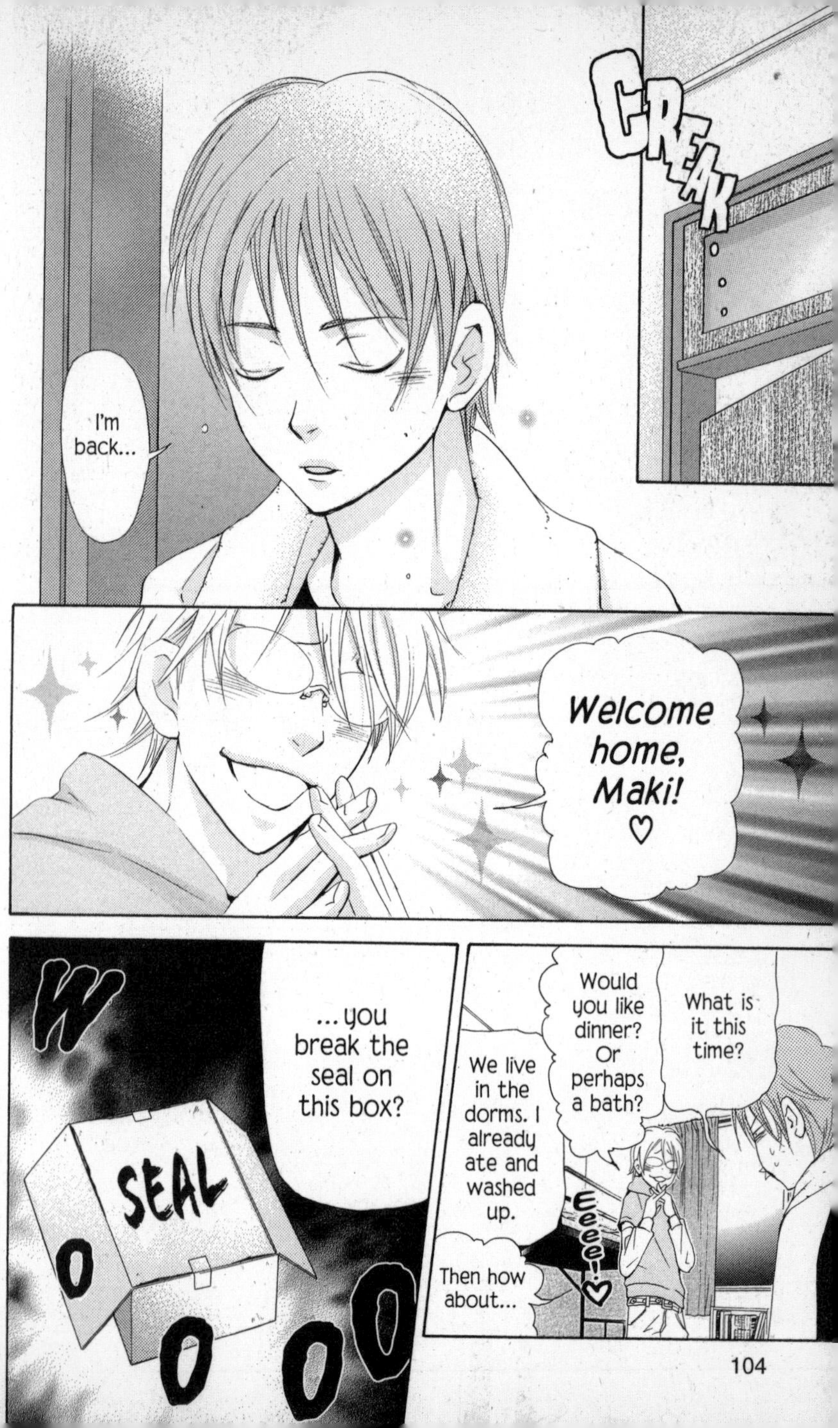
CREAK
I'm back...
Welcome home, Maki! ♡
What is it this time?
Would you like dinner? Or perhaps a bath?
Eeee!♡
We live in the dorms. I already ate and washed up.
Then how about...
...you break the seal on this box?
SEAL
WOOOOO

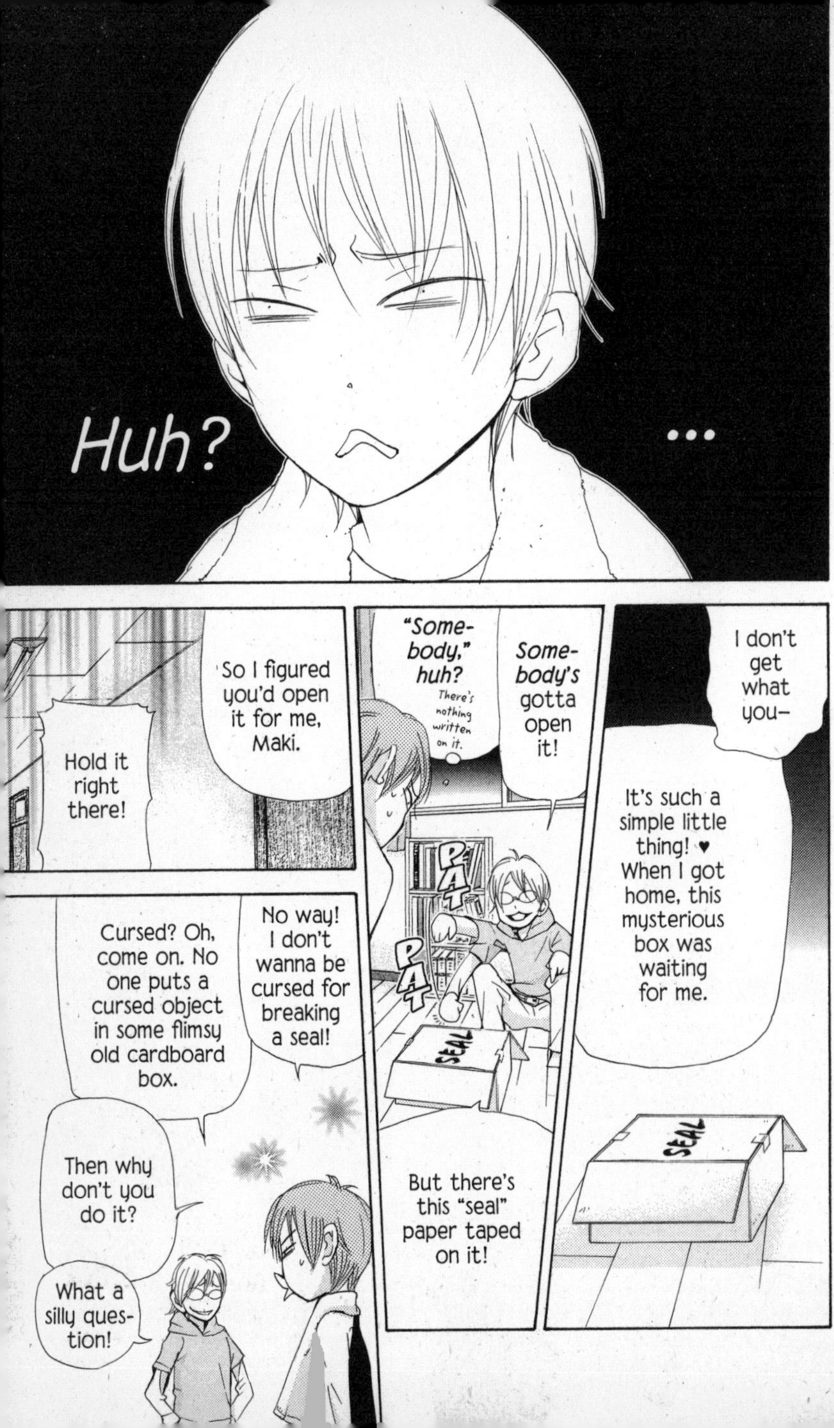
...
Huh?
I don't get what you–
It's such a simple little thing! ♥ When I got home, this mysterious box was waiting for me.
SEAL
Some-body's gotta open it!
"Some-body," huh?
There's nothing written on it.
PAT
PAT
SEAL
But there's this "seal" paper taped on it!
So I figured you'd open it for me, Maki.
Hold it right there!
No way! I don't wanna be cursed for breaking a seal!
Cursed? Oh, come on. No one puts a cursed object in some flimsy old cardboard box.
Then why don't you do it?
What a silly question!

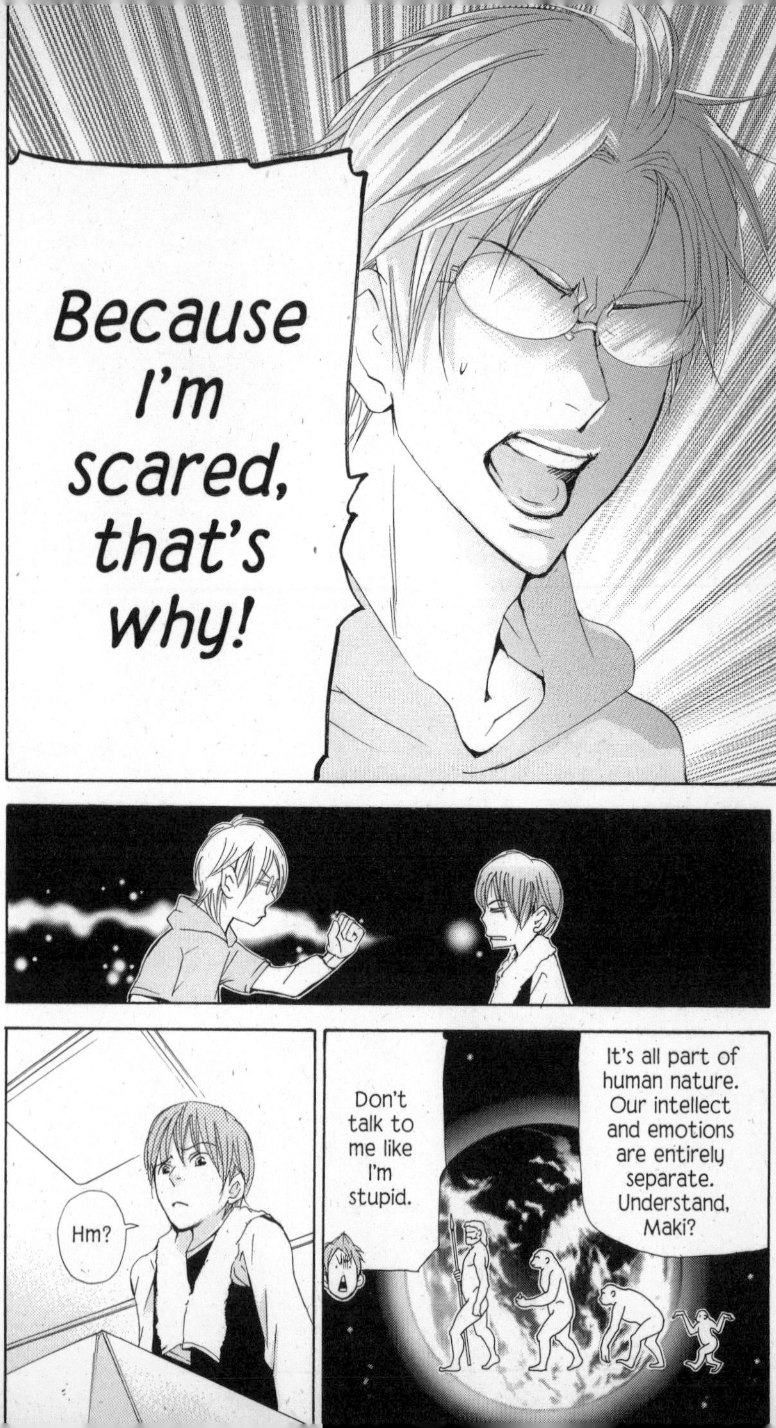
Because I'm scared, that's why!
It's all part of human nature. Our intellect and emotions are entirely separate. Understand, Maki?
Don't talk to me like I'm stupid.
Hm?

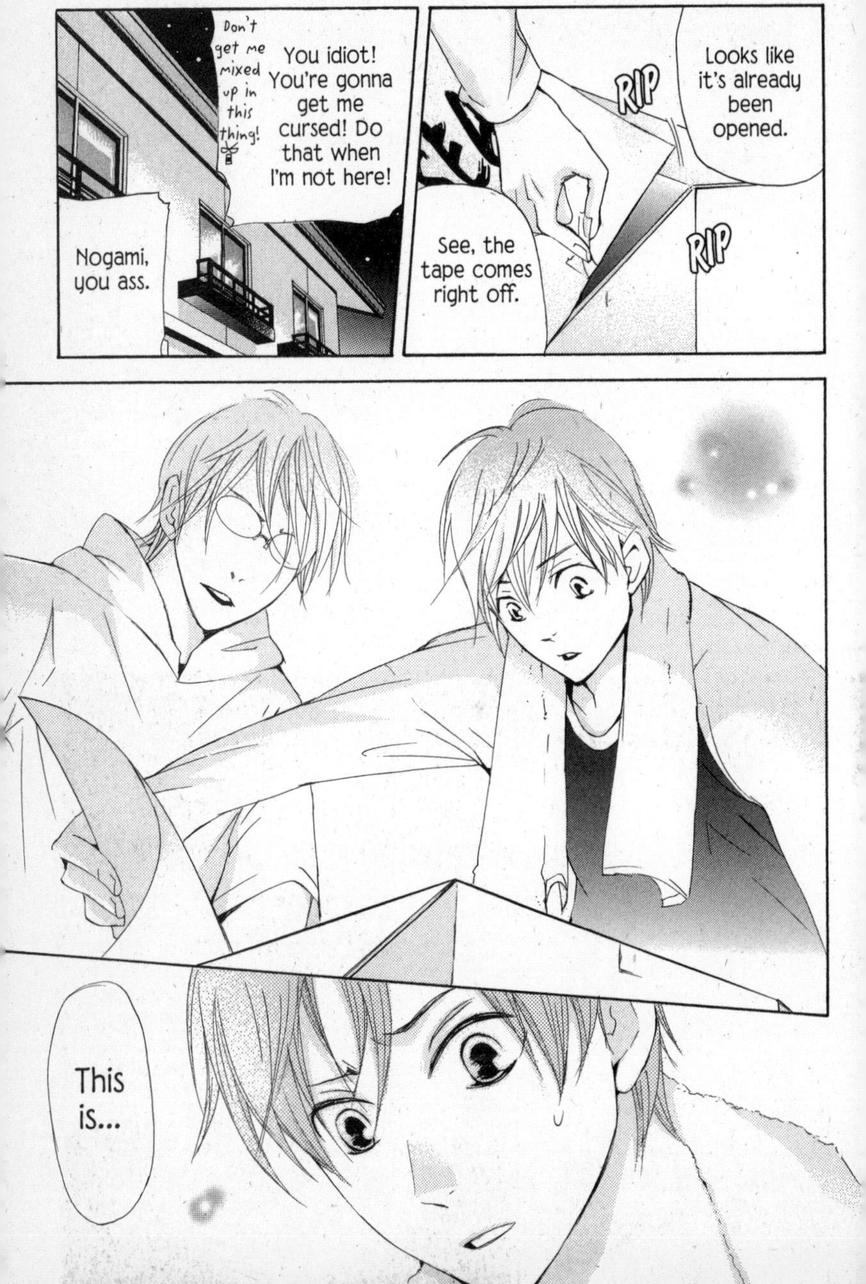
Looks like it's already been opened.
RIP
RIP
See, the tape comes right off.
You idiot! You're gonna get me cursed! Do that when I'm not here!
Don't get me mixed up in this thing!
Nogami, you ass.
This is...

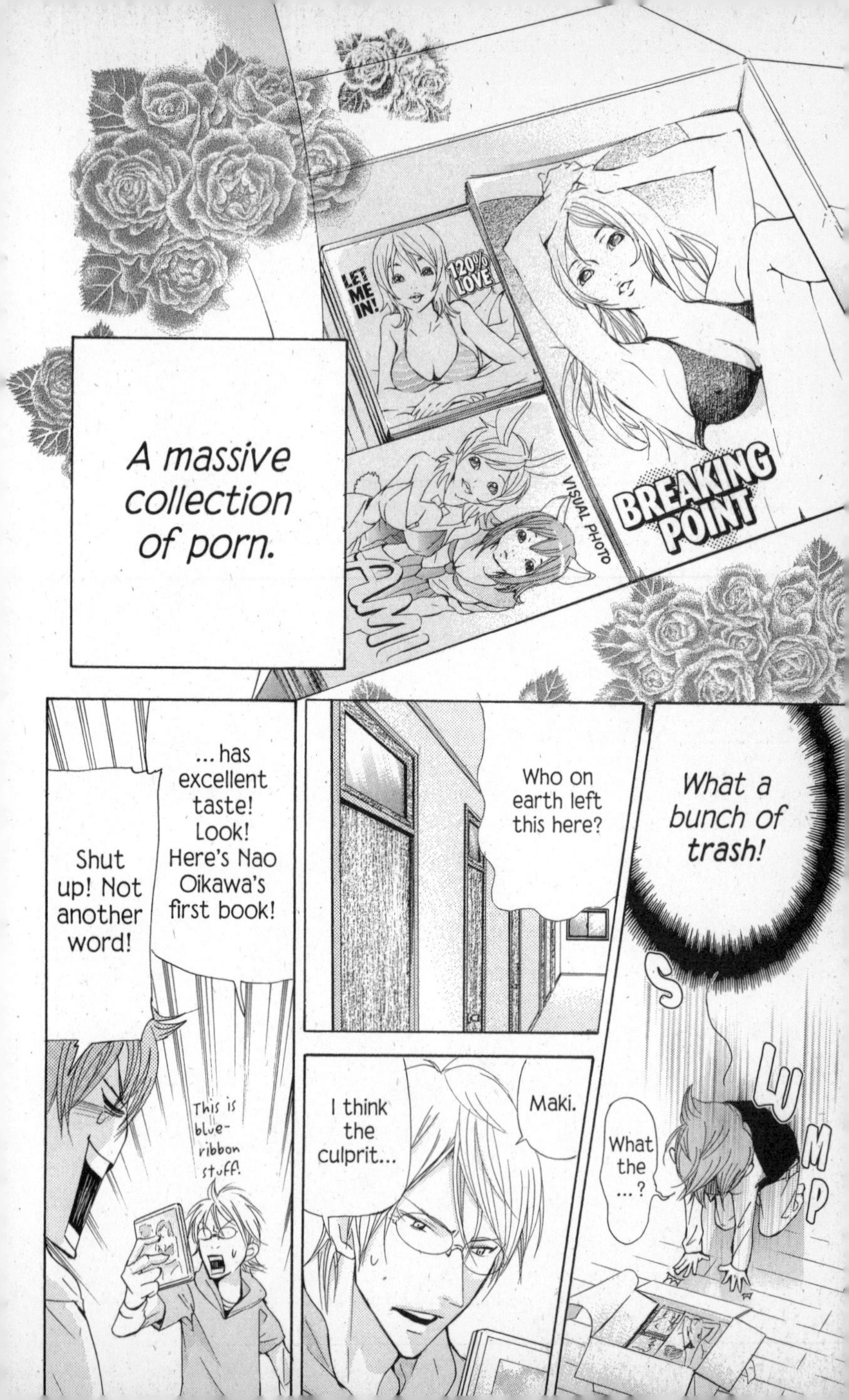
BREAKING POINT
120% LOVE
LET ME IN!
VISUAL PHOTO
A massive collection of porn.
What a bunch of trash!
SLUMP
What the ...?
Who on earth left this here?
Maki.
I think the culprit...
... has excellent taste! Look! Here's Nao Oikawa's first book!
Shut up! Not another word!
This is blue-ribbon stuff!

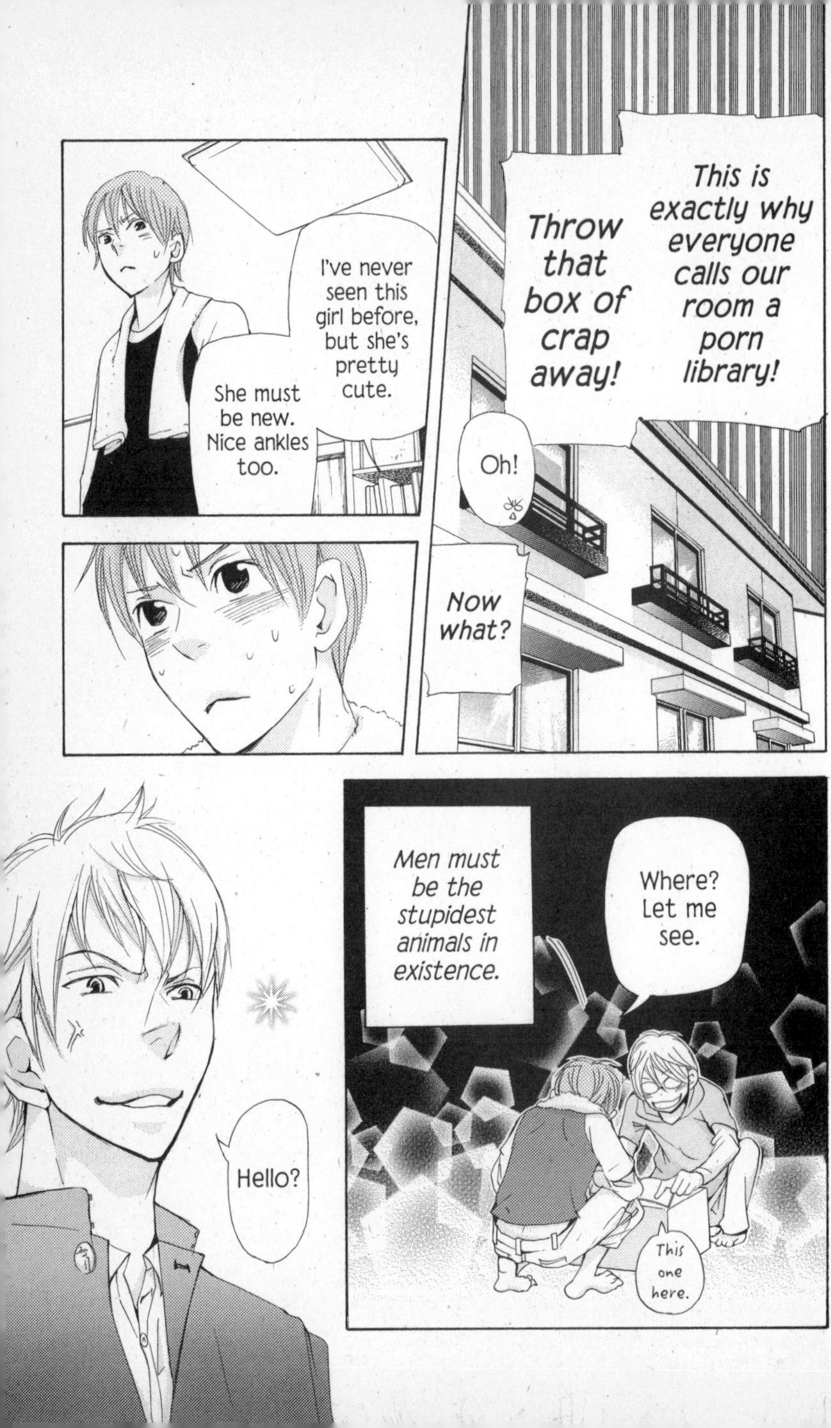
This is exactly why everyone calls our room a porn library!
Throw that box of crap away!
Oh!
Now what?
I've never seen this girl before, but she's pretty cute.
She must be new. Nice ankles too.
Where? Let me see.
Men must be the stupidest animals in existence.
This one here.
Hello?

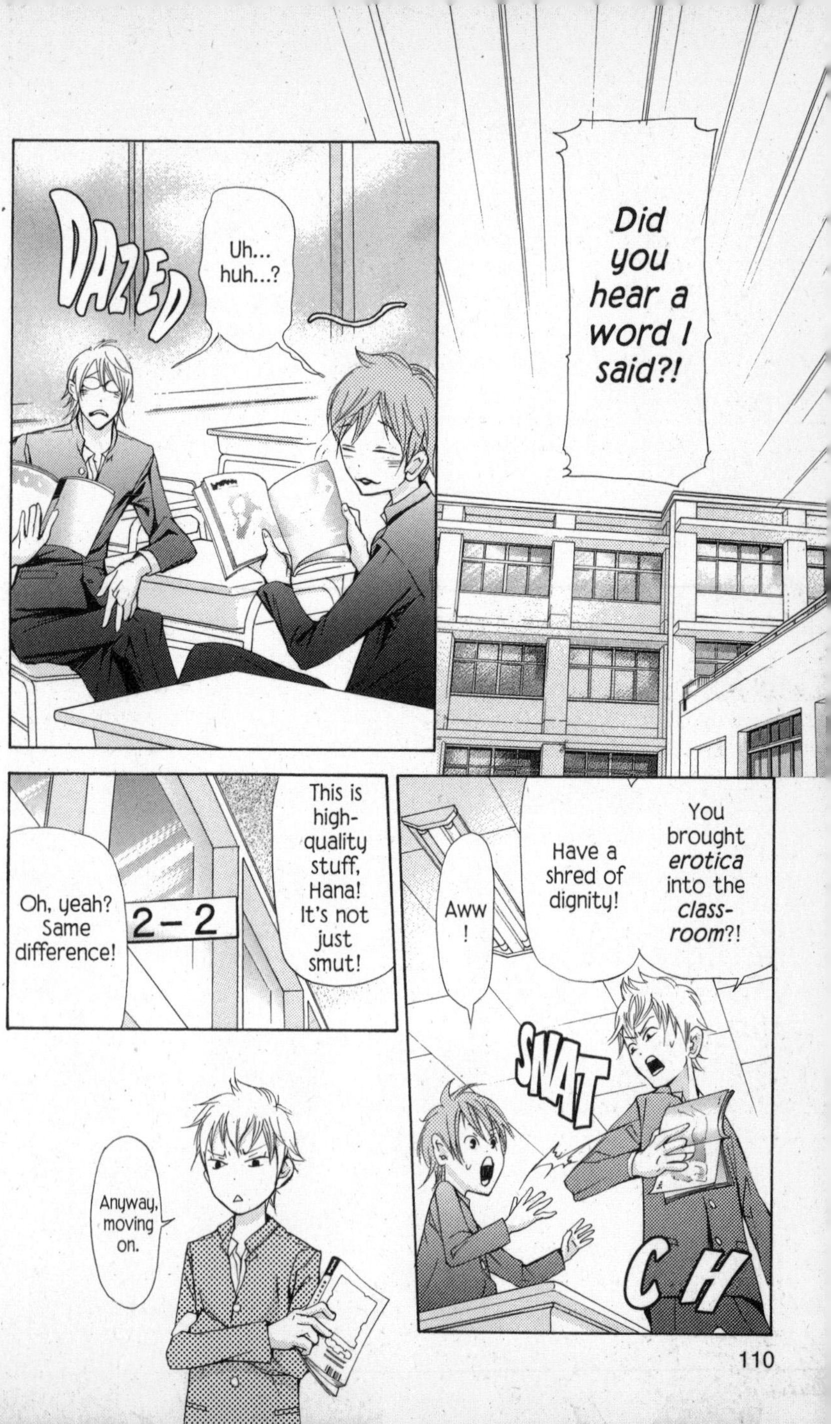
Did you hear a word I said?!
DAZED
Uh... huh...?
You brought *erotica* into the *class-room*?!
Have a shred of dignity!
Aww!
SNATCH
This is high-quality stuff, Hana! It's not just smut!
Oh, yeah? Same difference!
2-2
Anyway, moving on.

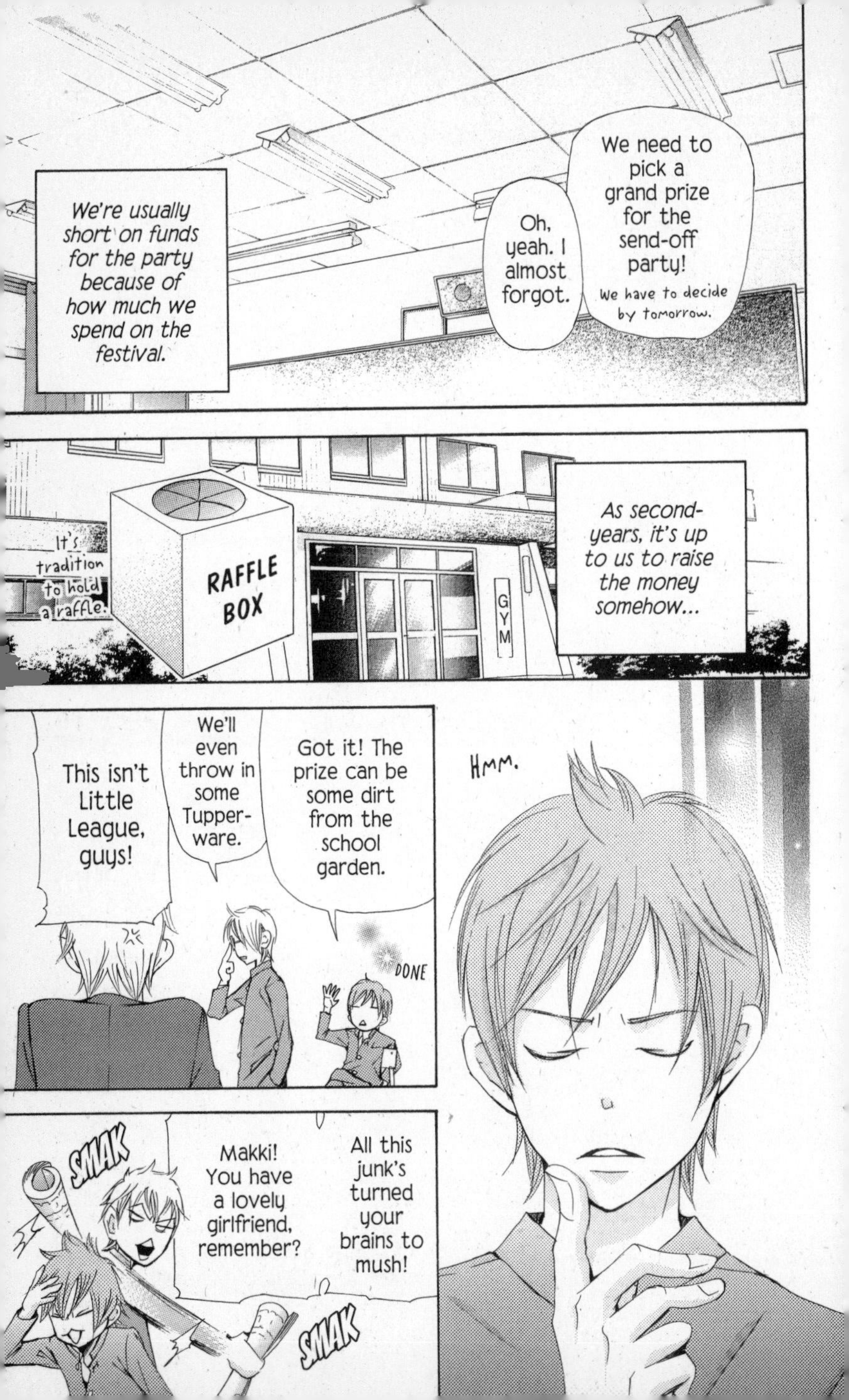
We need to pick a grand prize for the send-off party!
We have to decide by tomorrow.
Oh, yeah. I almost forgot.
We're usually short on funds for the party because of how much we spend on the festival.
As second-years, it's up to us to raise the money somehow...
GYM
RAFFLE BOX
It's tradition to hold a raffle.
HMM.
Got it! The prize can be some dirt from the school garden.
DONE
We'll even throw in some Tupperware.
This isn't Little League, guys!
All this junk's turned your brains to mush!
Makki! You have a lovely girlfriend, remember?
SMAK
SMAK

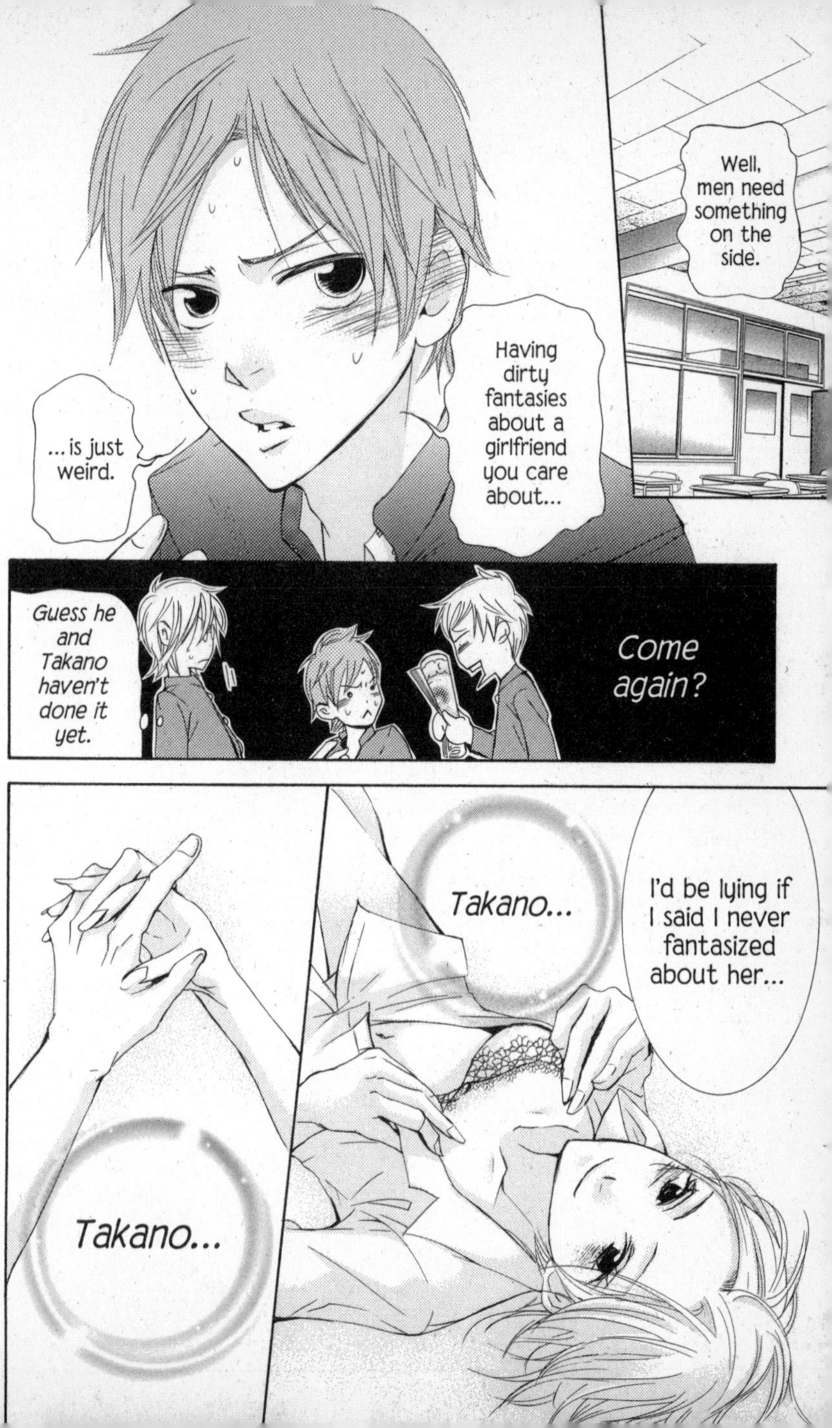
Well, men need something on the side.
Having dirty fantasies about a girlfriend you care about...
...is just weird.
Come again?
Guess he and Takano haven't done it yet.
I'd be lying if I said I never fantasized about her...
Takano...
Takano...

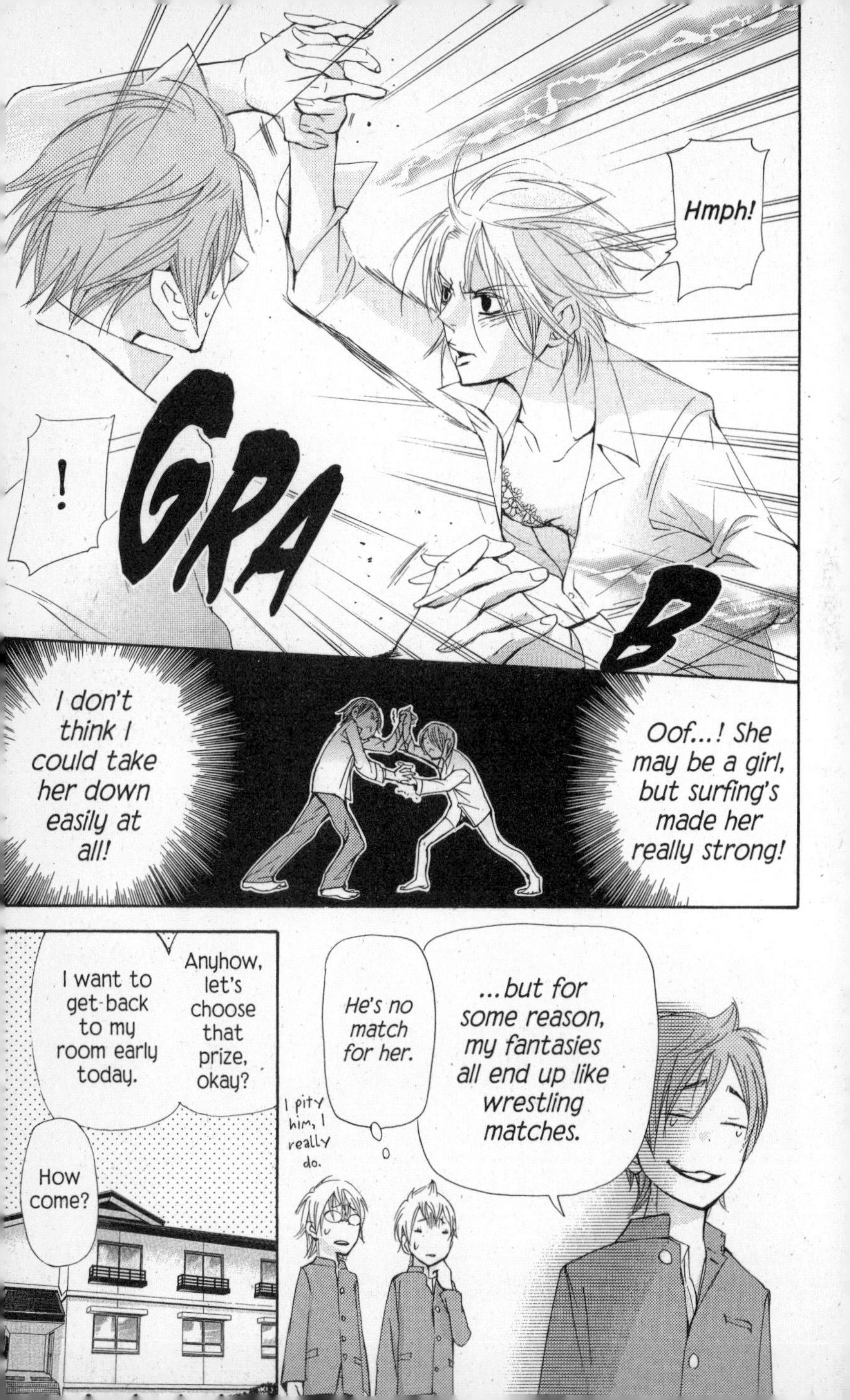
Hmph!
GRAB
!
Oof...! She may be a girl, but surfing's made her really strong!
I don't think I could take her down easily at all!
...but for some reason, my fantasies all end up like wrestling matches.
He's no match for her.
I pity him, I really do.
Anyhow, let's choose that prize, okay?
I want to get back to my room early today.
How come?

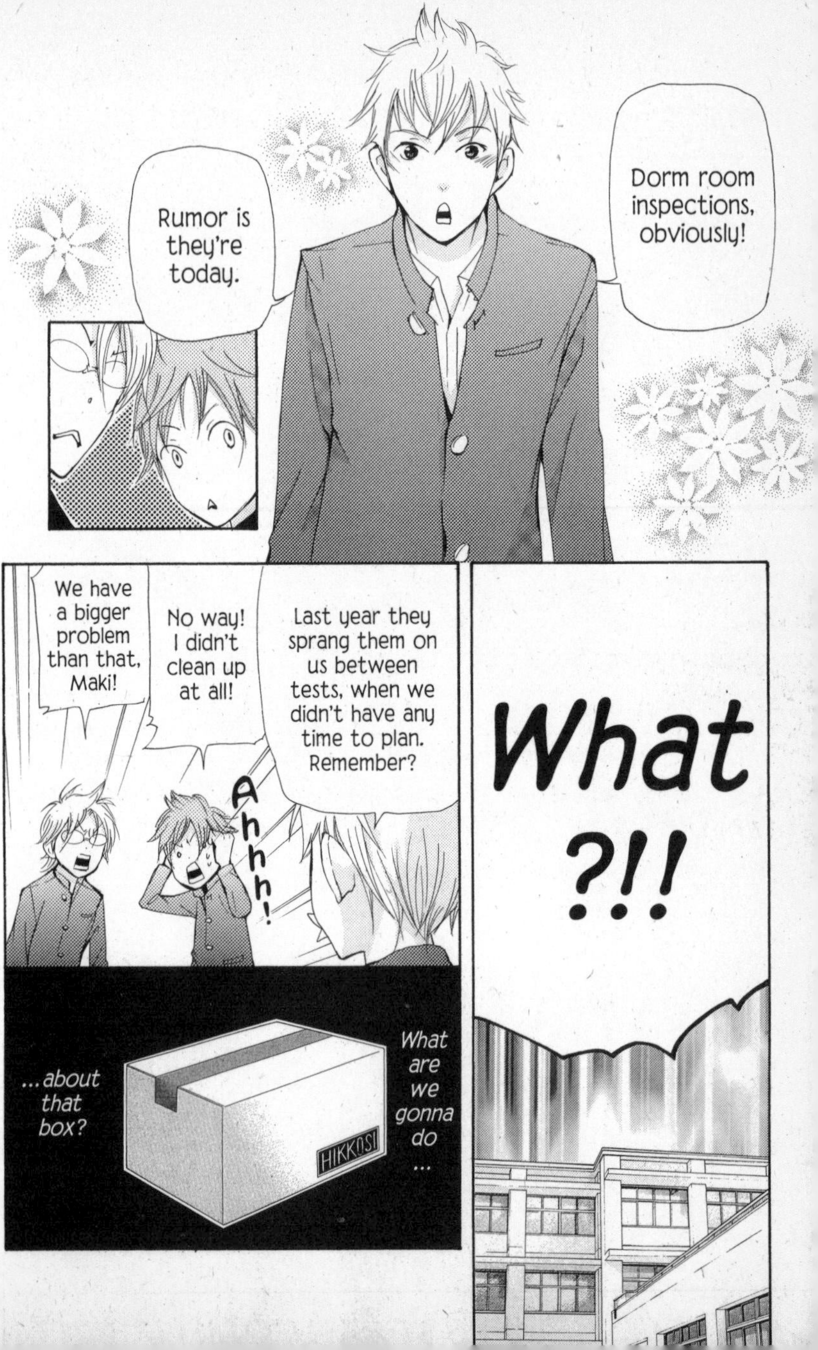
Dorm room inspections, obviously!
Rumor is they're today.
What ?!!
Last year they sprang them on us between tests, when we didn't have any time to plan. Remember?
No way! I didn't clean up at all!
Ahhh!
We have a bigger problem than that, Maki!
What are we gonna do ...
...about that box?
HIKKOSI

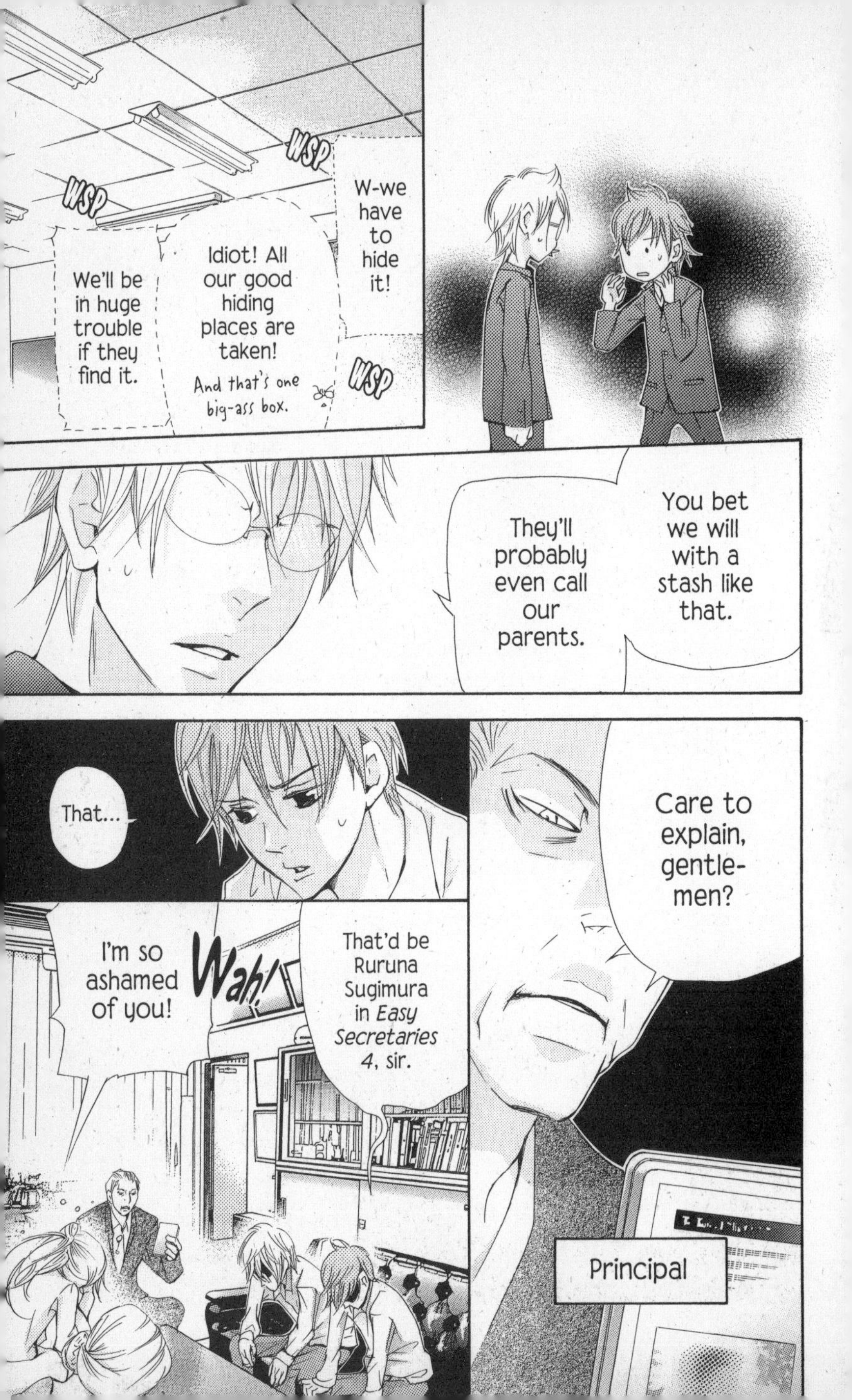
WSP
WSP
W-we have to hide it!
Idiot! All our good hiding places are taken!
And that's one big-ass box.
We'll be in huge trouble if they find it.
WSP
You bet we will with a stash like that.
They'll probably even call our parents.
Care to explain, gentle-men?
Principal
That...
That'd be Ruruna Sugimura in Easy Secretaries 4, sir.
Wah!
I'm so ashamed of you!

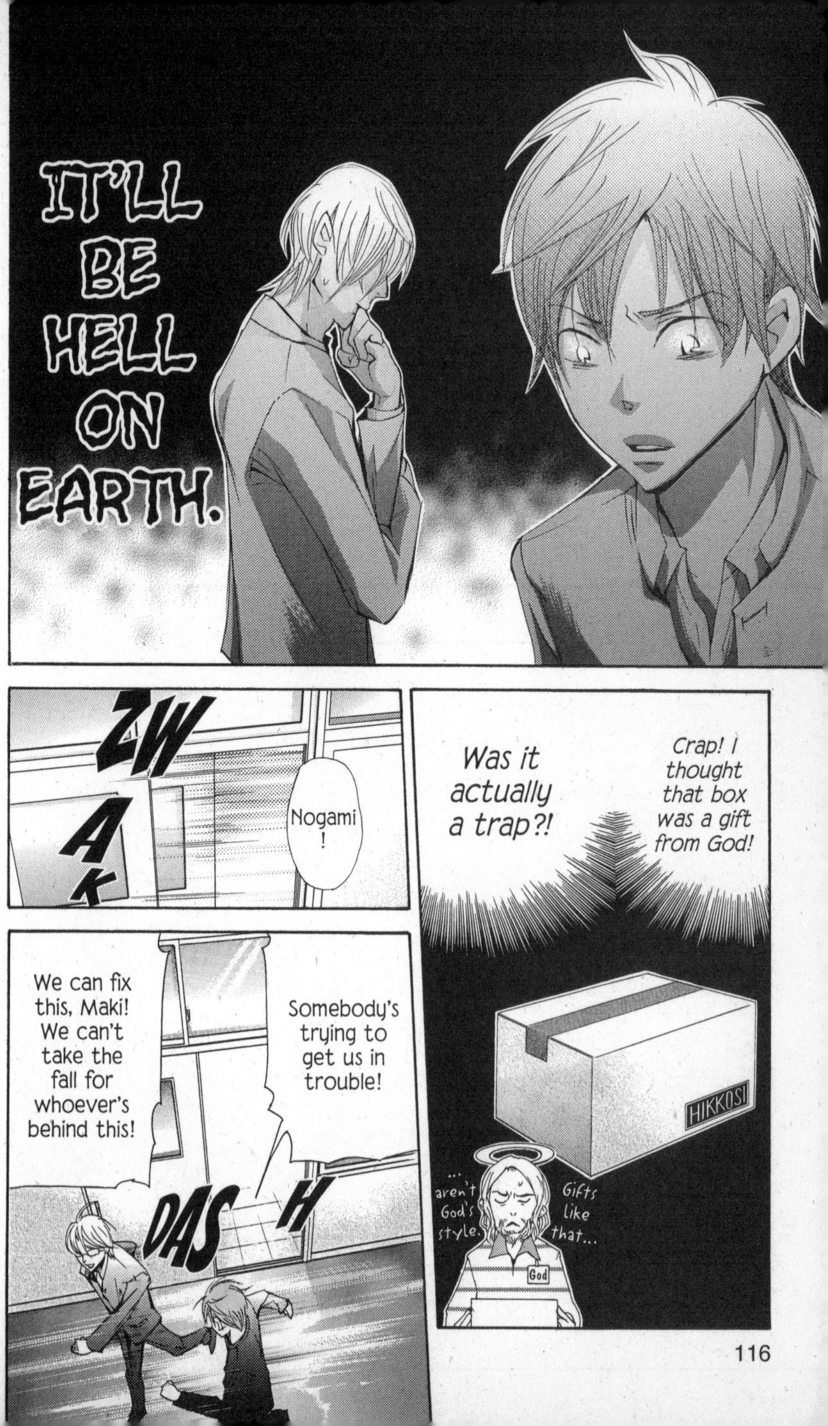
IT'LL BE HELL ON EARTH.
Crap! I thought that box was a gift from God!
Was it actually a trap?!
HIKKOSI
Gifts like that...
... aren't God's style.
God
ZWAK
Nogami!
Somebody's trying to get us in trouble!
We can fix this, Maki! We can't take the fall for whoever's behind this!
DASH

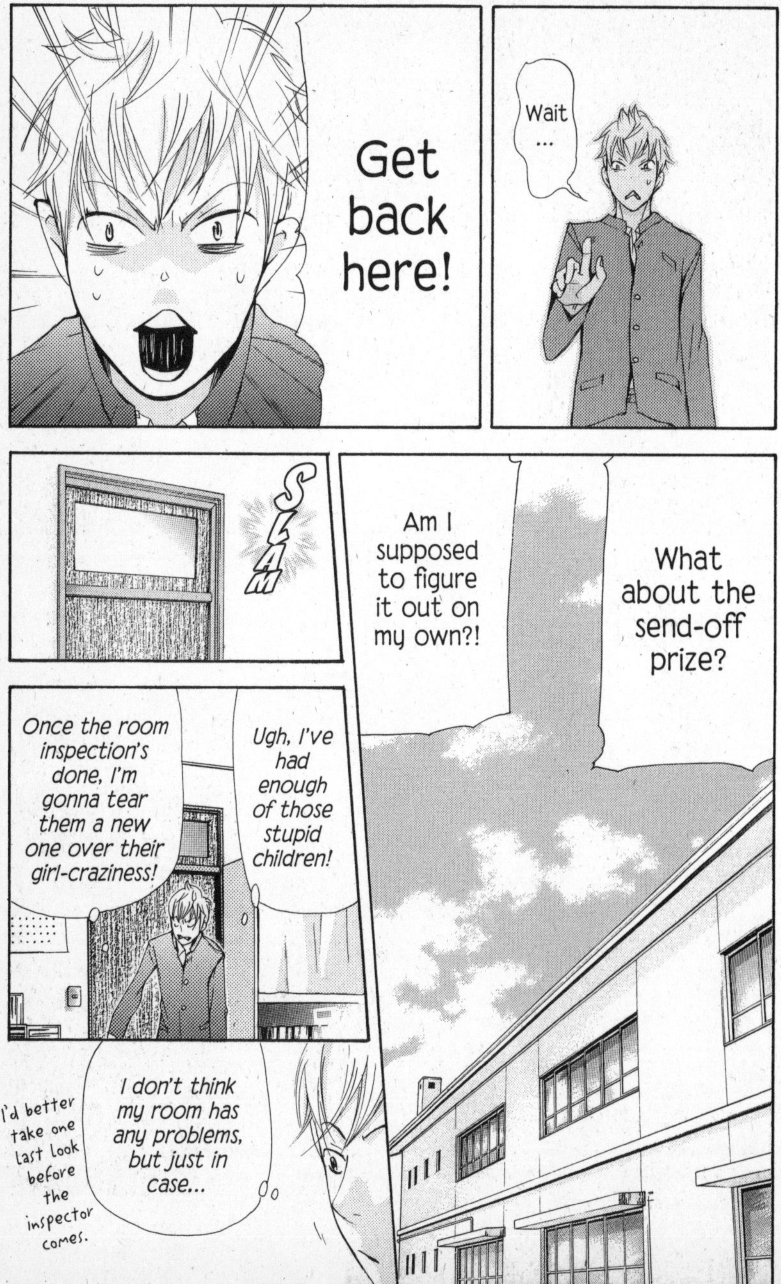
Wait ...
Get back here!
What about the send-off prize?
Am I supposed to figure it out on my own?!
SLAM
Ugh, I've had enough of those stupid children!
Once the room inspection's done, I'm gonna tear them a new one over their girl-craziness!
I don't think my room has any problems, but just in case...
I'd better take one last look before the inspector comes.

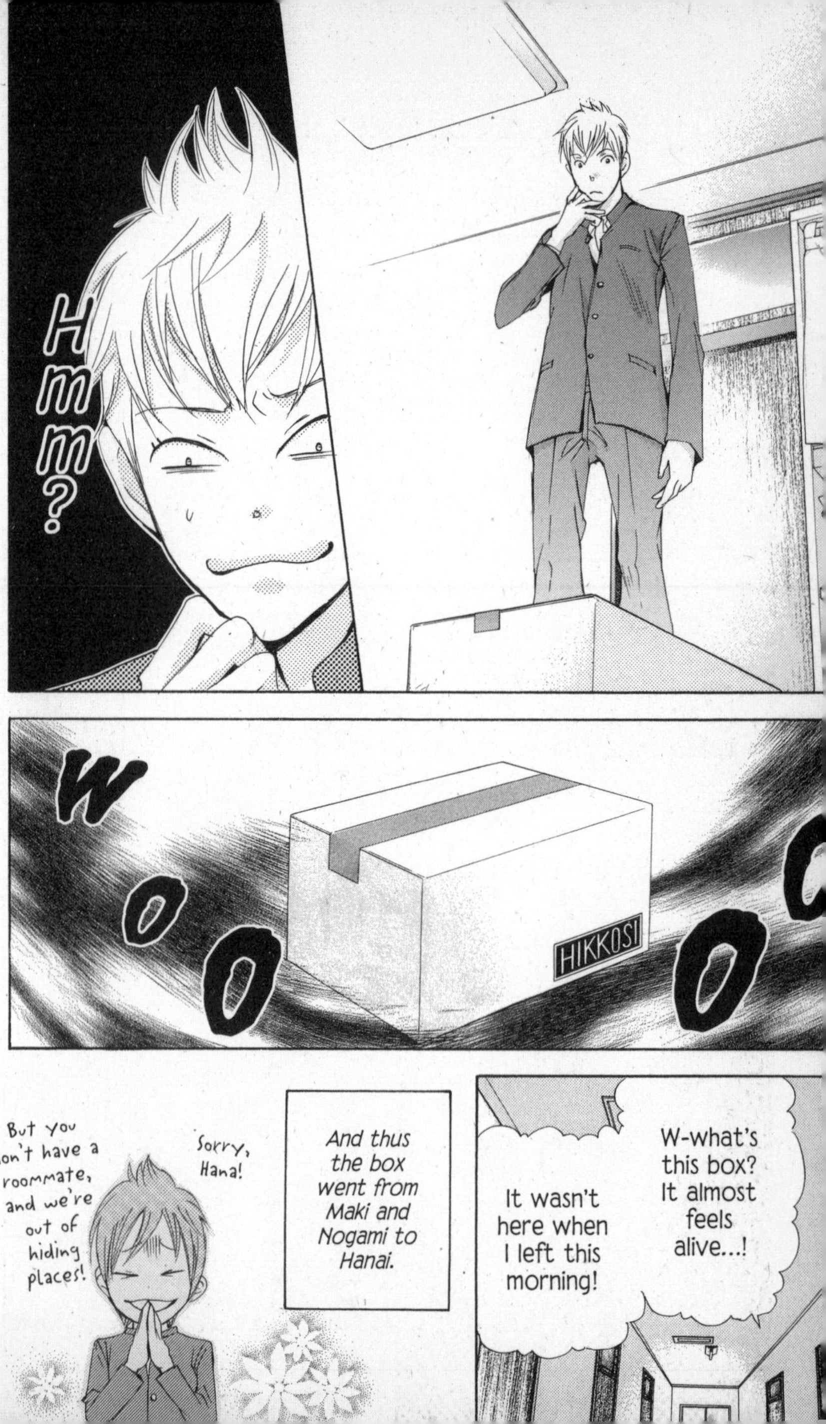
Hmm?
WOOOOO
W-what's this box? It almost feels alive...!
It wasn't here when I left this morning!
And thus the box went from Maki and Nogami to Hanai.
Sorry, Hana!
But you don't have a roommate, and we're out of hiding places!

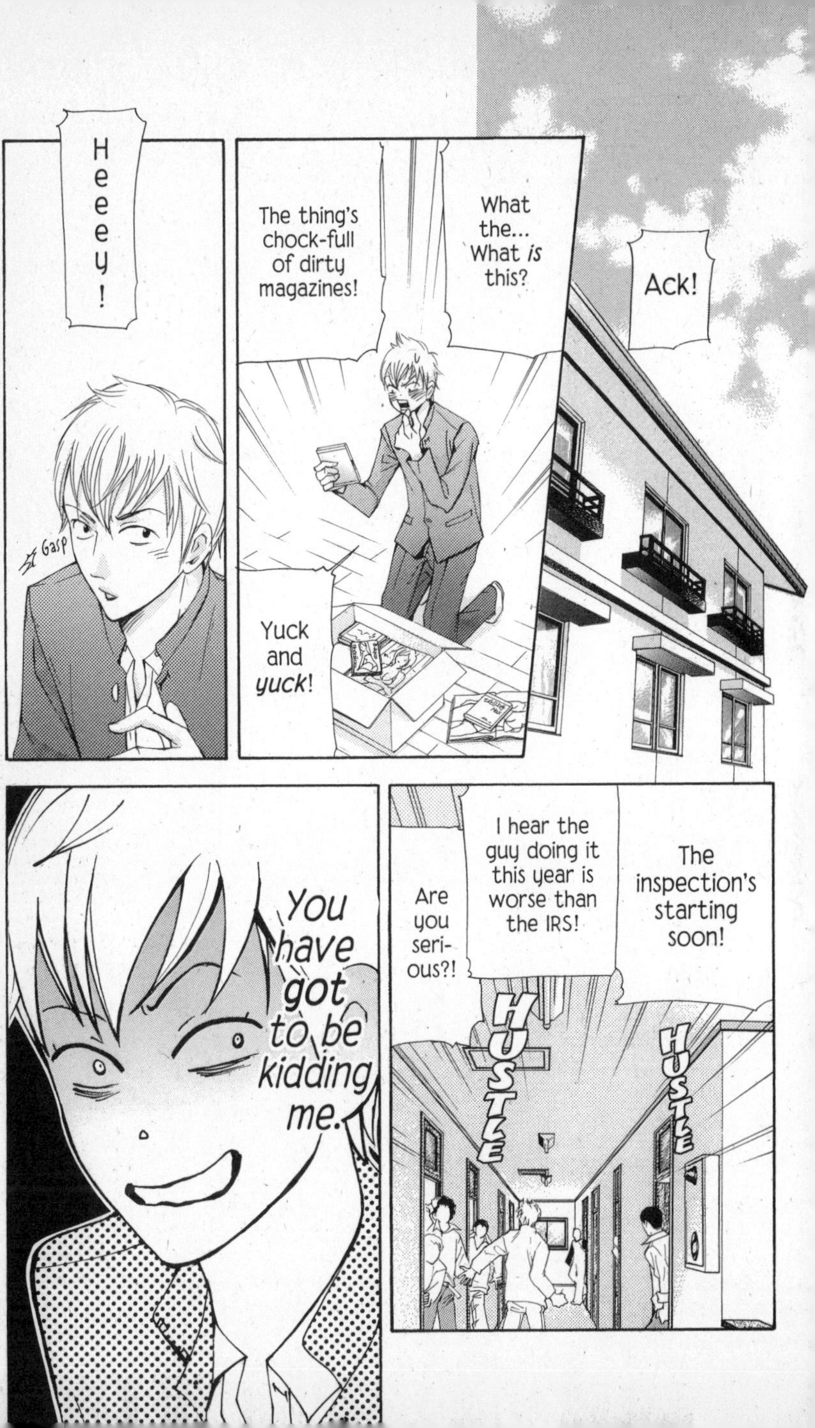
Ack!
What the... What *is* this?
The thing's chock-full of dirty magazines!
Yuck and *yuck*!
Heeey!
Gasp
The inspection's starting soon!
I hear the guy doing it this year is worse than the IRS!
Are you seri-ous?!
HUSTLE
HUSTLE
You have got to be kidding me.

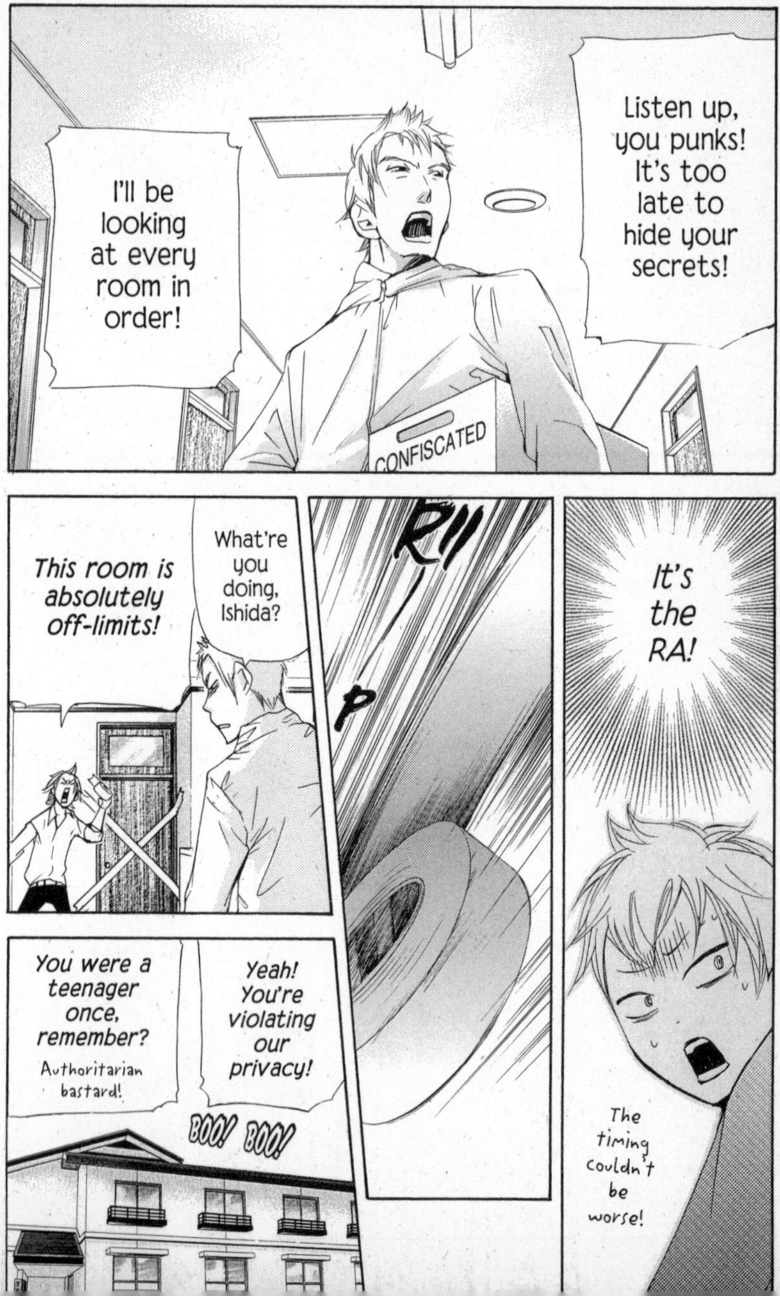

Listen up, you punks! It's too late to hide your secrets!
I'll be looking at every room in order!
CONFISCATED
It's the RA!
The timing couldn't be worse!
RIIP
What're you doing, Ishida?
This room is absolutely off-limits!
Yeah! You're violating our privacy!
You were a teenager once, remember?
Authoritarian bastard!
BOO! BOO!

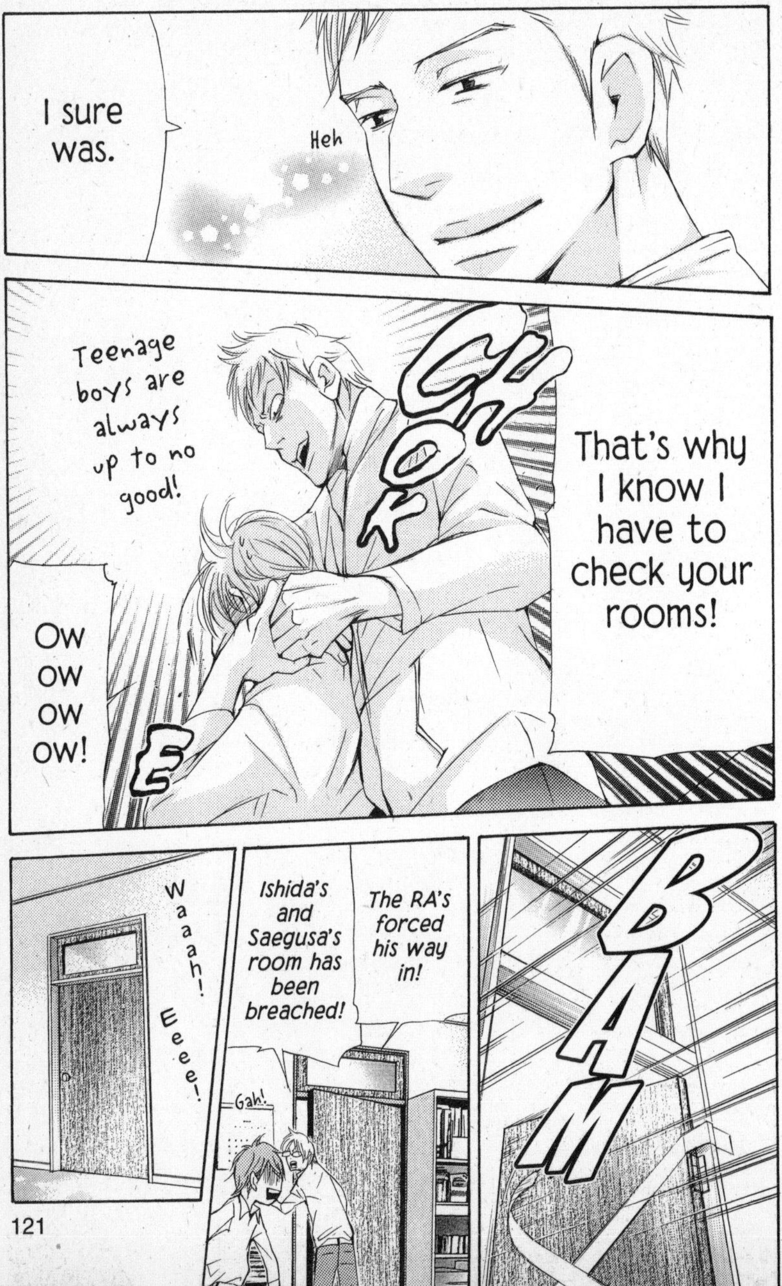
Heh
I sure was.
CHOK
That's why I know I have to check your rooms!
Teenage boys are always up to no good!
E
Ow ow ow ow!
BAM
The RA's forced his way in!
Ishida's and Saegusa's room has been breached!
Gah!
Waaah!
Eeee!

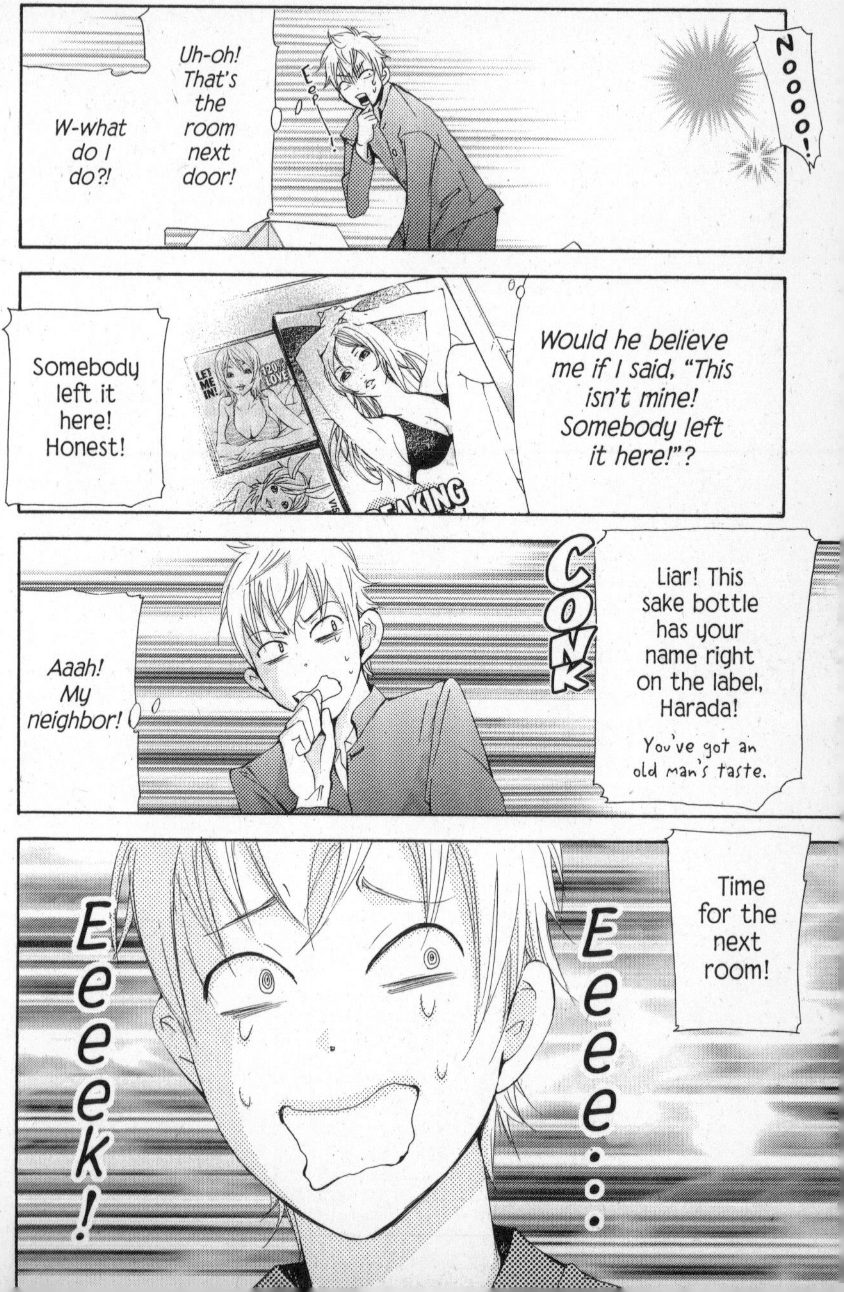

NOOOO!
Uh-oh! That's the room next door!
W-what do I do?!
Would he believe me if I said, "This isn't mine! Somebody left it here!"?
Somebody left it here! Honest!
Liar! This sake bottle has your name right on the label, Harada!
You've got an old man's taste.
CONK
Aaah! My neighbor!
Time for the next room!
Eeee...
Eeeek!

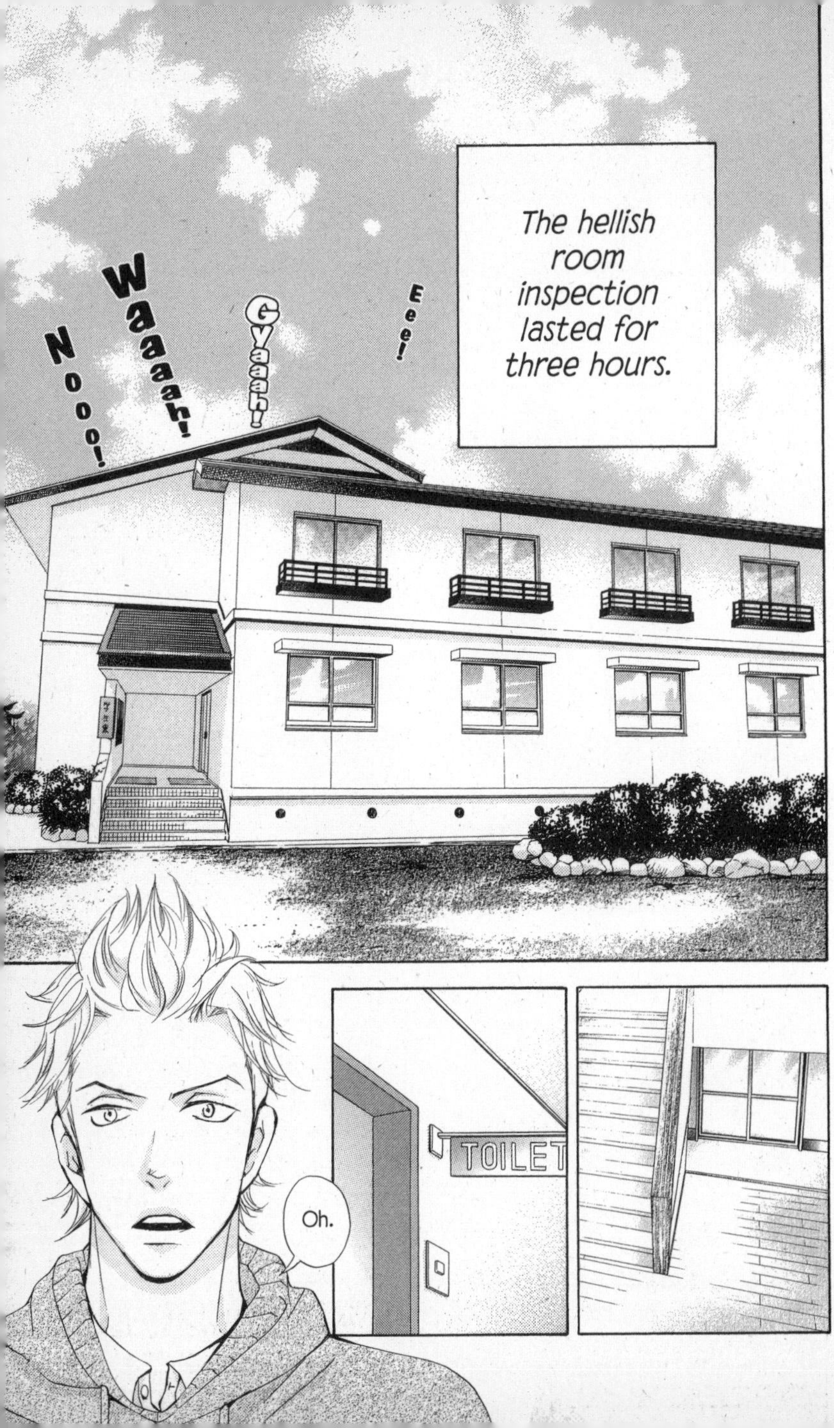
The hellish room inspection lasted for three hours.
Eee!
Gyaaah!
Waaaah!
Nooo!
TOILET
Oh.

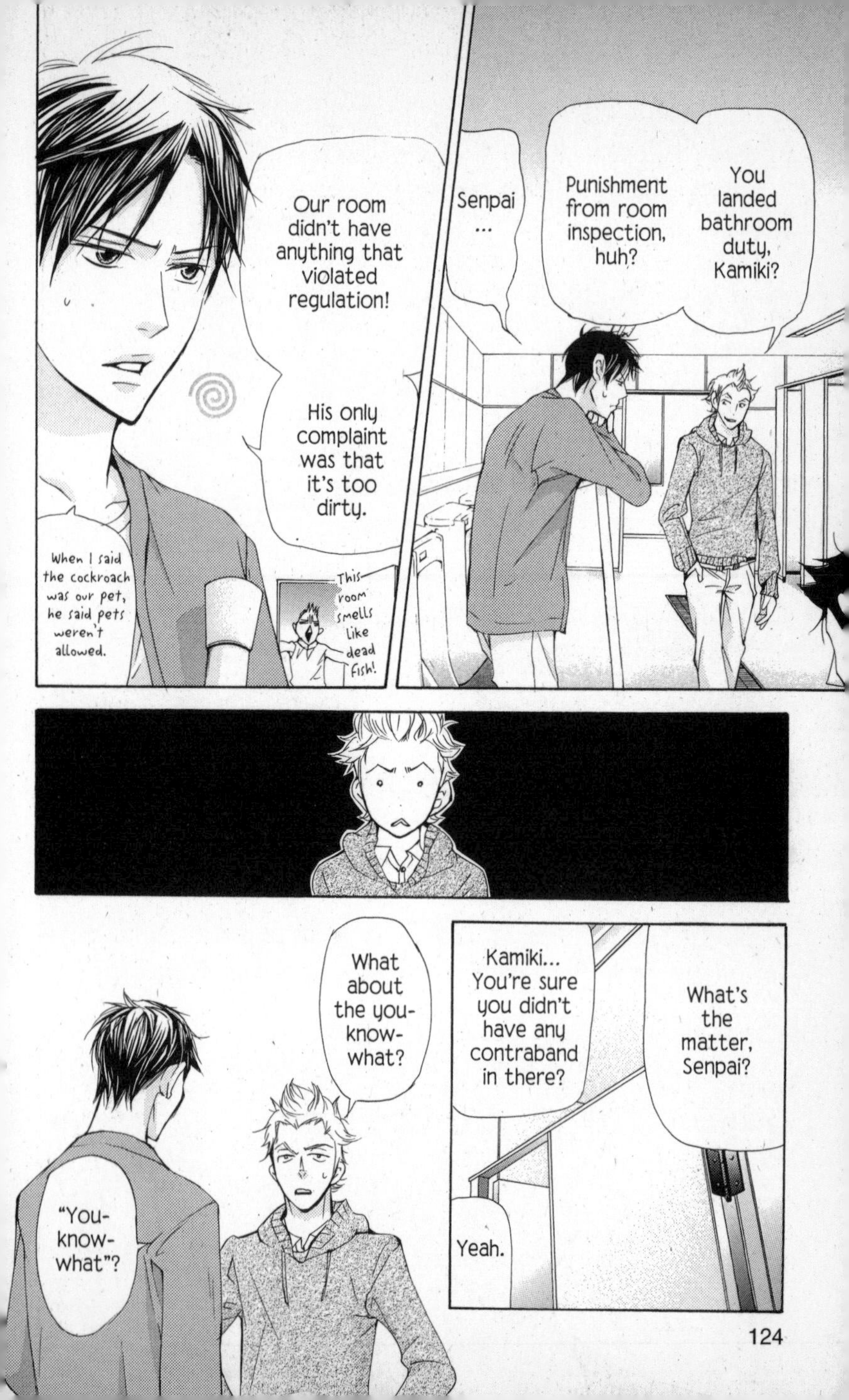
You landed bathroom duty, Kamiki?
Punishment from room inspection, huh?
Senpai ...
Our room didn't have anything that violated regulation!
His only complaint was that it's too dirty.
This room smells like dead fish!
When I said the cockroach was our pet, he said pets weren't allowed.
What's the matter, Senpai?
Kamiki... You're sure you didn't have any contraband in there?
Yeah.
What about the you-know-what?
"You-know-what"?

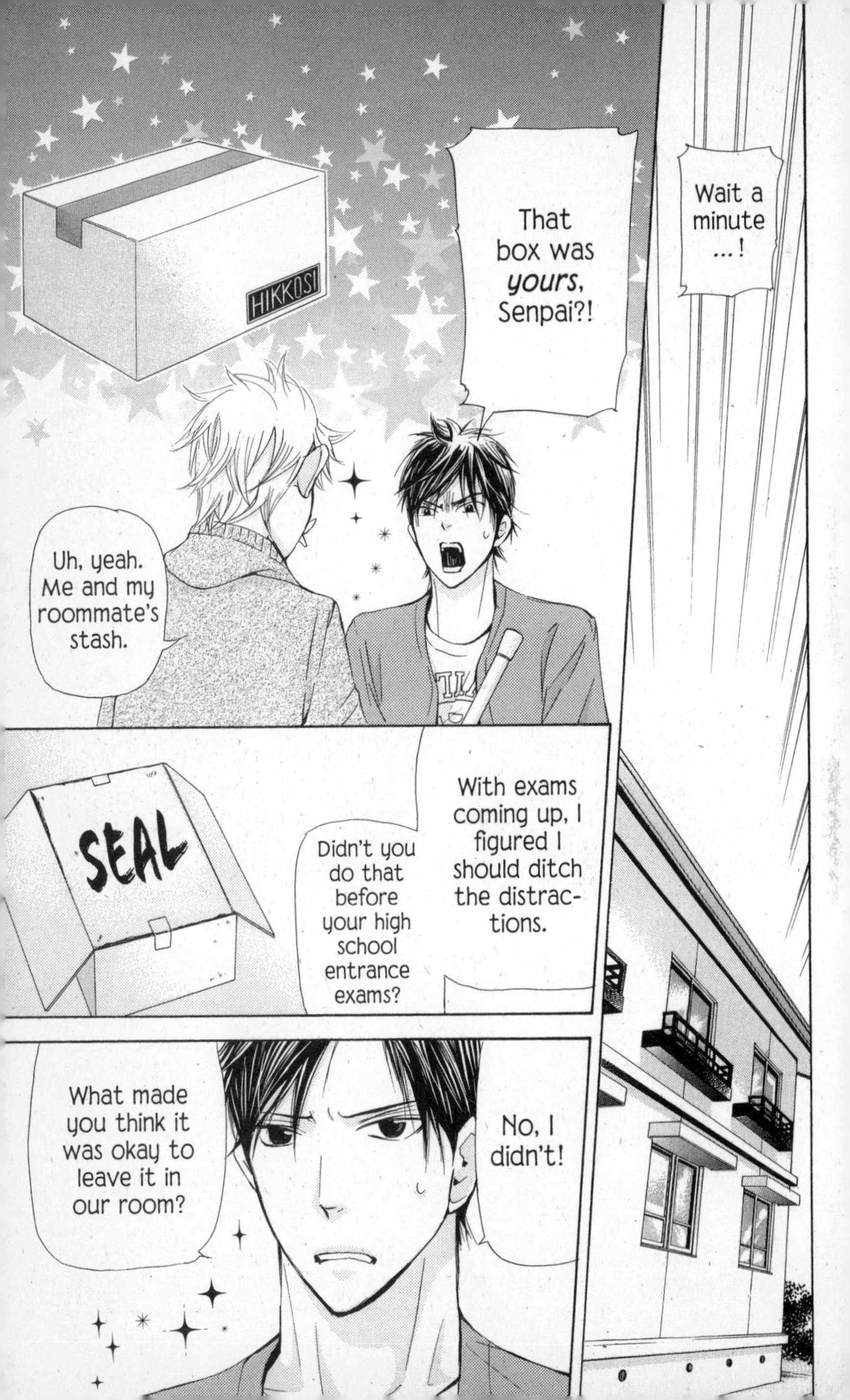
Wait a minute ...!
That box was *yours*, Senpai?!
HIKKOSI
Uh, yeah. Me and my roommate's stash.
With exams coming up, I figured I should ditch the distractions.
Didn't you do that before your high school entrance exams?
SEAL
No, I didn't!
What made you think it was okay to leave it in our room?

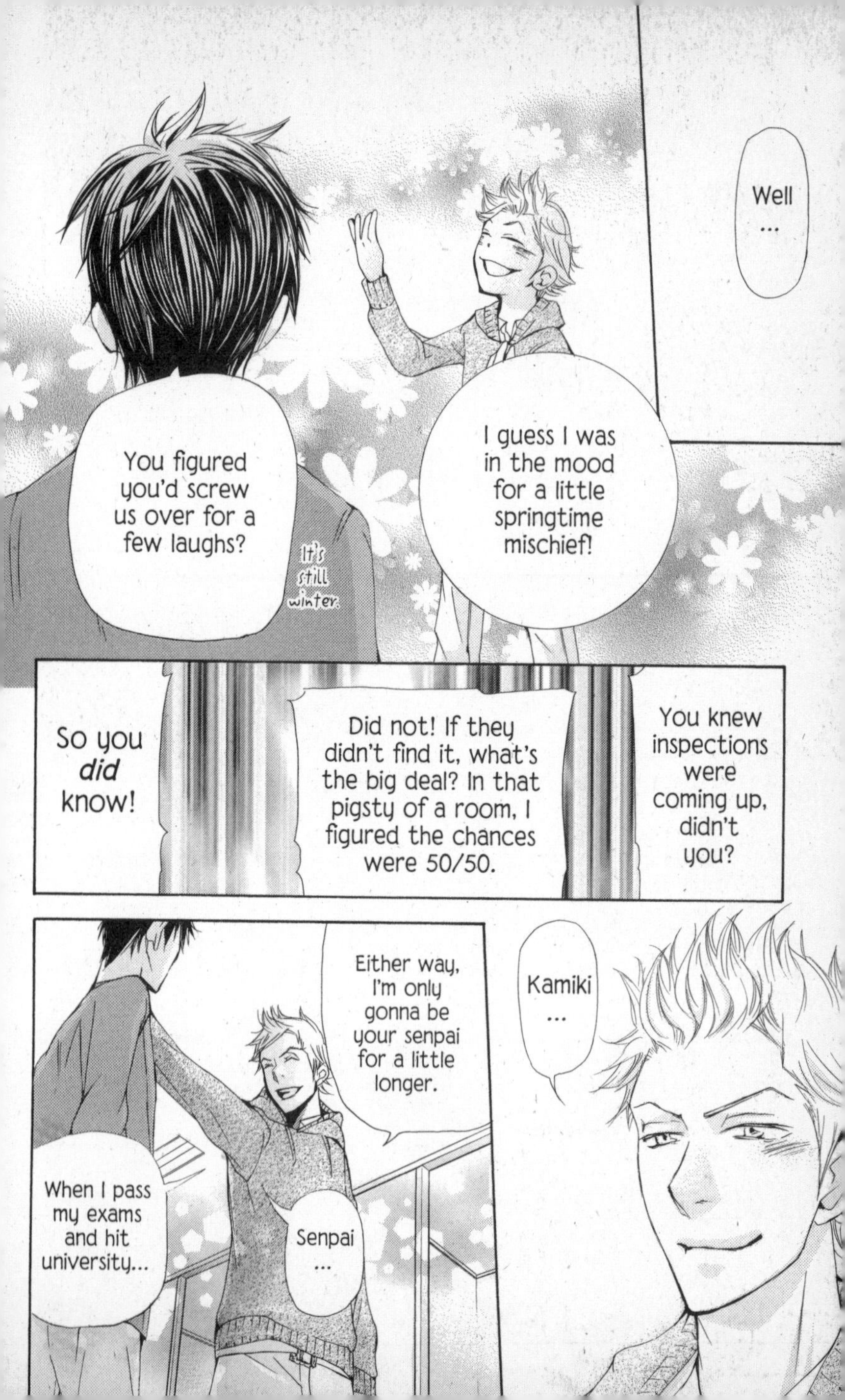
Well ...
I guess I was in the mood for a little springtime mischief!
You figured you'd screw us over for a few laughs?
It's still winter.
You knew inspections were coming up, didn't you?
Did not! If they didn't find it, what's the big deal? In that pigsty of a room, I figured the chances were 50/50.
So you *did* know!
Kamiki ...
Either way, I'm only gonna be your senpai for a little longer.
Senpai ...
When I pass my exams and hit university...

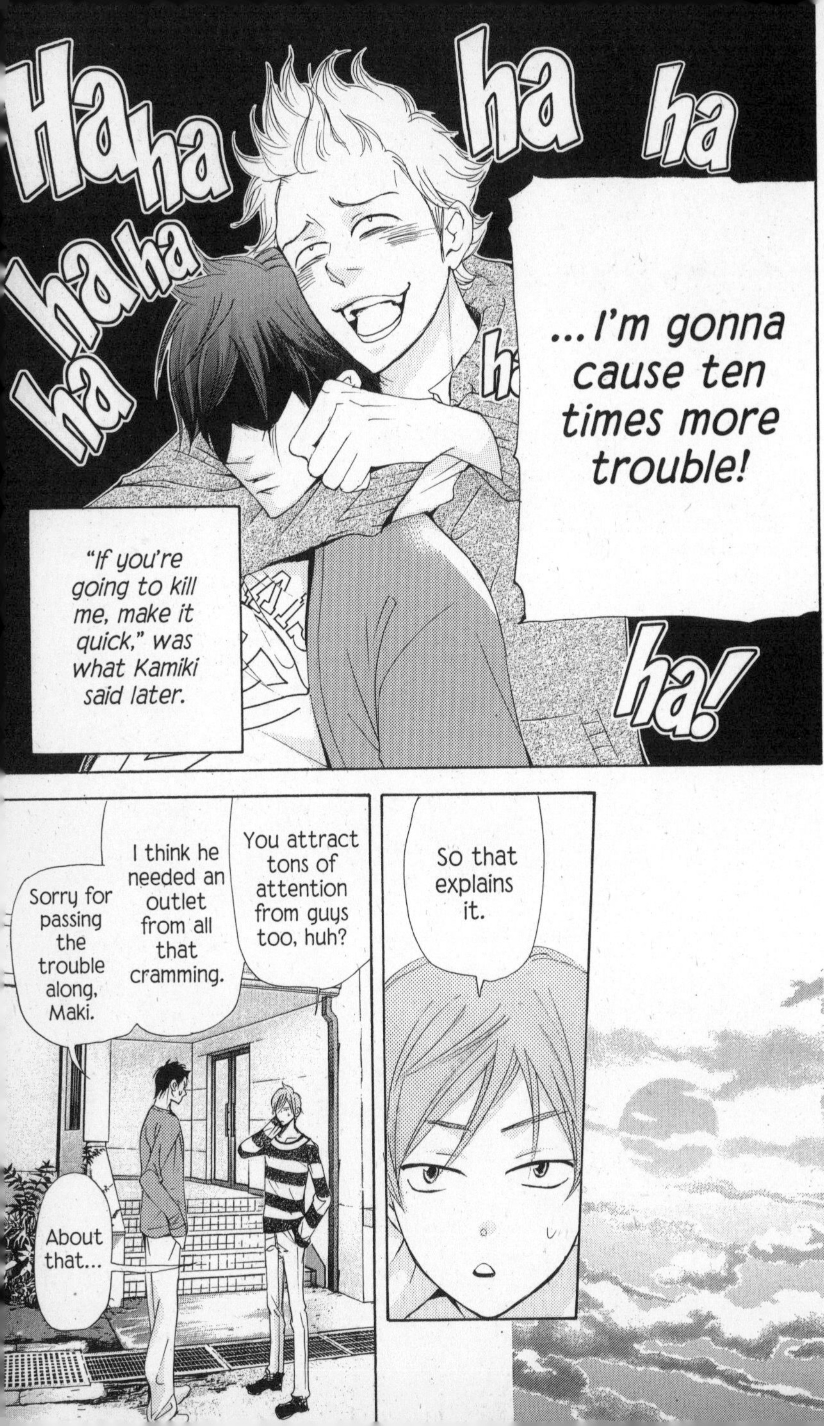
Ha ha ha ha ha ha ha ha ha
...I'm gonna cause ten times more trouble!
"If you're going to kill me, make it quick," was what Kamiki said later.
ha!
So that explains it.
You attract tons of attention from guys too, huh?
I think he needed an outlet from all that cramming.
Sorry for passing the trouble along, Maki.
About that...

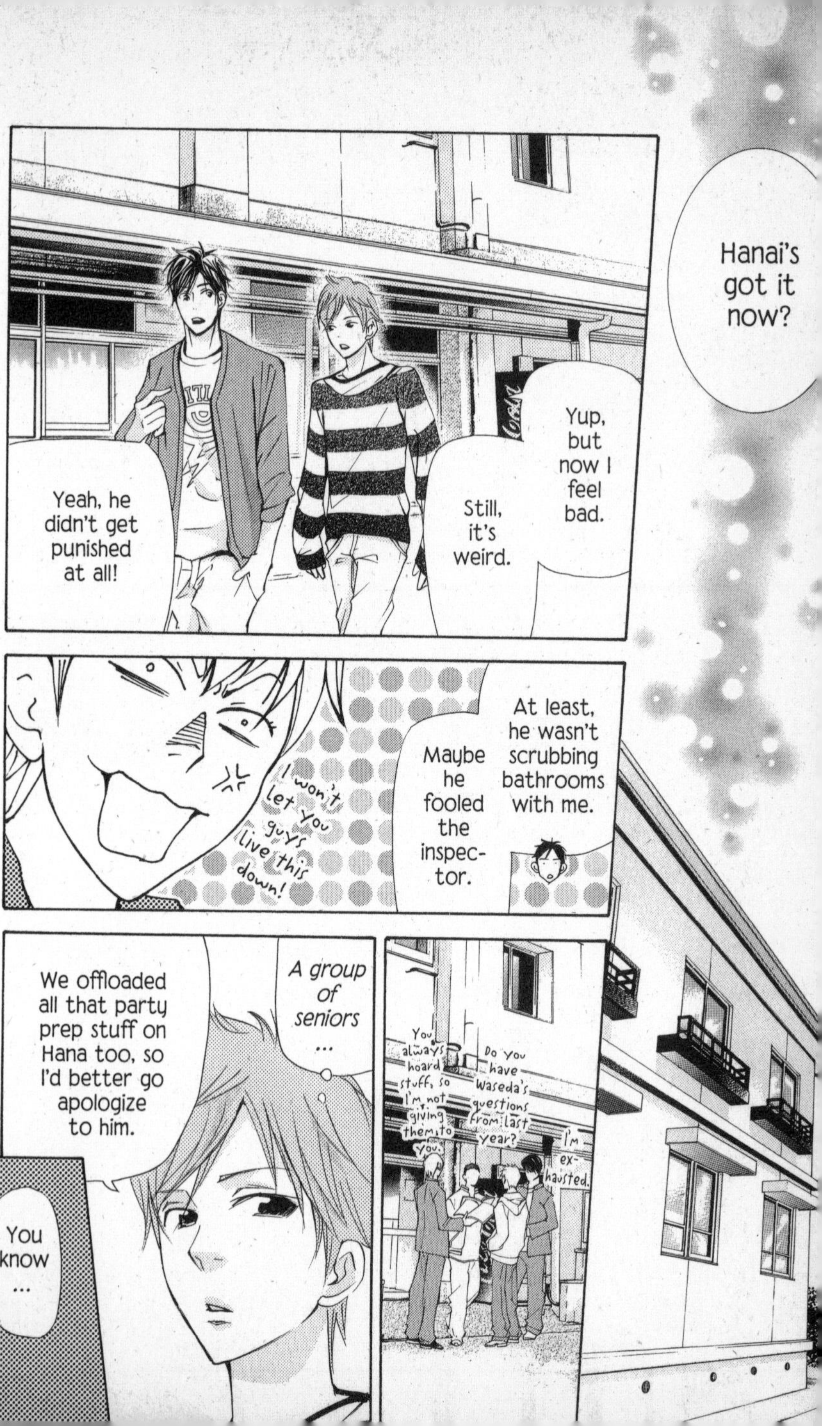
Hanai's got it now?
Yup, but now I feel bad.
Still, it's weird.
Yeah, he didn't get punished at all!
At least, he wasn't scrubbing bathrooms with me.
Maybe he fooled the inspector.
I won't let you guys live this down!
Do you have Waseda's questions from last year?
You always hoard stuff, so I'm not giving them to you.
I'm ex-hausted.
A group of seniors ...
We offloaded all that party prep stuff on Hana too, so I'd better go apologize to him.
You know ...

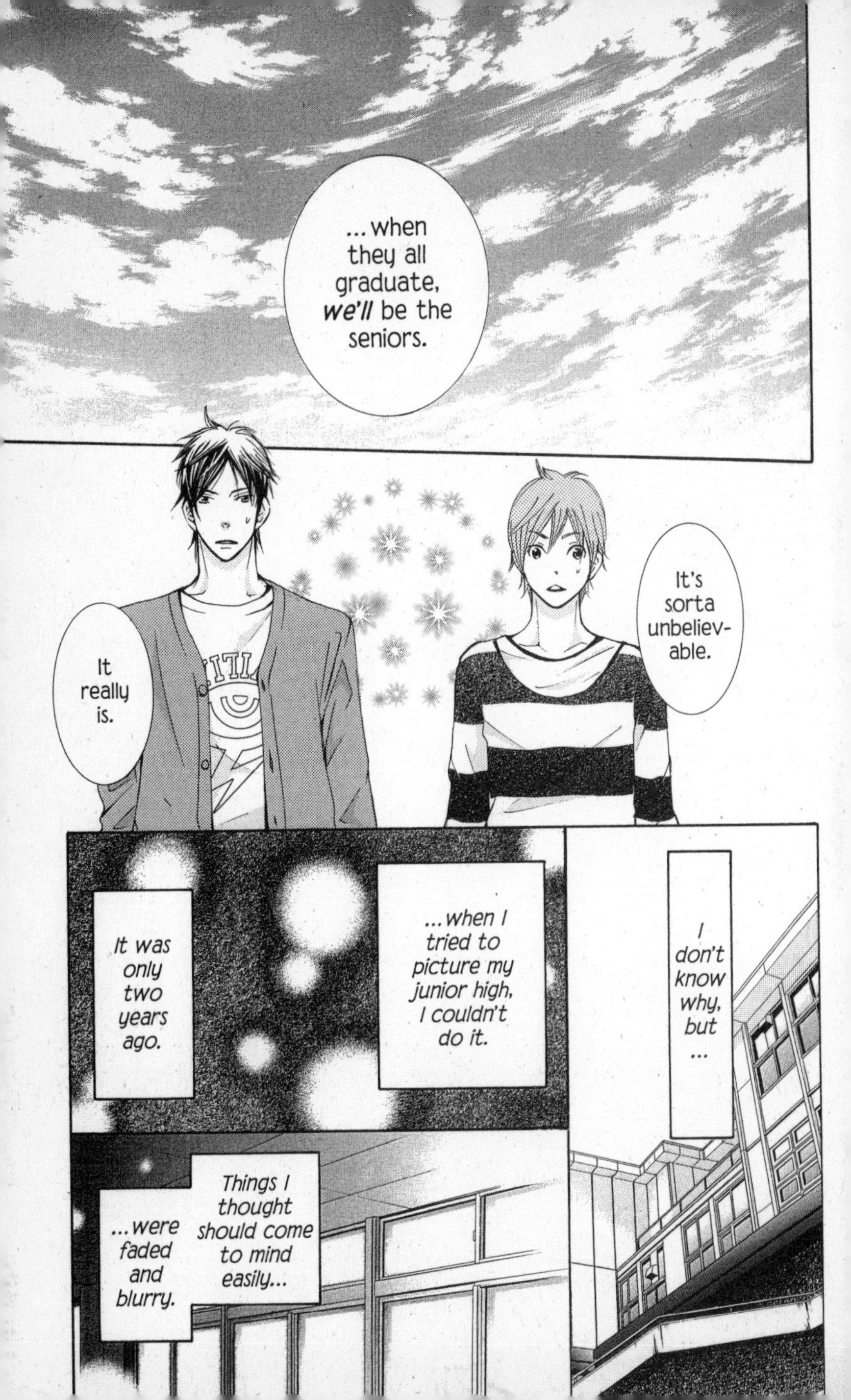
...when they all graduate, we'll be the seniors.
It's sorta unbelievable.
It really is.
I don't know why, but ...
...when I tried to picture my junior high, I couldn't do it.
It was only two years ago.
Things I thought should come to mind easily...
...were faded and blurry.

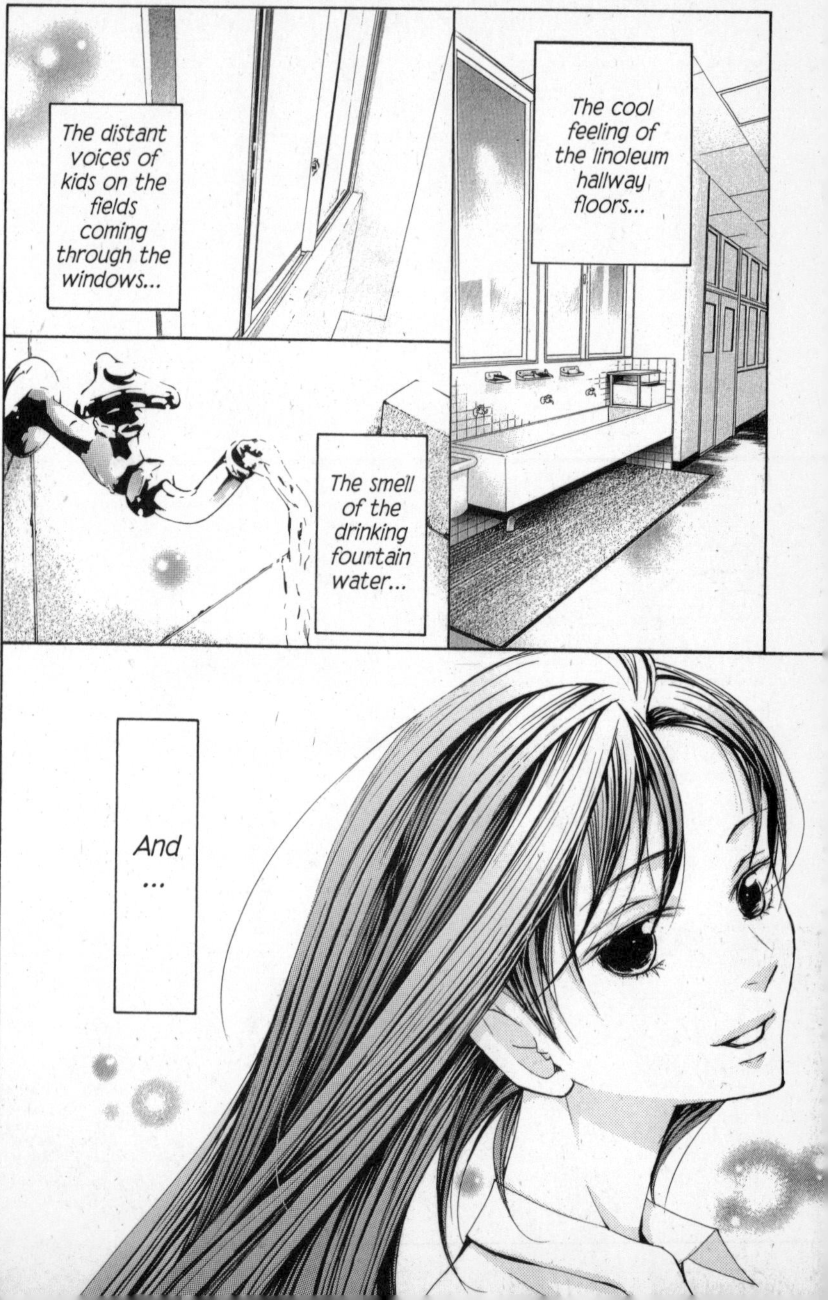
The cool feeling of the linoleum hallway floors...
The distant voices of kids on the fields coming through the windows...
The smell of the drinking fountain water...
And ...

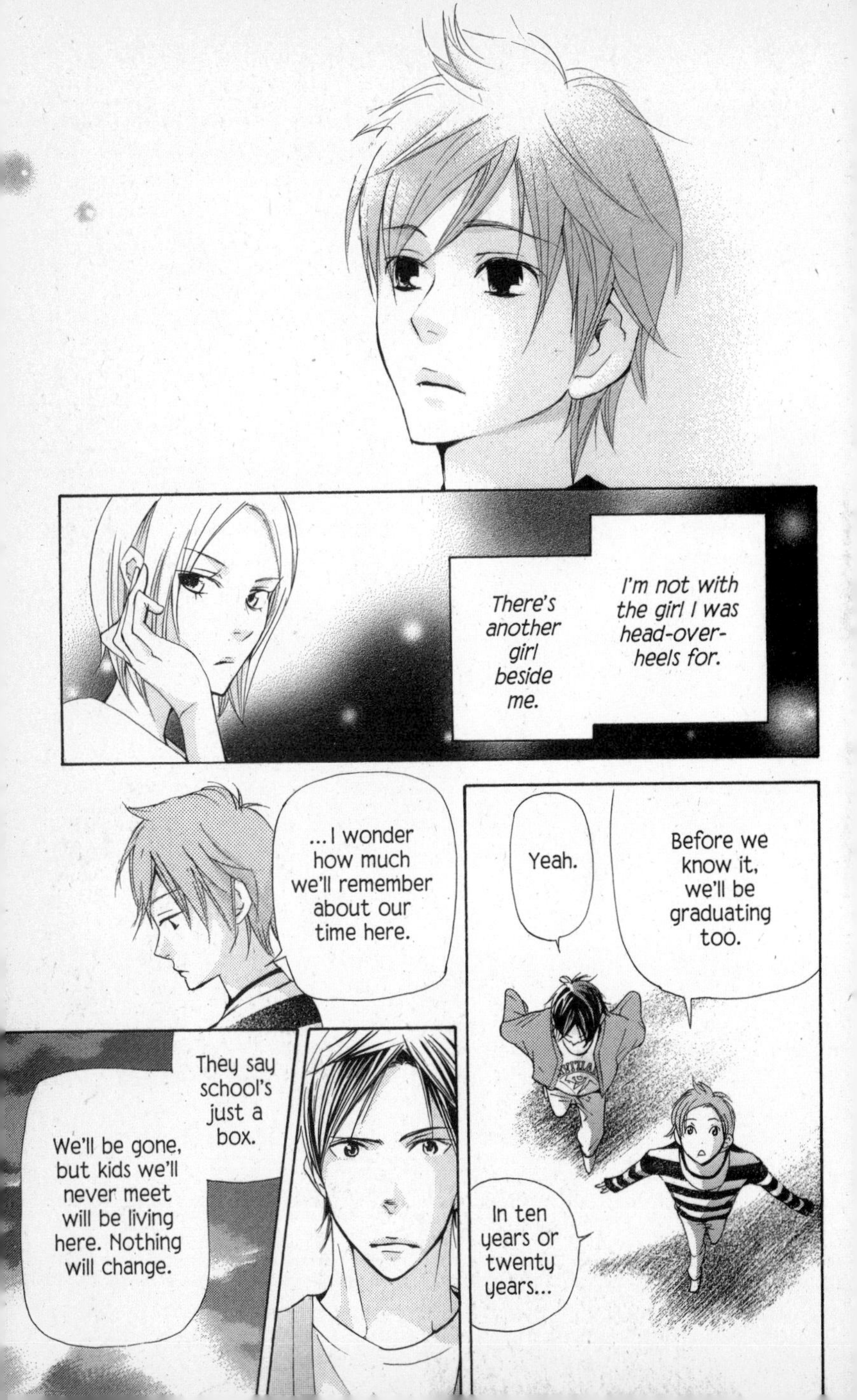
I'm not with the girl I was head-over-heels for.
There's another girl beside me.
Before we know it, we'll be graduating too.
Yeah.
In ten years or twenty years...
...I wonder how much we'll remember about our time here.
They say school's just a box.
We'll be gone, but kids we'll never meet will be living here. Nothing will change.

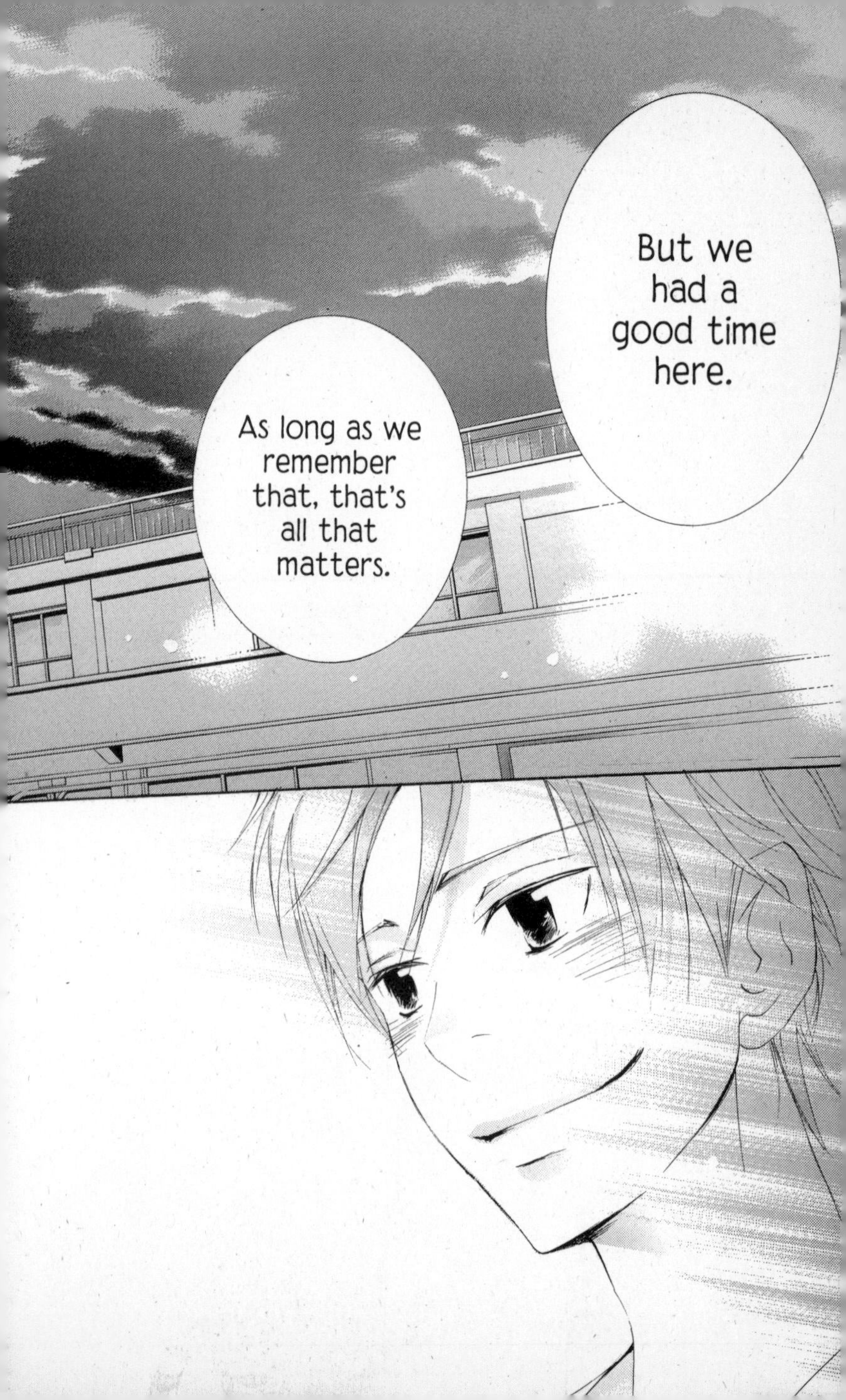
But we had a good time here.
As long as we remember that, that's all that matters.

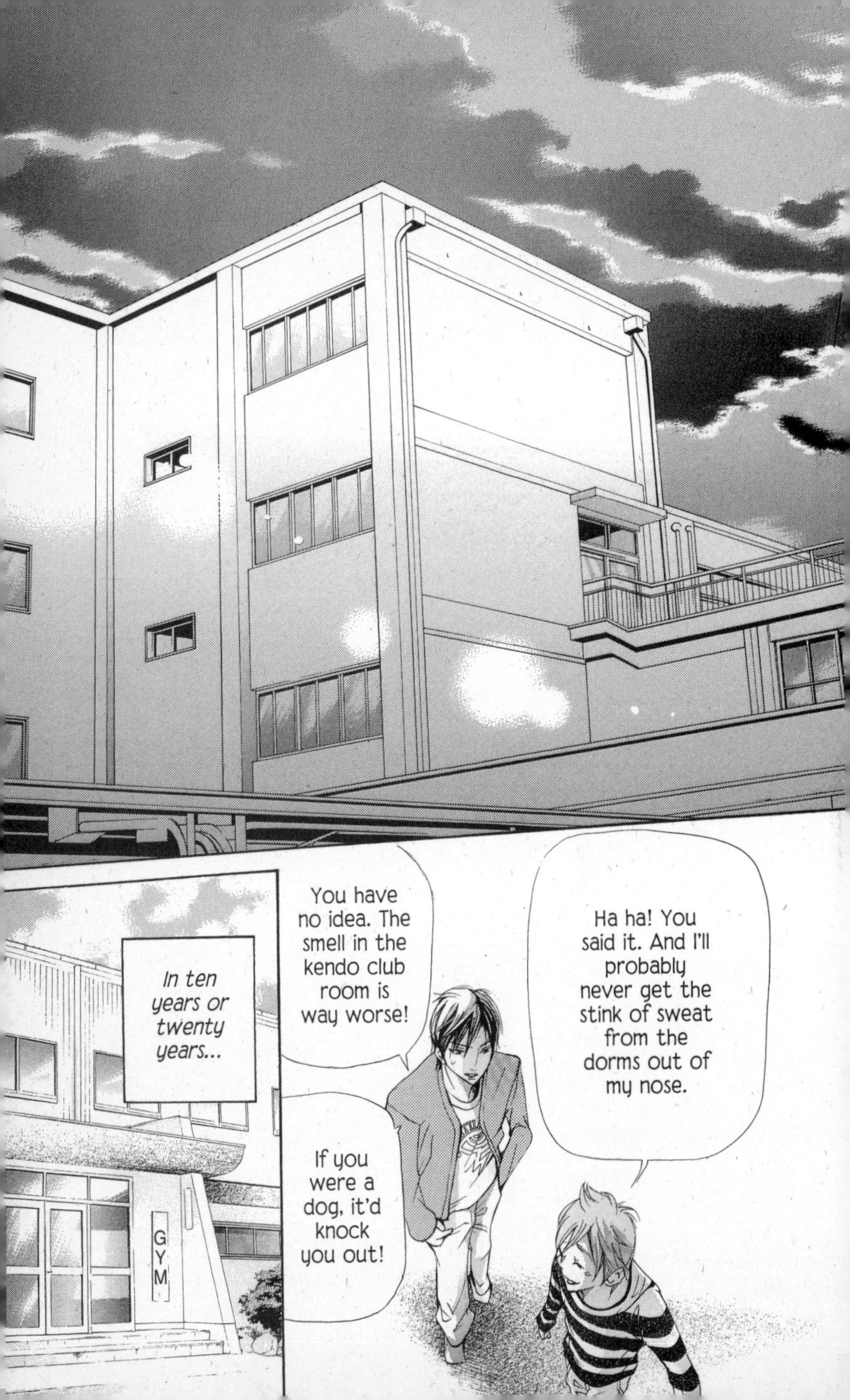
Ha ha! You said it. And I'll probably never get the stink of sweat from the dorms out of my nose.
You have no idea. The smell in the kendo club room is way worse!
If you were a dog, it'd knock you out!
In ten years or twenty years...
GYM

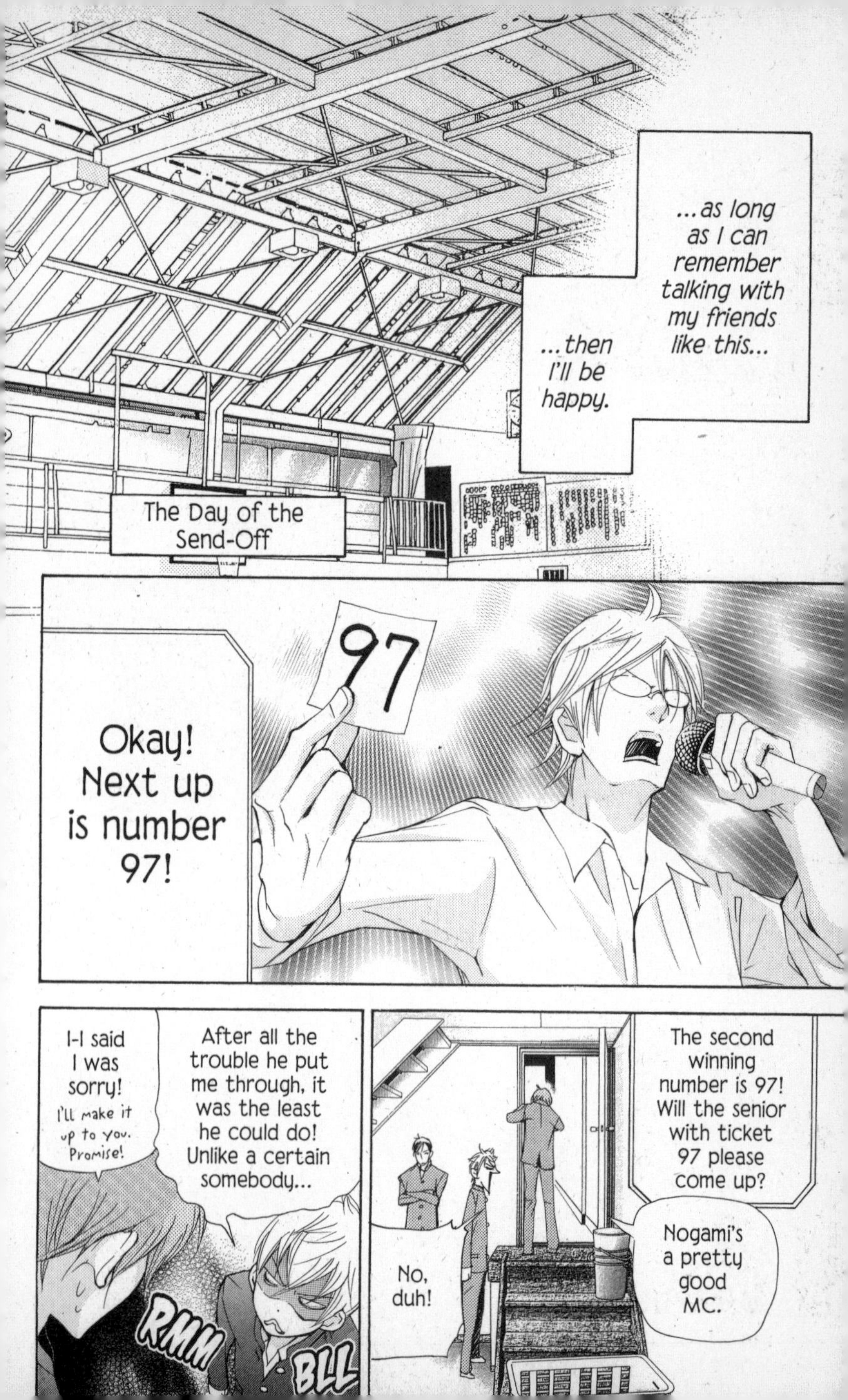
...as long as I can remember talking with my friends like this...
...then I'll be happy.
The Day of the Send-Off
97
Okay! Next up is number 97!
The second winning number is 97! Will the senior with ticket 97 please come up?
Nogami's a pretty good MC.
No, duh!
After all the trouble he put me through, it was the least he could do! Unlike a certain somebody...
I-I said I was sorry!
I'll make it up to you. Promise!
RMM
BLL

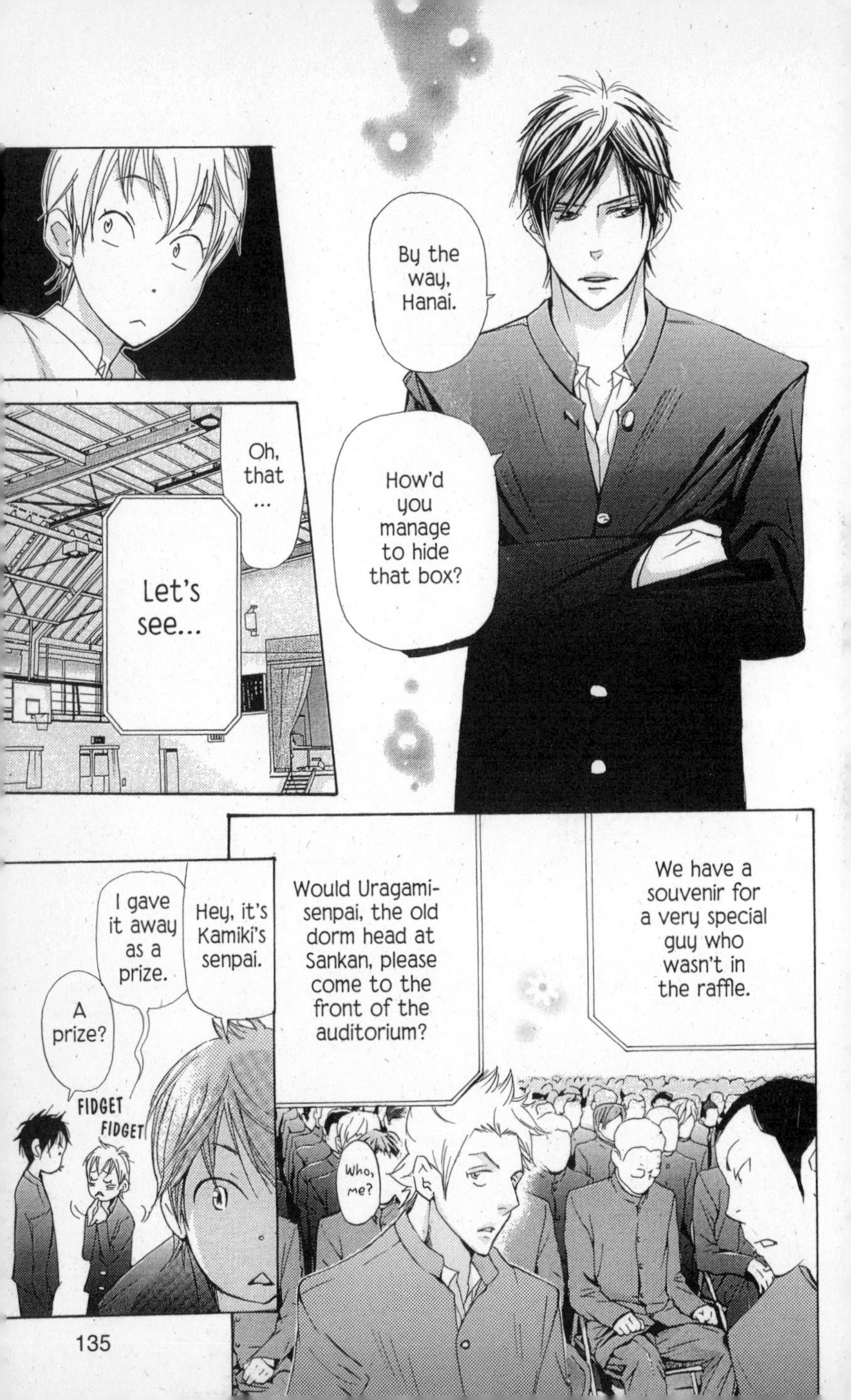
By the way, Hanai.
How'd you manage to hide that box?
Oh, that...
Let's see...
We have a souvenir for a very special guy who wasn't in the raffle.
Would Uragami-senpai, the old dorm head at Sankan, please come to the front of the auditorium?
Who, me?
Hey, it's Kamiki's senpai.
I gave it away as a prize.
A prize?
FIDGET
FIDGET

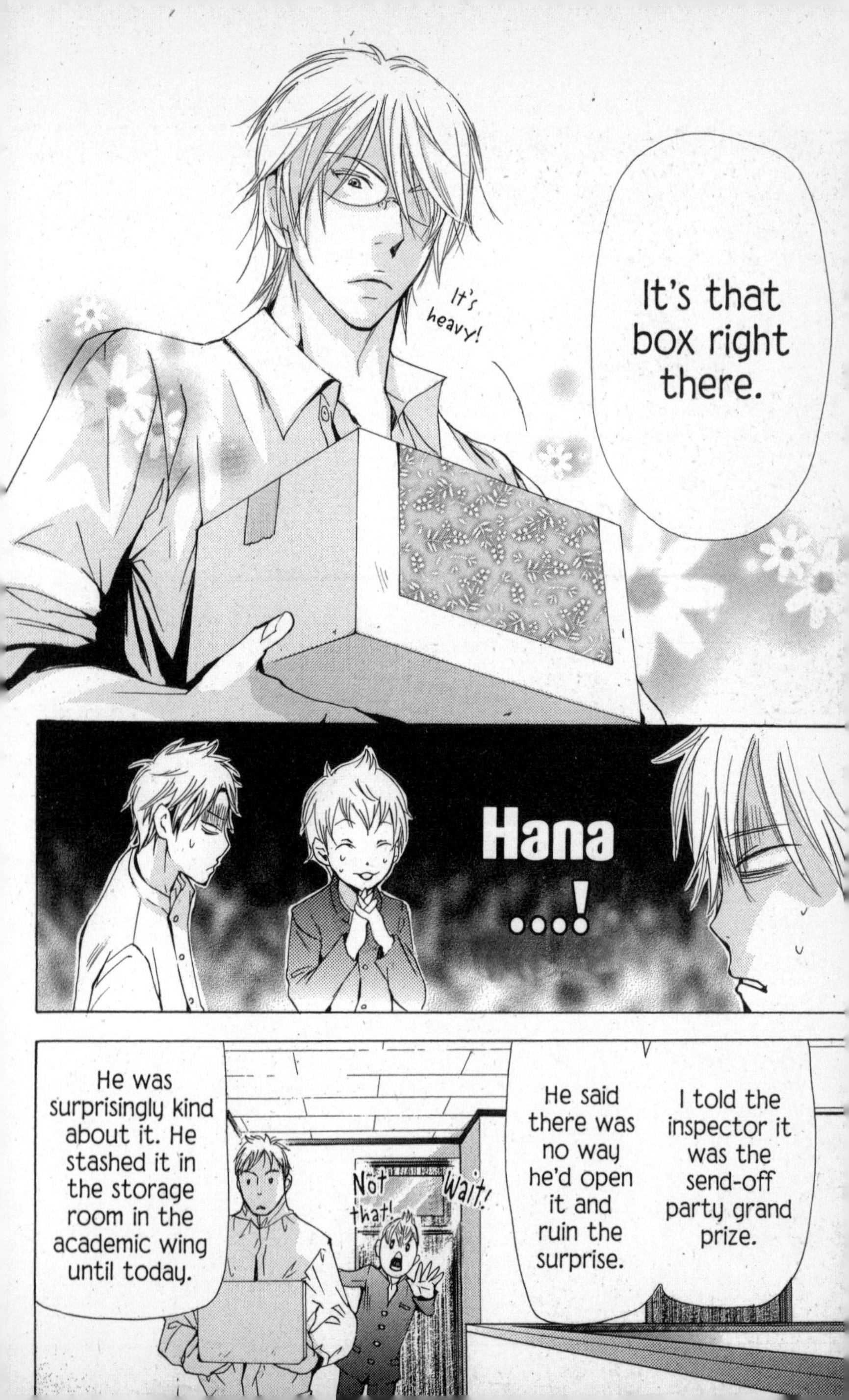
It's that box right there.
It's heavy!
Hana ...!
I told the inspector it was the send-off party grand prize.
He said there was no way he'd open it and ruin the surprise.
Wait!
Not that!
He was surprisingly kind about it. He stashed it in the storage room in the academic wing until today.

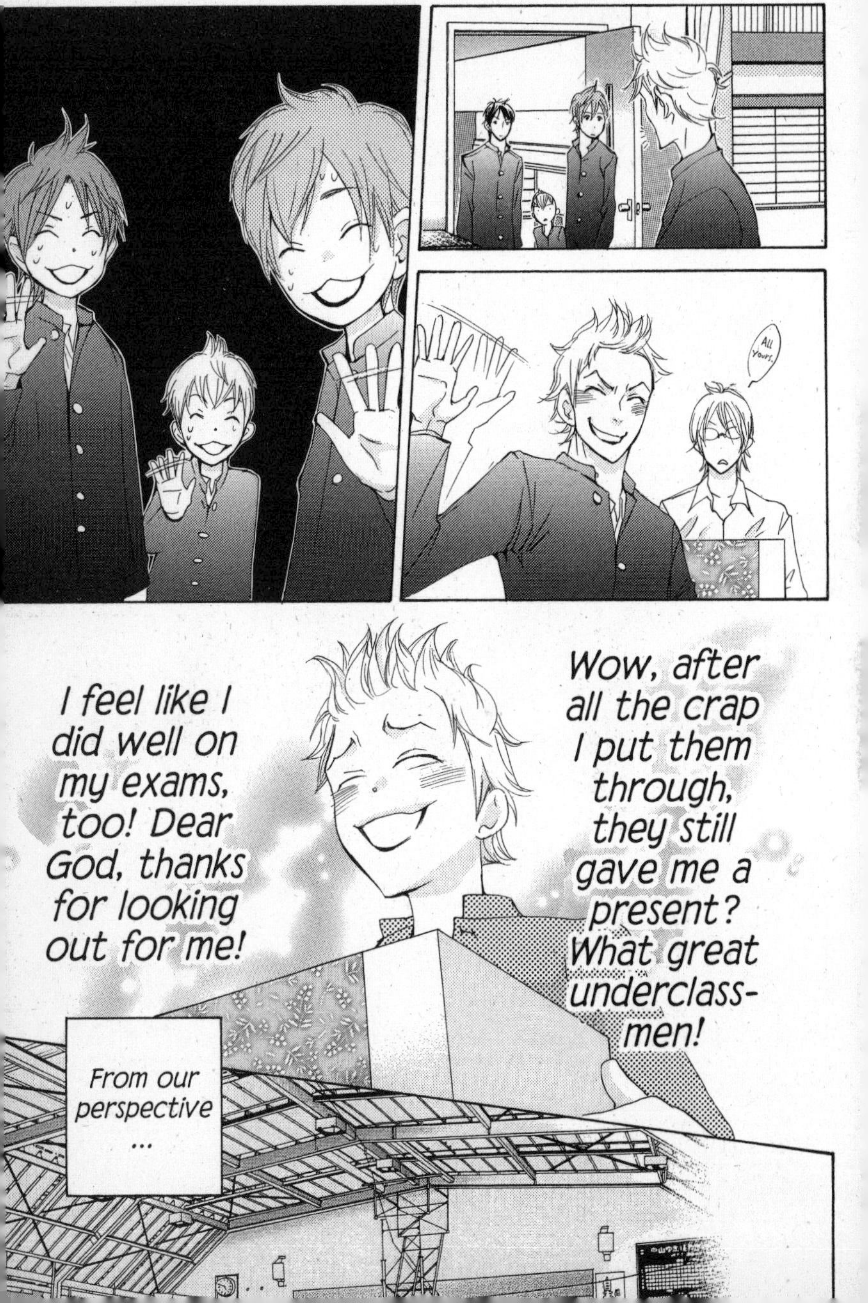
All Yours.
Wow, after all the crap I put them through, they still gave me a present? What great underclass-men!
I feel like I did well on my exams, too! Dear God, thanks for looking out for me!
From our perspective ...

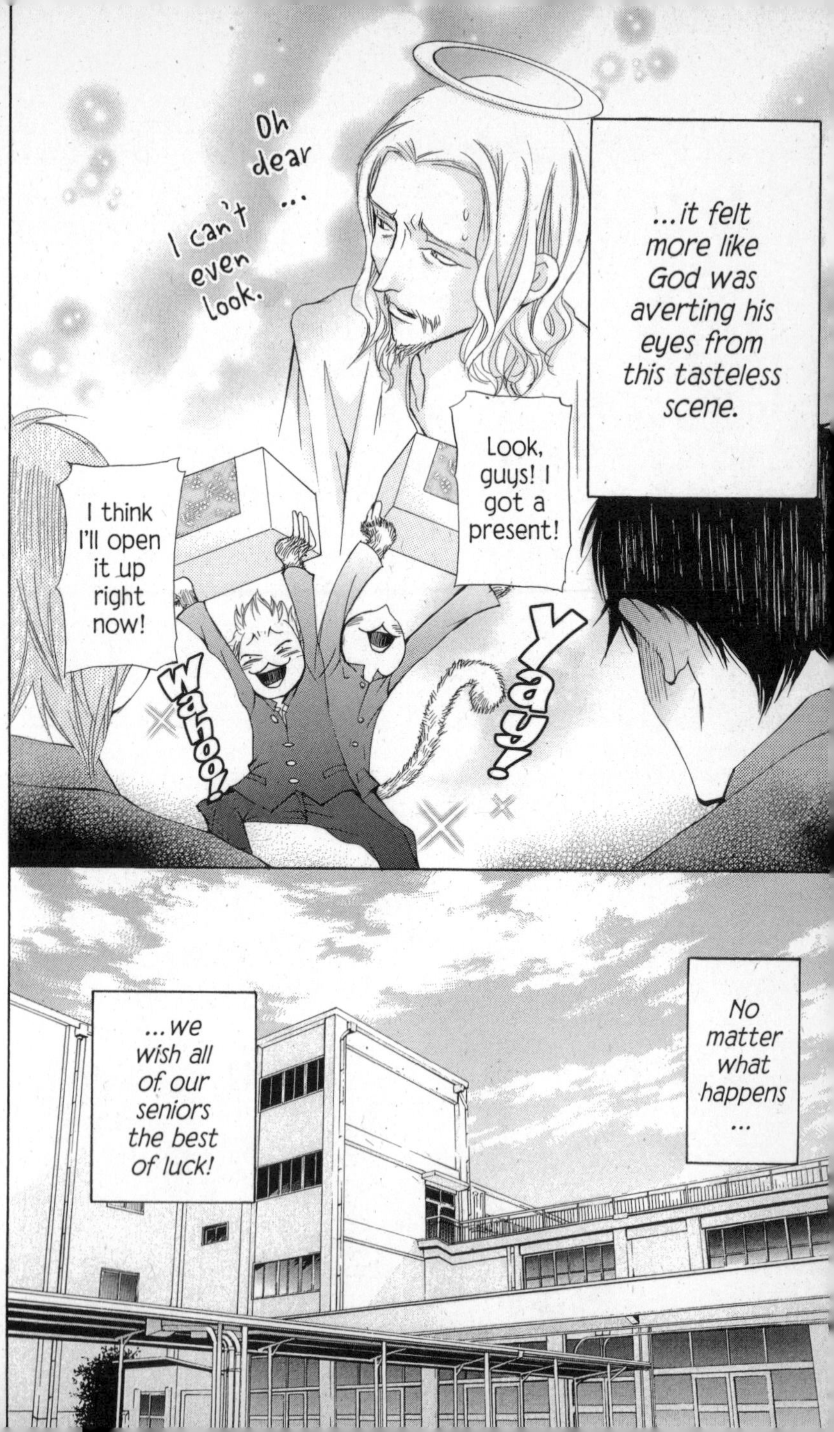
...it felt more like God was averting his eyes from this tasteless scene.
Oh dear ...
I can't even look.
Look, guys! I got a present!
Yay!
I think I'll open it up right now!
Wahoo!
No matter what happens ...
...we wish all of our seniors the best of luck!

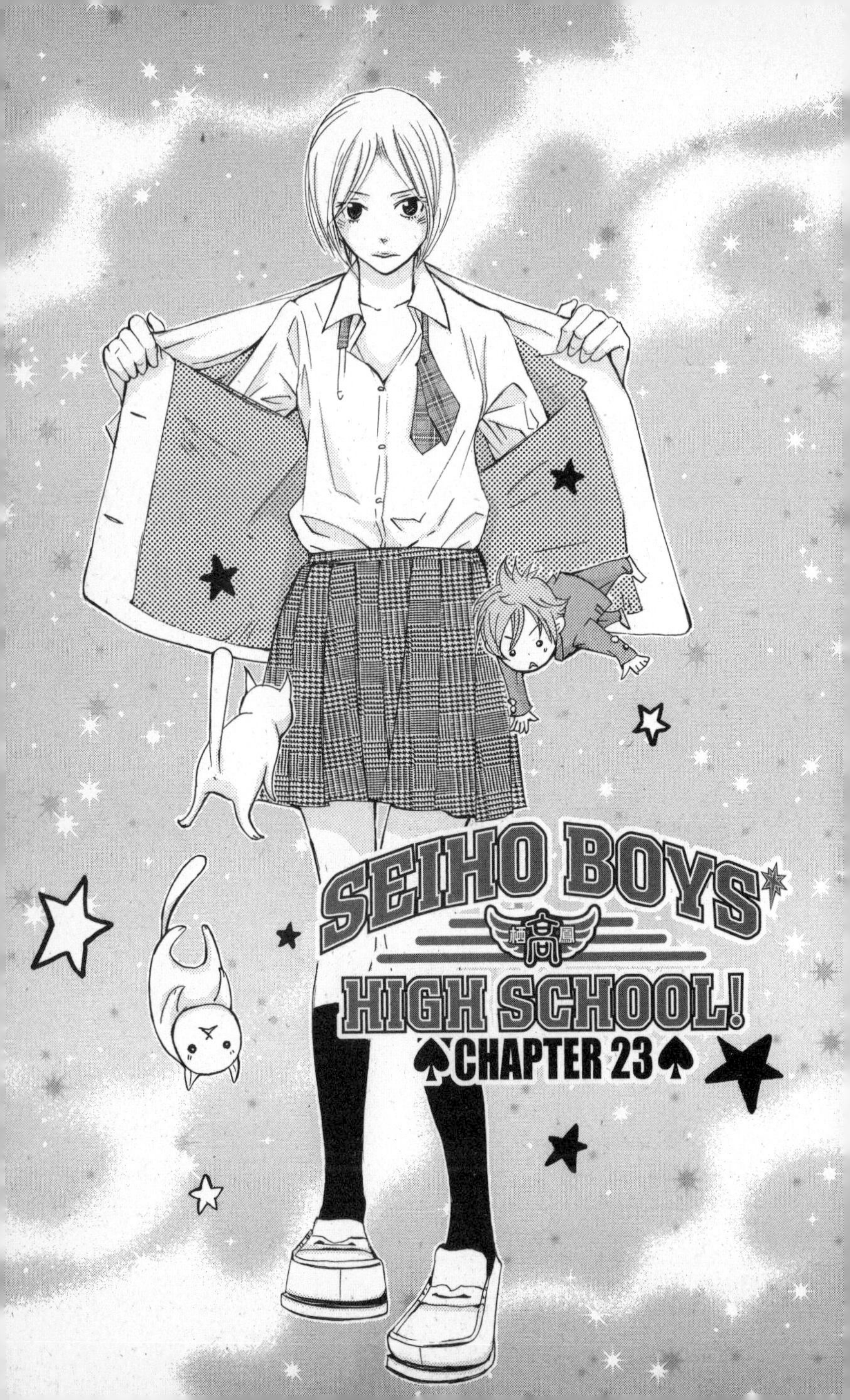
SEIHO BOYS'
HIGH SCHOOL!
CHAPTER 23

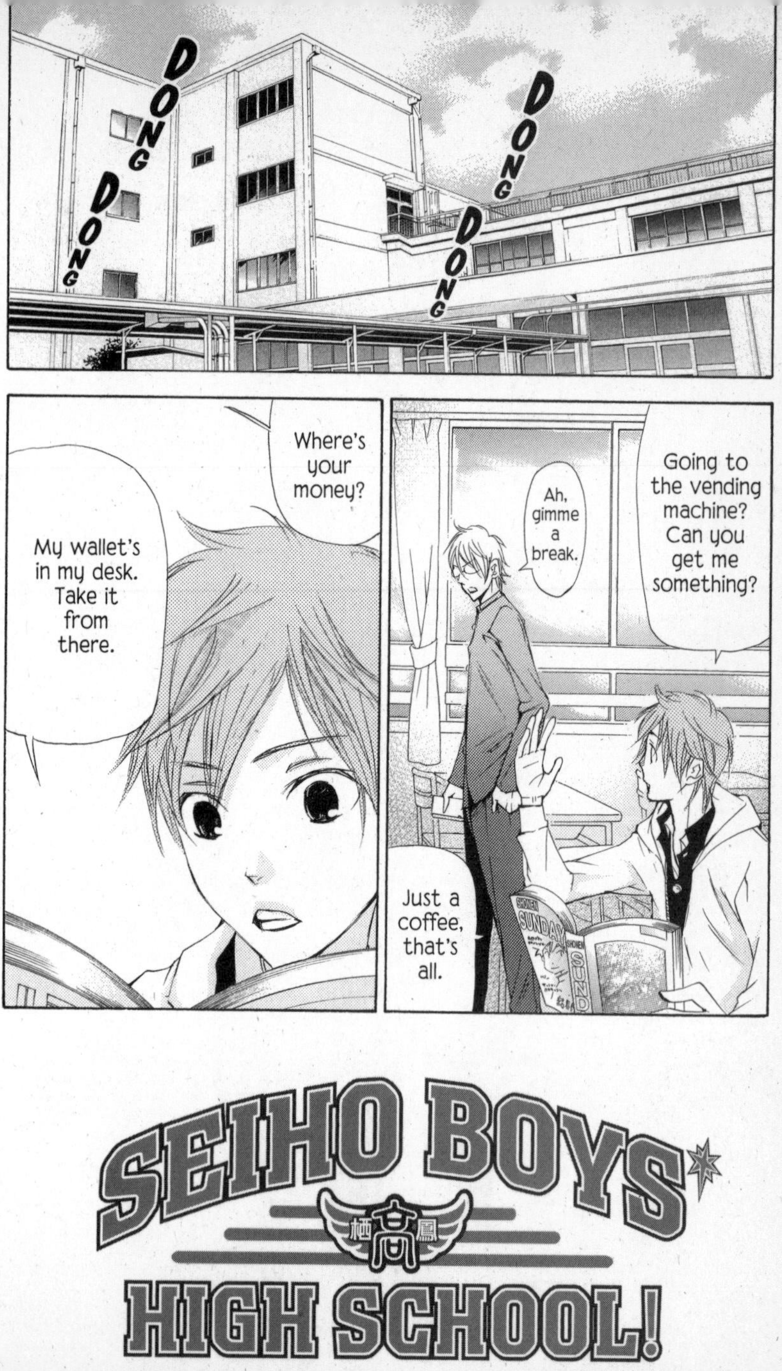
DONG DONG
DONG DONG
Going to the vending machine? Can you get me something?
Ah, gimme a break.
SHONEN SUNDAY
Just a coffee, that's all.
Where's your money?
My wallet's in my desk. Take it from there.

SEIHO BOYS HIGH SCHOOL!

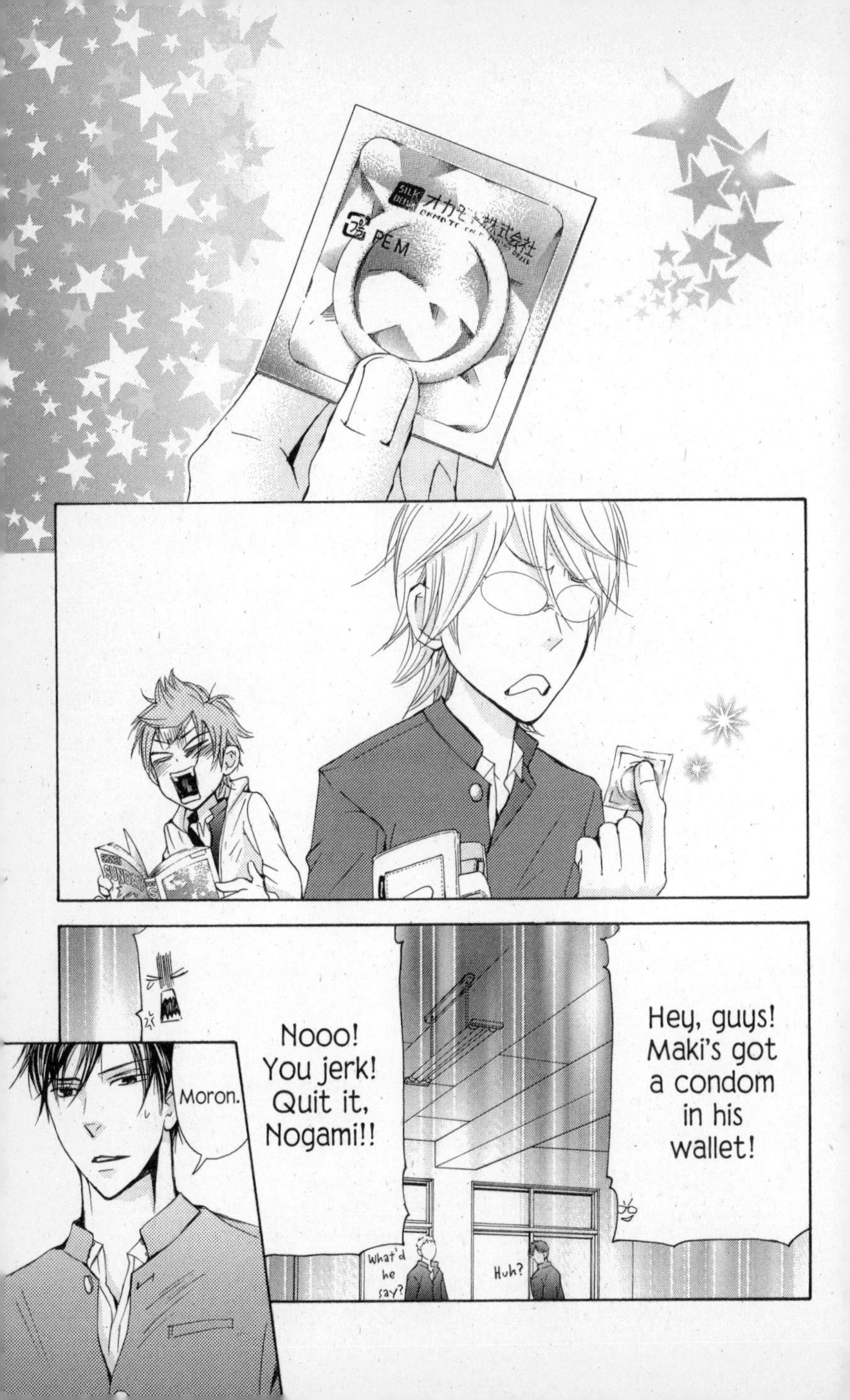
Hey, guys! Maki's got a condom in his wallet!
Huh?
What'd he say?
Nooo! You jerk! Quit it, Nogami!!
Moron.

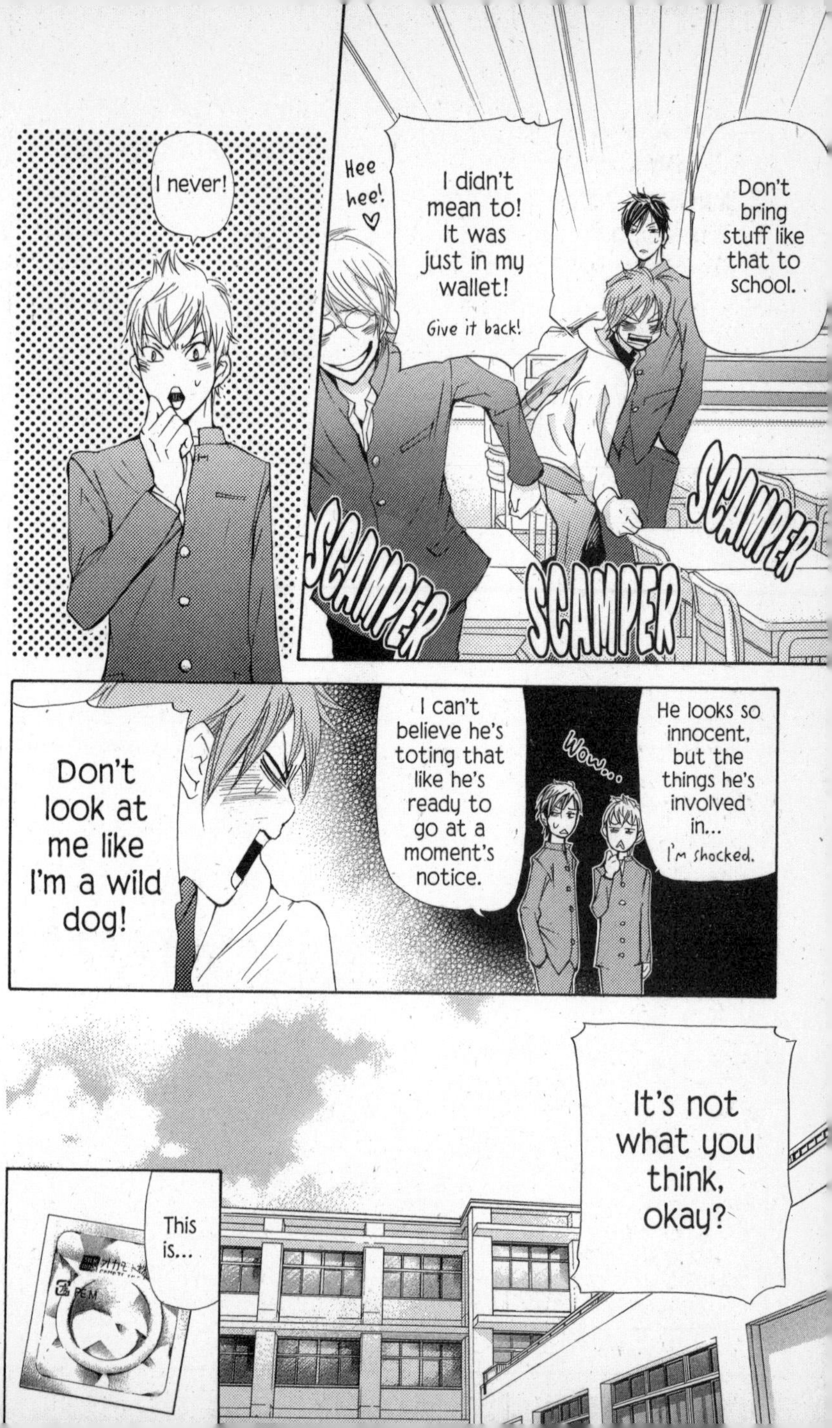
Don't bring stuff like that to school.
I didn't mean to! It was just in my wallet!
Hee hee! ♡
Give it back!
SCAMPER
SCAMPER
SCAMPER
I never!
He looks so innocent, but the things he's involved in...
I'm shocked.
Wow...
I can't believe he's toting that like he's ready to go at a moment's notice.
Don't look at me like I'm a wild dog!
It's not what you think, okay?
This is...

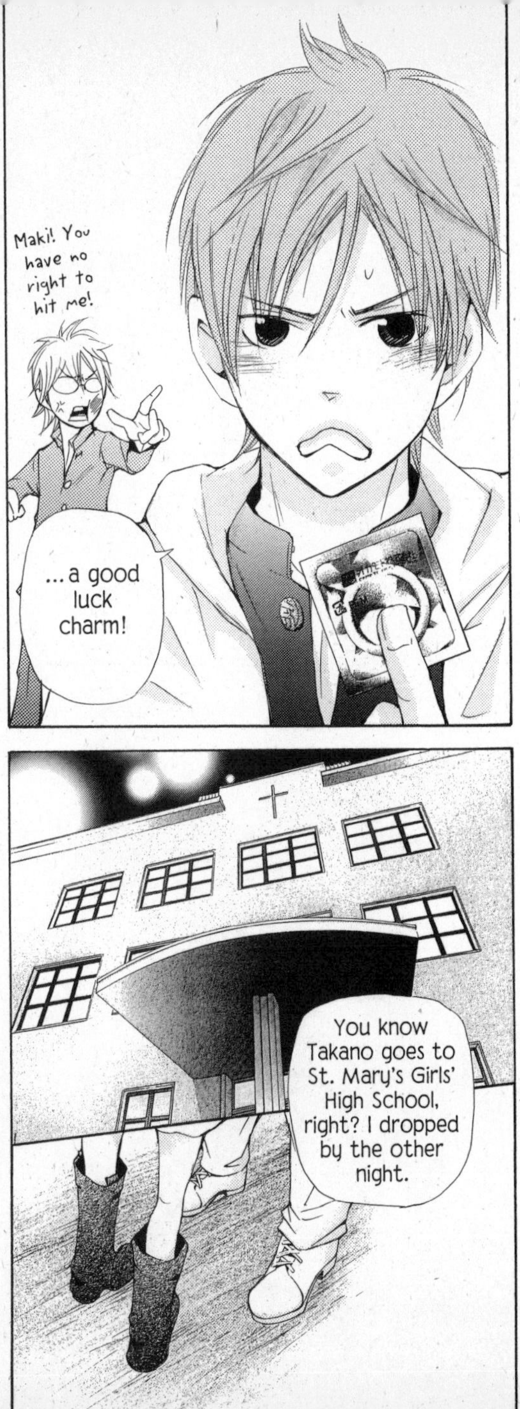
...a good luck charm!
Maki! You have no right to hit me!
You know Takano goes to St. Mary's Girls' High School, right? I dropped by the other night.

1/3 Filler Corner

AIRLINE FOOD The Opposite of a Gourmet Journey

Case 4

Air C

(China Domestic Flight)

The airline food was...

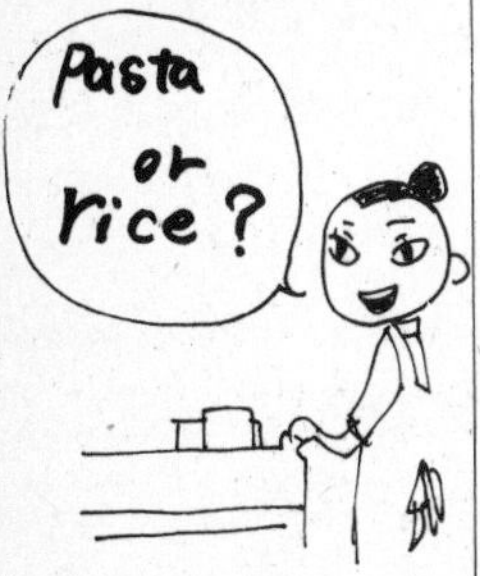
Pasta or rice?

When she asked me...

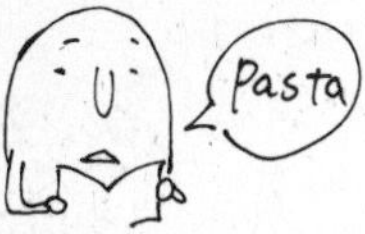
Pasta

...is what I said.

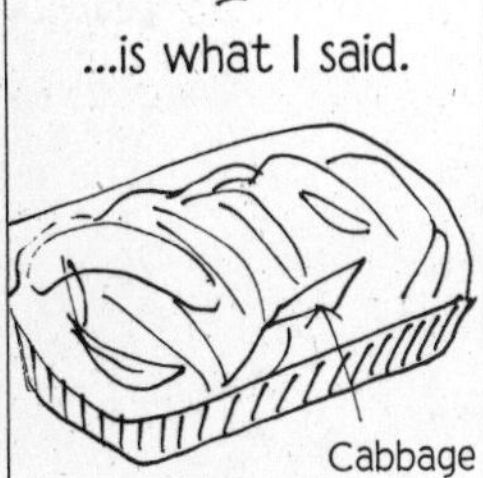
Cabbage

Fried noodles was what I got. I was very confused... Is this considered pasta...? Or noodles...?

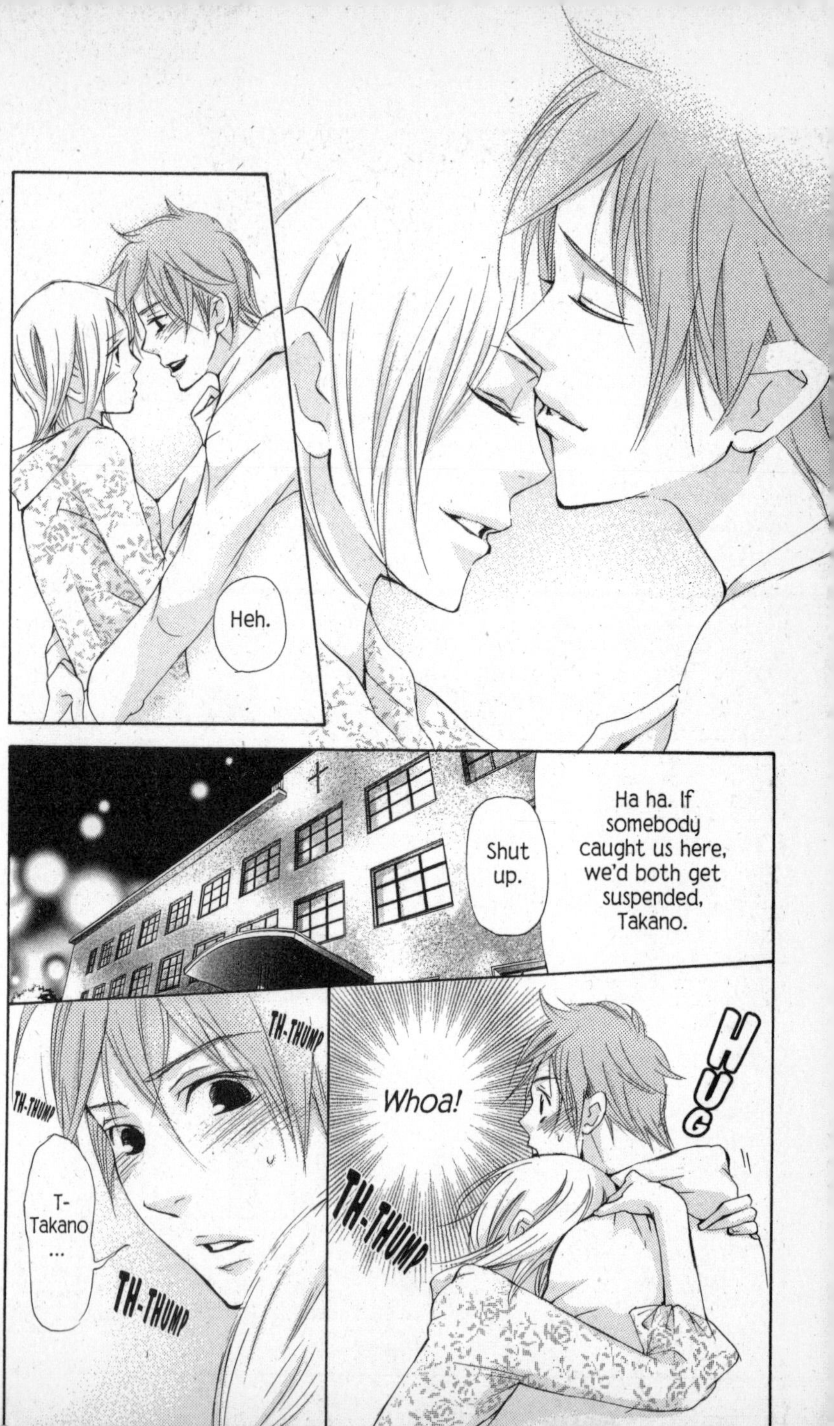
Heh.
Ha ha. If somebody caught us here, we'd both get suspended, Takano.
Shut up.
HUG
Whoa!
TH-THUMP
TH-THUMP
TH-THUMP
T-Takano...
TH-THUMP

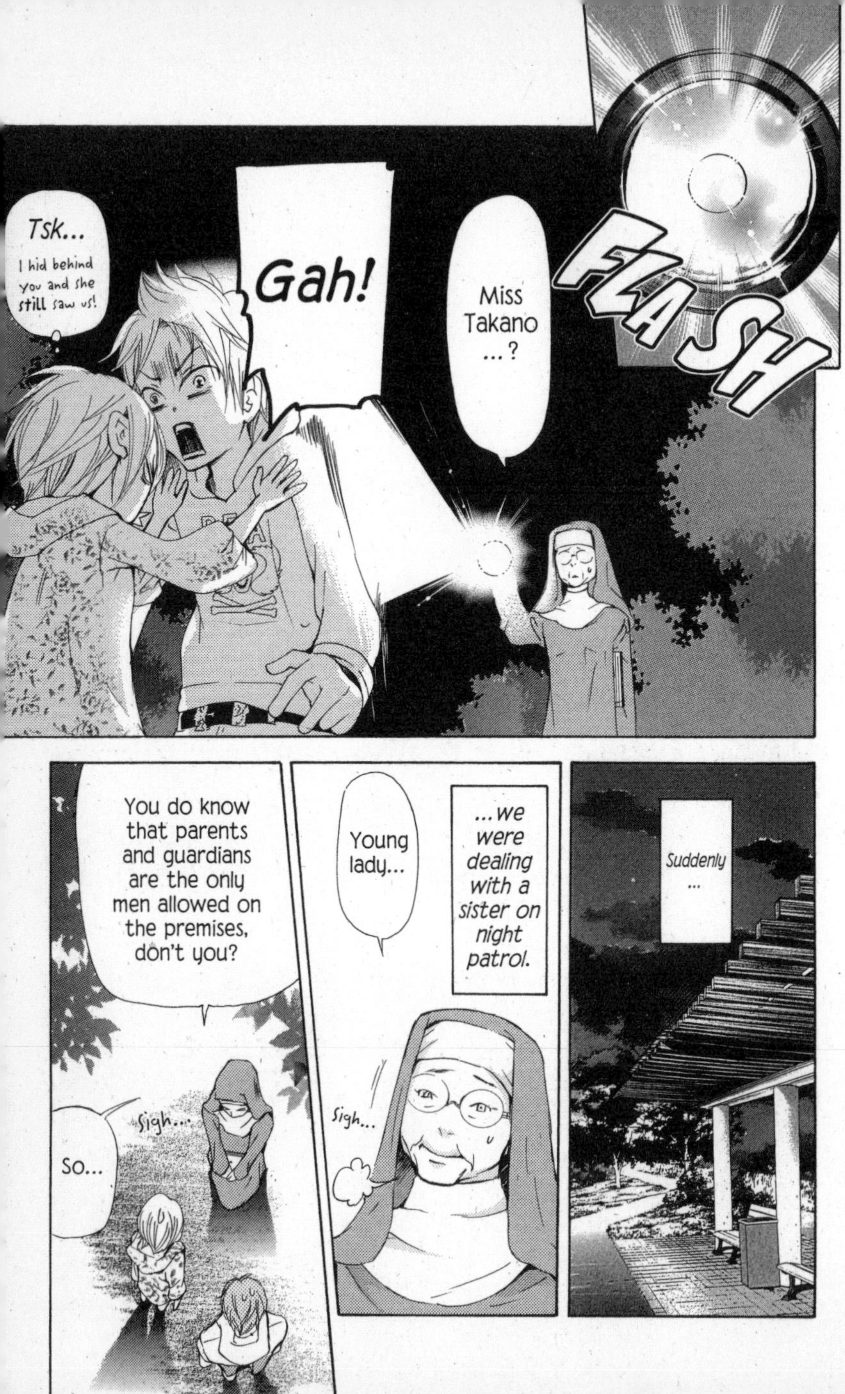
FLASH
Miss Takano ...?
Gah!
Tsk...
I hid behind you and she still saw us!
Suddenly ...
...we were dealing with a sister on night patrol.
Young lady...
Sigh...
You do know that parents and guardians are the only men allowed on the premises, don't you?
Sigh...
So...

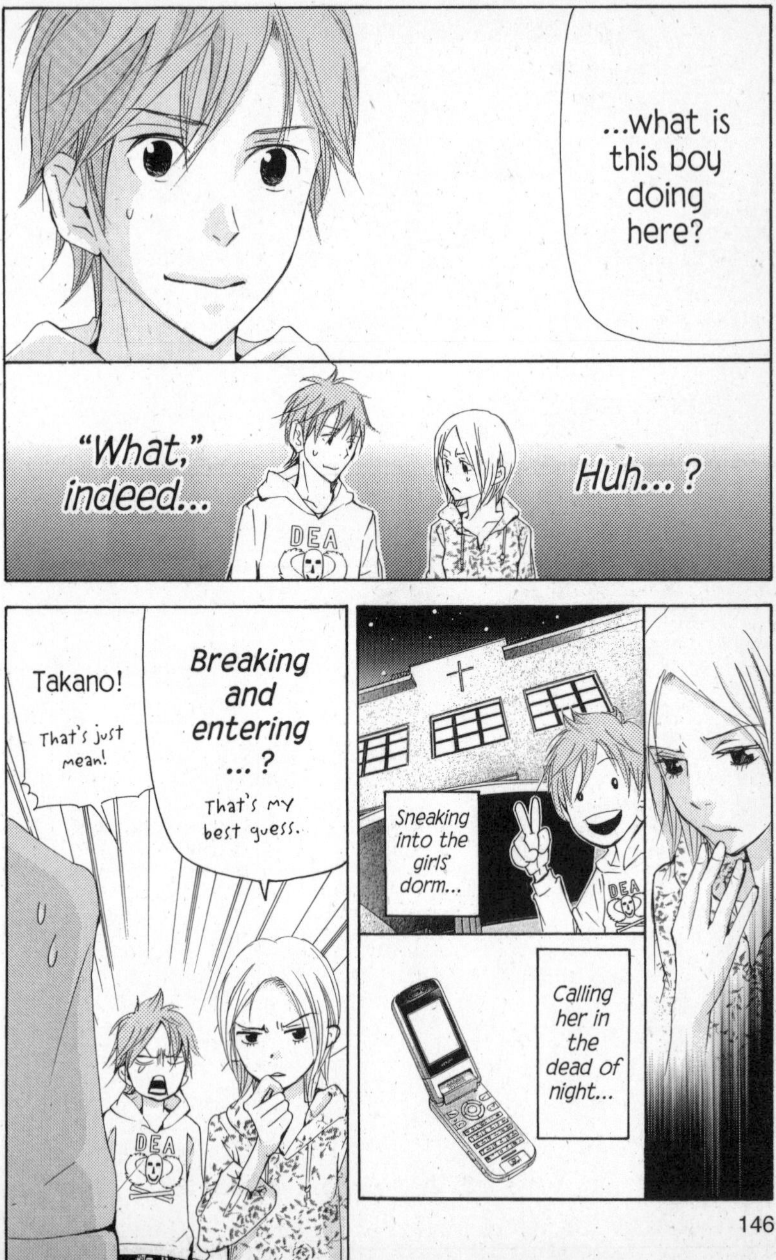
...what is this boy doing here?
Huh... ?
"What," indeed...
Sneaking into the girls' dorm...
Calling her in the dead of night...
Breaking and entering ...?
That's my best guess.
Takano!
That's just mean!

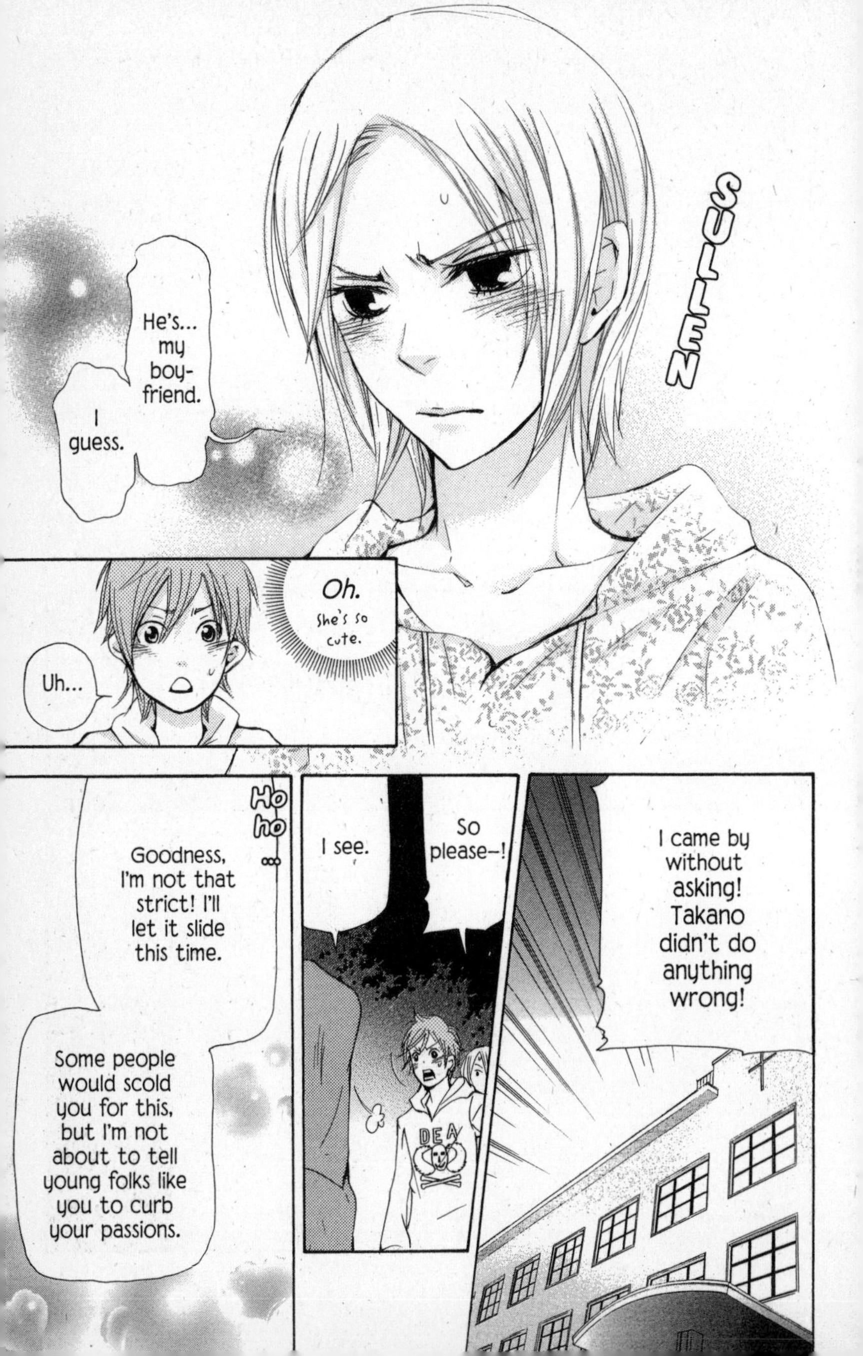
SULLEN
He's... my boy-friend.
I guess.
Oh.
She's so cute.
Uh...
I came by without asking! Takano didn't do anything wrong!
So please—!
I see.
Ho ho...
Goodness, I'm not that strict! I'll let it slide this time.
Some people would scold you for this, but I'm not about to tell young folks like you to curb your passions.

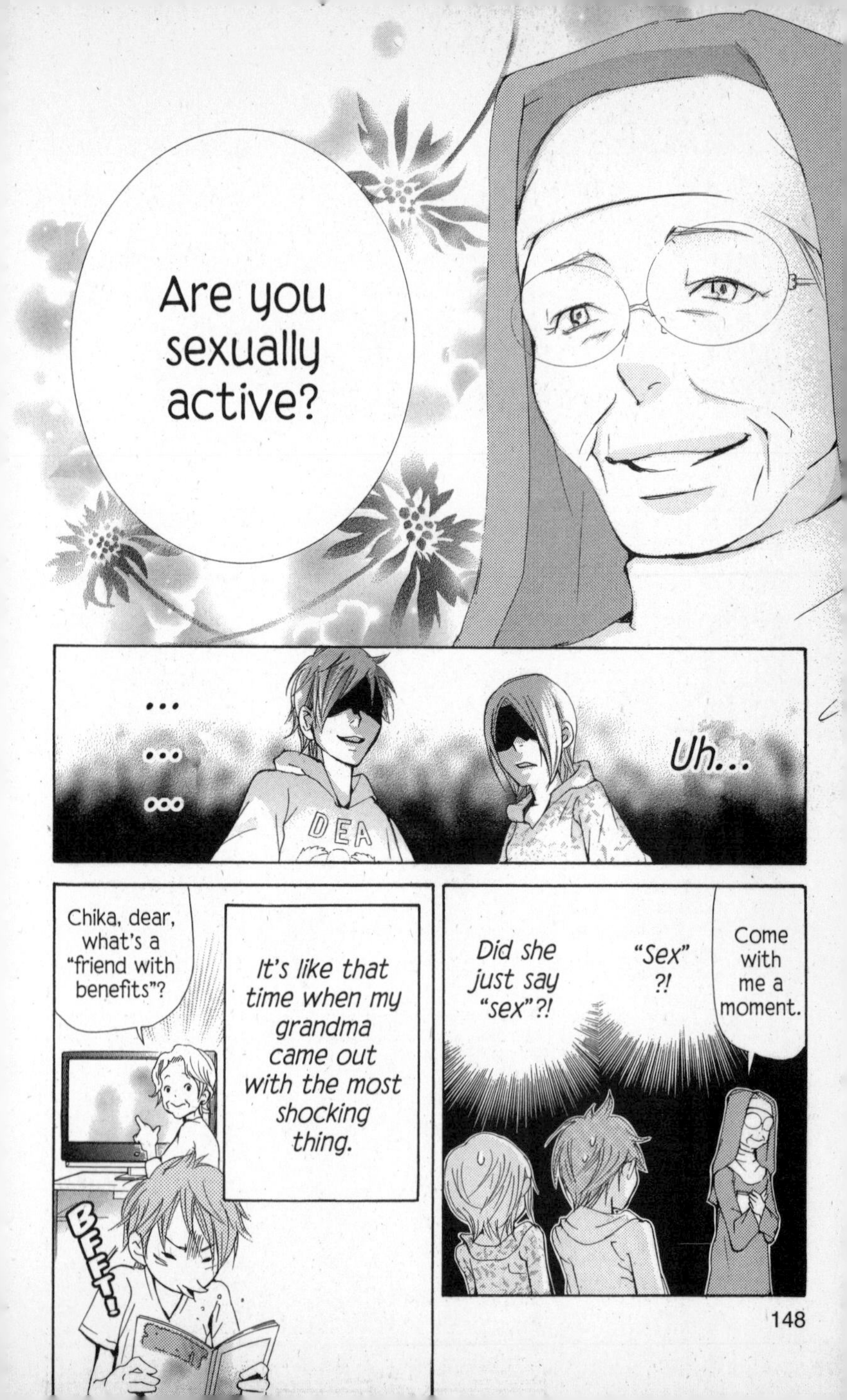

Are you sexually active?
Uh...
...
...
...
Come with me a moment.
"Sex" ?!
Did she just say "sex"?!
It's like that time when my grandma came out with the most shocking thing.
Chika, dear, what's a "friend with benefits"?
BFFT!

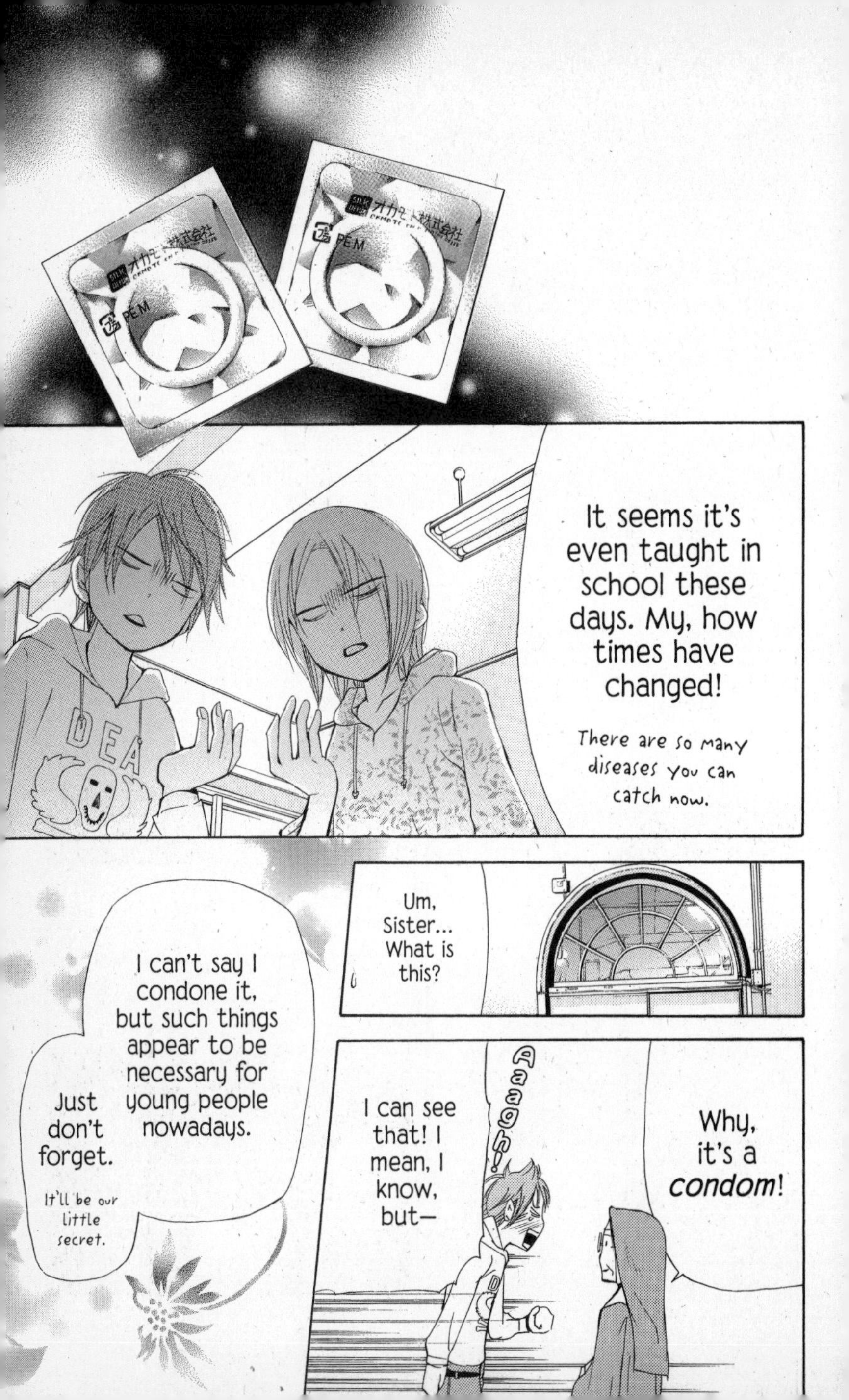
It seems it's even taught in school these days. My, how times have changed!
There are so many diseases you can catch now.
Um, Sister... What is this?
Why, it's a *condom*!
Aaaagh!
I can see that! I mean, I know, but—
I can't say I condone it, but such things appear to be necessary for young people nowadays.
Just don't forget.
It'll be our little secret.

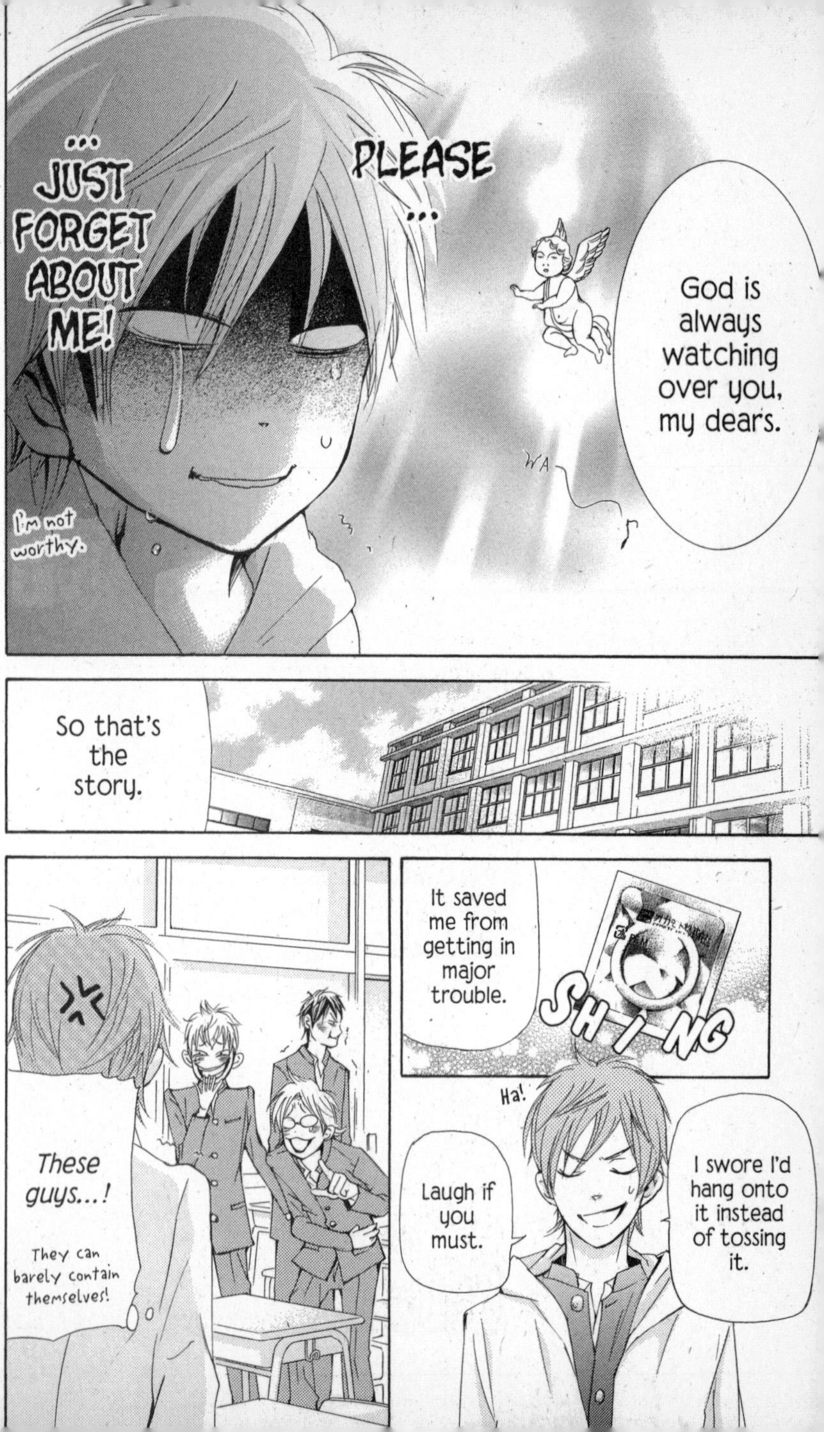
God is always watching over you, my dears.
WA
PLEASE...
...JUST FORGET ABOUT ME!
I'm not worthy.
So that's the story.
It saved me from getting in major trouble.
SHING
I swore I'd hang onto it instead of tossing it.
Laugh if you must.
Ha!
These guys...!
They can barely contain themselves!

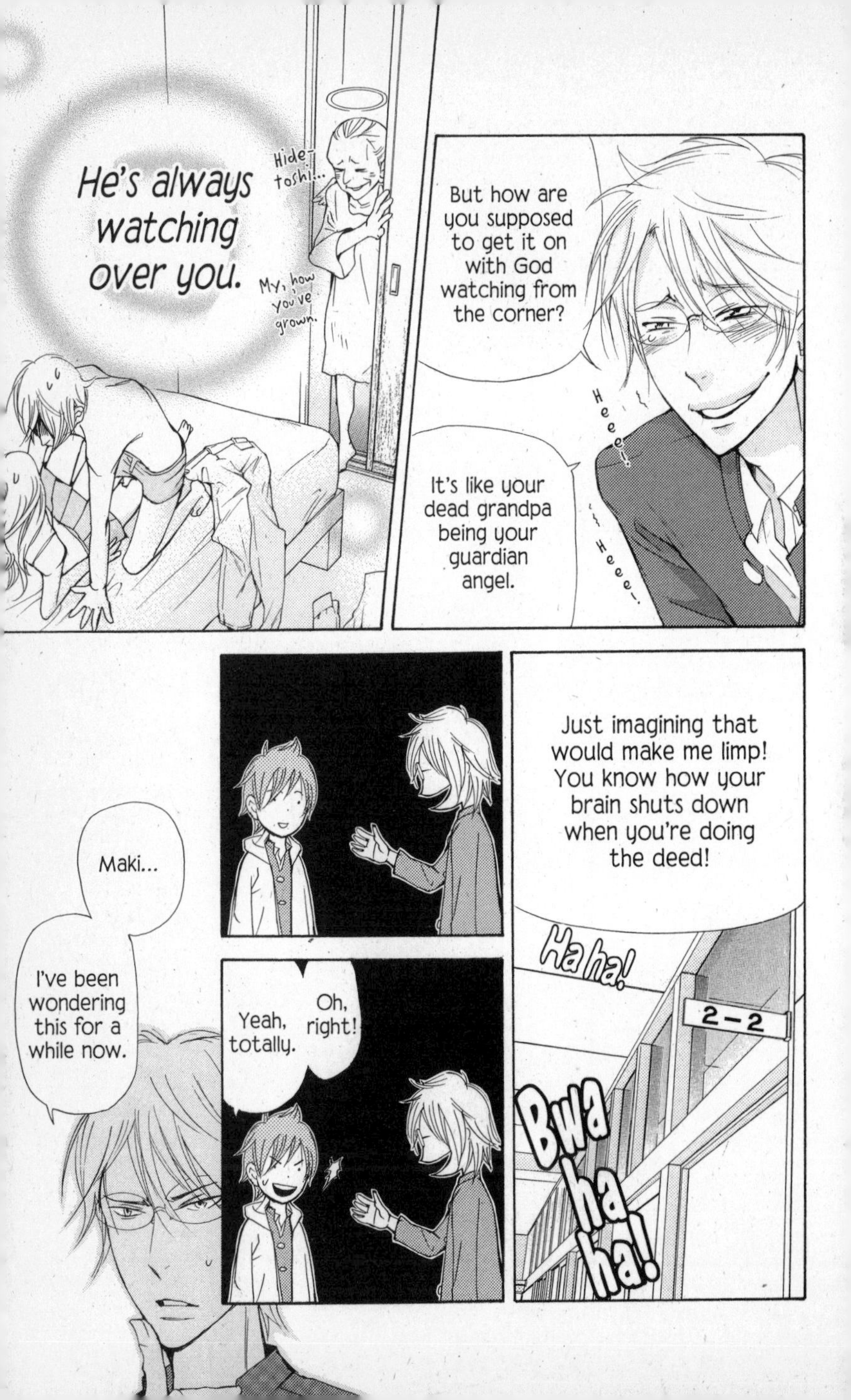
But how are you supposed to get it on with God watching from the corner?
It's like your dead grandpa being your guardian angel.
Heeee!
Heeee!
He's always watching over you.
Hide-toshi...
My, how you've grown.
Just imagining that would make me limp! You know how your brain shuts down when you're doing the deed!
Ha ha!
2-2
Bwa ha ha!
Oh, right!
Yeah, totally.
Maki...
I've been wondering this for a while now.

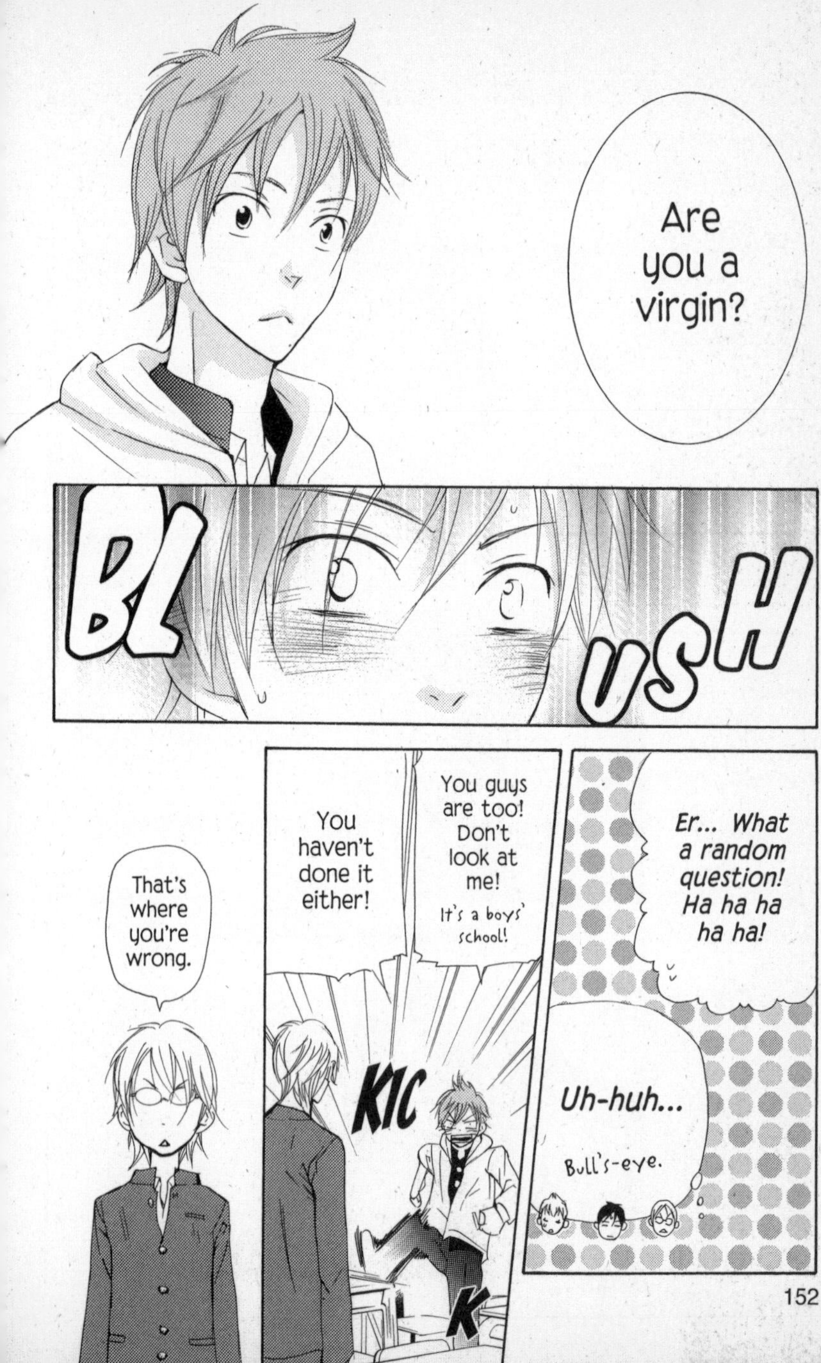
Are you a virgin?
BLUSH
Er... What a random question! Ha ha ha ha!
Uh-huh...
Bull's-eye.
You guys are too! Don't look at me!
It's a boys' school!
You haven't done it either!
KICK
That's where you're wrong.

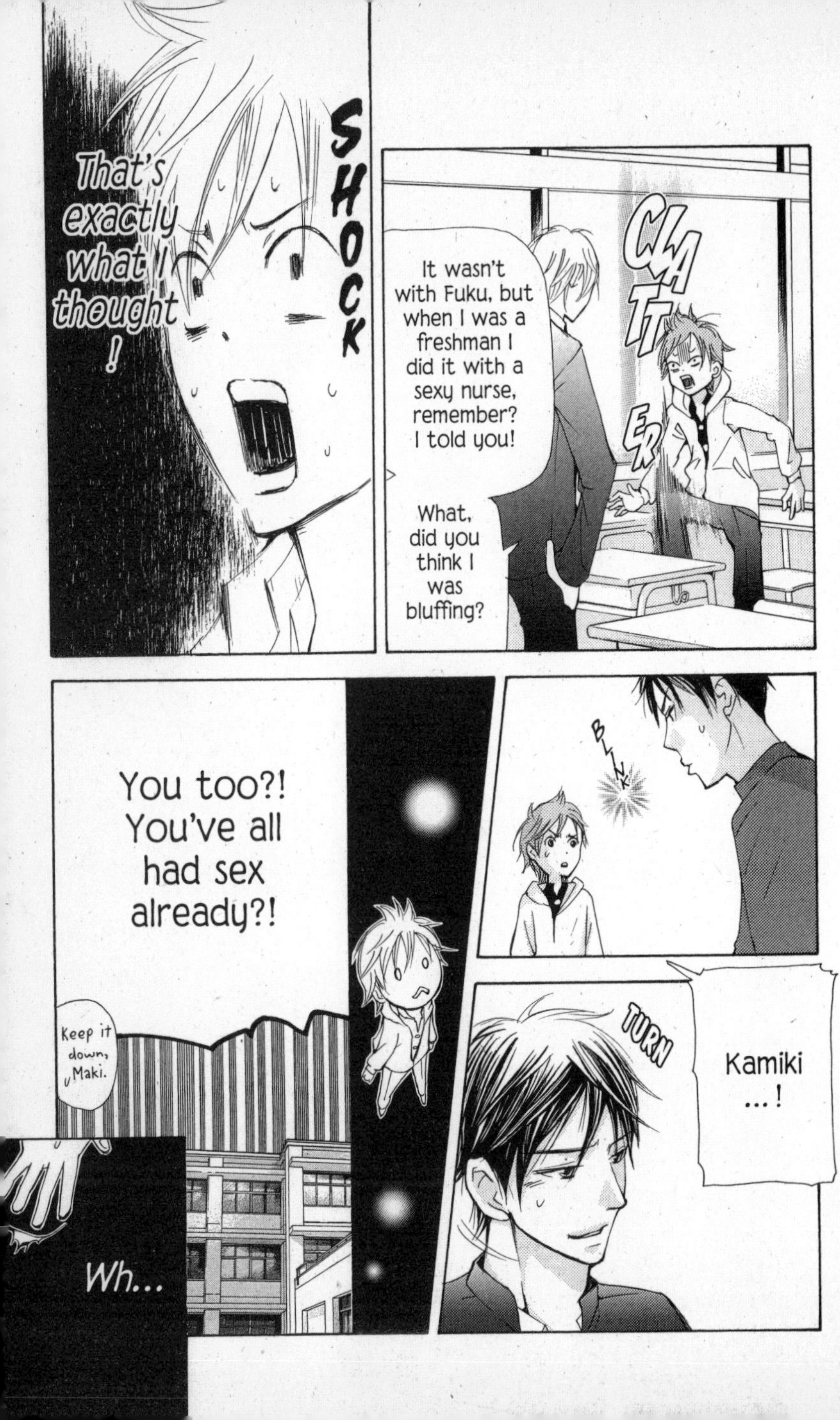
CLATTER
It wasn't with Fuku, but when I was a freshman I did it with a sexy nurse, remember? I told you!
What, did you think I was bluffing?
SHOCK
That's exactly what I thought!
BLINK
TURN
Kamiki ...!
You too?! You've all had sex already?!
Keep it down, Maki.
Wh...

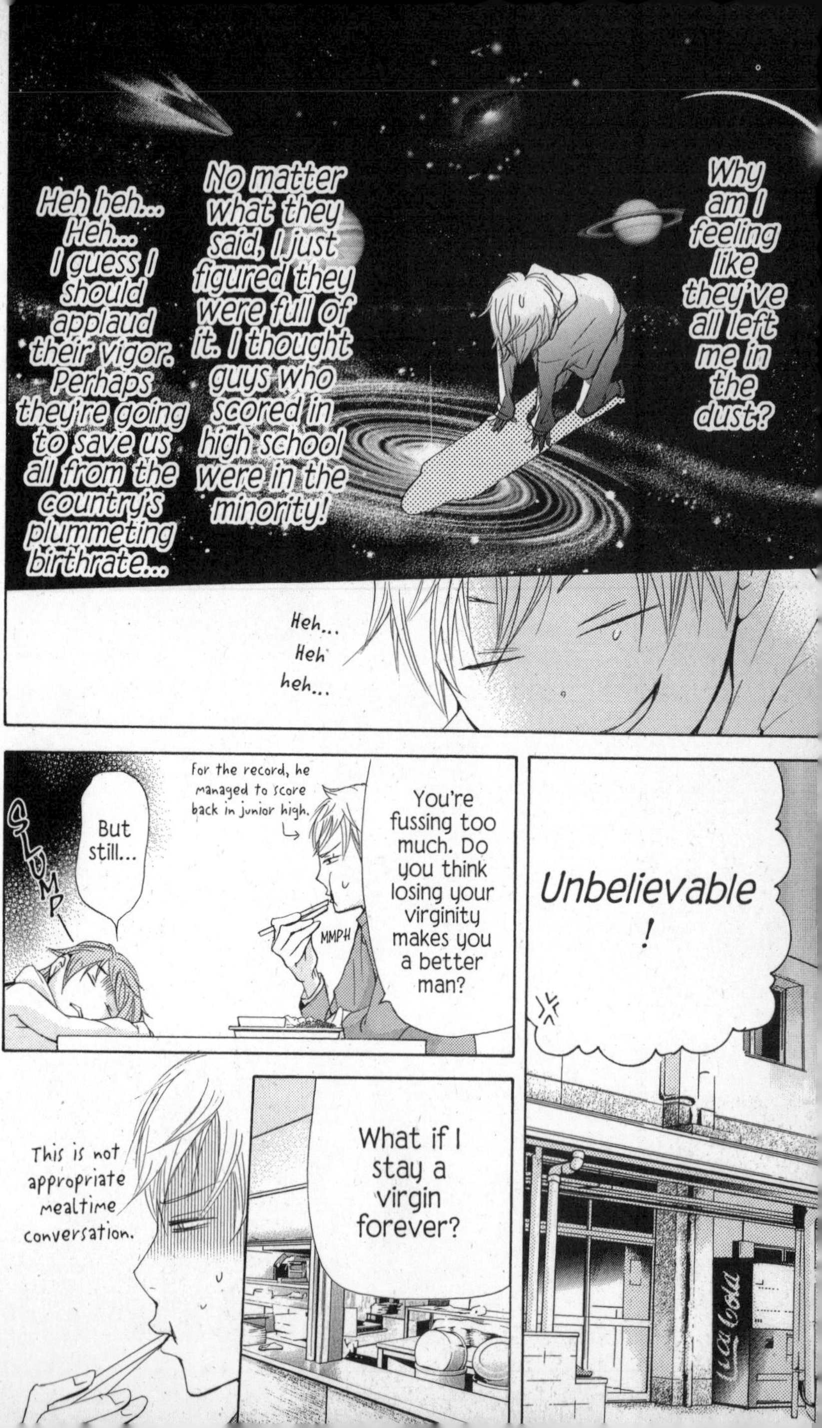
Why am I feeling like they've all left me in the dust?
No matter what they said, I just figured they were full of it. I thought guys who scored in high school were in the minority!
Heh heh... Heh... I guess I should applaud their vigor. Perhaps they're going to save us all from the country's plummeting birthrate...
Heh... Heh heh...
Unbelievable!
You're fussing too much. Do you think losing your virginity makes you a better man?
For the record, he managed to score back in junior high.
MMPH
But still...
SLUMP
What if I stay a virgin forever?
This is not appropriate mealtime conversation.
Coca-Cola

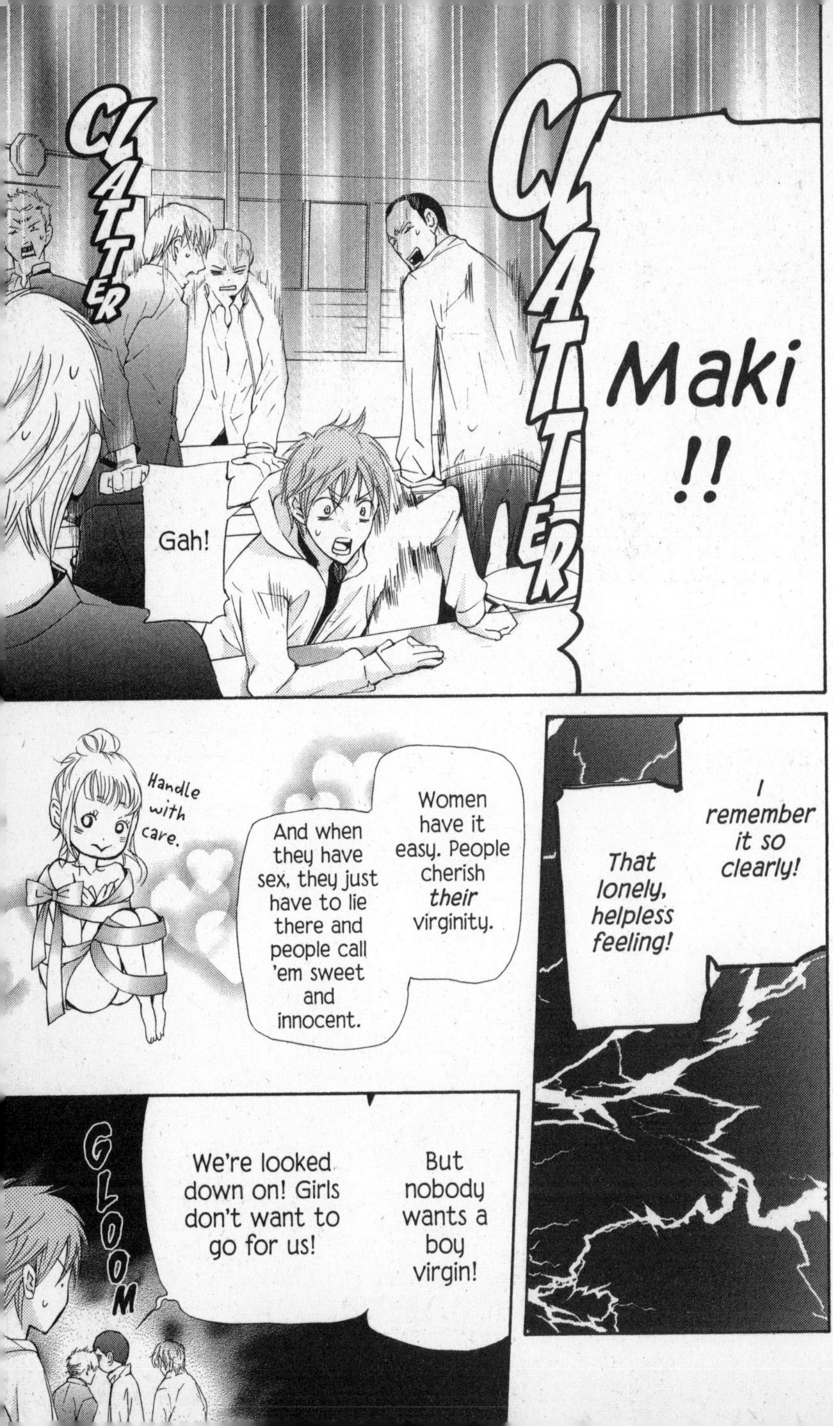
Maki !!
CLATTER
CLATTER
Gah!
I remember it so clearly!
That lonely, helpless feeling!
Women have it easy. People cherish *their* virginity.
And when they have sex, they just have to lie there and people call 'em sweet and innocent.
Handle with care.
But nobody wants a boy virgin!
We're looked down on! Girls don't want to go for us!
GLOOM

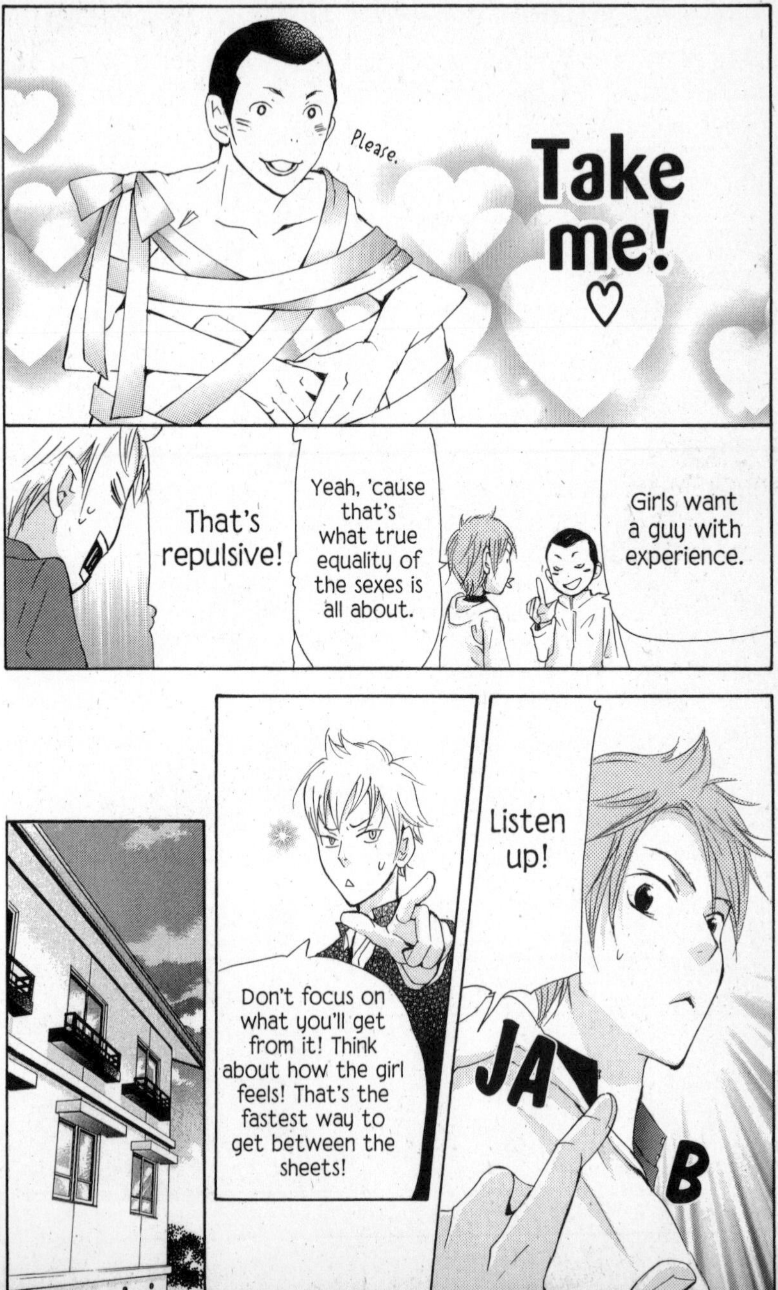
Take me! ♡
Please.
Girls want a guy with experience.
Yeah, 'cause that's what true equality of the sexes is all about.
That's repulsive!
Listen up!
JAB
Don't focus on what you'll get from it! Think about how the girl feels! That's the fastest way to get between the sheets!

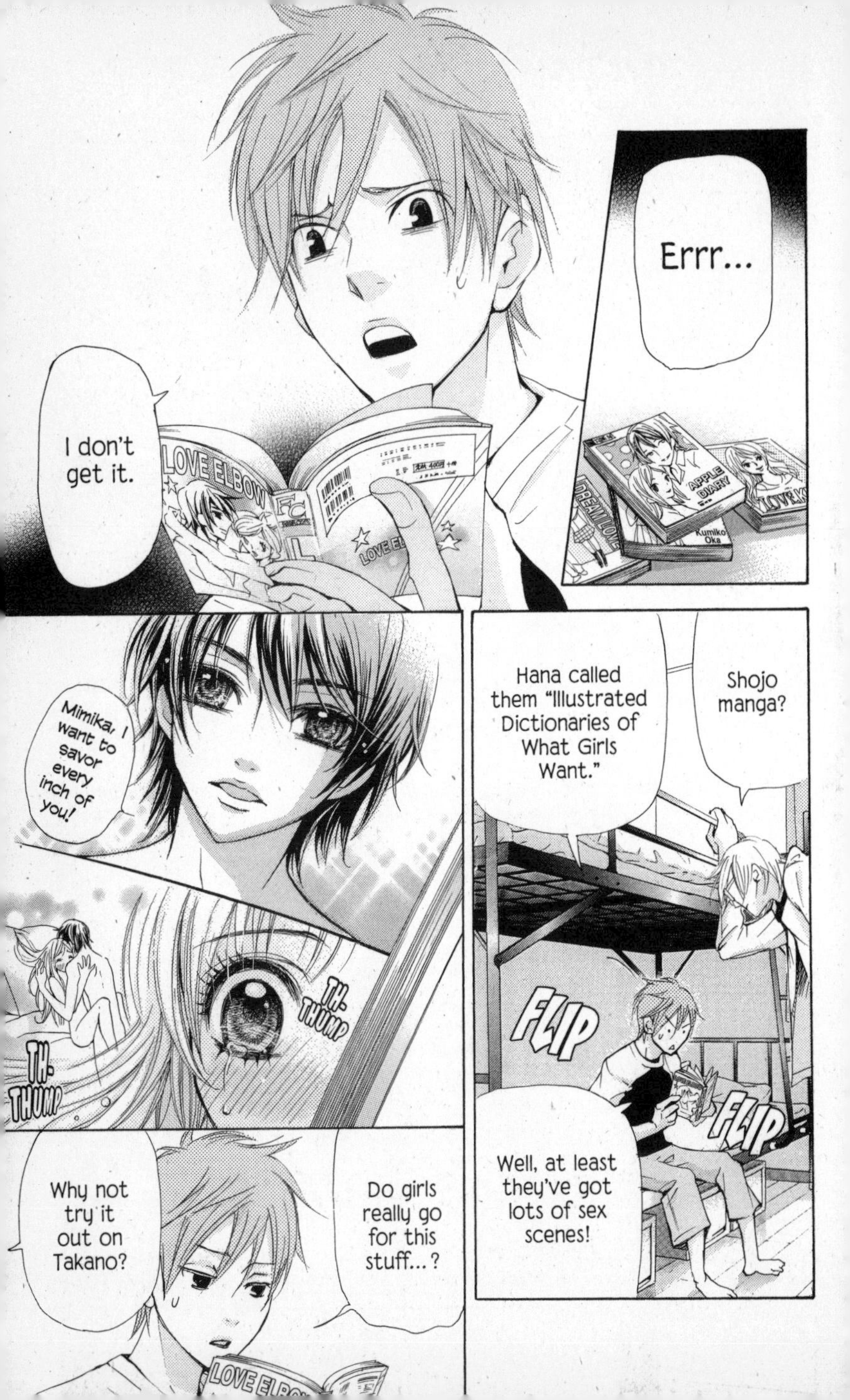
Errr...
APPLE DIARY
Kumiko Oka
DREAM LOVE
I don't get it.
LOVE ELBOW
Shojo manga?
Hana called them "Illustrated Dictionaries of What Girls Want."
FLIP
FLIP
Well, at least they've got lots of sex scenes!
Mimika, I want to savor every inch of you!
TH-THUMP
TH-THUMP
Do girls really go for this stuff...?
Why not try it out on Takano?
LOVE ELBOW

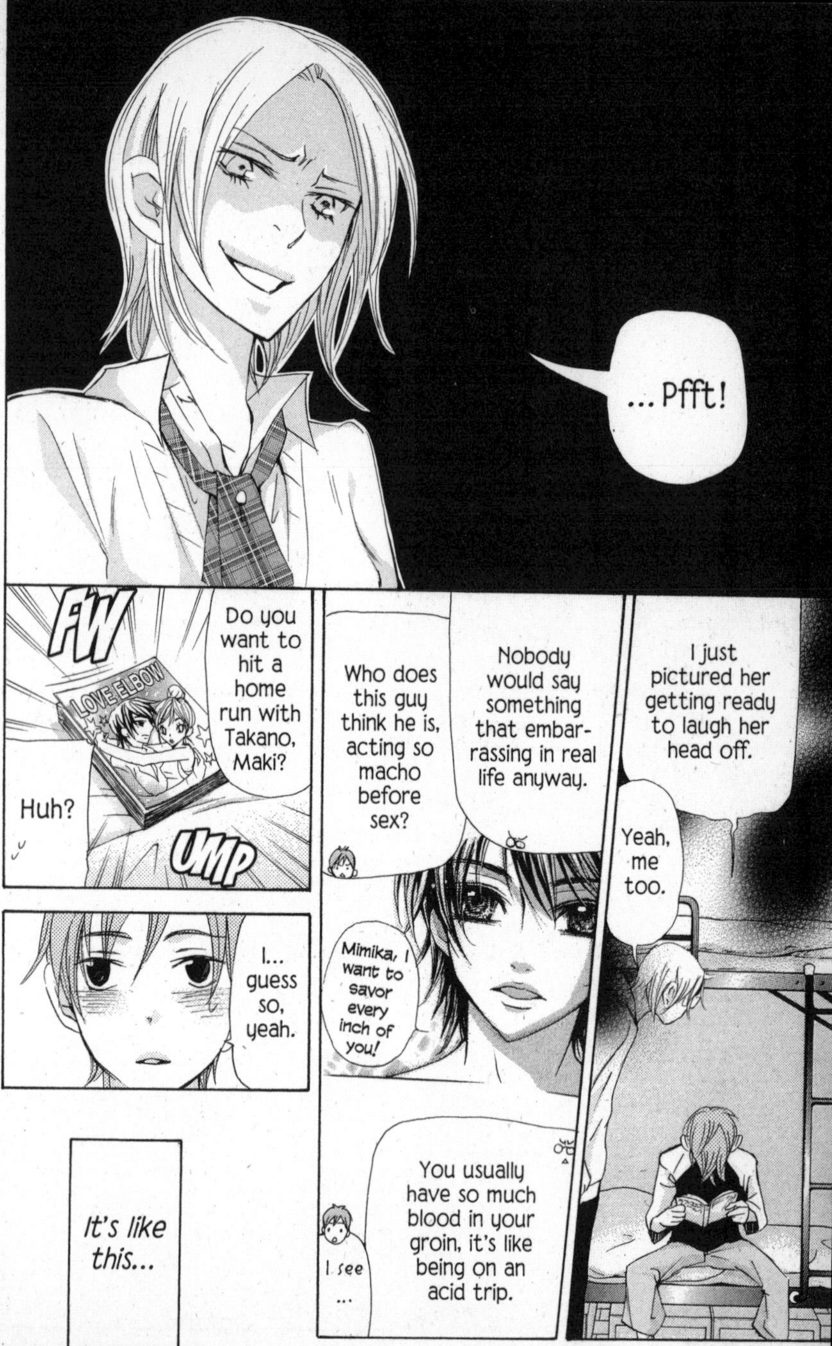
...Pfft!
I just pictured her getting ready to laugh her head off.
Yeah, me too.
Nobody would say something that embarrassing in real life anyway.
Who does this guy think he is, acting so macho before sex?
Mimika, I want to savor every inch of you!
You usually have so much blood in your groin, it's like being on an acid trip.
I see ...
FW
Do you want to hit a home run with Takano, Maki?
LOVE ELBOW
Huh?
UMP
I... guess so, yeah.
It's like this...

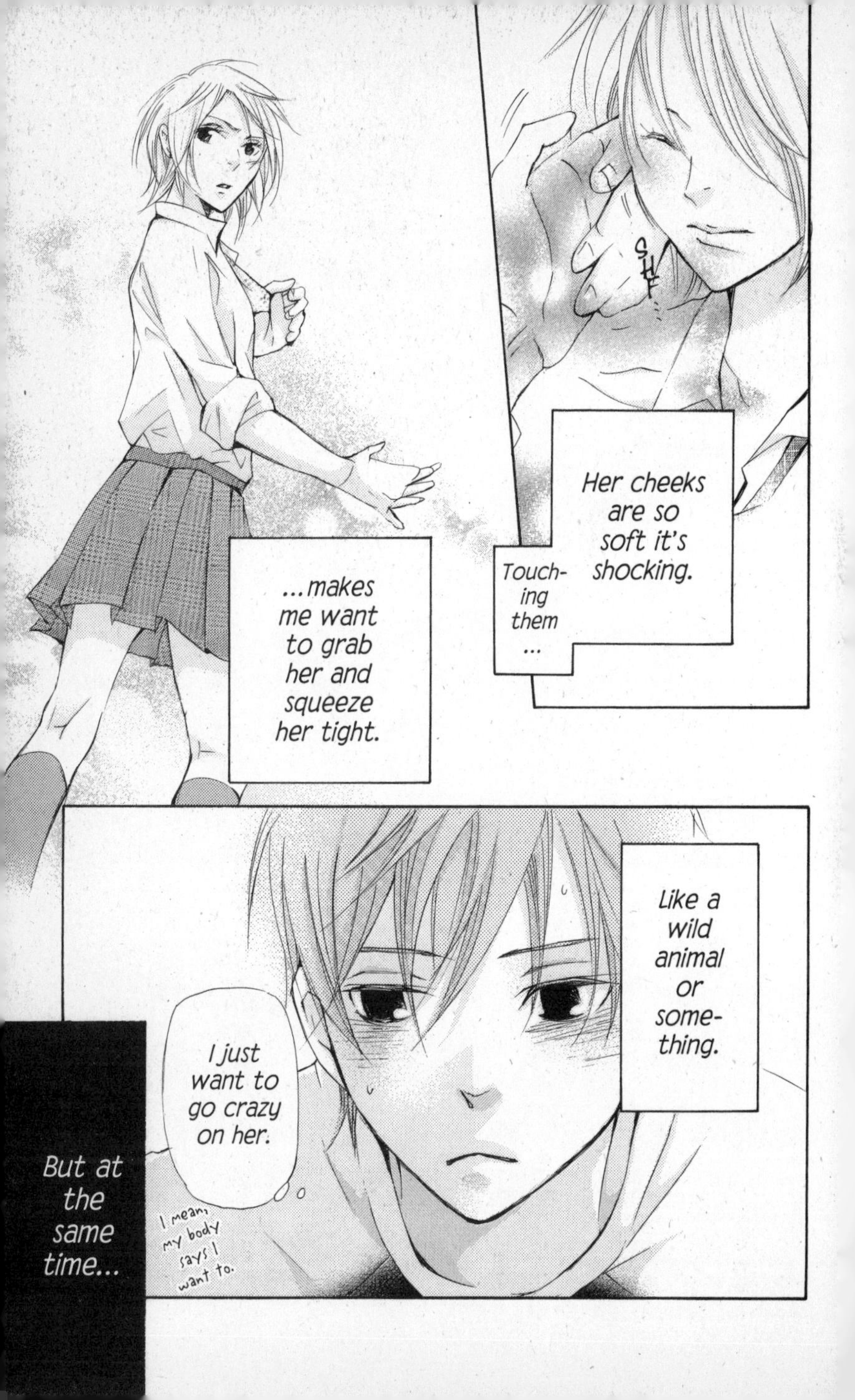
Her cheeks are so soft it's shocking.
Touching them...
...makes me want to grab her and squeeze her tight.
Like a wild animal or something.
I just want to go crazy on her.
I mean, my body says I want to.
But at the same time...

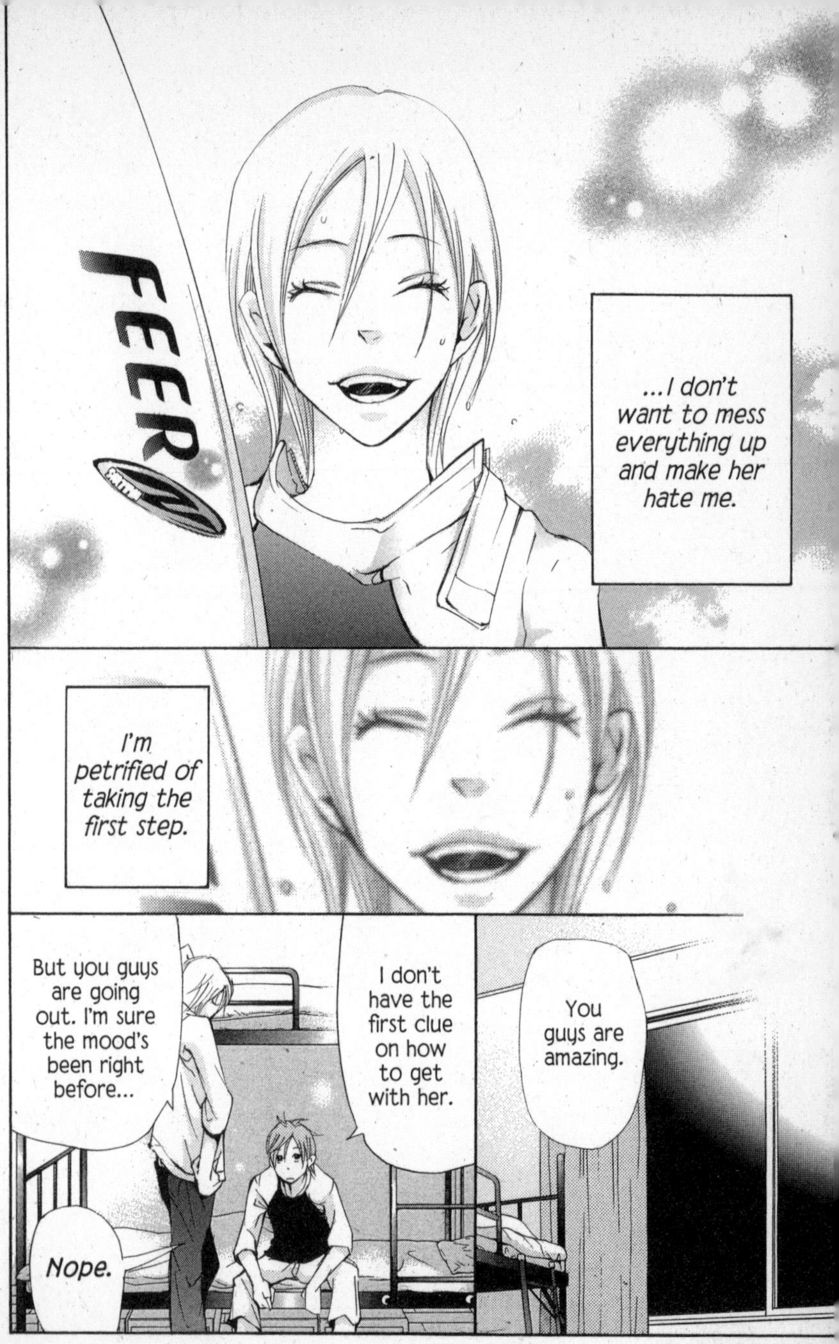
...I don't want to mess everything up and make her hate me.
FEER
I'm petrified of taking the first step.
You guys are amazing.
I don't have the first clue on how to get with her.
But you guys are going out. I'm sure the mood's been right before...
Nope.

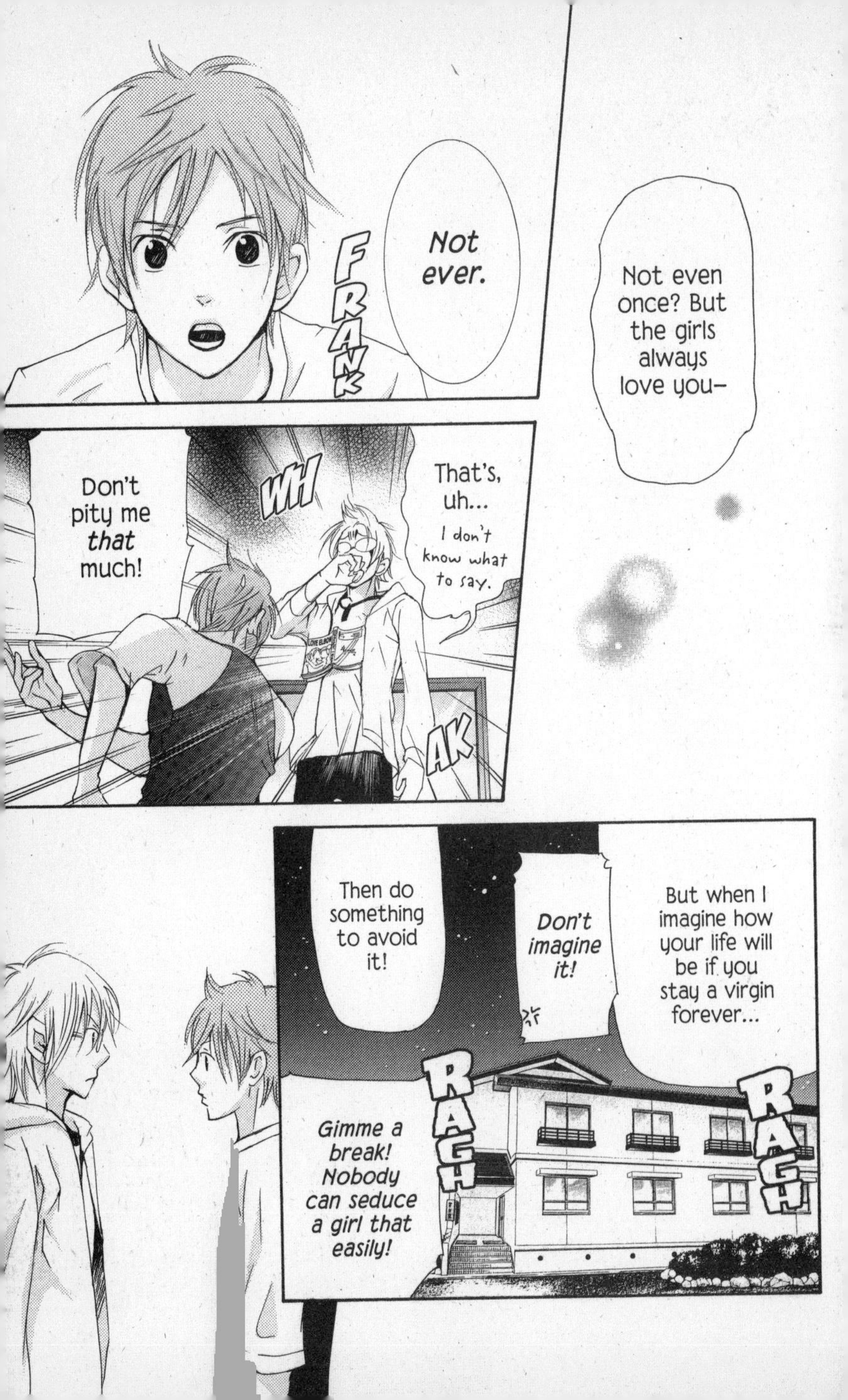
Not even once? But the girls always love you–
FRANK
Not ever.
That's, uh...
I don't know what to say.
WH
Don't pity me *that* much!
AK
But when I imagine how your life will be if you stay a virgin forever...
Don't imagine it!
Then do something to avoid it!
RAGH
Gimme a break! Nobody can seduce a girl that easily!
RAGH

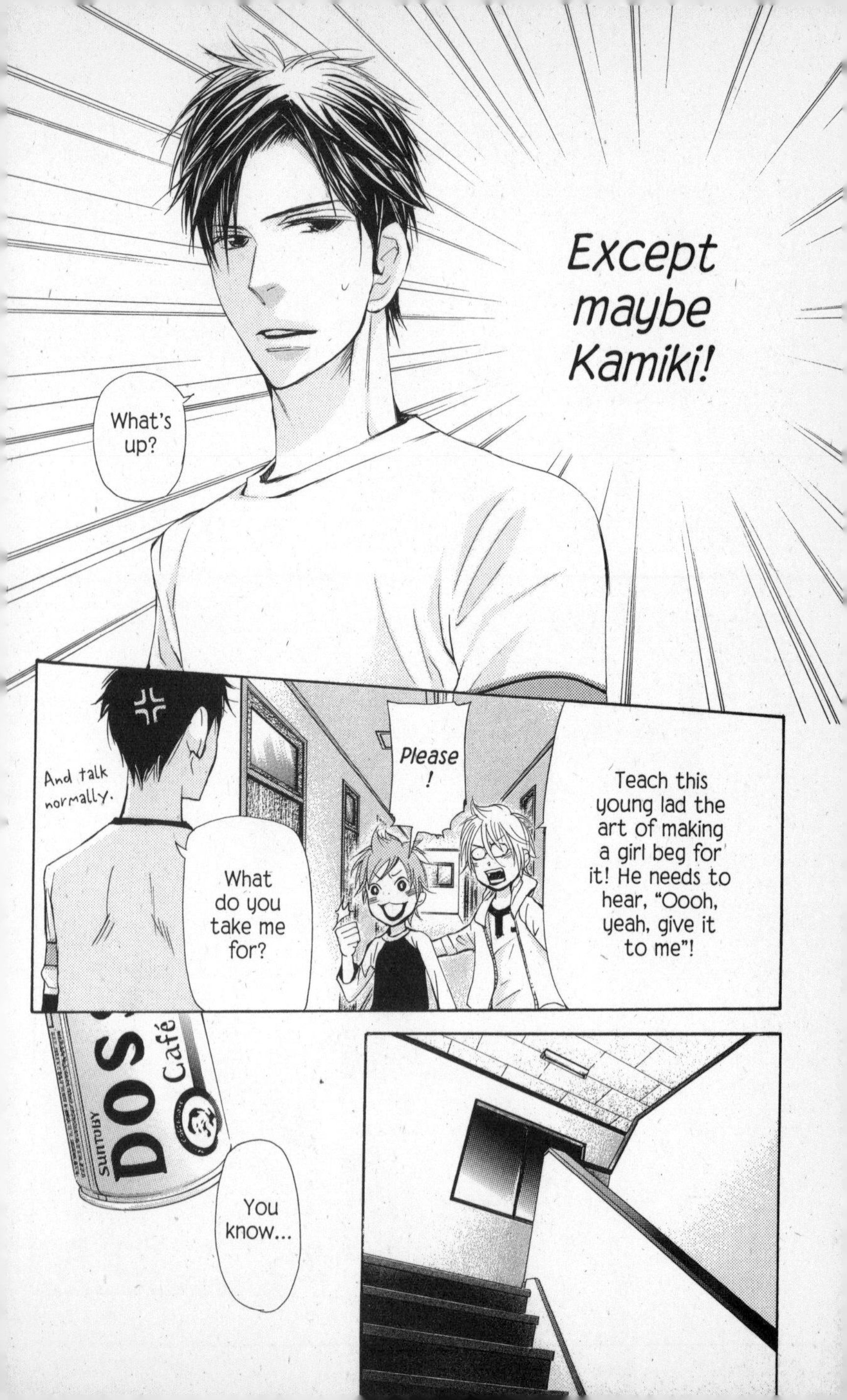
Except maybe Kamiki!
What's up?
Teach this young lad the art of making a girl beg for it! He needs to hear, "Oooh, yeah, give it to me"!
Please!
What do you take me for?
And talk normally.
SUNTORY
Café
You know...

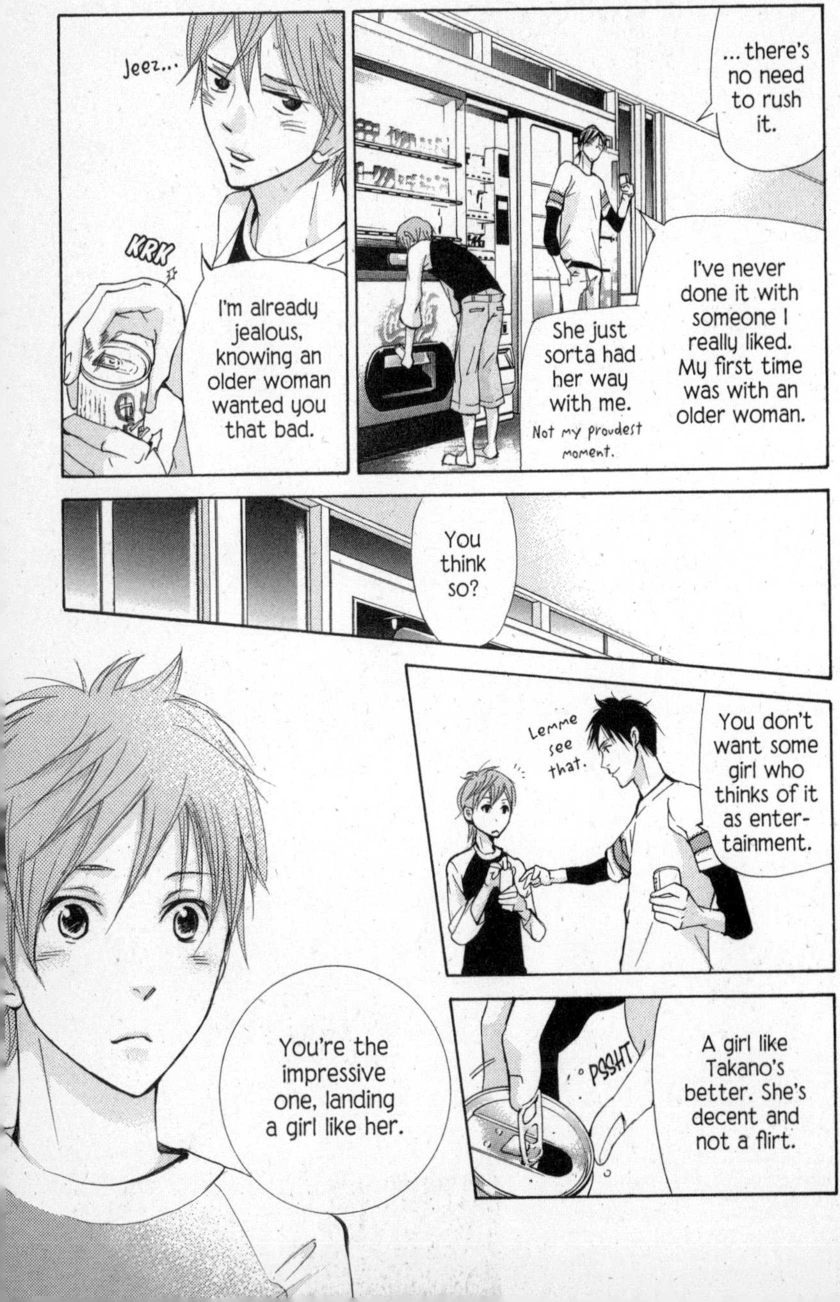
... there's no need to rush it.
I've never done it with someone I really liked. My first time was with an older woman.
She just sorta had her way with me.
Not my proudest moment.
Jeez...
KRK
I'm already jealous, knowing an older woman wanted you that bad.
You think so?
You don't want some girl who thinks of it as enter-tainment.
Lemme see that.
A girl like Takano's better. She's decent and not a flirt.
PSSHT
You're the impressive one, landing a girl like her.

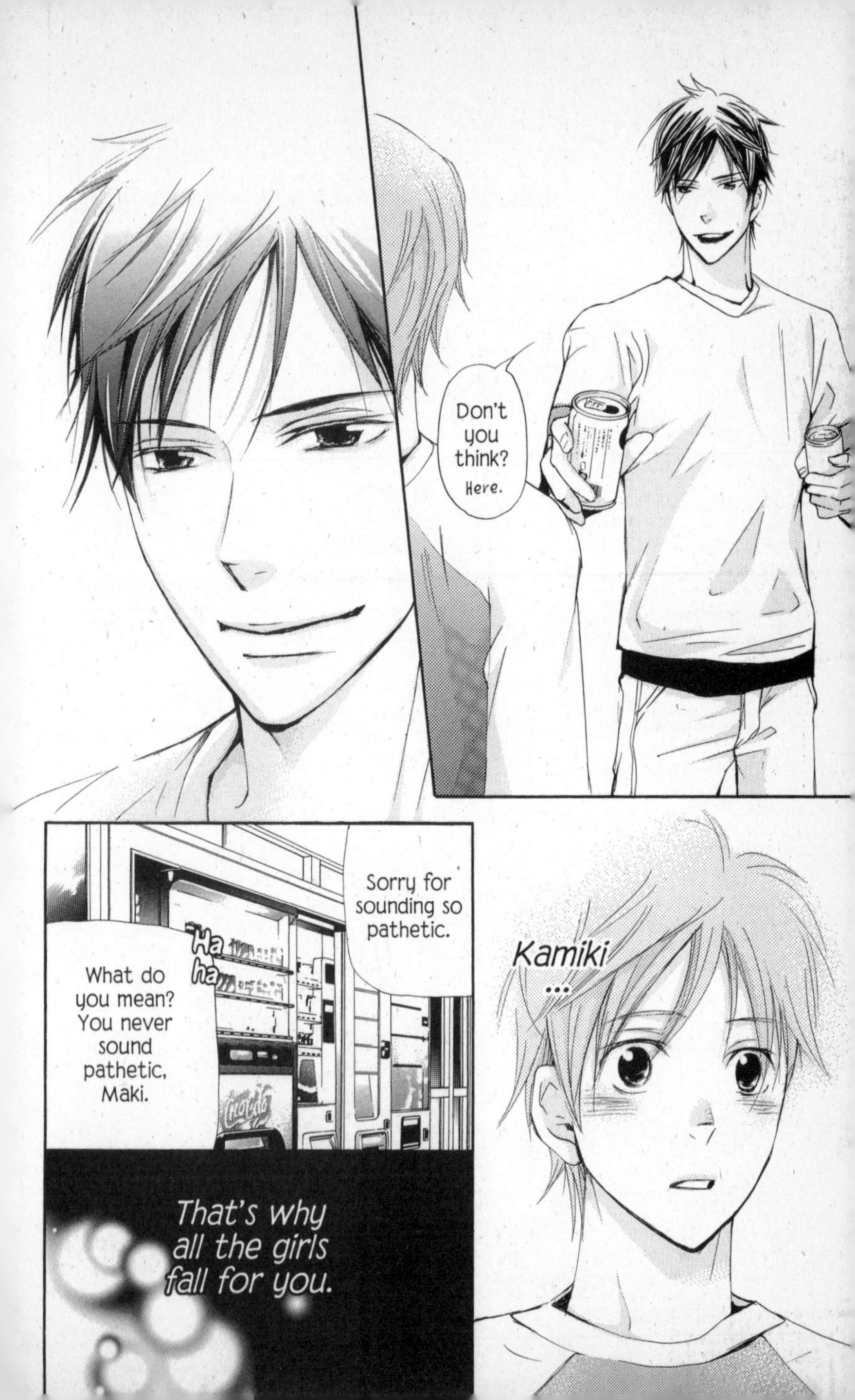
Don't you think?
Here.
Kamiki ...
Sorry for sounding so pathetic.
Ha ha
What do you mean? You never sound pathetic, Maki.
That's why all the girls fall for you.

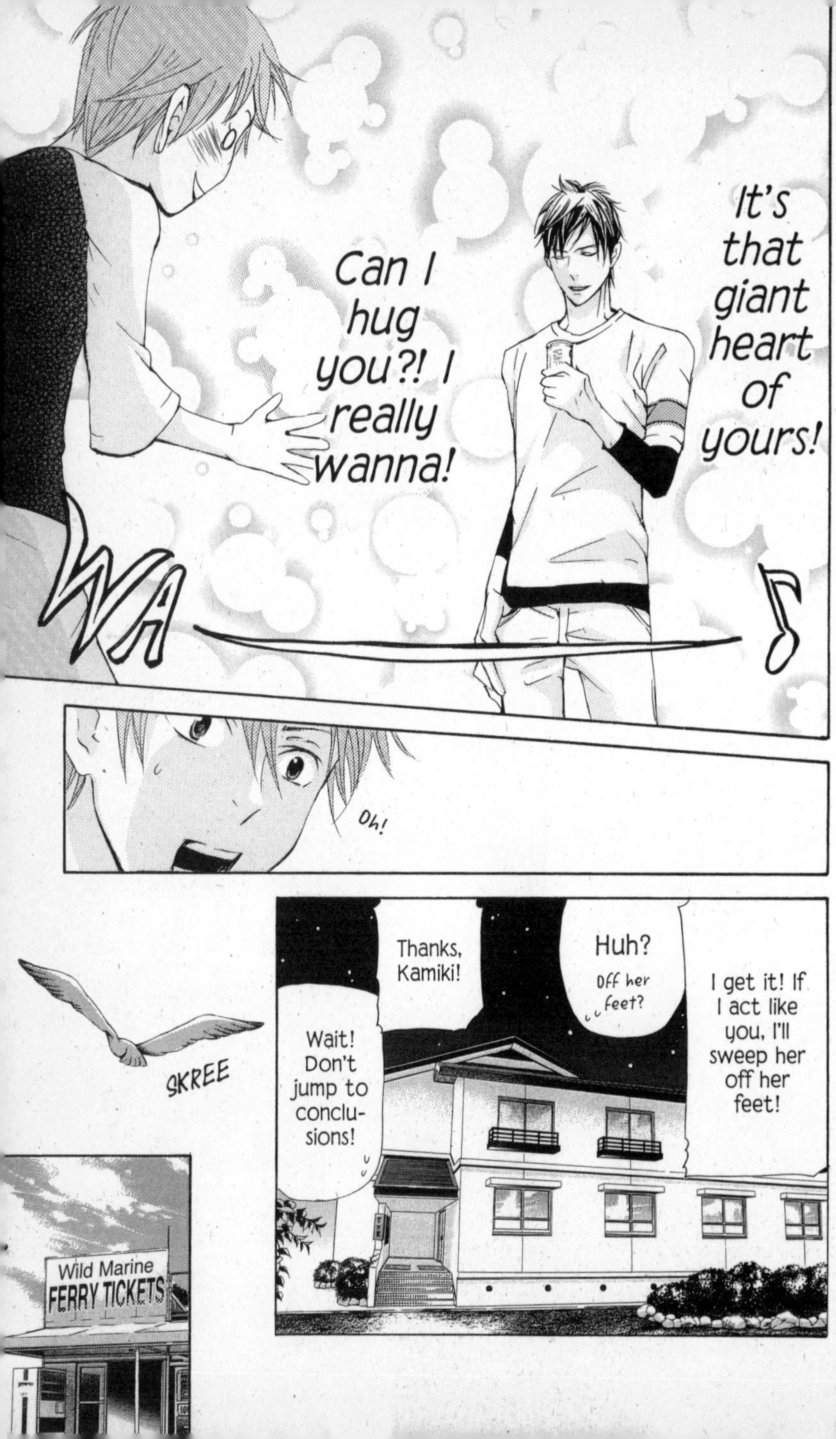
It's that giant heart of yours!
Can I hug you?! I really wanna!
WA
Oh!
I get it! If I act like you, I'll sweep her off her feet!
Huh?
Off her feet?
Thanks, Kamiki!
Wait! Don't jump to conclusions!
SKREE
Wild Marine
FERRY TICKETS

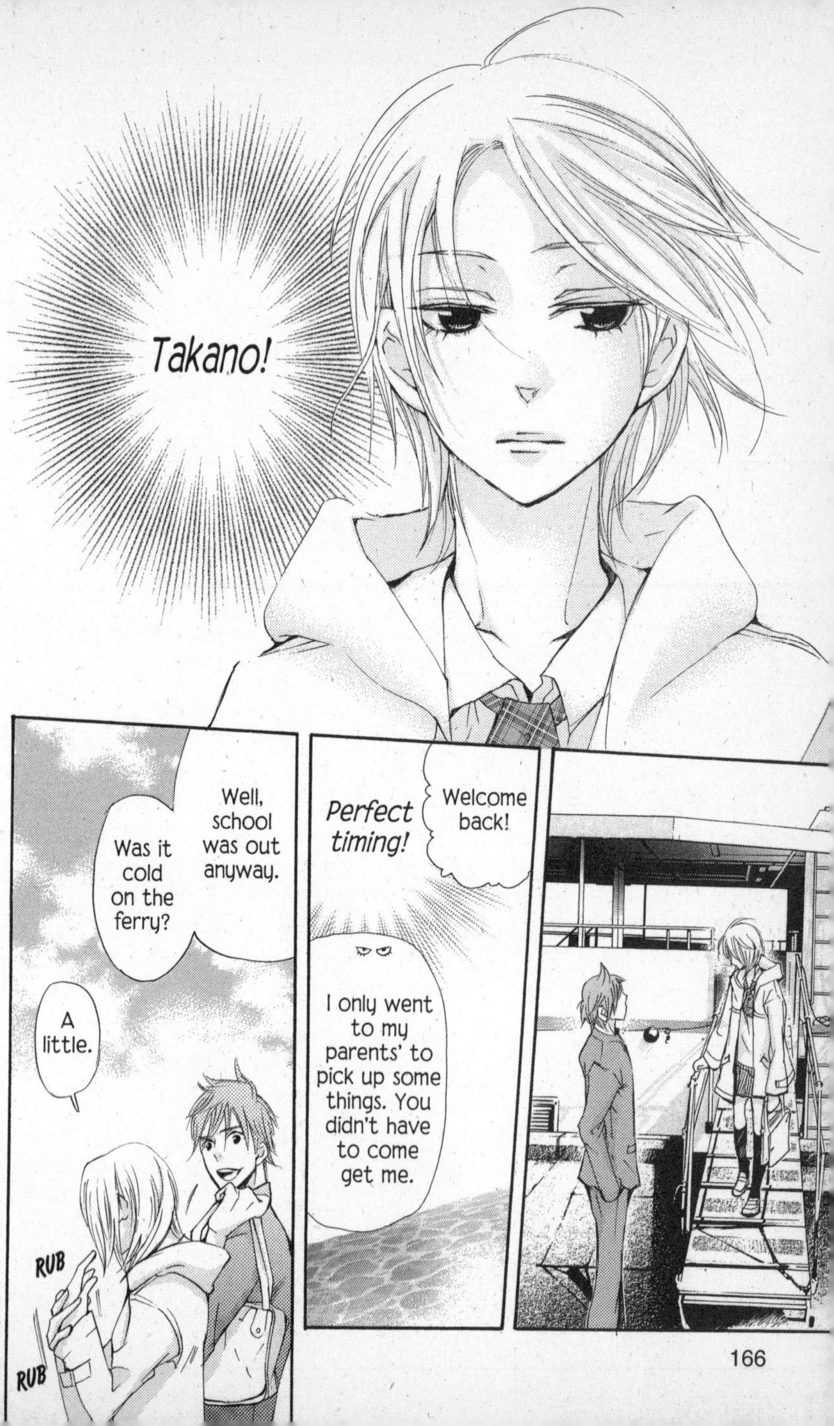
Takano!
Welcome back!
Perfect timing!
I only went to my parents' to pick up some things. You didn't have to come get me.
Well, school was out anyway.
Was it cold on the ferry?
A little.
RUB
RUB

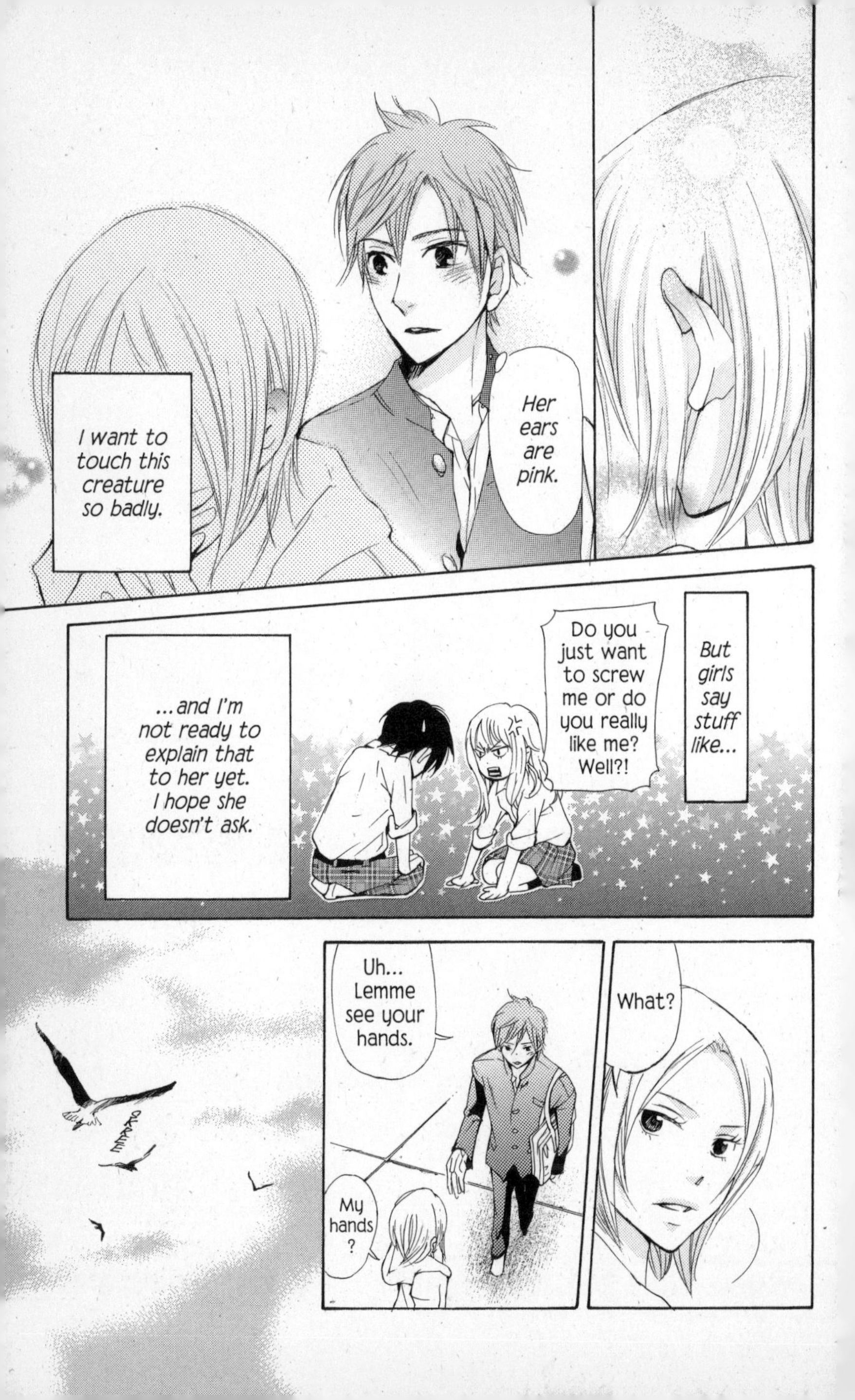
Her ears are pink.
I want to touch this creature so badly.
But girls say stuff like...
Do you just want to screw me or do you really like me? Well?!
...and I'm not ready to explain that to her yet. I hope she doesn't ask.
What?
Uh... Lemme see your hands.
My hands?
SKREEE

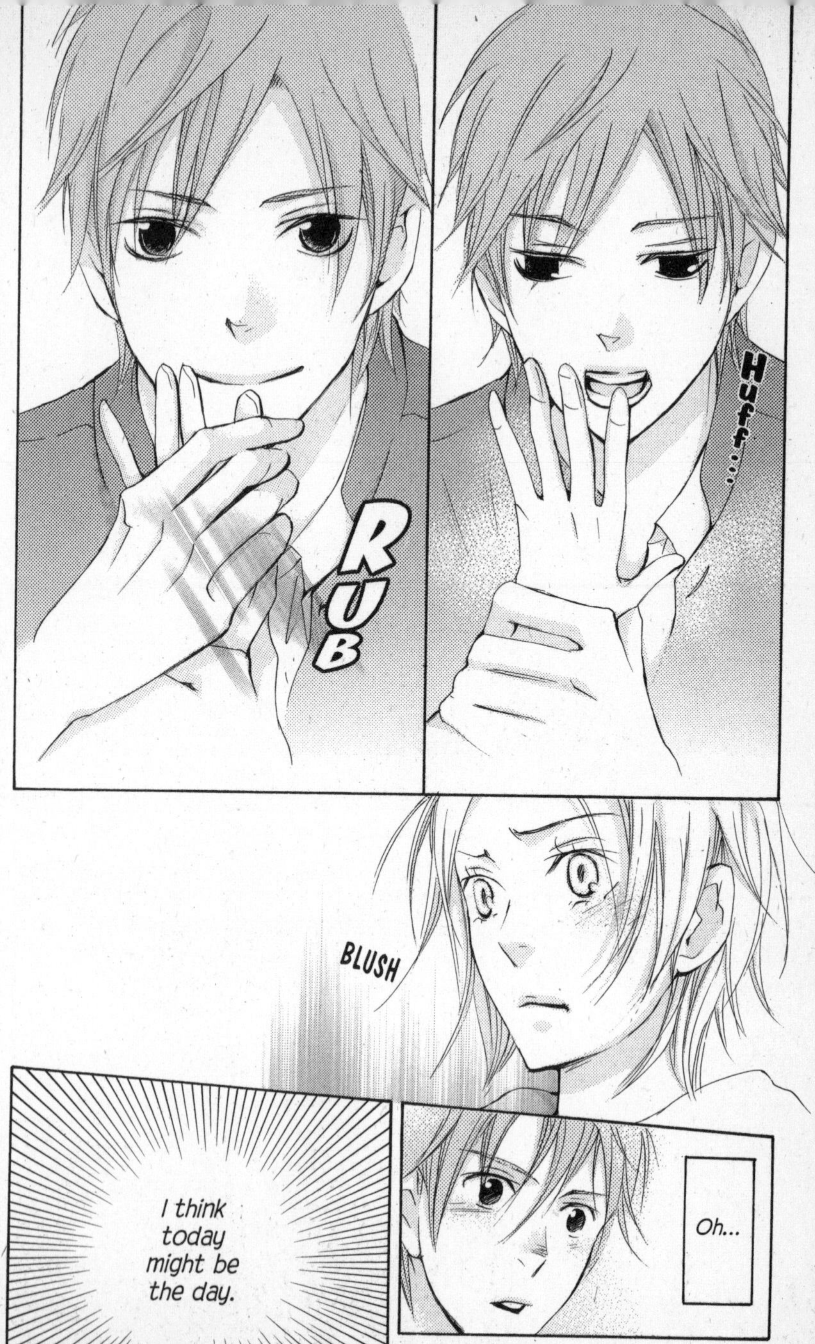
Huff...
RUB
BLUSH
Oh...
I think today might be the day.

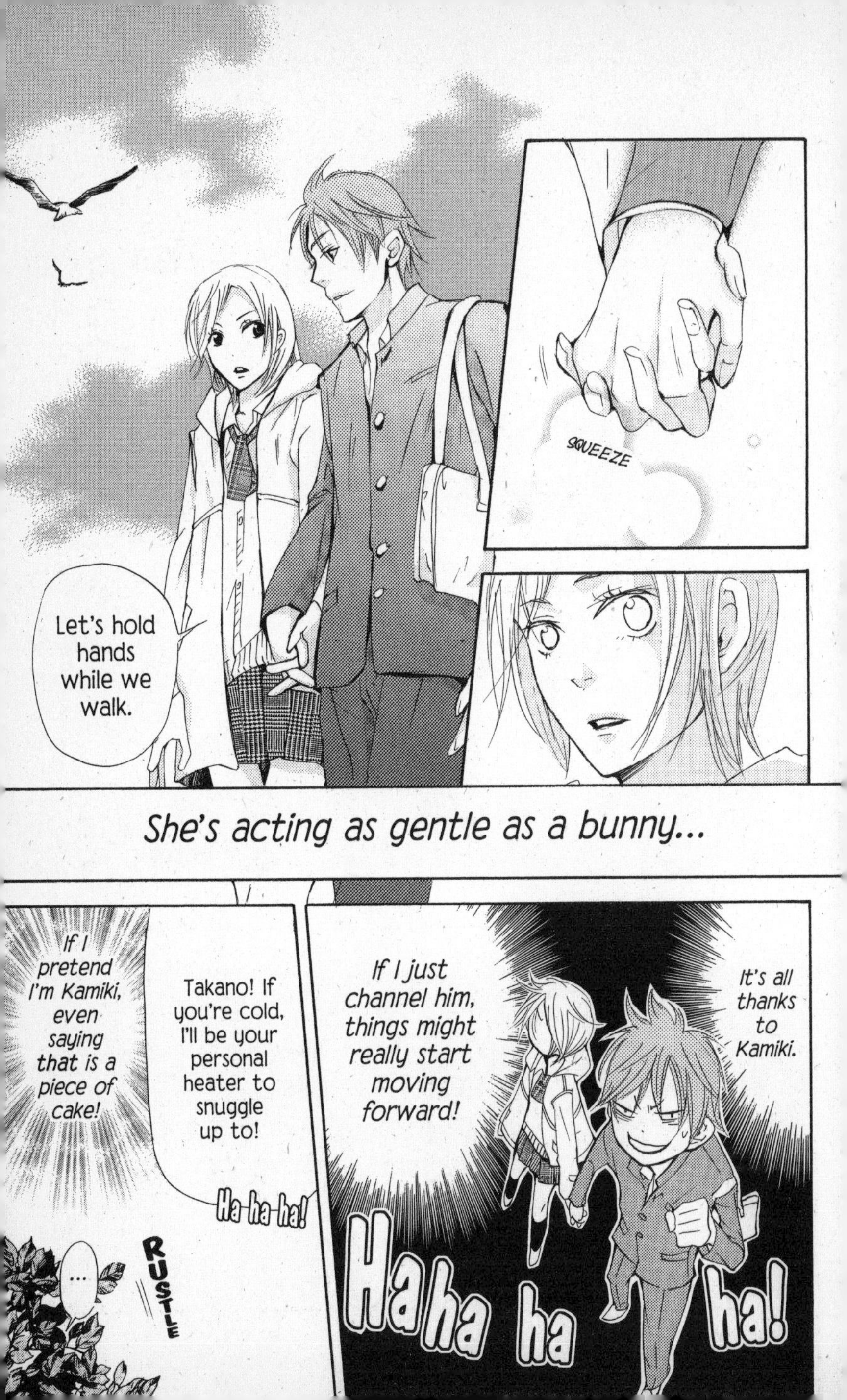
SQUEEZE
Let's hold hands while we walk.
She's acting as gentle as a bunny...
It's all thanks to Kamiki.
If I just channel him, things might really start moving forward!
Ha ha ha ha!
Takano! If you're cold, I'll be your personal heater to snuggle up to!
Ha ha ha!
If I pretend I'm Kamiki, even saying that is a piece of cake!
...
RUSTLE

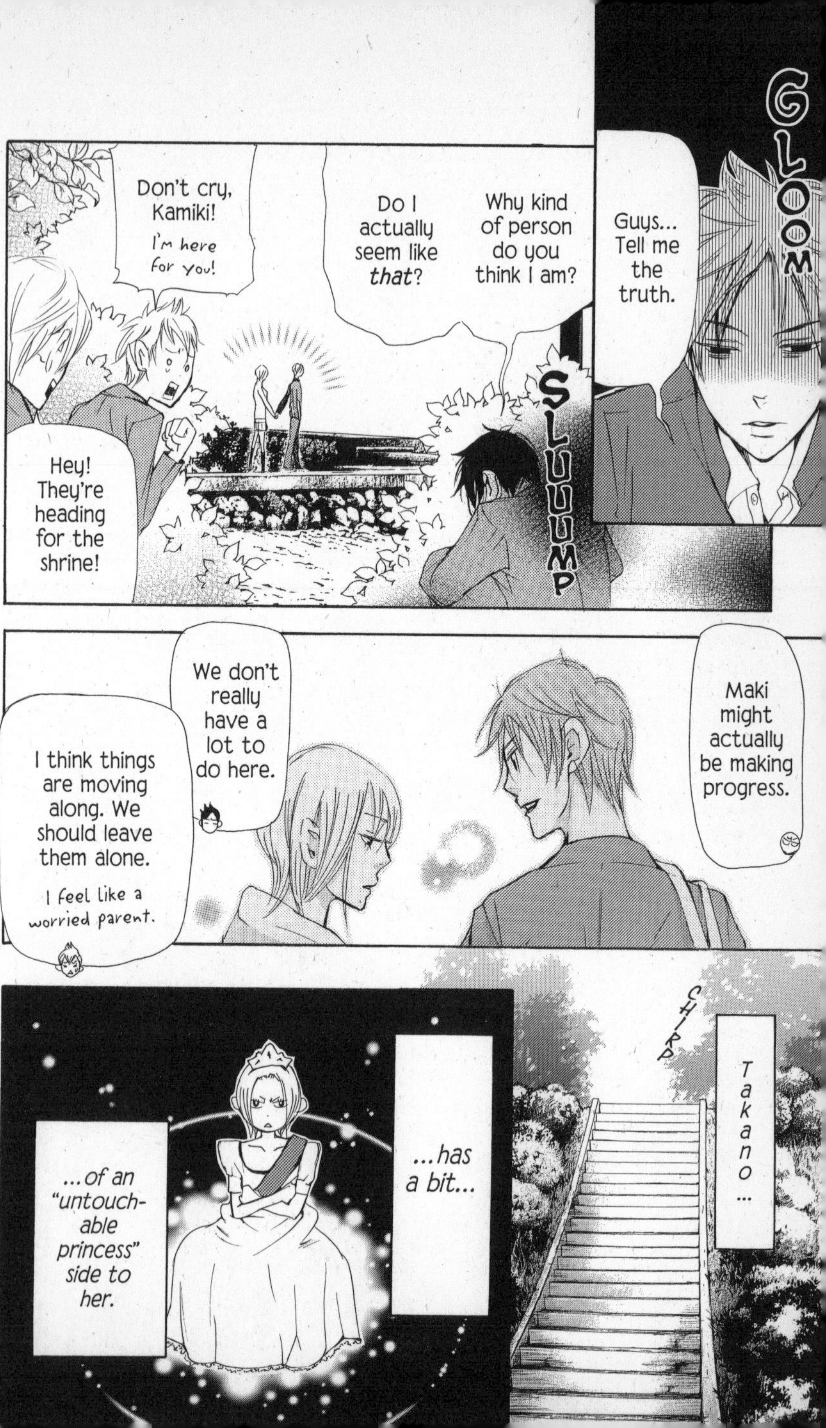
GLOOM
Guys... Tell me the truth.
Why kind of person do you think I am?
Do I actually seem like *that*?
SLUUUMP
Don't cry, Kamiki!
I'm here for you!
Hey! They're heading for the shrine!
Maki might actually be making progress.
We don't really have a lot to do here.
I think things are moving along. We should leave them alone.
I feel like a worried parent.
CHIRP
Takano...
...has a bit...
...of an "untouchable princess" side to her.

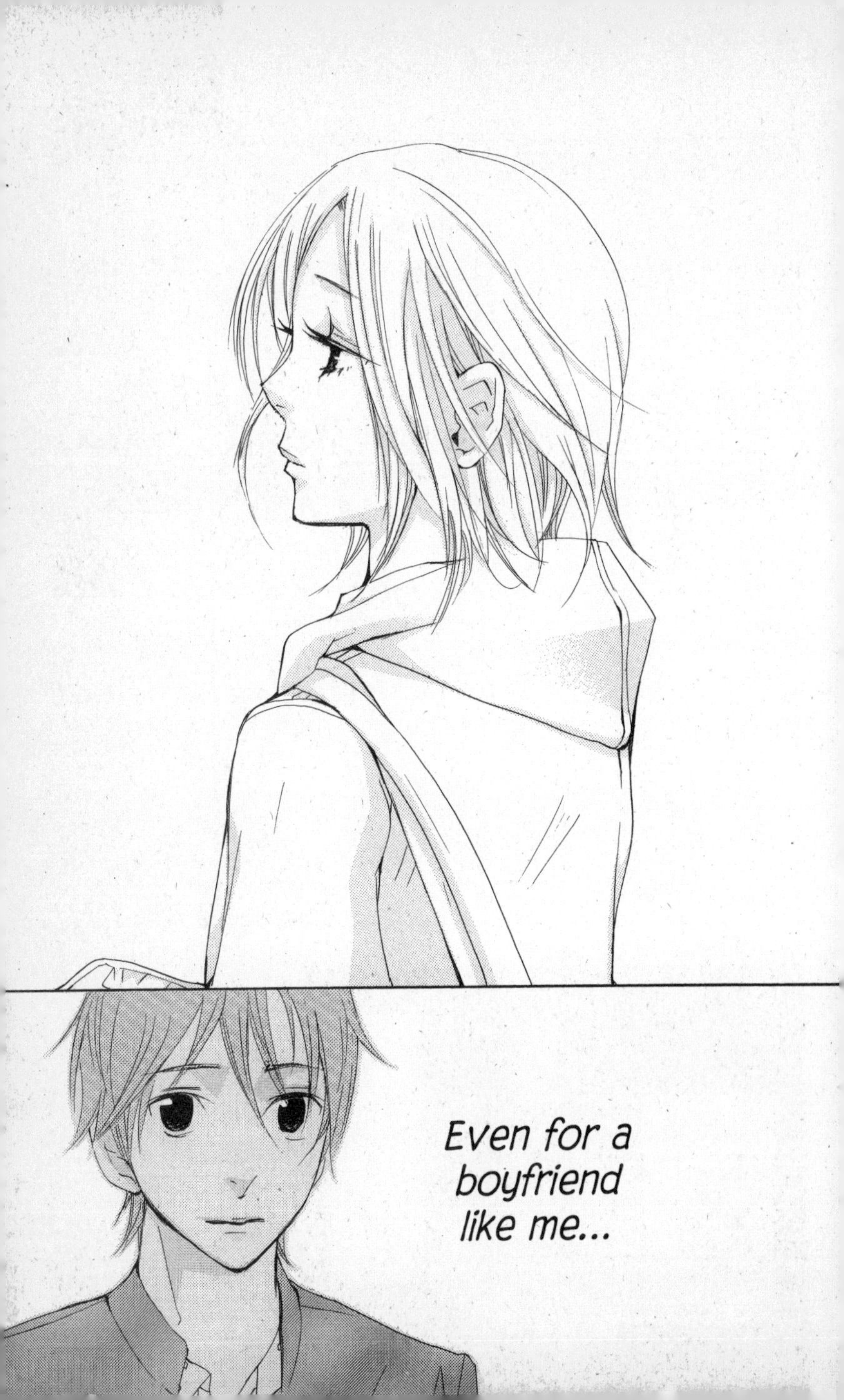
Even for a boyfriend like me...

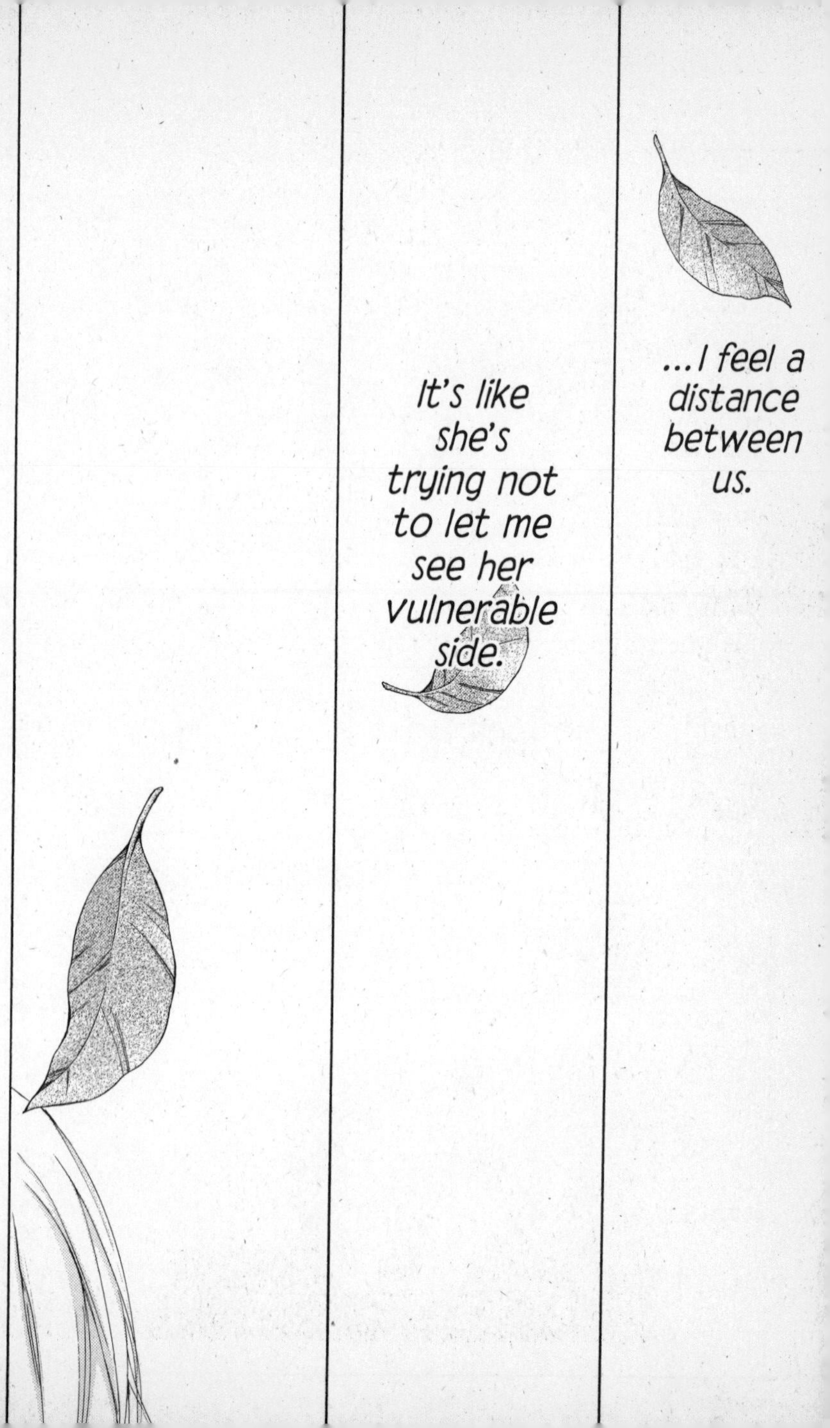

...I feel a
distance
between
us.

It's like
she's
trying not
to let me
see her
vulnerable
side.

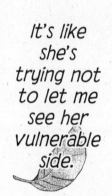

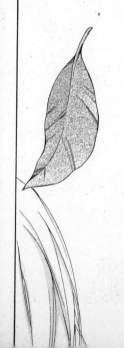

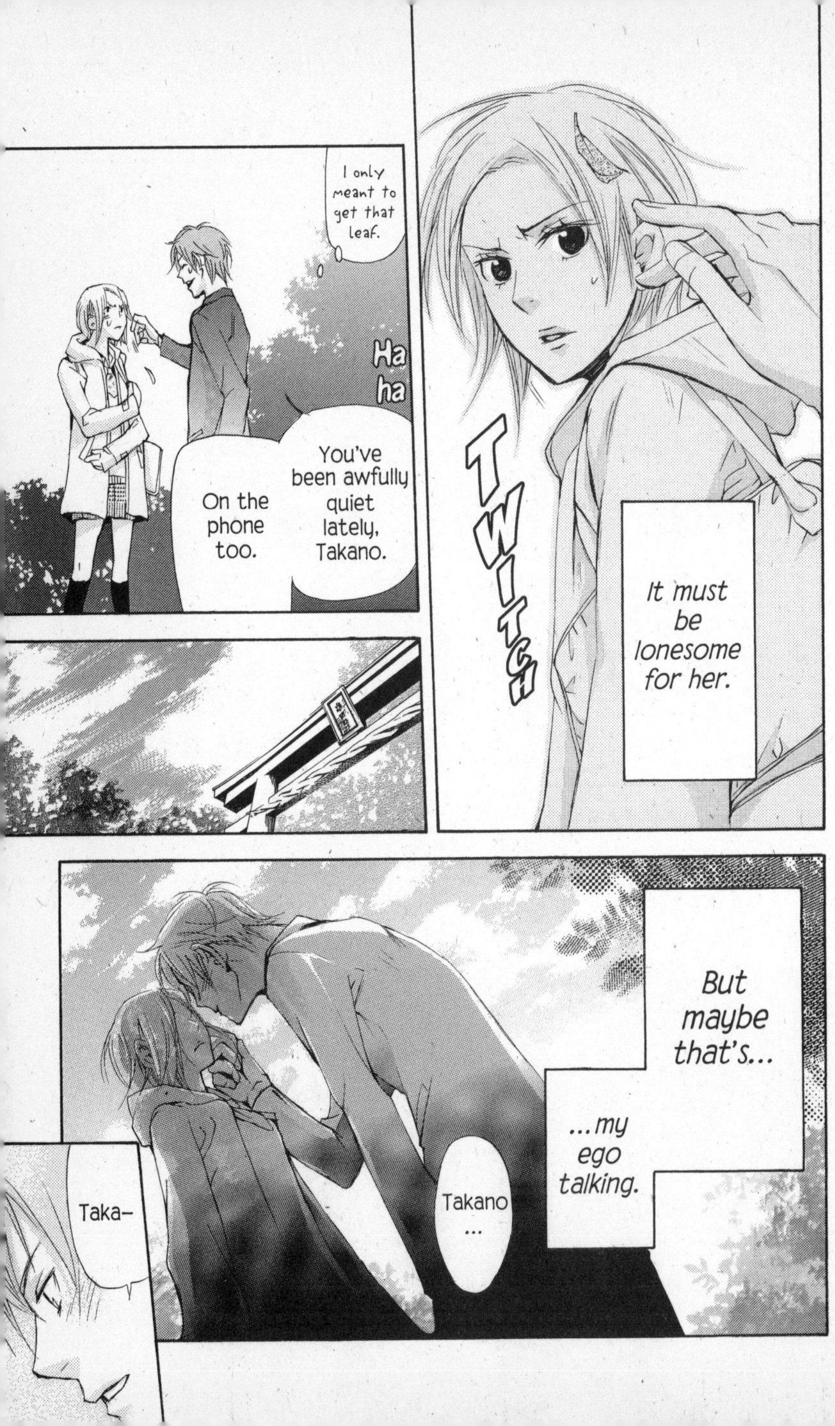
TWITCH
It must be lonesome for her.
I only meant to get that leaf.
Ha ha
You've been awfully quiet lately, Takano.
On the phone too.
But maybe that's...
...my ego talking.
Takano ...
Taka-

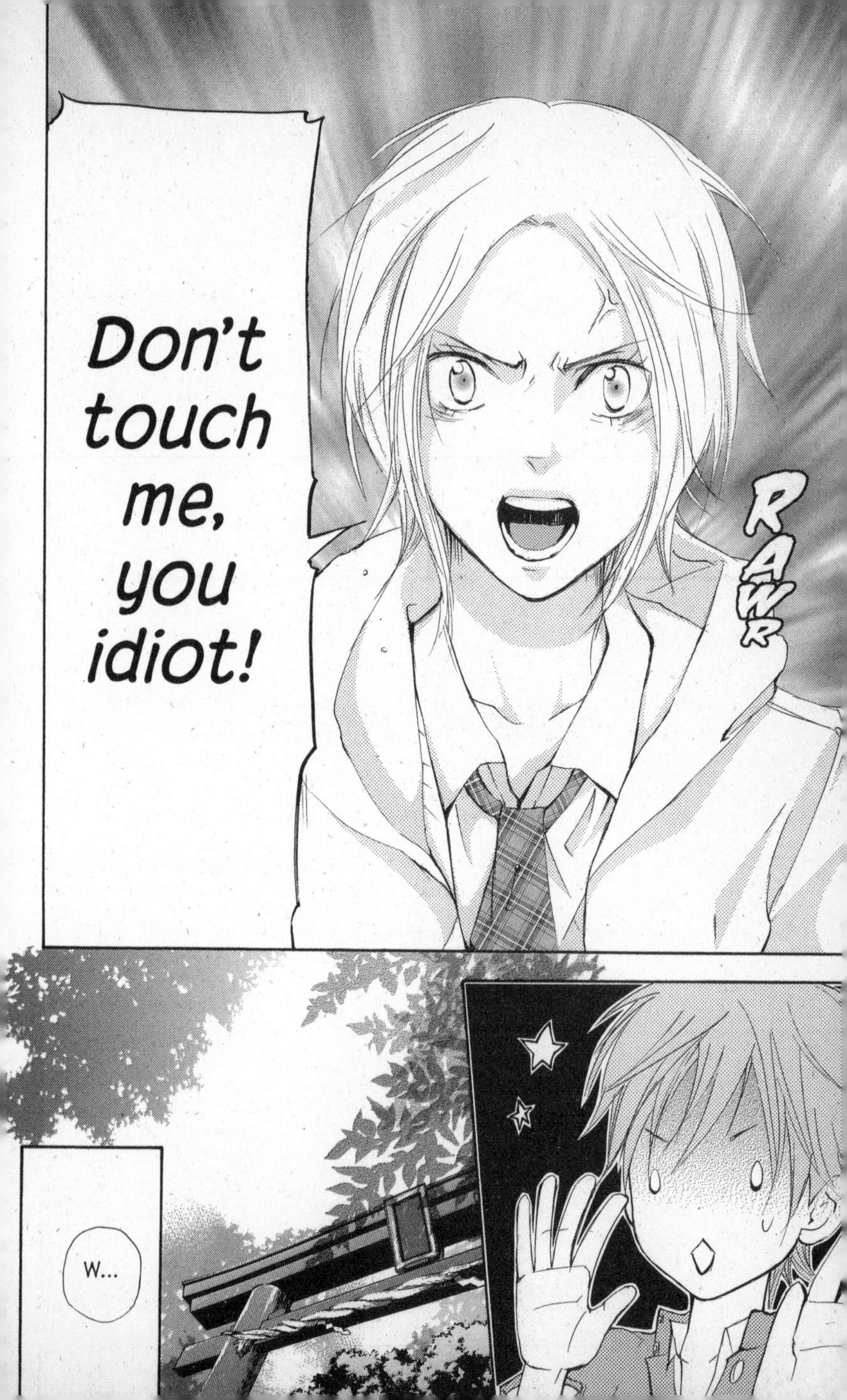
RAWR
Don't touch me, you idiot!
W...

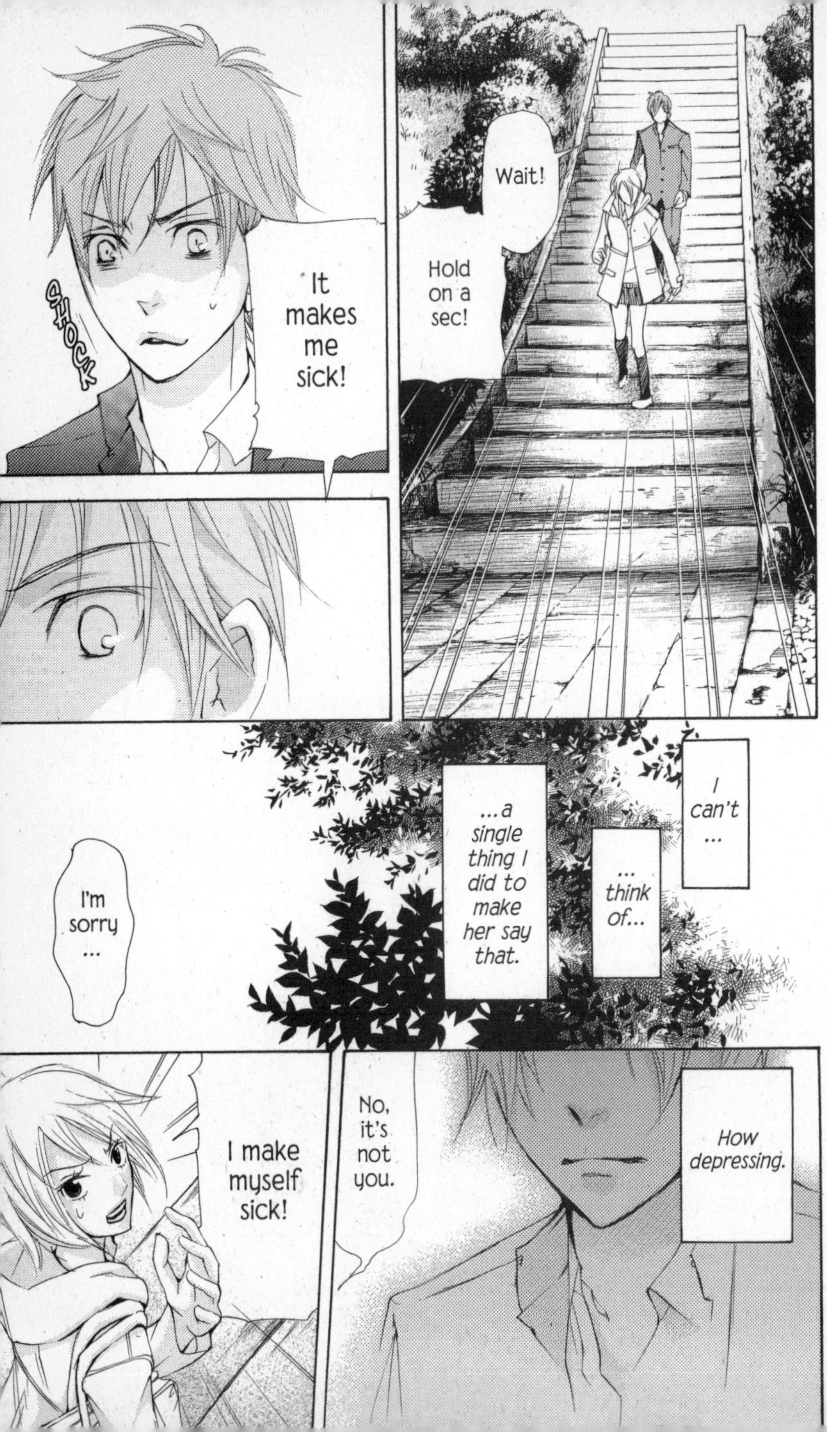
Wait!
Hold on a sec!
It makes me sick!
SHOCK
I can't...
...think of...
...a single thing I did to make her say that.
I'm sorry...
How depressing.
No, it's not you.
I make myself sick!

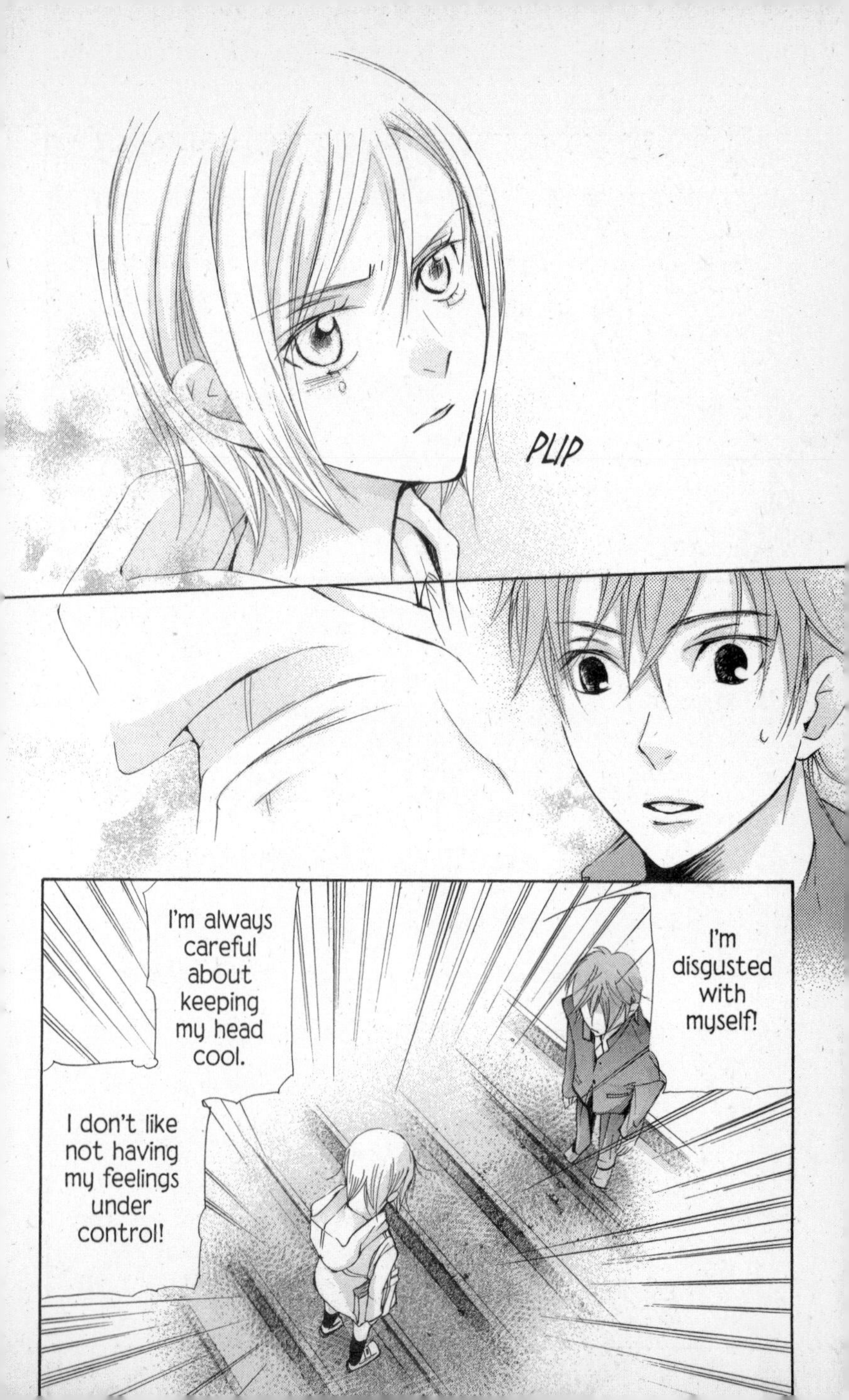
PLIP
I'm disgusted with myself!
I'm always careful about keeping my head cool.
I don't like not having my feelings under control!

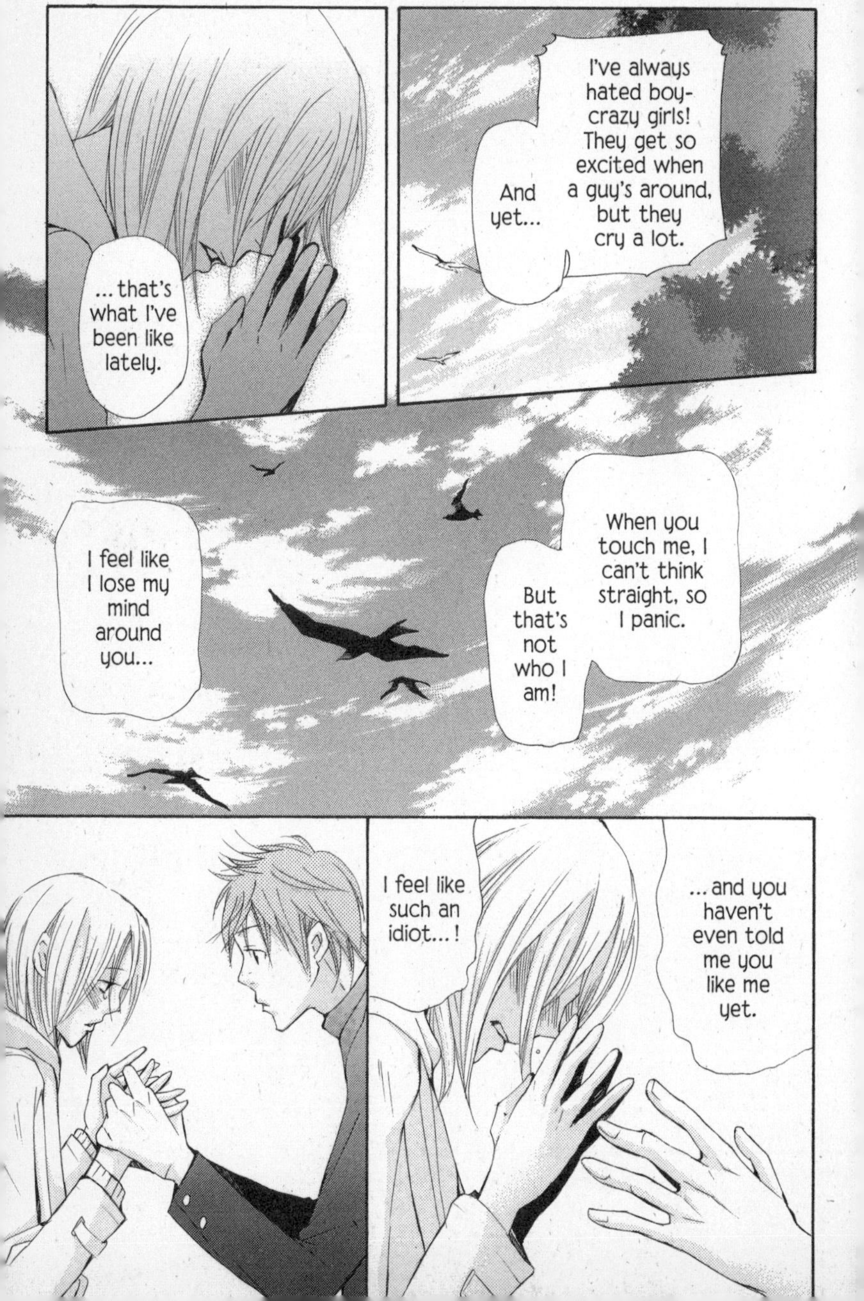
I've always hated boy-crazy girls! They get so excited when a guy's around, but they cry a lot.
And yet...
...that's what I've been like lately.
When you touch me, I can't think straight, so I panic.
But that's not who I am!
I feel like I lose my mind around you...
...and you haven't even told me you like me yet.
I feel like such an idiot...!

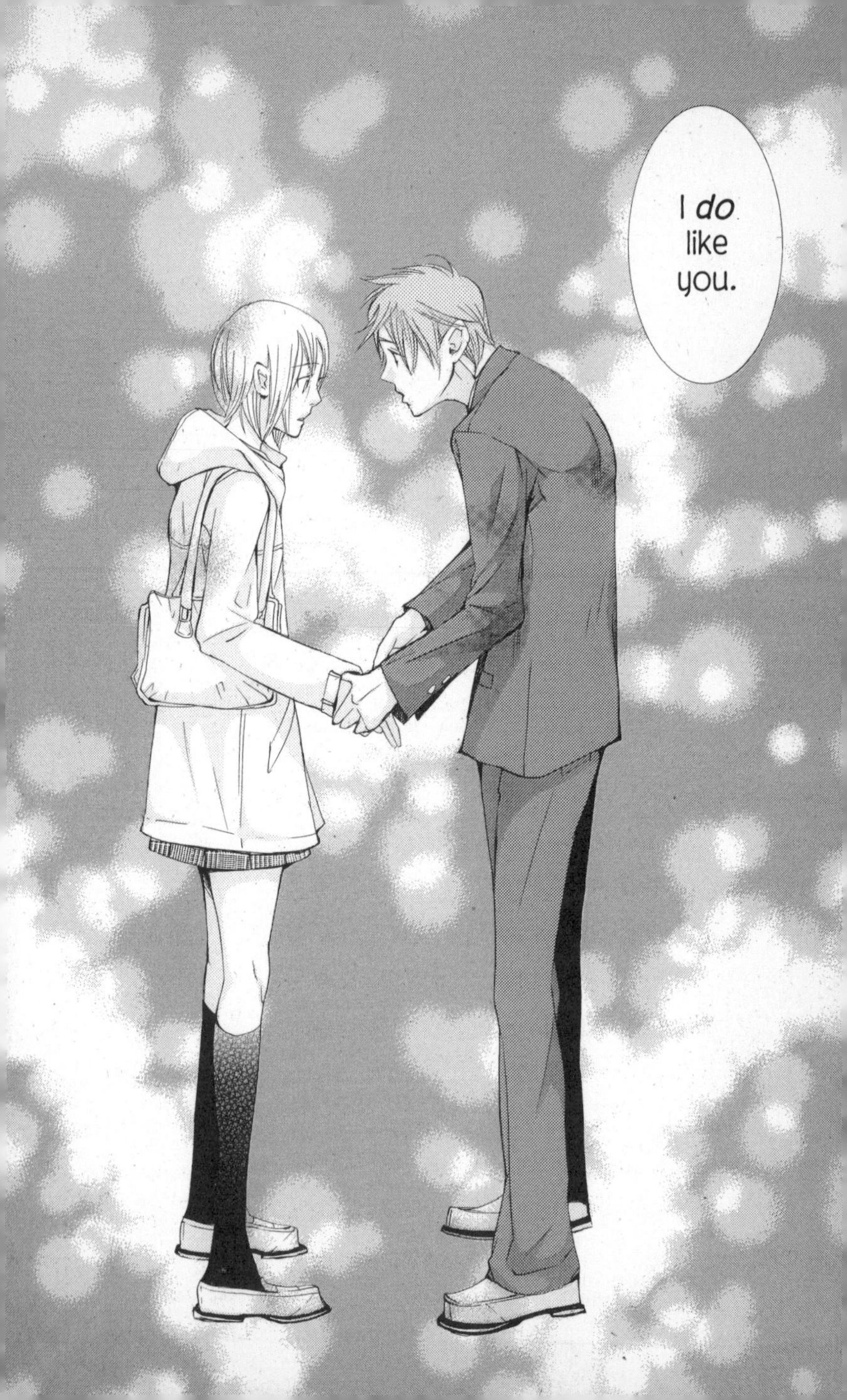
I *do* like you.

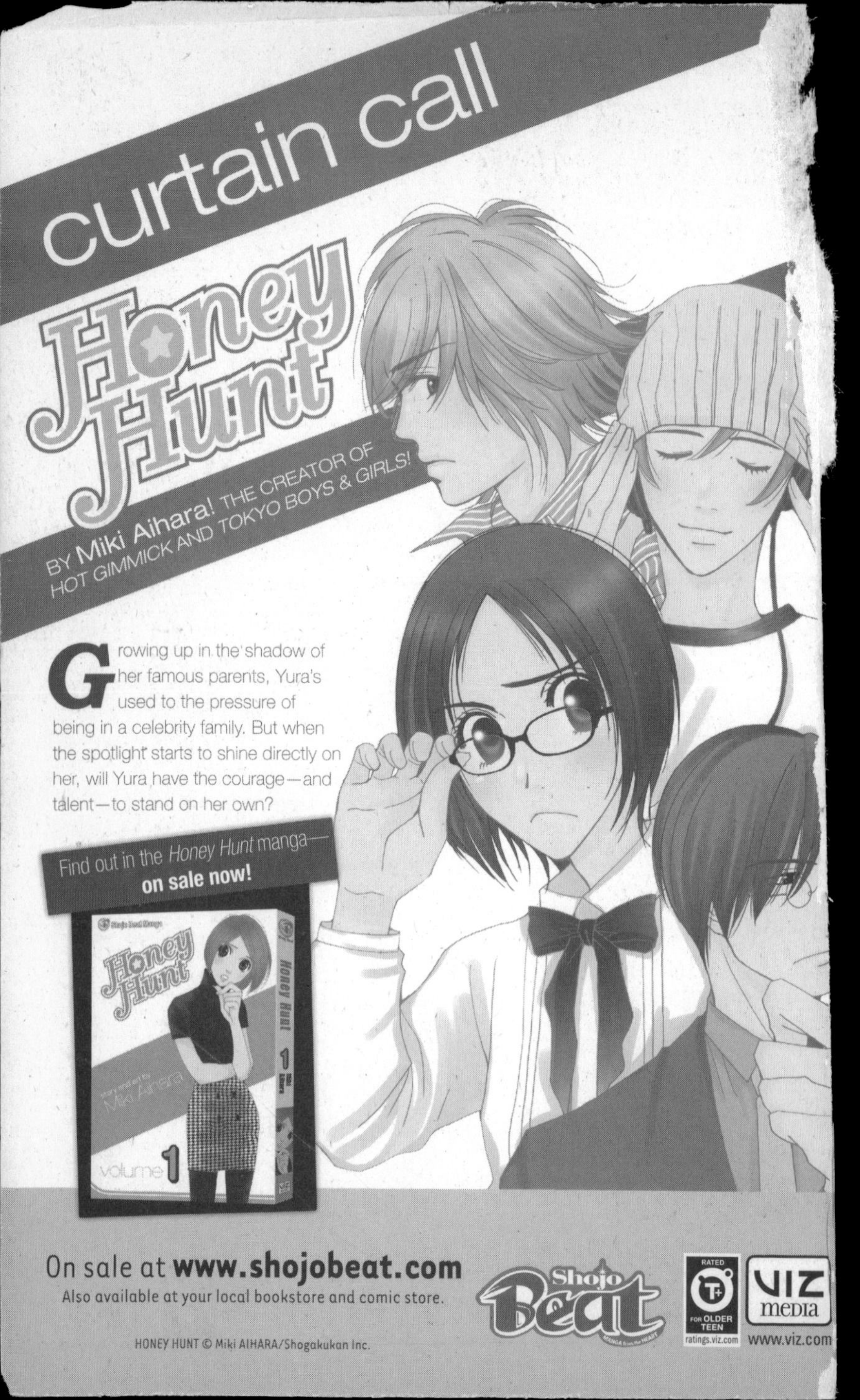
curtain call
Honey Hunt
BY Miki Aihara! THE CREATOR OF HOT GIMMICK AND TOKYO BOYS & GIRLS!
Growing up in the shadow of her famous parents, Yura's used to the pressure of being in a celebrity family. But when the spotlight starts to shine directly on her, will Yura have the courage—and talent—to stand on her own?
Find out in the Honey Hunt manga—
on sale now!
Honey Hunt
Honey Hunt
1
Miki Aihara
volume 1
On sale at www.shojobeat.com
Also available at your local bookstore and comic store.
HONEY HUNT © Miki AIHARA/Shogakukan Inc.
Shojo Beat
RATED T+ FOR OLDER TEEN
ratings.viz.com
VIZ media
www.viz.com

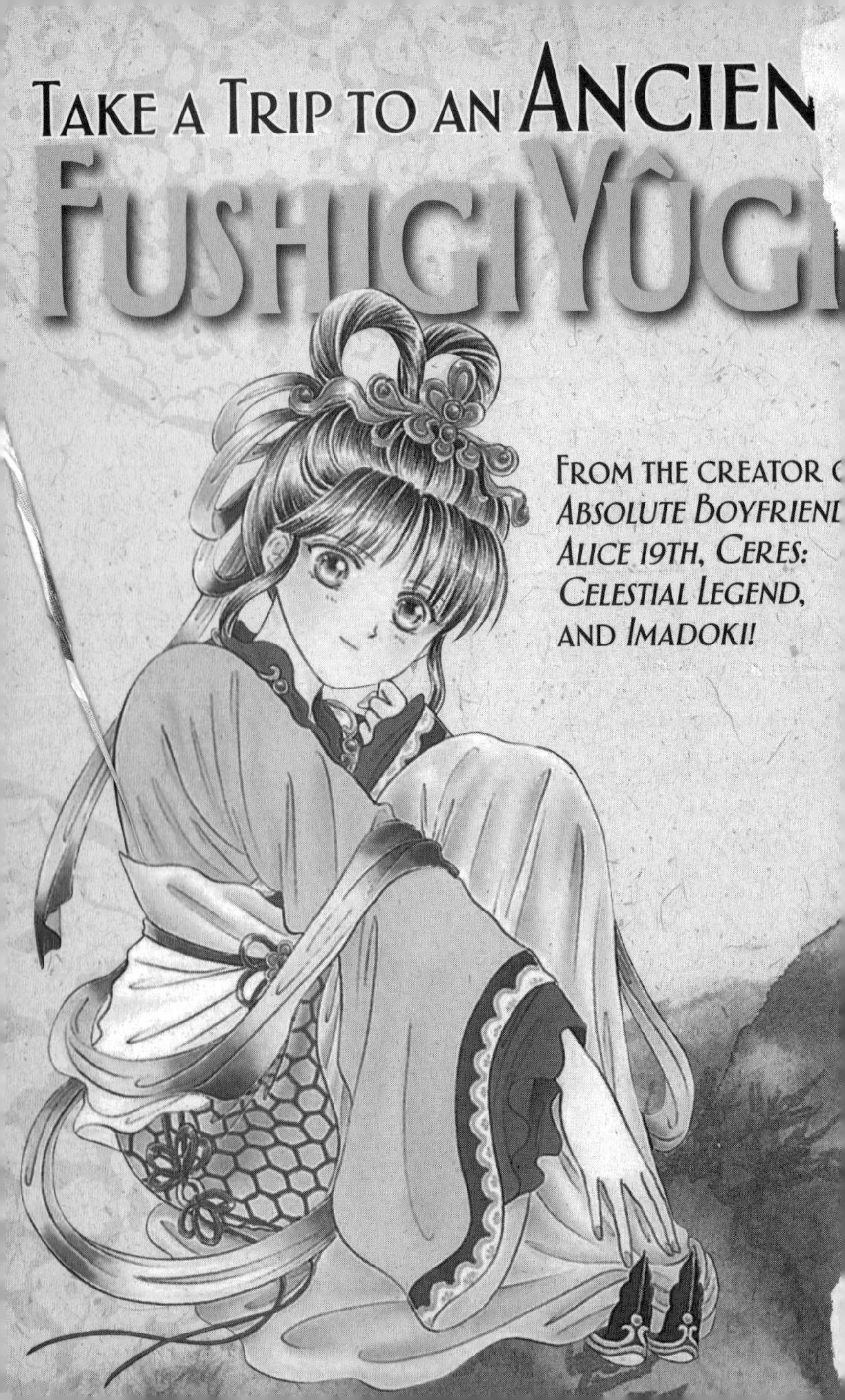
TAKE A TRIP TO AN ANCIEN
FUSHIGI YÛGI
FROM THE CREATOR O
ABSOLUTE BOYFRIEND
ALICE 19TH, CERES:
CELESTIAL LEGEND,
AND IMADOKI!

AND OF *Fantasy*

MIAKA YÛKI IS AN ORDINARY JUNIOR-HIGH STUDENT
WHO IS SUDDENLY WHISKED AWAY INTO THE WORLD OF A
BOOK, *THE UNIVERSE OF THE FOUR GODS*. WILL THE
BEAUTIFUL CELESTIAL BEINGS SHE ENCOUNTERS AND THE
CHANCE TO BECOME A PRIESTESS DIVERT MIAKA FROM
EVER RETURNING HOME?

THREE VOLUMES OF THE
ORIGINAL *FUSHIGI YÛGI*
SERIES COMBINED INTO A
LARGER FORMAT WITH AN
EXCLUSIVE COVER DESIGN
AND BONUS CONTENT

EXPERIENCE
THE BEAUTY OF
FUSHIGI YÛGI WITH
THE HARDCOVER
ART BOOK

ALSO AVAILABLE:
THE *FUSHIGI YÛGI:
GENBU KAIDEN* MANGA,
THE EIGHT VOLUME PREQUEL
TO THIS BEST-SELLING
FANTASY SERIES

Hot Gimmick

If you think being a teenager is hard, be glad your name isn't Hatsumi Narita

With scandals that would make any gossip girl blush and more triangles than you can throw a geometry book at, this girl may never figure out the game of love!

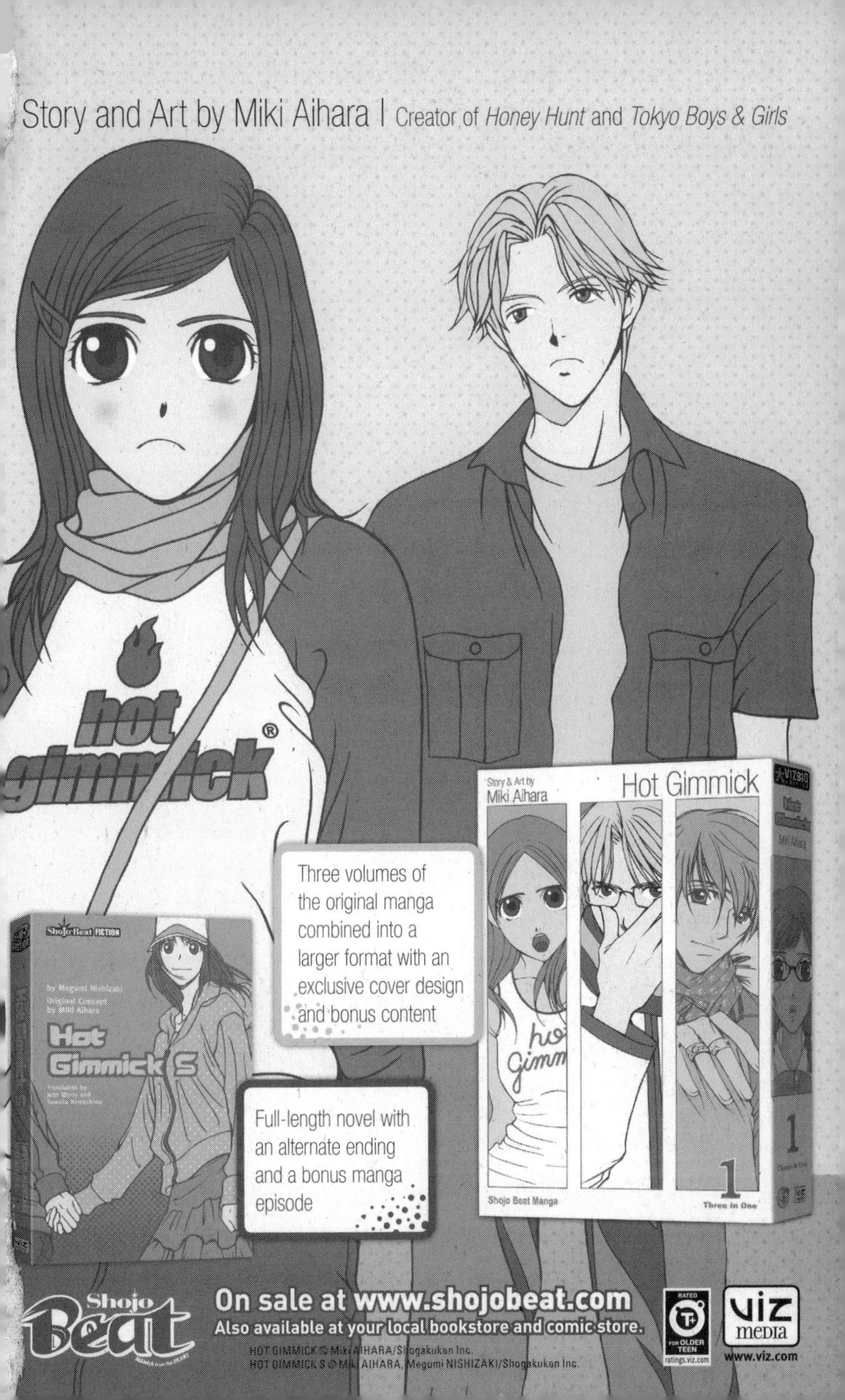
Story and Art by Miki Aihara | Creator of Honey Hunt and Tokyo Boys & Girls
hot gimmick®
Story & Art by Miki Aihara
Hot Gimmick
Shojo Beat Manga
1
Three in One
Three volumes of the original manga combined into a larger format with an exclusive cover design and bonus content
Shojo Beat FICTION
Hot Gimmick S
Full-length novel with an alternate ending and a bonus manga episode
Shojo Beat
On sale at www.shojobeat.com
Also available at your local bookstore and comic store.
HOT GIMMICK © Miki AIHARA/Shogakukan Inc.
HOT GIMMICK S © Miki AIHARA, Megumi NISHIZAKI/Shogakukan Inc.
RATED T+ FOR OLDER TEEN
ratings.viz.com
viz media
www.viz.com

SEIHO BOYS' HIGH SCHOOL
Volume 6
Shojo Beat Edition

STORY AND ART BY
KANEYOSHI IZUMI

© 2007 Kaneyoshi IZUMI/Shogakukan
All rights reserved.
Original Japanese edition "MEN'S KOU"
published by SHOGAKUKAN Inc.

English Adaptation/Ysabet MacFarlane
Translation/Katherine Schilling
Touch-up Art & Lettering/Maui Girl
Cover Design/Julie Behn
Interior Design/Ronnie Casson
Editor/Amy Yu

The stories, characters and incidents mentioned in this publication are entirely fictional.

Printed in Canada

Published by VIZ Media, LLC
P.O. Box 77010
San Francisco, CA 94107

10 9 8 7 6 5 4 3 2 1
First printing, June 2011

www.viz.com

www.shojobeat.com

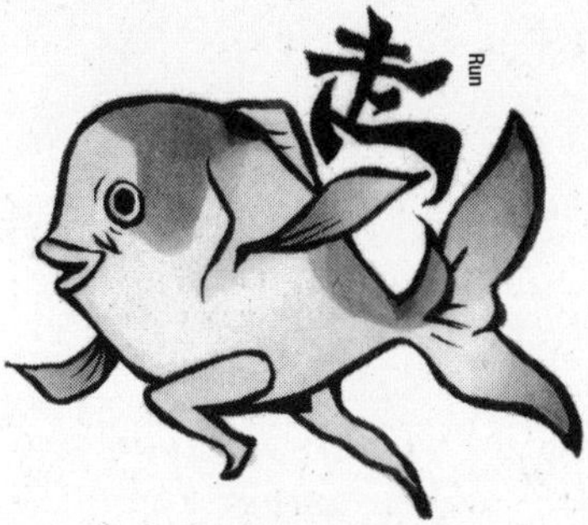
Run

Kaneyoshi Izumi

I want my life to be a bit more down-to-earth.

Kaneyoshi Izumi's birthday is April 1, and her blood type is probably type A (but she hasn't actually had it checked yet). Her debut story *Tenshi* (Angel) appeared in the September 1995 issue of *Bessatsu Shojo Comic* and won the 36th Shogakukan Shinjin (newbie) Comics Award. Her hobbies include riding motorcycles, playing the piano and feeding stray cats, and she continues to work as an artist for *Betsucomi.*

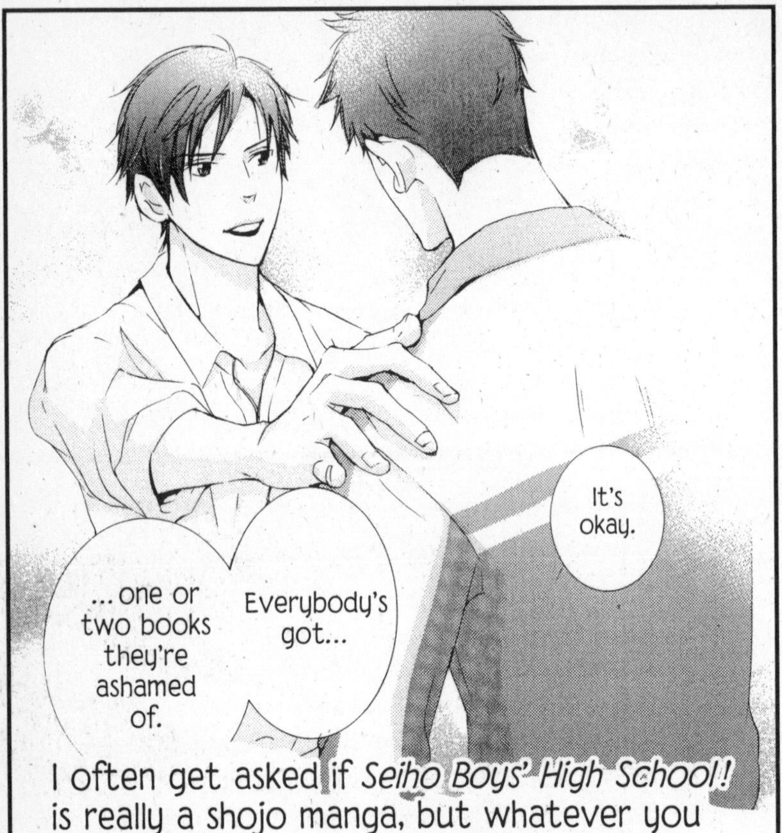
It's okay.
Everybody's got...
...one or two books they're ashamed of.

I often get asked if *Seiho Boys' High School!* is really a shojo manga, but whatever you care to call it, nothing makes me happier than knowing that people are reading and enjoying it.
It sounds like a surprising number of boys are reading it too. I hope you'll keep reading no matter how embarrassing it is for you.

Izumi

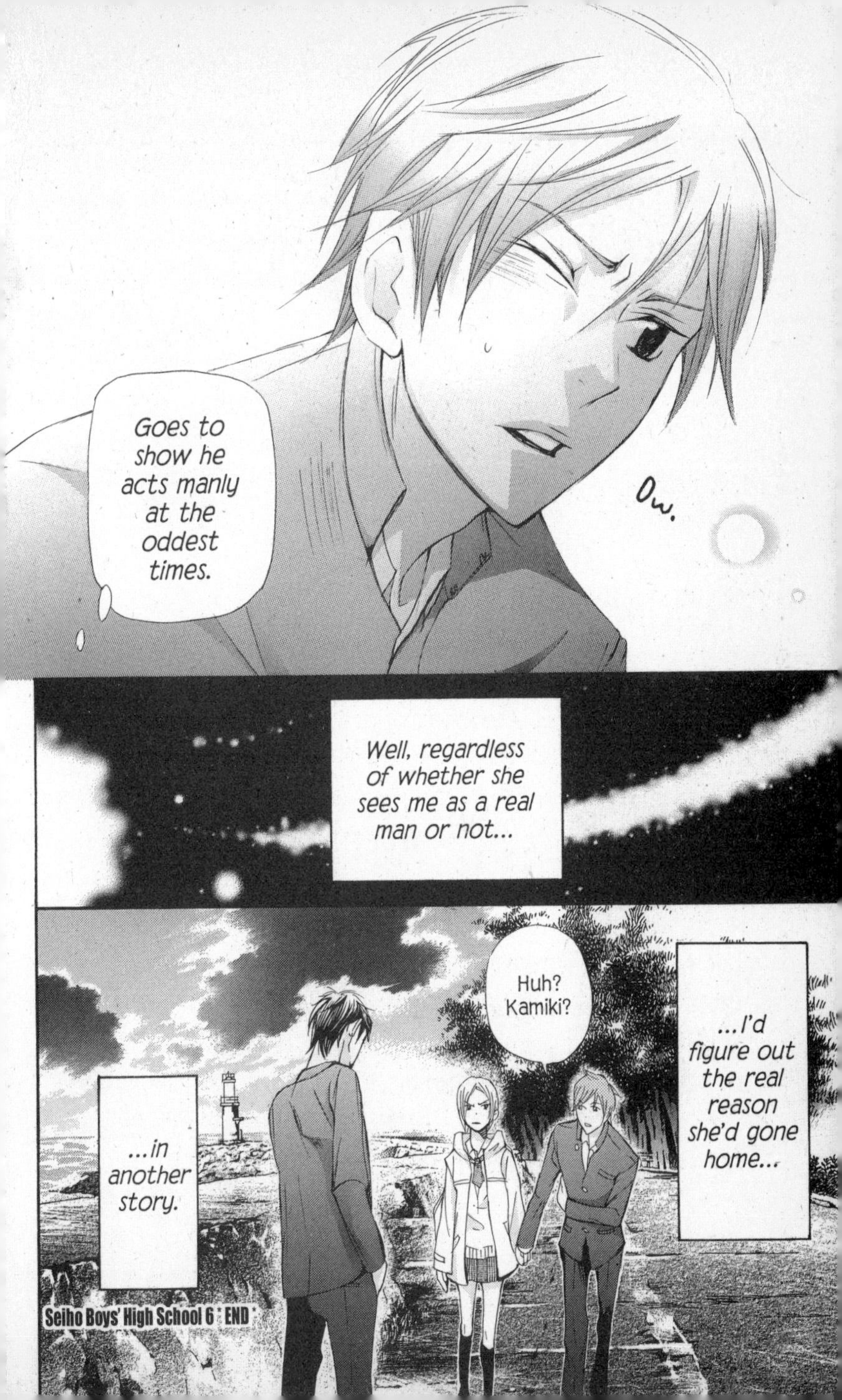
Ow.
Goes to show he acts manly at the oddest times.
Well, regardless of whether she sees me as a real man or not...
...I'd figure out the real reason she'd gone home...
Huh? Kamiki?
...in another story.
Seiho Boys' High School 6 END

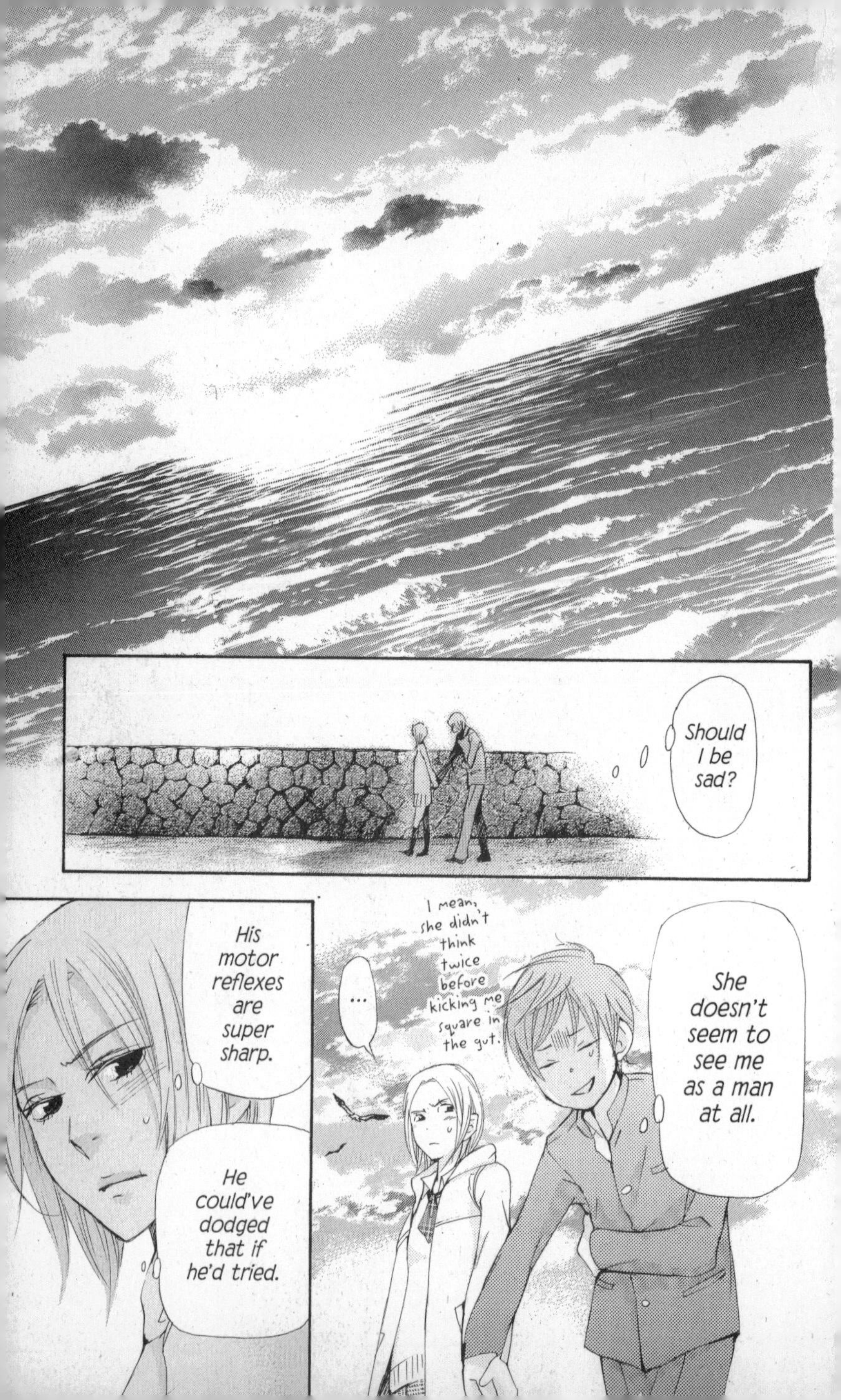
Should I be sad?
She doesn't seem to see me as a man at all.
I mean, she didn't think twice before kicking me square in the gut.
...
His motor reflexes are super sharp.
He could've dodged that if he'd tried.

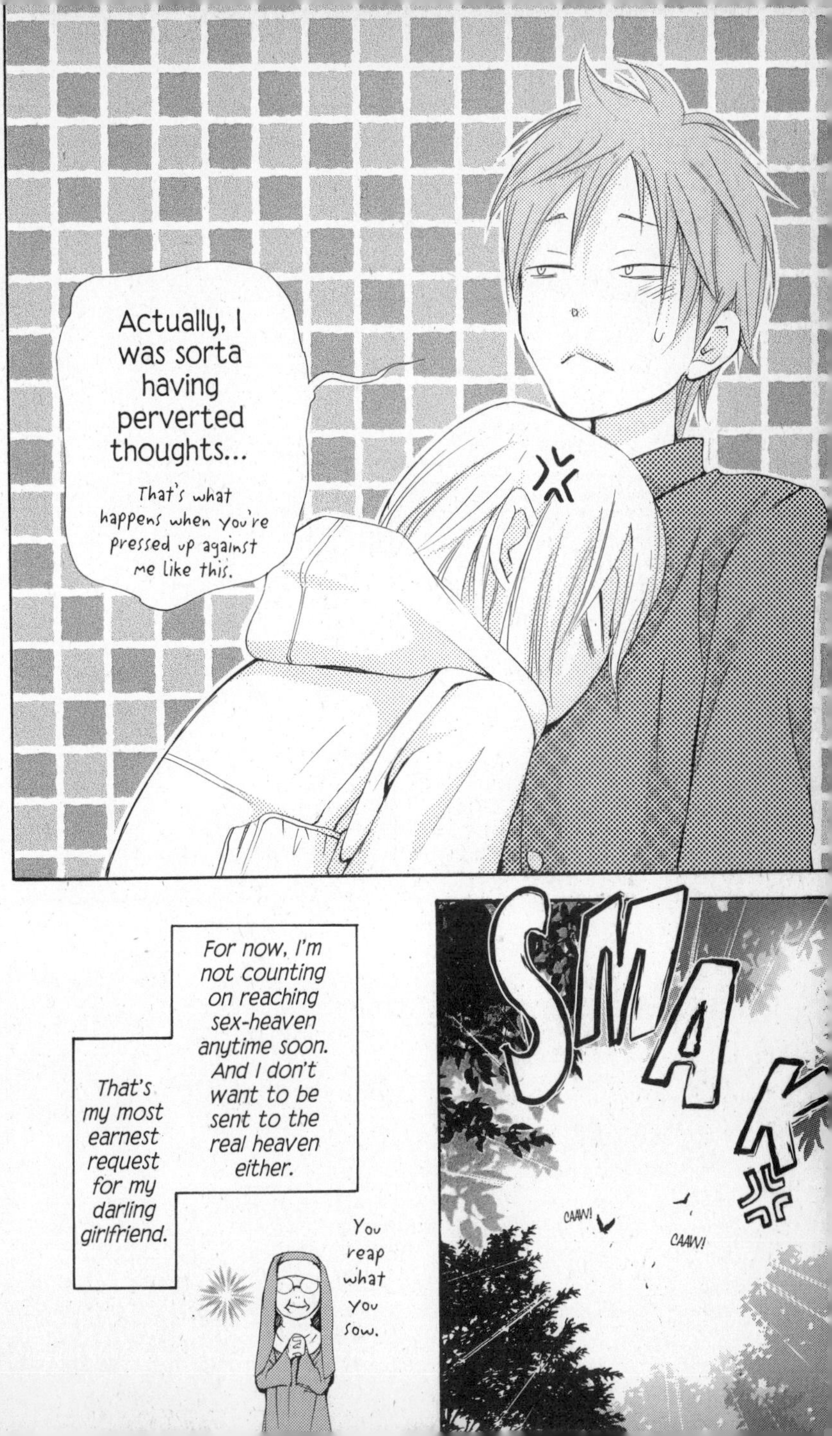
Actually, I was sorta having perverted thoughts...
That's what happens when you're pressed up against me like this.
SMAK
CAAW!
CAAW!
For now, I'm not counting on reaching sex-heaven anytime soon. And I don't want to be sent to the real heaven either.
That's my most earnest request for my darling girlfriend.
You reap what you sow.

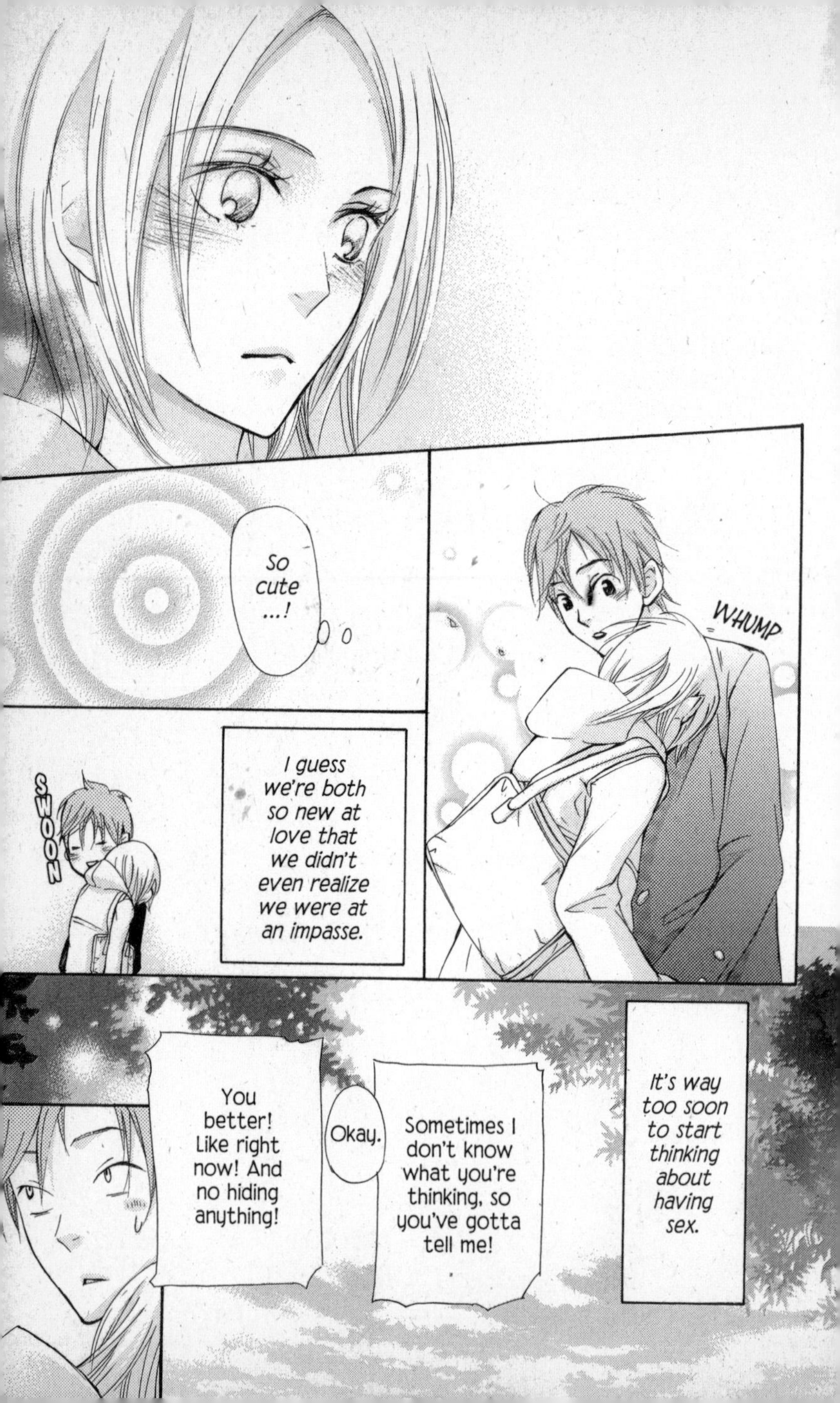
WHUMP
So cute ...!
I guess we're both so new at love that we didn't even realize we were at an impasse.
SWOON
It's way too soon to start thinking about having sex.
Sometimes I don't know what you're thinking, so you've gotta tell me!
Okay.
You better! Like right now! And no hiding anything!